Policing in Israel

Studying Crime Control, Community
Policing, and Counterterrorism

Advances in Police Theory and Practice Series

Series Editor: Dilip K. Das

Policing in Israel: Studying Crime Control, Community Policing, and Counterterrorism

Tal Jonathan-Zamir, David Weisburd, and Badi Hasisi

Policing Terrorism: Research Studies into Police Counterterrorism Investigations

David Lowe

Policing in Hong Kong: History and Reform

Kam C. Wong

Cold Cases: Evaluation Models with Follow-up Strategies for Investigators, Second Edition

James M. Adcock and Sarah L. Stein

Crime Linkage: Theory, Research, and Practice

Jessica Woodhams and Craig Bennell

Police Investigative Interviews and Interpreting: Context, Challenges, and Strategies

Sedat Mulayim, Miranda Lai, and Caroline Norma

Policing White Collar Crime: Characteristics of White Collar Criminals

Petter Gottschalk

Honor-Based Violence: Policing and Prevention

Karl Anton Roberts, Gerry Campbell, and Glen Lloyd

Policing and the Mentally Ill: International Perspectives

Duncan Chappell

Security Governance, Policing, and Local Capacity

Jan Froestad with Clifford D. Shearing

Policing in Hong Kong: History and Reform

Kam C. Wong

Police Performance Appraisals: A Comparative Perspective

Serdar Kenan Gul and Paul O'Connell

Los Angeles Police Department Meltdown: The Fall of the Professional-Reform Model of Policing

James Lasley

Financial Crimes: A Global Threat

Maximillian Edelbacher, Peter Kratcoski, and Michael Theil

Policing in Israel

Studying Crime Control, Community Policing, and Counterterrorism

Edited by

Tal Jonathan-Zamir
The Hebrew University of Jerusalem
Jerusalem, Israel

David Weisburd
The Hebrew University of Jerusalem
Jerusalem, Israel

George Mason University
Fairfax, Virginia, USA

Badi Hasisi
The Hebrew University of Jerusalem
Jerusalem, Israel

CRC Press
Taylor & Francis Group
Boca Raton London New York

CRC Press is an imprint of the
Taylor & Francis Group, an **informa** business

CRC Press
Taylor & Francis Group
6000 Broken Sound Parkway NW, Suite 300
Boca Raton, FL 33487-2742

© 2016 by Taylor & Francis Group, LLC
CRC Press is an imprint of Taylor & Francis Group, an Informa business

Library of Congress Cataloging-in-Publication Data

Policing in Israel : studying crime control, community policing, and counterterrorism / editors, Tal Jonathan-Zamir, David Weisburd, and Badi Hasisi.
    pages cm. -- (Advances in police theory and practice series ; 25)
    Includes bibliographical references and index.
    ISBN 978-1-4987-2256-8
    1. Police--Israel. 2. Internal security--Law and legislation--Israel. 3. Police regulations--Israel. 4. Terrorism--Prevention--Law and legislation--Israel. 5. Crime--Israel. 6. Police regulations. 7. Police corruption. I. Jonathan-Zamir, Tal, editor. II. Weisburd, David, editor. III. Hasisi, Badi, editor.

KMK1550.P65 2016
363.2095694--dc23
    2015013763

Visit the Taylor & Francis Web site at
http://www.taylorandfrancis.com

and the CRC Press Web site at
http://www.crcpress.com

Contents

Series Preface

While the literature on police and allied subjects is growing exponentially, its impact upon day-to-day policing remains small. The two worlds of research and practice of policing remain disconnected, even though cooperation between the two is growing. A major reason is that the two groups speak in different languages. The research work is published in hard-to-access journals and presented in a manner that is difficult to comprehend for a layperson. On the other hand, the police practitioners tend not to mix with researchers and remain secretive about their work. Consequently, there is little dialogue between the two and almost no attempt to learn from one another. Dialogues across the globe, among researchers and practitioners situated in different continents, are of course even more limited.

I attempted to address this problem by starting the IPES (http://www.ipes.info), where a common platform has brought the two together. IPES is now in its twenty-sixth year. The annual meetings that constitute most major annual events of the organization have been hosted in all parts of the world. Several publications have come out of these deliberations, and a new collaborative community of scholars and police officers has been created whose membership runs into several hundreds.

Another attempt was to begin a new journal, aptly called *Police Practice and Research: An International Journal* (*PPR*), that has opened the gate to practitioners to share their work and experiences. The journal has attempted to focus upon issues that help bring the two on a single platform. *PPR* is completing its 16 years in 2015. It is certainly an evidence of growing collaboration between police research and practice that *PPR*, which began with four issues a year, expanded into five issues in its fourth year, and now it is issued six times a year.

Clearly, these attempts, despite their success, remain limited. Conferences and journal publications do help create a body of knowledge and an association of police activists but cannot address substantial issues in depth. The limitations of time and space preclude larger discussions and more authoritative expositions that can provide stronger and broader linkages between the two worlds.

It is this realization of the increasing dialogue between police research and practice that has encouraged many of us—my close colleagues and I connected closely with IPES and *PPR* across the world—to conceive and implement a new attempt in this direction. This led to the book series *Advances in Police Theory and Practice*, that seeks to attract writers from all parts of the world. Further, the attempt is to find practitioner contributors. The objective is to make the series a serious contribution to our knowledge of the police as well as to improve police practices. The focus is not only in work that describes the best and successful police practices but also one that challenges current paradigms and breaks new ground to prepare a police for the twenty-first century. The series seeks a comparative analysis that highlights achievements in distant parts of the world as well as one that encourages an in-depth examination of specific problems confronting a particular police force.

The current book reports on the advancement of police research in Israel. The studies included make important contributions to the policing literature in at least one of three ways: they replicate findings from English-speaking countries (such as in the area of hot-spots policing), and thus provide support for their validity and generalizability; they utilize the unique Israeli conditions to address questions that are difficult to test in other countries, such as in the area of counterterrorism; and they ask innovative questions in the study of policing that are yet to be addressed elsewhere. These three types of contribution are made in the context of major areas of interest in the policing literature: crime control, police–community relationships, and policing terrorism. Thus, this book not only provides the reader with a broad picture of both Israeli policing and police research carried out in Israel in the past decade, but also has important implications for policing scholars and practitioners outside of Israel and throughout the democratic world.

It is hoped that through this series, it will be possible to accelerate the process of building knowledge about policing and help bridge the gap between the two worlds—the worlds of police research and police practice. This is an invitation to police scholars and practitioners across the world to come and join in this venture.

Dilip K. Das, PhD
Founding President,
International Police Executive Symposium,
IPES, www.ipes.info

Founding Editor-in-Chief,
Police Practice and Research: An International Journal,
PPR, www.tandf.co.uk/journals

Editors

Tal Jonathan-Zamir is a lecturer at the Institute of Criminology, Hebrew University of Jerusalem. She earned her PhD at Hebrew University in 2010 and spent a year as a Fulbright postdoctoral fellow at the Department of Criminology, Law, and Society at George Mason University. Her research interests include police–community relationships, police discretion, police legitimacy, and policing terrorism.

David Weisburd is a distinguished professor of criminology, law, and society at George Mason University in Fairfax, Virginia, and a Walter E. Meyer professor of law and criminal justice at Hebrew University Faculty of Law in Jerusalem. He is a recipient of many international awards including the 2010 Stockholm Prize in Criminology and the 2014 Sutherland Award from the American Society of Criminology. In 2015, he received the Israel Prize for his contributions to criminology.

Badi Hasisi serves as a chair of the Institute of Criminology, Hebrew University of Jerusalem. His main research focuses on policing divided societies, police–minority relations; law, history, and society; and terrorism and airport security.

Contributors

Nicole Adler
School of Business Administration
Hebrew University of Jerusalem
Jerusalem, Israel

Shai Amram
Faculty of Law
Institute of Criminology
Hebrew University of Jerusalem
Jerusalem, Israel

Itai Ater
Faculty of Management
Tel Aviv University
Tel Aviv, Israel

Gali Aviv
Faculty of Law
Institute of Criminology
Hebrew University of Jerusalem
Jerusalem, Israel

Juan Carlos Castillo
Institute of Sociology
Pontificia Universidad Católica de Chile
Santiago, Chile

Ehud Eldror
Department of Management
Research Institute of Human Factors of Road Safety
Bar Ilan University
Ramat Gan, Israel

Roni Factor
Faculty of Law
Institute of Criminology
Hebrew University of Jerusalem
Jerusalem, Israel

Yehonatan Givati
Faculty of Law
Hebrew University of Jerusalem
Jerusalem, Israel

Shalom Hakkert
Faculty of Civil and Environmental Engineering
Technion—Israel Institute of Technology
Haifa, Israel

Amikam Harpaz
Faculty of Law
Institute of Criminology
Hebrew University of Jerusalem
Jerusalem, Israel

Badi Hasisi
Faculty of Law
Institute of Criminology
Hebrew University of Jerusalem
Jerusalem, Israel

Tal Jonathan-Zamir
Faculty of Law
Institute of Criminology
Hebrew University of Jerusalem
Jerusalem, Israel

Jonathan Kornbluth
School of Business Administration
Hebrew University of Jerusalem
Jerusalem, Israel

Simon Perry
Faculty of Law
Institute of Criminology
Hebrew University of Jerusalem
Jerusalem, Israel

Arye Rattner
Department of Sociology
School of Criminology
Center for the Study of Crime, Law, and Society
University of Haifa
Haifa, Israel

Oren Rigbi
Department of Economics
Ben-Gurion University of the Negev
Beersheva, Israel

Tova Rosenbloom
Department of Management
Research Institute of Human Factors of Road Safety
Bar Ilan University
Ramat Gan, Israel

Revital Sela-Shayovitz
David Yellin Academic College
and
Faculty of Law
Institute of Criminology
Hebrew University of Jerusalem
Jerusalem, Israel

Mali Sher
Research Unit
Traffic Department
Israel National Police
Bet Dagan, Israel

David Weisburd
Faculty of Law
Institute of Criminology
Hebrew University of Jerusalem
Jerusalem, Israel

and

Department of Criminology, Law, and Society
George Mason University
Fairfax, Virginia

Policing in Israel: Studying Crime Control, Community, and Counterterrorism
Editors' Introduction*

1

TAL JONATHAN-ZAMIR
DAVID WEISBURD
BADI HASISI

Policing has become an important area of innovation in criminology and in practice over the past few decades. In methodology, policing has emerged as a key area of evidence-based policy in criminal justice (Lum, Koper, and Telep 2011; Sherman 1998; Weisburd and Neyroud 2011), and the police have become one of the most open agents of the criminal justice system to new ideas and new approaches (Weisburd and Braga 2006). The science of policing has advanced greatly, and there is now much evidence not only that the police can be effective (National Research Council 2004; Weisburd and Eck 2004) but also that policing and police data can play a role in advancing scientific understanding of crime and the relationships between the community and criminal justice (e.g., Gill et al. 2014; Telep and Weisburd 2012; Tyler 2011; Weisburd, Groff, and Yang 2012).

The advances in police science over the past few decades in the United States and the United Kingdom have also impacted scientific study of the police in many other countries. This edited book (developed from a special issue of *Police Practice and Research: An International Journal* and other recent studies) reports on the advancement of police research in Israel. As the studies suggest, cutting-edge methods and cutting-edge questions are being asked regarding Israeli policing. But the studies in this book suggest as well that there is much to learn about the police enterprise by looking to Israel.

Clearly, comparative studies are critical to identify whether phenomena observed in the United States, for example, can also be found in other settings. Thus, some of the studies reported in this book replicate findings in important areas such as crime and place and hot-spots policing (Chapter 2), attitudes of crime victims toward the police (Chapter 7), and police legitimacy (Chapter 8). However, Israel is not simply a different setting; it is also a setting with characteristics that make it particularly interesting to conduct police research. For example, although Israel has a long tradition of democratic government for a country outside the United States, Europe, and Australia, and its policing oversight has many characteristics similar to these democracies, it has faced terrorism often to a much greater degree, and its police have had a more critical role in controlling terrorism than that of police in other Western countries. Thus, several chapters of this book report on the implications of this policing role in terms of the ability of the police to control crime (Chapter 10), public attitudes toward the

* Adapted from Weisburd, D., B. Hasisi, and T. Jonathan-Zamir. 2014. Trends in Israeli policing: Terrorism, community, victimization and crime control. *Police Practice and Research: An International Journal*. 15(2): 97–100.

police (Chapter 12), and media coverage (Chapter 11). Finally, some of the chapters in this book address innovative questions in the study of police, raised and tested by Israeli scholars in the Israeli context, such as police officers' understanding of the sources of their legitimacy in the eyes of the public (Chapter 9), and the implications of shifting responsibilities from one criminal justice agency to another (Chapter 5).

These three axes (replications, the use of unique Israeli conditions, and innovative questions in the study of police) interact in this book with three themes that represent major areas of interest in the policing literature, and thus formed the organizational structure of the book: crime control, the police and the community, and policing terrorism. All studies reported in this book have already been published in peer-reviewed journals, but are brought together to provide a broad picture of both Israeli policing and police research carried out in Israel in the past decade. At the same time, however, and as illustrated in the specific chapters, the findings and conclusions of the studies bear important implications for policing scholars and practitioners outside of Israel and throughout the democratic world: they provide additional evidence for theories or approaches developed elsewhere and support their generalizability; they provide answers to contemporary questions that are being asked in many Western democracies, but are virtually impossible to test in these countries; and they raise new questions in the study of the police that are yet to be tested elsewhere. Some of the studies contribute in more than one way. For example, in Chapter 8 Factor et al. replicate the well-known legitimacy model (e.g., Sunshine and Tyler 2003) in the Israeli context, and thus provide additional evidence for its validity and generalizability, but at the same time add the religiosity component, which has not yet been tested in this context. Given the broad benefits emerging from the study of Israeli policing, we think this book also points to the advantages of conducting policing research outside English-speaking countries more generally.

The first theme of the book, crime control, includes four studies. The chapter by Weisburd and Amram (Chapter 2) provides a good example of the utility of examining key findings in different contexts. These researchers show that the concentration of crime at microgeographic units, or crime "hot spots," occurs in the city of Tel Aviv, Israel. Indeed, their results are strikingly similar to those reported in Seattle, Washington, and other American cities (e.g., Weisburd et al. 2012). They argue for a law of crime concentrations, and thus in order to be effective in controlling crime, the police should focus their efforts on these small areas where much of the crime in the city takes place. Examining crime hot spots in Israel provides accordingly important comparative data for advancing this area of study.

Another interesting replication can be found in Chapter 3. Rosenbloom and Eldror examine the deterrent effect of vehicle impoundment on both subjective perceptions (as reflected in survey responses) and actual driving behavior (using police records). They find that drivers whose vehicle was impounded report safer driving behaviors, and police records indeed show that these drivers committed fewer violations than the controls. At the same time, and in contrast to findings from California (see DeYoung 1999), no effects on involvement in traffic accidents were found. The authors suggest that a longer period (and thus more accident cases) may be required for statistically significant effects to emerge. Nevertheless, overall their findings provide further support for impoundment as a deterrent for several types of traffic violations.

Still in the area of traffic enforcement, Adler et al. (Chapter 4) develop an innovative road safety strategy. They use an optimization modeling approach from the operations management philosophy, which aims to increase the effect of police traffic enforcement given the budgetary and resource constraints imposed on the traffic police in Israel. They demonstrate the effectiveness of their strategy with a case study: their models were implemented by the Israel traffic police over 6 years (2004–2009) and, in turn, improved both the quality of the enforcement process and the process flow. Their analysis is the first to develop a model of road safety enforcement for the traffic-police ticketing process.

In Chapter 5, Ater, Givati, and Rigbi raise an innovative question in the study of police—whether the organizational structure of the criminal justice system affects crime control—and take advantage of a unique Israeli situation—shifting the responsibility for housing arrestees (who have not yet been convicted) from the Israel National Police to the Israel Prison Service. Their analysis took advantage of the fact that the reform diffused gradually throughout the country, allowing for the comparison of arrests and reported crime before and after the reform, both within and across the different Israeli regions. They found that, probably because of the externalization of financial and managerial costs, after the reform the police arrested more suspects and for longer periods (although the arrests were of lower quality and for less severe offenses). The reform also led to lower rates of reported crimes. They conclude that the organizational structure of criminal justice agencies does indeed affect both police activity and crime, and these effects should be considered when making similar reforms.

The second theme of this book, the police and the community, begins with an important examination of the relationship between the police and minority groups. Utilizing the unique political and cultural situation in Israel, in Chapter 6 Hasisi studies the views of Jews and Arabs toward the police, while tying the discussion to the concept of "deeply divided societies." Although most of this literature treated political differences as the primary explanation for relatively weak relationships between the police and minorities, Hasisi argues for the importance of the cultural component. Responses to a telephone survey indicate that, overall, Jews view the police more positively than Arabs. At the same time, Israeli Arabs are not homogeneous: Druze are similar in their political orientation to Jews, and as a result their perceptions of the police are more positive than those of Muslim and Christian Arabs. However, they appear to be culturally similar to Muslims, which explains why their responses to statements concerning receptivity to the police are closer to those of Muslim Arabs. Thus, Hasisi takes advantage of the unique characteristics of Israeli society to add an important dimension to the study of police in deeply divided societies more generally.

In Chapter 7, Aviv asks whether data on victims in Israel mirrors that of U.S. and European studies, but, importantly, also examines a broader set of attitudes than previously examined, which stem from the literature on police legitimacy (e.g., Tyler 2004). In line with previous studies carried out in Western democracies, her findings reveal that victims view the police less positively than nonvictims in terms of police treatment and performance. Victims also display significantly lower levels of trust in the police. Aviv's study provides important new data in a different national context in support of work that reveals differences between the way victims and nonvictims evaluate the police, but shows this gap in the specific context of the legitimacy model.

The legitimacy model also provided the background for the study by Factor, Castilo, and Rattner (Chapter 8). Although public views are often measured in Israel, the "legitimacy" of the police as frequently examined today (e.g., National Research Council 2004; Tyler 2004, 2009), its antecedents, and outcomes have rarely been examined in the Israeli context (see Jonathan-Zamir and Weisburd 2013, for an exception). Factor et al. replicate the process-based model established in an earlier work (Sunshine and Tyler 2003), and find support for the validity of the model in Israel. Similar to previous assessments, mostly in English-speaking countries, they find that the main predictor of police legitimacy is assessments of fair processes. Legitimacy, in turn, is associated with greater support for the police. Importantly, in addition to replicating the model, they examine the effect of religiosity, which has not yet been tested in this context. They find that, among the Jewish population, those who consider themselves more religious tend to view the police as less legitimate.

The last study in this section (Chapter 9) takes an innovative approach to the study of police legitimacy. To date, police legitimacy has mostly been examined from the perspective of citizens. Recently, Bottoms and Tankebe (2012) have argued that the way the police perceive their own legitimacy should also be considered. In this study, Jonathan-Zamir and Harpaz examine Israeli police officers' understanding of the factors that affect their external legitimacy ("What makes citizens view us as legitimate?"). They find that in contrast to citizen priorities as reflected in surveys, Israeli police believe that their legitimacy in the eyes of the public depends more on their accomplishments in fighting crime than on procedural justice. This study is an important example of pioneering investigations of police carried out in Israel that should be replicated in other local/national contexts.

The studies in the last section of the book, policing terrorism, make use of unique Israeli circumstances to answer important questions that are being asked in many Western democracies, particularly since the terror attack of 9/11, but often cannot be empirically tested in those countries because of relatively low rates of terrorist attacks, and because their local police have relatively little experience in facing terrorism threats. The Israel National Police resembles local police agencies in many Western democracies in its core functions and restrains, but, at the same time, has been responsible for "internal security" since the early 1970s, and over the years has faced numerous and diverse terrorism threats.

Weisburd, Hasisi, Jonathan-Zamir, and Aviv (Chapter 10) take advantage of the diversity in terrorism threats across Israeli communities during the period of the "Second Intifada," and examine if and how terrorism threats have affected police performance in fighting crime, as reflected in clearance rates. They also examine if terrorism threats have a different effect in majority-Jewish versus minority-Arab communities. They find that in Jewish communities, probably as a result of limited resources and changing priorities, as terrorism threats increase—the ability of the police to solve crime decreases. At the same time, the effect is opposite in Arab communities: the higher the terrorism threats, the higher the clearance rates. They attribute this effect to growing surveillance in these communities as a result of heightened suspicion in high-threat periods.

Sela-Shayovitz (Chapter 11) also uses the high-threat period of the Second Intifada and examines media coverage of the police within the framework of police legitimacy, comparing the way the police were portrayed before and during the Intifada period. She finds that the high-threat period resulted in more media coverage that both reflects and encourages trust in the Israel National Police. Periods of intense terrorism threats also led to favorable coverage of police performance and fair treatment. Multivariate analyses showed the important effect of high terrorism threats on trust in the police (as reflected in media coverage) independent of other variables often associated with police legitimacy. Thus, this study supports earlier findings regarding the effects of external threats on internal cohesion, while tying the findings to the legitimacy model (e.g., Sunshine and Tyler 2003).

In Chapter 12, Hasisi and Weisburd use the Israeli situation to examine the extent to which the Arab minority in Israel differs in its evaluations of policing terrorism and its impacts on traditional policing and the community. Their research reinforces findings that minorities with national or religious affiliations with the sources of terrorism in a country will feel particularly vulnerable and threatened by a police focus on terrorism. However, their survey also suggests that even in Israel, where minority/majority relationships are complicated by national identities, there is much commonality between the majority and minority communities. Both recognize the importance of policing terrorism, and both are aware that such an emphasis in policing may negatively impact police performance in other areas and complicate the relationships of the police with minority communities.

The chapter by Jonathan-Zamir and Aviv (Chapter 13) focuses on how the police have understood their counterterrorism role and its implications over the years. Centering on three critical periods, they analyze Israeli police annual reports and find that fighting terrorism was not always perceived as an easy and natural role for the Israeli police, and it often took precedence over traditional crime-fighting roles in Israel. Their analysis also reveals that this agency shows only partial acknowledgment of the potential outcomes of counterterrorism functions, particularly with regard to the relationship between the police and the public.

Finally, Perry and Jonathan-Zamir (Chapter 14) review recent research on policing in Israel. They focus on two important areas—policing terrorism and police–community relationships, and thus this chapter is relevant to both the second and third themes of this book. They identify that most studies on policing terrorism in Israel highlight the unintended outcomes of excessive focus on counterterrorism, both with regard to the ability of the police to solve crime and in terms of police–community relationships, particularly with the Arab minority. Studies on the relationship between the police and the public not only reveal a long-term drop in public support for the Israeli police but, taken together, suggest that this drop is largely the result of disregard for the principles of procedural justice.

This edited book illustrates the important advances in Israeli police science over the past decade. It also shows that studying Israeli policing can provide important knowledge for advancing police science more generally. Empirical research in Israel, or other countries outside the traditional research domains of the United States, Europe and Australia, can provide important comparative data about key concepts and findings in policing. This was the case, for example, for hot spots research, examination of crime victims' attitudes, and police legitimacy here. However, the book also suggests that new knowledge that raises new questions can be identified in such comparative studies.

Some of the studies reported in this book, such as testing the outcomes of shifting responsibilities from one agency in the criminal justice system to another, developing models for the purpose of improving traffic enforcement effectiveness given budgetary and resource constraints, or examining police legitimacy from the perspective of the police rather than the public, suggest innovative outlooks to the study of police. Moreover, the Israeli setting provides an important laboratory for testing questions related to policing terrorism in a democratic society, particularly the outcomes of such "high policing" roles (see Bayley and Weisburd 2009). These questions would be difficult to examine in other countries where terrorism threats were less intense or have not varied over time, or where the police are not bound by democratic principles. Israel also shows a continuing drop in public trust, which raises broader questions about maintaining long-term public support. We believe that other democratic societies, with their distinctive features, allow for the examination of similarly important and unique questions. We hope that this book on Israel will lead to greater focus on research in other comparative settings. We also think that it is important in illustrating the advances in police science in Israel.

References

Bayley, D. and D. Weisburd. 2009. Cops and spooks: The role of police in counter terrorism. In *To protect and to serve: Policing in an age of terrorism*, eds. D. Weisburd., T. E. Feucht, I. Hakimi, L. F. Mock and S. Perry, 81–99. New York: Springer.

Bottoms, A. and J. Tankebe. 2012. Beyond procedural justice: A dialogic approach to legitimacy in criminal justice. *The Journal of Criminal Law and Criminology* 102(1): 119–170.

DeYoung, D. J. 1999. An evaluation of the specific deterrent effects of vehicle impoundment on suspended, revoked, and unlicensed drivers in California. *Accident Analysis and Prevention* 31: 45–53.

Gill, C. E., D. Weisburd, T. Bennett, C. W. Telep and Z. Vitter. 2014. Community-oriented policing to reduce crime, disorder, and fear and increase satisfaction and legitimacy among citizens: A systematic review. *Journal of Experimental Criminology* 10(4): 399–428.

Jonathan-Zamir, T. and D. Weisburd. 2013. The effects of security threats on antecedents of police legitimacy: Findings from a quasi-experiment in Israel. *Journal of Research in Crime and Delinquency* 50(1): 3–32.

Lum, C., C. S. Koper and C. Telep. 2011. The evidence-based policing matrix. *Journal of Experimental Criminology* 7: 3–26.

National Research Council. 2004. *Fairness and effectiveness in policing: The evidence.* Committee to Review Research on Police Policy and Practices. W. Skogan and K. Frydl (Eds.), Committee on Law and Justice, Division of Behavioral and Social Sciences and Education. Washington, DC: The National Academies Press.

Sherman, L. W. 1998. *Evidence-based policing.* Washington, DC: Police Foundation.

Sunshine, J. and T. R. Tyler. 2003. The role of procedural justice and legitimacy in shaping public support for policing. *Law and Society Review* 37: 513–548.

Telep, C. W. and D. Weisburd. 2012. What has been learned from systematic reviews in policing? Paper presented May 1 at the conference: *What has been learned from systematic reviews in criminology?* Jerusalem, Israel.

Tyler, T. R. 2004. Enhancing police legitimacy. *The Annals of the American Academy of Political and Social Science* 593(1): 84–99.

Tyler, T. R. 2009. Legitimacy and criminal justice: The benefits of self-regulation. *Ohio State Journal of Criminal Law* 7(1): 307–359.

Tyler, T. R. 2011. Trust and legitimacy: Policing in the USA and Europe. *European Journal of Criminology* 8(4): 254–266.

Weisburd, D. and A. Braga. 2006. *Police innovation: Contrasting perspectives.* Cambridge, UK: Cambridge University Press.

Weisburd, D. and J. E. Eck. 2004. What can police do to reduce crime, disorder and fear? *Annals of the American Academy of Political and Social Science* 593: 42–65.

Weisburd, D. and P. Neyroud. 2011. Police science: Toward a new paradigm. *New Perspectives in Policing.*

Weisburd, D., E. R. Groff and S. M. Yang. 2012. *The criminology of place: Street segments and our understanding of the crime problem.* New York: Oxford University Press.

Crime Control

I

Law of Concentrations of Crime at Place
Case of Tel Aviv-Jaffa*

2

DAVID WEISBURD
SHAI AMRAM

Contents

Although the individual and "macro" units of place such as the community have long been a focus of research and theory regarding social problems, only recently have scholars begun to explore crime and other antisocial behavior at very small "micro" units of geography. The roots of such approaches can be found in the efforts of scholars to identify the relationship between specific aspects of urban design (Jeffery 1971) or urban architecture (Newman 1972) and antisocial behavior, but broadened to take into account a much larger set of characteristics of physical space and criminal opportunity (e.g., Brantingham and Brantingham 1975). These studies drew important distinctions between the specific location of antisocial behavior and the larger geographical area (such as neighborhood, community, police beat, or city) that surrounds it.

The main theoretical impetus to the micro place approach to antisocial behavior is found in a group of theoretical perspectives that emerged in the late 1970s. In a seminal article on routine activities and crime, for example, Cohen and Felson (1979) suggested that a fuller understanding of crime must include a recognition that the availability of suitable crime targets and the presence or absence of capable guardians influence crime events. Routine activities focused attention on the specific ecological contexts in which suitable targets, motivated offenders, and the absence of capable guardians occurred. Researchers at the British Home Office, in a series of studies examining the effects of "situational crime prevention," also challenged the traditional focus on offenders and communities (e.g., see Clarke 1983). In contrast to offender-based approaches to crime prevention, which usually focus on the dispositions of criminals, situational crime prevention begins with the opportunity structure (and immediate physical context) of the crime situation (Felson and Clarke 1998). Paul and Patricia Brantingham also emphasized the role of place characteristics in shaping the type and frequency of human interaction in their work on environmental criminology (Brantingham and Brantingham 1991).

* Reproduced from Weisburd, D. and S. Amram. *Police Practice and Research: An International Journal* 15(2): 101–114, 2014.

One implication of these emerging perspectives was that places at a "micro" geographic level should be an important focus of scholarly inquiry. Although concern with the relationship between social problems and place is not new and indeed goes back to the founding generations of modern criminology, the "micro" approach to places suggested by recent theories has just begun to be examined (Weisburd, Bernasco, and Bruinsma 2009). Places in this "micro" context are specific locations within the larger social environments of communities and neighborhoods (Eck and Weisburd 1995). Recent studies point to the potential theoretical and practical benefits of focusing research on crime places. In particular, there has been a consistent finding that crime is tightly concentrated at just a small number of micro places in a city. For example, in one of the pioneering studies in this area, Sherman, Gartin, and Buerger (1989) found that only 3.5% of the addresses in Minneapolis, Minnesota, produced 50% of all calls to the police. Fifteen years later, in a retrospective longitudinal study in Seattle, Washington, Weisburd et al. (2004) reported that between 4% and 5% of street segments in the city accounted for 50% of crime incidents for each year over 14 years.

The findings of remarkable concentrations of crime at place raise a more general question about the phenomenon of crime in cities. Is there some general law that applies across cities that dictates the general concentration of crime? This is the question raised in a recent book by Weisburd, Groff, and Yang (2012) titled *The Criminology of Place*. Studying crime at street segments in Seattle, they found a remarkable stability of crime concentrations each year over a 16-year period. They argue that these data, as well as prior studies showing similar concentrations of crime for specific years in other cities (e.g., see Pierce, Spaar, and Briggs 1988; Sherman et al. 1989) suggest that crime concentrations at micro places are relatively constant with about 5% of places producing about 50% of crime in a city each year (see also Weisburd, Telep, and Lawton 2014).

The idea of a "law" of crime rates is not a new one. Emile Durkheim raised this possibility more than a century ago. Durkheim suggested that crime was not indicative of pathology or illness in society, but at certain levels was simply evidence of the normal functioning of communities (Durkheim 1895, 1964). For Durkheim, the idea of a normal level of crime reinforced his theoretical position that crime helped to define and solidify norms in society. Although Durkheim's proposition regarding a normal level of crime in society does not seem to fit recent experience and is seldom discussed by criminologists today, Weisburd et al. (2012) argue that there is indeed a "normal level of crime" in cities, but one that relates to the concentration of crime at place and not to the overall rate of crime. Whereas the absolute levels of crime in cities vary from year to year, the extent of crime concentrations remains similar (Pierce et al. 1988; Sherman et al. 1989; Weisburd et al. 2004).

Weisburd et al. (2004) conclusions are based primarily on data on crime concentrations in Seattle and other American cities. In this paper, we examine such concentrations in Tel Aviv-Jaffa, Israel. If the "law of crime concentrations" applies to Tel Aviv-Jaffa, then we have another important data point for advancing this proposition about crime concentrations in modern urban areas.

Concentration of Crime at Place

A number of studies, beginning in the late 1980s, suggest that significant clustering of crime at place exists, regardless of the specific unit of analysis defined (see Brantingham and

Brantingham 1999; Crow and Bull 1975; Pierce et al. 1988; Roncek 2000; Sherman et al. 1989; Weisburd and Green 1994; Weisburd, Maher, and Sherman 1992; Weisburd et al. 2004, 2009). Perhaps the most influential of these was Sherman et al.'s (1989) analysis of emergency calls to street addresses over a single year. Sherman et al. (1989) found that only 3.5% of the addresses in Minneapolis produced 50% of all calls to the police. They regarded these results as so startling that they called for a new area of study, which they termed the "criminology of place."

Other studies produced similar evidence of the concentration of crime in crime hot spots. Weisburd and Mazerolle (2000), for example, found that approximately 20% of all disorder crimes and 14% of crimes against persons were concentrated in just 56 drug crime hot spots in Jersey City, New Jersey, an area that comprised only 4.4% of street segments and intersections in the city. Similarly, Eck, Gersh, and Taylor (2000) found that the most active 10% of places (in terms of crime) in the Bronx, New York, and Baltimore, Maryland, accounted for approximately 32% of a combination of robberies, assaults, burglaries, grand larcenies, and auto thefts. A study conducted by Weisburd et al. (2004) not only confirms the concentration of crime, but also the stability of such concentrations across a long time span. Weisburd et al. examined street segments in the city of Seattle from 1989 through 2002. They found that 50% of crime incidents over the 14-year period occurred at only 4.5% of the street segments. Crime concentrations appear to be greater in examining specific types of crime. In another study in Seattle, Weisburd et al. (2009) examined the concentration of crime incidents in which a juvenile was arrested. They found that only 86 street segments out of more than 25,000 accounted for one-third of all official juvenile arrest incidents over a 14-year period.

In a recent study extending the research of Weisburd et al. (2004) in Seattle, Weisburd, Groff, and Yang (2012) found that crime concentrations continued at similar levels over the additional 2-year period examined. Moreover, they found that the 1% of street segments in the city accounted for fully 23% of crime incidents. They also examined the extent to which such crime concentrations represented larger community area effects, or local processes generated at the street segment level. Their analyses suggest overall that there is a tremendous level of street-by-street variability in developmental patterns of crime at street segments in Seattle (see also Groff, Weisburd, and Yang 2010). For example, simple descriptive maps pointed to the spread of crime hot spots across Seattle. Although certain areas, such as the downtown center of the city, evidenced larger numbers of chronic hot spots, hot spot street segments were generally dispersed throughout the city. They concluded that an approach that assumed that hot spots were clustered only in a few "very bad" neighborhoods would misrepresent the spread of such problems in the city.

Similarly, drawing conclusions from spatial statistics, they found that trajectory patterns are interspersed, for example, with crime-free street segments often likely to be bounded by higher crime street segments, or chronic hot spots near street segments evidencing less serious developmental patterns. Indeed, 85% of street segments within 800 ft (nearly 244 m) of chronic crime hot spots were places with little or no crime. While acknowledging that community and larger area processes are important for understanding crime, they conclude that the action of crime begins at a very micro level of geography—in their case, the street segment.

Although these studies suggest that there is indeed a law of concentrations of crime operating across cities, and that these crime concentrations at micro places are not simply a reflection of larger area trends, there is little known about the concentration of crime outside of the United States, and to some extent Australia, the United Kingdom, and Europe, where such studies are just beginning to emerge. In the following discussion, we test the law of crime concentrations in the context of one such city, Tel Aviv-Jaffa, Israel.

The Study

Our data are drawn from the city of Tel Aviv-Jaffa, which is the heart of Israel's largest metro-politan urban area. The city itself had a population of 404,400 for the year 2010, which makes it the second largest city in the country behind Jerusalem. However, the metropolitan area of Tel Aviv-Jaffa includes a population of 3.3 million, nearly 43.4% of the total population of Israel. The city was established in 1909 and played a central role in the development of the Zionist movement in the country as the first new city in Palestine. It was the center of the political renaissance of Jewish institutions in Palestine, and of the new socialist labor move-ment of the twentieth century. Today, it is the economic and cultural capital of Israel. It is the home of the Israeli stock exchange, and includes the corporate offices of many international companies based in Israel. It is also home to such key cultural institutions as the Israeli Opera and Israel's most prestigious theater, "HaBima." And as a tourist attraction with entertain-ment available 24 hours a day, it is nicknamed in Israel as "the city that never sleeps."

The city population is primarily of Jewish background (92%), although it includes a significant minority population composed of Arab Muslims and Christians and non-Arab Christians. The Arab population (3.9%) is concentrated in the old city of Jaffa, incorpo-rated into Tel Aviv-Jaffa in 1948, and is primarily Muslim. Tel Aviv-Jaffa, like other major cities around the world, includes an overrepresentation of older citizens, younger profes-sionals, and students. The rate of elderly persons (aged 65 years or older) in Tel Aviv-Jaffa is 14.2%, which is higher than the average number of elderly in the general population (9.7%). The rate of the younger population in the city aged 21–39 years is 38.8%, whereas the national rate is 29.2%.

The city has emerged in recent years as a major urban center, which is reflected by the large growth of urban business towers and residences across the city. Tel Aviv-Jaffa's property crime rate was 54 incidents per 1000 persons, which placed it first among cities in Israel in 2010, the year of our study data. Tel Aviv-Jaffa's violent crime rate of 10.8 per 1000 persons is also one of the highest among Israeli cities.

Crime Incidents at Street Segments

We used computerized records of written reports for the calendar year of 2010, often referred to as "incident reports," to examine crime trends. Tel Aviv-Jaffa experienced a total of 43,258 crime incidents during the research period. Incident reports are generated in Tel Aviv-Jaffa by police officers or detectives after an initial response to a request for police service or as a result of a crime identified by the police. In this sense, incident reports are more inclusive than arrest reports but less inclusive than calls for service. Incident reports have been used in a series of other studies examining crime at place including those conducted by Weisburd and colleagues (see Weisburd and Green 1995; Weisburd and Mazerolle 2000; Weisburd et al. 2004, 2012, 2014), thus allowing us to make direct comparisons to prior research.

The geographic unit of interest for this study is the street segment (sometimes referred to as a street block or face block), defined as the two block faces on both sides of a street between two intersections. We follow Weisburd et al. (2004, 2012) in choosing this unit of analysis and also follow their general logic for its utility. It is important to note that the street segment approach fit easily to Tel Aviv-Jaffa in part because it is a new city that was created using the street grid model.

Scholars have long recognized the street segment's relevance in organizing life in the city (Appleyard 1981; Brower 1980; Jacobs 1961; Taylor, Gottfredson, and Brower 1984; Unger and Wandersman 1983). Taylor (1997, 1998), for example, argues that the visual closeness of block residents, interrelated role obligations, acceptance of certain common norms and behavior, common regularly recurring rhythms of activity, the physical boundaries of the street, and the historical evolution of the street segment make the street block or street segment a particularly useful unit for analysis of place (see also Hunter and Baumer 1982; Taylor et al. 1984).

Beyond the theoretical reasons for using street segments to understand crime at place, there are other advantages. Unlike neighborhood boundaries, street segments are easily recognized by residents and have well-defined boundaries (Taylor 1988). Moreover, the small size of street segments minimizes spatial heterogeneity and makes for easier interpretation of significant effects (Rice and Smith 2002; Smith, Frazee, and Davison 2000), and processes of informal social control and territoriality (Taylor et al. 1984) are more effective in smaller settings such as street segments.

Operationally, the choice of street segments over even smaller units such as addresses (see Sherman et al. 1989) also minimizes the error likely to develop from miscoding of addresses in official data (see Klinger and Bridges 1997; Weisburd and Green 1994). We recognize, however, that crime events may be linked across street segments. For example, a drug market may operate across a series of blocks (Weisburd and Green 1995; Worden, Bynum, and Frank 1994), and a large housing project and problems associated with it may transverse street segments in multiple directions (see Skogan and Annan 1994). Nonetheless, the street segment offers a useful compromise because it allows a unit of analysis large enough to avoid unnecessary crime coding errors, but small enough to avoid aggregation that might hide specific trends. Importantly, as well, a number of prior studies have utilized the street segment when examining crime concentrations at places.

Following Weisburd et al. (2012; see also Groff et al. 2010), we operationalized the definition of street segments by referring directly to the geography of streets in Tel Aviv-Jaffa. Prior studies have generally relied on what are often defined as hundred blocks to approximate the geography of street segments (e.g., Groff, Weisburd, and Morris 2009; Weisburd et al. 2004, 2009). In this approach, researchers assume that the actual streets in a city follow the overall rule that a street segment includes addresses ranging a hundred numbers, for example, from 1 to 100 or from 101 to 200. Although this approach is common and identifies broadly the geography of street segments in the city, we wanted our study to match as much as possible the reality of the behavioral settings of streets between intersections. We defined 17,160 valid street segments in Tel Aviv-Jaffa. The average length of a street segment was 205 ft (or 62 m). The majority of the streets (roughly 75%) are between 163 and 220 ft (50–67 m). Using our definition, very few streets (less than 3%) ended up longer than 330 ft (101 m).

In linking crime incidents to street segments, we exclude records of crimes that occur on the Tel Aviv-Jaffa beach, the central station area, and for nonresidential or business road types such as highways and regional roads. We geocoded the remaining incident reports (excluding those without address identifiers) and were left with 39,392 incidents, nearly

91% of the total recorded crime incidents during that period. The geocoding process was carried out using Arc GIS 10 with a geocoding locator used by the police information technology unit. To convert a crime point's location into a street segment ($N = 17,160$), we used the Spatial Join tool to join attributes from one feature, the point location, to another attribute, the street segment, based on a spatial relationship.

Results

Concentration of Crime at Place

Figure 2.1 presents the overall concentration of crime incidents at street segments in Tel Aviv-Jaffa. The results are startling in their similarity to the findings of studies in U.S. cities. As we noted earlier, studies of crime concentrations have generally found that between 3% and 6% of places produce about 50% of crimes or crime calls to the police. In the most comparable study conducted to date in Seattle, Washington (Weisburd et al. 2012), between 4.7% and 6% of street segments over a 16-year period produced 50% of crime incidents. In Tel Aviv-Jaffa in 2010, 4.5% of the street segments produced approximately 50% of the crime. This consistency is striking, and reinforces the proposition that we posed earlier of a law of concentrations of crime at place.

When we examine where 25% of crime is located in the city, our findings are reinforced. Just 0.9% of street segments in Tel Aviv-Jaffa accounted for one-quarter of all crimes. This means that just 159 street segments in the city are responsible for a quarter of the crime at street segments. Again, this is very similar to the results of the study in Seattle, conducted by Weisburd et al. (2012). As we noted earlier, they found that the 1% of street segments that were the most chronic hot spots of crime in the city included about 23% of all crime incidents over a 16-year period.

It is also the case that in Tel Aviv-Jaffa, as well as in American cities that have been studied, most street segments have little or no crime. Comparing Tel Aviv-Jaffa to Seattle in this case, Tel Aviv-Jaffa seems to have even a larger proportion of crime-free street segments. In Tel Aviv-Jaffa, about two-thirds of the street segments did not have a reported crime in all of 2010, whereas in Seattle the number across the study period averaged about 40% (see Weisburd et al. 2014).

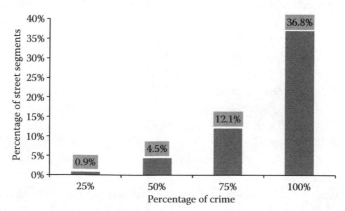

Figure 2.1 Crime concentrations in Tel Aviv-Jaffa. Note: Street segments = 17,160; crime incidents = 39,392.

A key question in prior studies has been whether crime at place varies significantly within larger areas. If, for example, crime was concentrated at a small number of streets, but all of those streets were clustered together in a single community, then the concept of hot spots of micro crime places would be challenged. Rather, it would be relevant to speak of hot neighborhoods, as has long been a tradition in criminology (e.g., Bursik and Grasmick 1993; Greenberg, Rohed, and Williams 1982; Sampson, Raudenbush, and Earls 1997). We noted earlier that prior studies in the United States have found that there is important street-by-street variability in crime. Is the concentration of crime at micro places in Tel Aviv-Jaffa a reflection of micro areas processes?

Looking at Tel Aviv-Jaffa tells a very similar story in this regard to U.S. studies. Figures 2.2–2.4 show street-by-street crime counts for Tel Aviv-Jaffa. The darker the shading, the higher the number of crime incidents at that street. For purposes of simplification, we divide counts into five groups. The most serious crime hot spots are represented in black (51+ crime incidents). They include just 0.3% of the street segments of Tel Aviv-Jaffa but some 15% of the crime. The next group, coded dark gray, also includes crime hot spots in the city but with lower intensity (16–50 crime incidents). At the other end of the scale are the two-thirds of street segments with no crimes during the study period (colored white).

There are clearly area influences. For example, Figure 2.2 shows the wealthier, more residential northern part of Tel Aviv-Jaffa, including Tel Aviv University, which is dominated

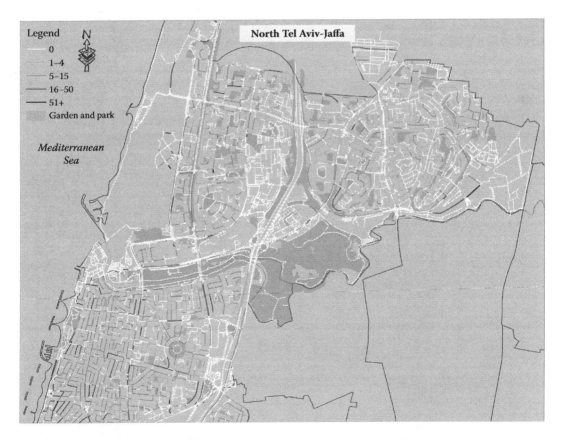

Figure 2.2 North Tel Aviv-Jaffa.

by streets with little or no crime. At the same time, even in the northernmost part of the city, which is affluent and highly residential, there are pockets of gray-colored streets that had between 5 and 15 crime incidents in 1 year. And there are scattered dark gray and black lines, representing more chronic hot spot street segments as you move toward Central Tel Aviv-Jaffa.

The central area of Tel Aviv-Jaffa (see Figure 2.3), including the main business district, has many more streets with serious crime problems. But even here, the vast majority of streets have little or no crime as represented by the white and light gray lines. Note the tremendous street-to-street variability of crime levels in this map, with white, light gray, and gray street segments interspersed. And in this case, there are a number of chronic hot spot street segments as represented by the black and dark gray lines. Importantly, although there is some clustering of such high crime streets in specific areas, there is still a considerable level of street-by-street variability, for example, with gray, light gray, and white lines often adjacent or close by.

The southern neighborhoods of Tel Aviv-Jaffa (Figure 2.4), which includes an area around the Central Bus Station—known for high numbers of illegal immigrants and homeless individuals, does indeed have higher crime concentrations on average. And the area around the Central Bus Station has the highest concentration of chronic crime hot spots (black and dark gray lines) in the city. However, such hot spots can also be found in other areas here, and there is a substantial amount of street-by-street variability in the

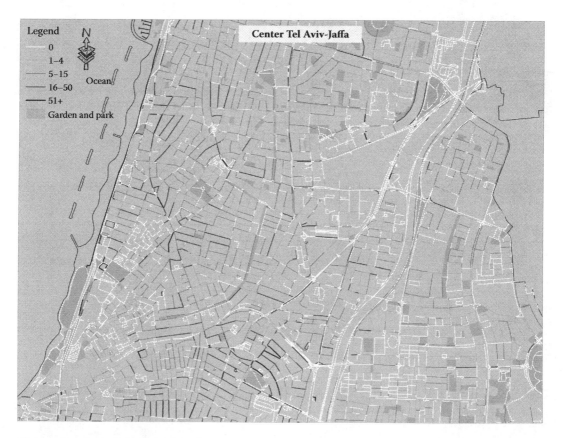

Figure 2.3 Central Tel Aviv-Jaffa.

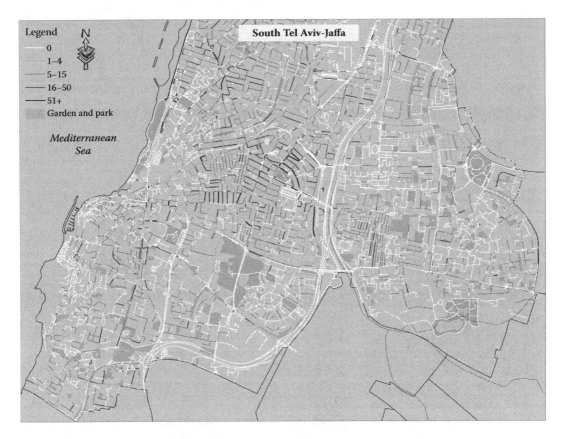

Figure 2.4 South Tel Aviv-Jaffa.

colors observed across the areas, as was true of the earlier maps. Importantly, most streets even in what is generally described as a high crime area of Tel Aviv-Jaffa have little or no crime as evidenced by the light gray and white colored streets.

Discussion and Conclusions

Looking at crime incidents in Tel Aviv-Jaffa, we find that crime is tightly concentrated at place. Just 4.5% of the street segments in the city account for 50% of crime incidents, and just 0.9% of the street segments account for 25% of crime incidents over a 1-year period. Moreover, these crime concentrations at street segments are not simply reflective of neighborhood trends. Although there are clearly larger area influences on crime in Tel Aviv-Jaffa, there is also a tremendous amount of street-to-street variability within neighborhoods. Even in the "best neighborhoods" in Tel Aviv-Jaffa, there are crime hot spots. And in the neighborhoods that are often seen as problematic, most streets have little or no crime, and there is often variability in crime from street to street.

Our findings, as noted in the preceding discussion, are particularly interesting in light of Emile Durkheim's classic proposition that the level of crime is stable in society, or rather that there was a "normal level" of crime in society. For Durkheim, this meant that crime was not necessarily an indication of an illness or pathology in society, but rather that healthy societies would inevitably have some normal level of crime. Crime waves and crime drops, in this context, can be seen as the result of some "abnormality" in society that results from crisis or dramatic social change.

Underlying Durkheim's proposition is his understanding of crime as a product of social definition. Erickson (1966) was to build on this idea in his classic study, *Wayward Puritans*, where he sought to show that the definition of crime had a social function. By defining others as deviant, society can help draw the boundaries between acceptable and unacceptable conduct (see also Adler and Adler 2009; Becker 1963). Defining people as criminal in this sense serves a function in defining the moral boundaries of society. We can know the boundaries of acceptable behavior by observing "deviants" who are sanctioned for violating societal norms.

Crime rates over the past few decades would seem to strongly contradict Durkheim's conception of normal levels of crime in society. Between 1973 and 1990 violent crime doubled (Reiss and Roth 1993), and in the 1990s the United States experienced a well-documented "crime drop" (Blumstein and Wallman 2000). In the 1970s, Alfred Blumstein and colleagues (Blumstein and Cohen 1973; Blumstein, Cohen, and Nagin 1976; Blumstein and Moitra 1979) hypothesized that Durkheim's proposition could be applied to punishment in America, where imprisonment rates had remained static for a long time (see also Tremblay 1986). However, recent dramatic increases in U.S. incarcerations in the 1980s and 1990s would seem inconsistent with the normal crime, or "normal punishment" (Blumstein and Cohen 1973), hypothesis. Unless, of course, we were to postulate that these are periods of dramatic social change.

Weisburd et al. (2012) argue that there is indeed a "normal level of crime" in cities, but one that relates to the concentration of crime at place and not to the overall rate of crime. They claim that a different proposition from Durkheim's can be raised at this juncture, and should be examined in future studies. There appears to be a "law of concentrations" of crime at place. Our study provides important support for this proposition as it is one of the first studies of crime concentrations at micro places outside of the United States. The consistency of crime concentrations at micro places in Tel Aviv-Jaffa and American cities suggests that there is some underlying social process pushing crime to certain levels of concentration in modern cities.

Can we use Durkheim's initial insights to consider possible reasons for this law of concentrations of crime at place? If we follow Durkheim and other theorists that built on his work, we would look to the role of crime at place in defining normative boundaries in society. In this case, we might argue that a certain number of places in the city with severe crime problems serve as lessons for the city more generally. This would fit well with our finding that crime hot spots are found throughout the city. Accordingly, we all have direct visceral experiences with the "bad places" in the city, and perhaps that serves to define for the rest of us the "moral boundaries" of place. The normal level of crime concentrations in this context would relate to the proportion of problem places that are needed to bring the lessons of moral boundaries to the city's residents.

Another possible explanation for a law of concentrations comes from the concentration of other characteristics of places in the city. For example, Weisburd et al. (2012) note that the concentrations of bus stops or number of public facilities, like crime, stays relatively stable over long periods. Perhaps the law of concentrations of crime is related to the overall distribution of social and environmental characteristics of places in cities. Does the stability of patterns of business and employment in a city, for example, reflect more general patterns of concentration that are related to the growth and development of urban areas? Certainly, cities regulate such concentrations, by defining commercial, business, and industrial use of property. Perhaps the normal concentrations of crime are simply a reflection of the normal concentrations of other social activities in the city. The law of concentrations of crime at place may simply be a reflection of a more general law of the stability of concentrations of specific aspects of social and economic life in the city. This is suggested by Juran (1951), who first noted a general rule for the concentration of social and economic activities. He called this rule the Pareto Principle, coining the phrase "the vital few and the trivial many."

But this brings us back to Durkheim, because crime is a social phenomenon, and its tolerance is a social construct. Is society willing to tolerate crime at only a certain proportion of the landscape of a city? Is the law of concentrations a result of the boundaries of crime at place that citizens are willing to tolerate? Will people become worried and call for action when crime hot spots increase beyond a specific proportion of places in the city, and will they become more lax when the concentrations are below that level?

We think that our data in Tel Aviv-Jaffa add a strong reason to continue to explore explanations for a law of concentrations of crime at place. The fact that cities thousands of miles apart from each other, with very different populations and social norms, have virtually identical crime concentrations at micro places is an intriguing and important finding. Certainly, this law of concentrations needs to be studied across other metropolitan centers around the world to see how widely it applies. More generally, it is time for scholars to explore more directly the explanation for the law of concentrations of crime trends at micro places. In the spatial context, scholars should explore street segment characteristics, social and environmental, that are important to understanding the concentration of crime at place.

Finally, we want to emphasize the crime prevention policy implications of our study for Israel. Our data reinforce the importance of crime places in the production of crime, and suggest that Israel is no different from American cities. Given that crime in Tel Aviv-Jaffa is concentrated at micro places, so too should police activity be concentrated at this geographic level. The Israeli National Police has generally considered crime problems at macro geographic levels such as neighborhoods or cities. It is time to recognize that the action of crime is often at a much more local geographic level, such as the street segment. Evidence from hot spot policing programs suggests that the police can be effective in preventing crime when they focus on micro geographic hot spots (e.g., see Braga and Bond 2008; Sherman and Weisburd 1995; Weisburd and Green 1995). Our data show that such an approach is relevant to the Israeli case.

References

Adler, P. A. and P. Adler. 2009. *Constructions of deviance: Social power, context, and interaction.* 6th ed. Belmont, CA: Wadsworth Publishing.

Appleyard, D. 1981. *Livable streets.* Berkeley, CA: University of California Press.

Becker, H. S. 1963. *Outsiders: Studies in the sociology of deviance.* Glencoe, IL: Free Press of Glencoe.

Blumstein, A. J. and J. Cohen. 1973. A theory of the stability of punishment. *The Journal of Criminal Law and Criminology* 64: 198–207.

Blumstein, A. and S. Moitra. 1979. An analysis of the time series of the imprisonment rate in the states of the United States: A further test of the stability of punishment hypothesis. *The Journal of Criminal Law and Criminology* 70: 376–390.

Blumstein, A. and J. Wallman. 2000. The recent rise and fall of American violence. In *The crime drop in America*, eds. A. Blumstein, and J. Wallman, 1–12. Cambridge, UK: Cambridge University Press.

Blumstein, A., J. Cohen and D. S. Nagin. 1976. The dynamics of a homeostatic punishment process. *Journal of Criminal Law and Criminology* 67: 317–334.

Braga, A. A. and B. J. Bond. 2008. Policing crime and disorder hot spots: A randomized controlled trial. *Criminology* 46: 577–608.

Brantingham, P. L. and P. J. Brantingham. 1975. Residential burglary and urban form. *Urban Studies* 12: 104–125.

Brantingham, P. J. and P. L. Brantingham. 1991. *Environmental criminology*. Prospect Heights, IL: Waveland Press.

Brantingham, P. L. and P. J. Brantingham. 1999. Theoretical model of crime hot spot generation. *Studies on Crime and Crime Prevention* 8: 26–27.

Brower, S. 1980. Territory in urban settings. In *Human behavior and environment: Current theory and research*, eds. I. Altman, and C. M. Werner, 4: 179–207. New York: Plenum.

Bursik, R. J. Jr. and H. G. Grasmick. 1993. *Neighborhoods and crime: The dimensions of effective community control*. New York: Lexington Books.

Clarke, R. V. 1983. Situational crime prevention: Its theoretical basis and practical scope. In *Crime and Justice: A Review of Research*, eds. M. Tonry, and N. Morris, 14: 225–256. Chicago: University of Chicago Press.

Cohen, L. E. and M. Felson. 1979. Social change and crime rate trends: A routine activity approach. *American Sociological Review* 44: 588–608.

Crow, W. J. and J. L. Bull. 1975. *Robbery deterrence: An applied behavioral science demonstration—Final report*. La Jolla, CA: Western Behavioral Sciences Institute.

Durkheim, E. 1895, 1964. *The rules of sociological method*. Edited by G. E. G. Catlin, Translated by S. A. Solovay, and J. H. Mueller. New York: Free Press.

Eck, J. E. and D. Weisburd. 1995. Crime places in crime theory. In *Crime and place. Crime Prevention Studies*, eds. J. E. Eck, and D. Weisburd, 4: 1–33. Monsey, NY: Willow Tree Press.

Eck, J. E., J. S. Gersh and C. Taylor. 2000. Finding crime hot spots through repeat address mapping. In *Analyzing crime patterns: Frontiers of practice*, eds. V. Goldsmith., P. McGuir, J. H. Mollenkopf and T. A. Ross, 49–64. Thousand Oaks, CA: Sage Publications.

Erickson, K. T. 1966. *Wayward puritans: A study in the sociology of deviance*. New York: Wiley.

Felson, M. and R. V. Clarke. 1998. Opportunity makes the thief: Practical theory for crime prevention. *Police Research Group: Police Research Series*. Paper 98:36.

Greenberg, S. W., W. M. Rohed and J. R. Williams. 1982. Safety in urban neighborhoods: A comparison of physical characteristics and informal territorial control in high and low crime neighborhoods. *Population and Environment* 5: 141–165.

Groff, E. R., D. Weisburd and N. Morris. 2009. Where the action is at places: Examining spatio-temporal patterns of juvenile crime at places using trajectory analysis and GIS. In *Putting crime in its place: Units of analysis in spatial crime research*, eds. D. Weisburd., W. Bernasco and G. Bruinsma, 61–86. New York: Springer.

Groff, E. R., D. Weisburd and S. M. Yang. 2010. Is it important to examine crime trends at a local "micro" level?: A longitudinal analysis of street to street variability in crime trajectories. *Journal of Quantitative Criminology* 26: 32–37.

Hunter, A. and T. L. Baumer. 1982. Street traffic, social integration, and fear of crime. *Sociological Inquiry* 52(2): 122–131.

Jacobs, J. 1961. *The death and life of great American cities*. New York: Vintage Books.

Jeffery, C. R. 1971. *Crime prevention through environmental design*. Beverly Hills, CA: Sage Publications.

Juran, J. M. 1951. *Quality control handbook*. New York: McGraw-Hill.

Klinger, D. and G. Bridges. 1997. Measurement error in calls-for-service as an indicator of crime. *Criminology* 35: 705–726.

Newman, O. 1972. *Defensible space: Crime prevention through environmental design*. New York: Macmillan.

Pierce, G., S. Spaar and L. R. Briggs. 1988. *The character of police work: Strategic and tactical implications.* Boston: Center for Applied Social Research, Northeastern University.

Reiss, A. J. Jr. and J. A. Roth. 1993. *Understanding and preventing violence.* National Research Council. Washington, DC: National Academy Press.

Rice, K. J. and W. R. Smith. 2002. Sociological models of automotive theft: Integrating routine activity and social disorganization approaches. *Journal of Research in Crime and Delinquency* 39: 304–336.

Roncek, D. W. 2000. Schools and crime. In *Analyzing crime patterns: Frontiers of practice,* eds. V. Goldsmith., P. G. McGuire, J. H. Mollenkopf and T. A. Ross, 153–165. Thousand Oaks, CA: Sage Publications.

Sampson, R. J., S. W. Raudenbush and F. Earls. 1997. Neighborhoods and violent crime: A multilevel study of collective efficacy. *Science* 277: 918–924.

Sherman, L. W. and D. Weisburd. 1995. General deterrent effects of police patrol in crime "hot spots": A randomized, controlled trial. *Justice Quarterly* 12(4): 625–648.

Sherman, L. W., P. Gartin and M. E. Buerger. 1989. Hot spots of predatory crime: Routine activities and the criminology of place. *Criminology* 27: 27–55.

Skogan, W. G. and S. Annan. 1994. Drugs and public housing: Toward an effective police response. In *Drugs and crime: Evaluating public policy initiatives,* eds. D. MacKenzie, and C. D. Uchida, 129–150. Thousand Oaks, CA: Sage Publications.

Smith, W. R., S. G. Frazee and E. L. Davison. 2000. Furthering the integration of routine activity and social disorganization theories: Small units of analysis and the study of street robbery as a diffusion process. *Criminology* 38: 489–523.

Taylor, R. B. 1988. *Human territorial functioning: An empirical, evolutional perspective on individual and small group territorial cognitions, behaviors and consequences.* Cambridge, UK: Cambridge University Press.

Taylor, R. B. 1997. Social order and disorder of street blocks and neighborhoods: Ecology, micro-ecology, and the systemic model of social disorganization. *Journal of Research in Crime and Delinquency* 34: 113–155.

Taylor, R. B. 1998. Crime and small-scale places: What we know, what we can prevent, and what else we need to know. In *Crime and place: Plenary papers of the 1997 conference on criminal justice research and evaluation,* eds. R. B. Taylor., G. Bazemore, B. Boland, T. R. Clear, R. P. J. Corbett, J. Feinblatt, G. Berman, M. Sviridoff and C. Stone, 1–22. Washington, DC: National Institute of Justice.

Taylor, R. B., S. D. Gottfredson and S. Brower. 1984. Block crime and fear: Defensible space, local social ties, and territorial functioning. *Journal of Research in Crime and Delinquency* 21: 303–331.

Tremblay, P. 1986. The stability of punishment: A follow-up of Blumstein's hypothesis. *Journal of Quantitative Criminology* 2: 157–180.

Unger, D. and A. Wandersman. 1983. Neighboring and its role in block organizations: An exploratory report. *American Journal of Community Psychology* 11: 291–300.

Weisburd, D. and S. Amram. 2014. The law of concentrations of crime at place: The case of Tel Aviv-Jaffa. *Police Practice and Research: An International Journal* 15(2): 101–114.

Weisburd, D. and L. Green. 1994. Defining the drug market: The case of the Jersey City DMA system. In *Drugs and crime: Evaluating public policy initiatives,* eds. D. L. MacKenzie, and C. D. Uchida. Thousand Oaks, CA: Sage Publications.

Weisburd, D. and L. Green. 1995. Policing drug hot spots: The Jersey City drug market analysis experiment. *Justice Quarterly* 12: 711–735.

Weisburd, D. and L. G. Mazerolle. 2000. Crime and disorder in drug hot spots: Implications for theory and practice in policing. *Police Quarterly* 3: 331–349.

Weisburd, D., W. Bernasco and G. J. N. Bruinsma. 2009. *Putting crime in its place: Units of analysis in spatial crime research.* New York: Springer-Verlag.

Weisburd, D., S. Bushway, C. Lum and S. M. Yang. 2004. Trajectories of crime at places: A longitudinal study of street segments in the city of Seattle. *Criminology* 42: 283–321.

Weisburd, D., E. R. Groff and S. M. Yang. 2012. *The criminology of place: Street segments and our understanding of the crime problem.* New York: Oxford University Press.

Weisburd, D., L. Maher and L. Sherman. 1992. Contrasting crime general and crime specific theory: The case of hot spots of crime. In *New directions in criminological theory, Advances in criminological theory*, eds. F. Adler, and W. Laufer, 4: 45–69. New Brunswick, NJ: Transaction Press.

Weisburd, D., C. Telep and B. Lawton. 2014. Could innovations in policing have contributed to the New York City crime drop even in a period of declining police strength?: The case of stop, question and frisk as a hot spots policing strategy. *Justice Quarterly*, 31: 129–153.

Worden, R., T. Bynum and J. Frank. 1994. Police crackdowns on drug abuse and trafficking. In *Drugs and crime: Evaluating public policy initiatives*, eds. D. MacKenzie, and C. D. Uchida, 95–113. Thousand Oaks, CA: Sage Publications.

Vehicle Impoundment Regulations as a Means of Reducing Traffic Violations and Road Accidents in Israel*

3

TOVA ROSENBLOOM
EHUD ELDROR

Contents

Introduction

Road crashes are a major cause of death and serious injuries in many countries and extract a high cost on society (Tay 2003). A prevalent approach in many countries involves high levels of enforcement supported by intensive publicity campaigns (e.g., Tay 2005). Traffic laws sanctions tend to yield regional, short-term mild deterring effects (Hakkert et al. 2001; Sanderson and Cameron 1983) and are more effective when applied in temporal proximity to the actual violation (Yu and Williford 1995). Sanction severity appears to be of less consequence on short-term deterrence, sometimes yielding similar results for both strict and lenient sanctions, e.g., actual license revocation vs. suspended revocation, (DeYoung 1997; Siskind 1996; Watson 1998; Watson and Siskind 1997) fines vs. short time imprisonment (Martin, Annan, and Forst 1993).

Research on sanctions focusing on licensure, such as revocation or suspension, found these sanctions as effective in the reduction of subsequent involvement in traffic violations and accidents (Kim, Myeong, and Kweon 2011; Ross and Gonzales 1988), although they are relatively difficult to enforce (Gebers, DeYoung, and Peck 1997). Stricter sanctions apply limitations not only on the offending driver but also on the vehicle, such as vehicle impoundment. Evidence to the effect of vehicle impoundment varies, indicating mainly a decrease in repeat convictions, especially for first-time offenders (Beirness et al. 1997; Crosby 1995; DeYoung 1998, 1999; Laurence, Simon, and Cleary 1996; Rodgers 1997). Although vehicle impoundment was followed by lower rates of accident involvement, these became evident only after a period of 2–3 years, and were apparently affected by other police activities used during that period (Cooper, Chira-Chavala, and Gillen 2000; DeYoung 1998, 1999; Sweedler and Stewart 1997). These effects were limited to the offenders only and were not carried out to the general population (DeYoung 2000). Further variability is attributable to local differences in the violations to which the sanction applies, the impounding agency, and the duration of the impoundment (DeYoung 1998). In summary, vehicle impoundment and confiscation can be effective in the prevention of various repeat offenses, even after the vehicle is returned to its owner. Impoundment is most effective when it is applied immediately after the actual violation; yet, it is mostly a specific—rather than a general—deterrent, and yielding a significant effect usually requires several years.

Impoundment, as an additional measure to license suspension, was applied in Israel since June 2006. The Israeli impoundment regulation authorizes police officers to impound vehicles on-site for a 30-day period, in addition to license revocation pending trial, for the following violations: driving without a valid license, driving with a suspended or revoked license, driving under the influence (DUI) of intoxicating beverages or drugs, passenger over quota, cargo overload, driving over hours limit, unaccompanied new driver or allowing a new driver to drive unaccompanied, and involvement in a hit-and-run accident. The initial effects of this regulation are the focus of this study.

The current study aimed at examining the effects of the impoundment regulation in Israel, subjectively, by surveying the perceived effects of impoundment on driving and daily behaviors, and the level of familiarity and agreement with the sanctions and the violations to which it applies; and objectively, by analyzing the police data on the consequent effects of vehicle impoundment on traffic violations and accidents.

Methods

This section as well as "Results" deal first with the impoundment's subjective effects as measured in a telephone survey, followed by the objective effects analyzed from police records data.

Participants

Telephone Survey

The aim of the telephone survey was to explore the subjective impoundment effects. The participants consisted of 378 drivers randomly sampled from the 14,873 entries in the police impoundment records for the period of June 1, 2006 to December 31, 2007 (confidence interval [CI] 95% ± 5%). Table 3.1 presents the distribution characteristics of survey participants.

Table 3.1 Distribution Characteristics of Survey Participants (N = 378)

Variable	Category	Prevalence	Relative Frequency
Sex	Males	334	(88.4%)
	Females	44	(11.6%)
Age groups (years)	18–24	130	(34.5%)
	25–34	119	(31.6%)
	35–44	65	(17.2%)
	45–54	35	(9.3%)
	55–64	19	(5.0%)
	65+	9	(2.4%)
Marital status	Single	213	(56.3%)
	Married	139	(36.8%)
	Divorced	24	(6.3%)
	Widower	2	(0.5%)
Education	High school	270	(72.2%)
	Associate degree	41	(11.0%)
	Academic degree	63	(16.8%)
Monthly income (NIS)	0–5000	98	(30.0%)
	5001–7000	86	(26.3%)
	7001–10,000	100	(30.6%)
	10,001–12,000	24	(7.3%)
	12,001+	19	(5.8%)
License tenure	Up to 2 years	34	(9.0%)
	Up to 5 years	107	(28.3%)
	Up to 10 years	94	(24.9%)
	Up to 20 years	77	(20.4%)
	More than 20 years	66	(17.5%)
Daily driving hours	Up to 1 h	111	(30.5%)
	Up to 2 h	95	(26.1%)
	Up to 3 h	52	(14.3%)
	Up to 4 h	22	(6.0%)
	Up to 5 h	13	(3.6%)
	More than 5 h	71	(19.5%)
Vehicle class	Motorcycle	11	(2.9%)
	Passenger car	296	(78.3%)
	Commercial	54	(14.3%)
	Public/heavy vehicle	17	(4.5%)
Vehicle ownership	Self-owned	223	(59.0%)
	Owned by a family member	88	(23.3%)
	Company-owned/ rental	67	(17.7%)
Previous revocation	Yes	274	(72.5%)
	No	104	(27.5%)

Table 3.2   Violations Distribution in Police Records Data Analysis Samples

Violation	Impoundment Sample	Controls Sample	Total	% Out of Total Sample	% Out of Impoundment Sampling Framework
Driving without a valid license	528 (34.1%)	392 (29.0%)	920	(35.9%)	(36.3%)
Driving while revoked/suspended	100 (6.5%)	208 (15.4%)	308	(6.6%)	(5.1%)
Driving under the influence	529 (34.2%)	494 (36.5%)	1023	(35.0%)	(37.4%)
Passenger over quota	99 (6.4%)	95 (7.0%)	194	(6.6%)	(4.4%)
Driving over hours limit	97 (6.3%)	100 (7.4%)	197	(6.6%)	(2.2%)
Unaccompanied new driver	196 (12.7%)	65 (4.8%)	261	(9.4%)	(14.1%)
Total	1549 (100.0%)	1354 (100.0%)	2903	–	–

Police Records Data Analysis

Police records data analysis focused on the objective effect of impoundment on subsequent involvement in traffic accidents and violations. Data analysis was performed for records of 1549 drivers whose vehicles were impounded (M_{Age} = 28.62, SD_{Age} = 10.30), and 1354 drivers who performed matching violations before the application of the impoundment sanction (M_{Age} = 30.86, SD_{Age} = 10.29; t_{Age}(2901) = 5.86, p < 0.001). The impoundment group data were sampled from police impoundment records for the period of June 1, 2006 to May 31, 2007, using random stratified sampling from each violation included in the regulation. The sample size was set to 1500 cases (CI 99.5% ± 3%) with a correction applied to violations samples consisting of less than 100 cases (driving while revoked, passenger over quota, and driving over hours limit violations) for which the sample size was randomly set at 100 cases.* The control group data were sampled from traffic-violation conviction records for the period of June 1, 2004 to May 31, 2005, using a random stratified sample, proportionally matching the impoundment sample violation distribution. Female drivers were dropped as they comprised less than 5% of either group (impoundment, 75 women (4.6%); Controls, 68 women (4.8%); χ^2 (1, N = 3046) = 0.50^{ns}), that is, outside the CI. The final violation distribution in both data analysis samples, percentage of the total sample, and of the impoundment framework is presented in Table 3.2.

Materials

Telephone Survey

A survey questionnaire was constructed, requiring respondents to identify the set penalties (knowledge), opine as to appropriate penalty (opinion), and report self-behavior on several traffic violations, including eight impoundment violations and four "distracter" violations. Knowledge and opinion were scored on a 5-point Likert scale, ranging from

---

* Compared to their proportional representation in the original sampling framework, these violations were overrepresented in the final sample to allow a wider coverage of the effect in various violations.

fines through license revocation to vehicle impoundment. Additionally, the questionnaire addressed the justification and effect of the impoundment on daily life and consequent driving behaviors, allowing for several effects to be specified simultaneously.

Procedure

Telephone Survey

The telephone survey was conducted during September and October 2008, by trained police officers to ensure the respondents' legal privileges.

Police Records Data Analysis

Police records analysis included traffic violations and accident involvement in 3 years preceding the sampling violation date and in the following year, similar to the period range estimated by DeYoung (1997, 1999). Final analyses were conducted using count data regression models. Data variables included information pertaining to the violations' verdict, such as punitive measures and penalties; traffic accident data included the accident type and severity, and the number of people and vehicles involved. Sociodemographic data in police records were limited to sex, date of birth, and date of driving licensure, as other variables contained datum pertaining to the date of retrieval rather than the actual recording date. Preliminary analyses entered each data variable in a series of bivariate regression analyses as a regressor for both subsequent year's convictions and traffic accidents, and only significant variables were included in the subsequent analyses.

Results

Telephone Survey

The knowledge questions demonstrated a pattern of 50% correct responses for only three of the eight impoundment violations, intimating a failure to clearly state all the violations punishable by impoundment (see Table 3.3). Although overall nearly one-third of the respondents opined that impoundment is the appropriate penalty for the impound-regulation violation in general, the opinions on specific violations varied between violations, ranging between 6% and 68%. Knowledge and opinion highly correlated with each other. The self-reports of violation committed in the previous year indicated that nearly a third of the sample committed DUI violations in the previous year.

Only 79% of the respondents (297 respondents) answered questions pertaining to the justification and the effect of their impoundment. Half of those who did respond viewed the impoundment as justified ($N = 151$; 50.8%). The self-reported effects of the impoundment on daily life and consequent driving behaviors (see Table 3.4) intimated nearly all the responses indicated an increased safety effect on consequent driving behaviors, coupled with an exacting range of negative effects on daily life.

Police Records Data Analysis

An initial analysis of the count data indicated excess zero counts (indicating either no violations or no accidents in the year subsequent to the sampling violation date),

Table 3.3 Percentage (Standard Deviation) of Knowledge Opinions and Self-Reports Regarding Impoundment Violations

Violation	% Knowledge of Impoundment as Set Penalty	% Opinion of Impoundment as Appropriate Penalty	Correlation between Knowledge and Opinion Responses	% Self-Reported Violations Committed in Previous Year
Driving without a valid license	5.82 (0.23)	5.82 (0.23)	0.69*	8.20 (0.27)
Driving while revoked/suspended	51.85 (0.50)	56.61 (0.50)	0.64*	4.76 (0.21)
Driving under the influence	78.04 (0.41)	66.40 (0.47)	0.35*	30.42 (0.46)
Hit and run	58.99 (0.49)	68.25 (0.47)	0.68*	0.26 (0.05)
Passenger over quota	14.81 (0.36)	8.20 (0.27)	0.48*	11.11 (0.31)
Driving over hours limit	4.76 (0.21)	8.99 (0.29)	0.79*	2.12 (0.14)
Cargo overload	8.20 (0.27)	10.32 (0.30)	0.73*	2.38 (0.15)
Unaccompanied new driver	29.10 (0.45)	21.69 (0.41)	0.60*	9.79 (0.30)
Total impound violations	31.45 (0.18)	30.79 (0.17)	0.55*	8.63 (0.10)

*$p < 0.001$.

Table 3.4 Reported Effect on Daily Life and Driving Behaviors (Multiple Answers Are Applicable)

Effect of Impoundment On	Category	N	% of Total Responses	% per Respondent
Subsequent driving	No effect	62	12.3%	20.9%
	Increased caution	181	35.8%	60.9%
Behaviors	Obeying traffic laws	138	27.3%	46.5%
	Informing/warning others	109	21.6%	36.7%
	Other	0	0.0%	0.0%
	Don't know	15	3.0%	5.1%
	Total responses	505	100.0%	170.0%
Daily life	Limited mobility	186	27.7%	62.6%
	Increased expenses	203	30.2%	68.4%
	Inconvenience	183	27.2%	61.6%
	Impeding business/work	83	12.4%	28.0%
	Other	17	2.5%	5.7%
	Total responses	672	100.0%	226.3%

suggesting a zero-inflated distribution (see Table 3.5). The preliminary analyses compared the fit of one of three count data models: (1) a negative binomial model, with more lenient requirements on variance compared to Poisson models, while allowing for overdispersion; (2) a zero-inflated negative binomial model, allowing for both overdispersion and excess zeros; (3) zero-inflated Poisson model, providing a better fit should the overdispersion result from a high frequency of zero counts (Liu and Cela 2008).* Table 3.6

---

* One of the Poisson models' assumptions requires that variances are not much larger than the mean, i.e., that the model is not overdispersed. However, when the overdispersion originates from the high frequency of zero counts, the zero-inflated Poisson model provides a better fit than negative binomial or zero-inflated negative binomial models (Liu and Cela 2008).

Table 3.5 Frequencies (Percentages) for Subsequent Traffic Accidents and Violations

| Count | Accident | Violation Type | | |
		Any	Impound	Same
0	2696 (92.87%)	2225 (76.64%)	2551 (87.87%)	2740 (94.39%)
1	195 (6.72%)	288 (9.92%)	180 (6.20%)	103 (3.55%)
2	10 (0.34%)	138 (4.75%)	78 (2.69%)	26 (0.90%)
3	2 (0.07%)	86 (2.96%)	43 (1.48%)	15 (0.52%)
4	–	58 (2.00%)	16 (0.55%)	6 (0.21%)
5	–	33 (1.14%)	12 (0.41%)	4 (0.14%)
6	–	27 (0.93%)	9 (0.31%)	6 (0.21%)
7	–	13 (0.45%)	5 (0.17%)	2 (0.07%)
8	–	10 (0.34%)	2 (0.07%)	1 (0.03%)
9	–	10 (0.34%)	3 (0.10%)	–
10	–	4 (0.14%)	3 (0.10%)	–
11	–	5 (0.17%)	–	–
12	–	–	–	–
13	–	–	1 (0.03%)	–
14	–	1	–	–
15	–	1 (0.03%)	–	–
16	–	–	–	–
17	–	2 (0.07%)	–	–
18	–	1 (0.03%)	–	–
27	–	1 (0.03%)	–	–

presents the dispersion data both with and without the excess zero (coefficients of variance, means, and standard deviations) and the model fit criteria of deviance, and Akaike information criteria (AIC) for each model, where smaller criterion values indicate a better fit (Kibria 2006). The zero-inflated negative binomial models converged poorly and were subsequently dropped. Data dispersion indicated evidence for overdispersion, and the comparisons of data dispersion with and without the excess zeros implied that the overdispersion results from the high frequencies of zero counts, in which case, zero-inflated Poisson models provide a better fit than negative binomial or zero-inflated negative binomial models (Liu and Cela 2008). Based on the model fit criteria (deviance and AIC), the models selected were zero-inflated Poisson regressions for subsequent involvement in traffic accidents and for subsequent convictions in the same traffic violations; and negative binomial regressions for subsequent convictions in any traffic violations or in impound violations.

The appropriate count data regressions were performed, assessing the effects of impoundment group (impoundment/control) and prior convictions (first offense/repeat offense) separately on four measures: (1) subsequent accident involvement, (2) subsequent overall traffic-violation convictions, (3) subsequent convictions of traffic violations included in the impoundment regulation, and (4) subsequent convictions of the same traffic violation (as a measure of recidivism). Significant regressors from the preliminary analyses were entered as additional regressors. The means and standard errors of the

Table 3.6 Overdispersion Data (CVs Means and SD with and without Zeros) and Model-Fit Summary

Dependent Variable		Variation	Overdispersion Data			Model-Fit Summary (N = 2903)							
						Negative Binomial				Zero-Inflated Poisson			
			Coefficient	Mean	SD	Log Likelihood	df	Deviance	AIC	Log Likelihood	df	Deviance	AIC
Subsequent accidents		Zeros	374.7	0.1	0.3	−976.88	2894	1642.30	2014.78	−767.89	2894	1556.81	1592.81
		No zeros	26.9	1.1	0.3	–	–	–	–	–	–	–	–
Subsequent violations	Any	Zeros	266.3	0.6	1.7	−662.21	2884	1436.01	4331.57	−698.04	2884	4363.24	4439.24
		No zeros	94.3	2.7	2.6								
	Impound	Zeros	362.6	0.3	1.0	−794.62	2884	916.63	2566.69	−790.42	2884	2518.30	2594.30
		No zeros	84.7	2.2	1.8								
	Same	Zeros	530.7	0.1	0.6	−485.46	2884	−635.70	1311.41	−464.87	2884	1230.24	1306.24
		No zeros	80.1	1.9	1.5	–	–	–	–	–	–	–	–

Note: AIC, Akaike information criteria; CV, coefficients of variance; df, degree of freedom; SD, standard deviation.

mean for the dependent variables and for the regressors are shown in Tables 3.7 and 3.8, respectively.

1. Subsequent involvement in traffic accidents. The zero-inflated Poisson regression model's parameter estimates and measures of goodness of fit are presented in Table 3.9, indicating that both impoundment group and prior convictions failed to predict traffic accident involvement in the subsequent year.

Table 3.7 Means (Standard Error) for Dependent Variables Used in Regression Models

	Controls		Impounds	
Variables	First-Time Offenders	Repeat Offenders	First-Time Offenders	Repeat Offenders
Subsequent year accidents	0.07 (0.01)	0.06 (0.01)	0.07 (0.01)	0.07 (0.05)
Subsequent year convictions in any traffic violation	0.44 (0.01)	0.62 (0.02)	0.00 (0.01)	0.68 (0.06)
Subsequent year convictions in impound violations	0.21 (0.01)	0.39 (0.02)	0.00 (0.01)	0.39 (0.06)
Subsequent year convictions in the same violation	0.06 (0.01)	0.31 (0.01)	0.00 (0.01)	0.25 (0.04)

Table 3.8 Means (Standard Error) for Covariates Used in Regression Models

	Controls		Impounds	
Covariates	First-Time Offenders	Repeat Offenders	First-Time Offenders	Repeat Offenders
Age	30.77 (0.32)	31.19 (0.59)	28.60 (0.26)	29.57 (1.95)
License tenure	9.95 (0.28)	11.45 (0.51)	9.13 (0.22)	10.56 (1.66)
No. of accidents with light injuries	0.24 (0.02)	0.24 (0.03)	0.23 (0.01)	0.18 (0.10)
No. of light injuries	0.40 (0.04)	0.40 (0.07)	0.37 (0.03)	0.43 (0.22)
Total injuries in accidents	0.41 (0.04)	0.41 (0.07)	0.38 (0.03)	0.46 (0.23)
Prior convictions in any traffic violation	4.79 (0.17)	10.74 (0.31)	0.07 (0.14)	13.64 (1.01)
Prior convictions in the same violations	0.00 (0.05)	3.72 (0.09)	0.00 (0.04)	6.07 (0.30)
Prior fines	0.61 (0.04)	2.13 (0.07)	0.02 (0.03)	5.11 (0.24)
Sum of prior fines	484.82 (44.51)	2015.08 (82.38)	15.52 (36.95)	5498.93 (272.33)
Maximum prior fine	285.08 (14.47)	991.20 (26.79)	8.35 (12.01)	1598.21 (88.55)
Total license revocations	0.24 (0.03)	1.00 (0.05)	0.01 (0.02)	3.43 (0.17)
Total suspended license revocations	0.39 (0.03)	1.46 (0.06)	0.01 (0.03)	3.68 (0.19)
Maximum revocation period	19.47 (4.12)	143.95 (7.62)	1.19 (3.42)	237.50 (25.18)
Maximum suspended revocation period	21.36 (1.18)	69.35 (2.19)	0.64 (0.98)	134.64 (7.23)
Total revocation period	27.16 (7.72)	213.25 (14.29)	2.17 (6.41)	777.64 (47.25)
Total suspended revocation period	31.96 (3.04)	128.07 (5.63)	1.35 (2.53)	405.89 (18.61)

Table 3.9 Regression Models: Subsequent Convictions in Traffic Accidents and in Traffic Violations by Violation Type (Any Impoundment Violations or Same)

	Traffic Accidents						Traffic Violations											
	Zero-Inflated Poisson						Any Violation			Impound Violation			Same Violation					
	Logit Part			Poisson Part			Negative Binomial			Negative Binomial			Zero-Inflated Poisson					
													Logit Part			Poisson Part		
Variable	B	SE	OR	B	SE	OR	B	SE	OR	B	SE	OR	β	SE	OR	β	SE	OR
Intercept	0.16^{NS}	0.79	–	−1.45**	0.44	0.24	−3.35**	0.19	0.04	−4.50**	0.29	0.01	4.20**	0.72	66.47	−0.78	0.55	–
Age	0.01^{NS}	0.02	–	−0.01^{NS}	0.01	–	−0.01*	0.00	0.99	0.00^{NS}	0.01	–	0.03*	0.01	1.03	0.01	0.01	–
License tenure	0.00^{NS}	0.00	–	0.00*	0.00	0.99	0.00^{NS}	0.00	–	0.00^{NS}	0.00	–	0.00	0.00	–	0.00	0.00	–
No. of accidents with light injuries	−0.19^{NS}	0.39	–	0.27^{NS}	0.23	–	−0.02^{NS}	0.10	–	−0.16^{NS}	0.16	–	1.37*	0.61	3.95	0.23	0.34	–
No. of light injuries	3.58^{NS}	2.54	–	0.27^{NS}	0.56	–	−0.13^{NS}	0.33	–	−0.12^{NS}	0.48	–	4.44	3.38	–	1.29	0.84	–
Total injuries in accidents	−3.32^{NS}	2.51	–	−0.15^{NS}	0.52	–	0.15^{NS}	0.32	–	0.13^{NS}	0.46	–	−4.93	3.39	–	−1.47	0.78	–
Prior convictions in any traffic violation	−0.38*	0.16	0.68	−0.02^{NS}	0.02	–	0.09**	0.01	1.09	0.10**	0.01	1.10	−0.03	0.03	–	−0.02	0.01	–
Prior convictions in the same violation	–	–	–	–	–	–	−0.03^{NS}	0.02	–	−0.05^{NS}	0.03	–	−0.11	0.07	–	0.09*	0.03	1.10
Prior fines	–	–	–	–	–	–	0.11^{NS}	0.07	–	0.12^{NS}	0.10	–	−0.24	0.19	–	−0.03	0.09	–
Sum of prior fines	–	–	–	–	–	–	0.00*	0.00	1.00	0.00^{NS}	0.00	–	0.00*	0.00	1.00	0.00	0.00	–
Maximum prior fine	–	–	–	–	–	–	0.00**	0.00	1.00	0.00*	0.00	1.00	0.00*	0.00	1.00	0.00	0.00	–
Total license revocations	–	–	–	–	–	–	0.13^{NS}	0.09	–	−0.03^{NS}	0.13	–	0.95*	0.33	2.58	0.48*	0.14	1.61
Total suspended license revocations	–	–	–	–	–	–	−0.37*	0.13	0.69	−0.26^{NS}	0.18	–	0.05	0.43	–	−0.17	0.20	–
Maximum revocation period	–	–	–	–	–	–	0.00*	0.00	1.00	0.00*	0.00	1.00	0.00	0.00	–	0.00	0.00	–

(Continued)

Table 3.9 (Continued) Regression Models: Subsequent Convictions in Traffic Accidents and in Traffic Violations by Violation Type (Any Impoundment Violations or Same)

	Traffic Accidents						Traffic Violations											
	Zero-Inflated Poisson						Any Violation			Impound Violation			Same Violation					
													Zero-Inflated Poisson					
	Logit Part			Poisson Part			Negative Binomial			Negative Binomial			Logit Part			Poisson Part		
Variable	B	SE	OR	B	SE	OR	B	SE	OR	B	SE	OR	β	SE	OR	β	SE	OR
Maximum suspended revocation period	–	–	–	–	–	–	0.00*	0.00	1.00	0.00^{NS}	0.00	–	0.00	0.01	–	0.00	0.00	–
Total revocation period	–	–	–	–	–	–	0.00^{NS}	0.00	–	0.00^{NS}	0.00	–	0.00	0.00	–	0.00**	0.00	1.00
Total suspended revocation period	–	–	–	–	–	–	0.01*	0.00	1.01	0.00^{NS}	0.00	–	–0.01	0.01	–	0.00	0.00	–
Impoundment group	–0.28^{NS}	0.76	–	–0.28^{NS}	0.76	–	3.03**	0.16	20.69	2.83**	0.24	16.97	–2.57**	0.58	0.08	0.46	0.40	–
Prior convictions	0.87^{NS}	1.33	–	0.87^{NS}	1.33	–	0.54**	0.13	1.71	0.61*	0.19	1.85	–1.42**	0.39	0.24	0.35	0.27	–
χ^2	40.71**	–	–	–	–	–	1275.04**	–	–	663.31**	–	–	486.58**	–	–	–	–	–
Cox and Snell's R^2_{CS}	0.01	–	–	–	–	–	0.36	–	–	0.20	–	–	0.15	–	–	–	–	–
Nagelkerke's R^2_N	0.03	–	–	–	–	–	0.42	–	–	0.20	–	–	0.35	–	–	–	–	–

Note: Impoundment group is coded 0 for impoundment and 1 for controls; Prior convictions are coded 0 for first-time offenders and 1 for repeat offenders. NS, non-significant; OR, odds ratio; SE, standard error.

$*p < 0.05$; $**p < 0.001$.

2. Subsequent convictions in any traffic violation. Table 3.9 presents the model's parameter estimates and measures of goodness-of-fit for predicting subsequent convictions in any traffic violations. The negative binomial model indicated that both impoundment group and prior convictions were significant predictors of subsequent convictions. Specifically, holding all other variables constant, the odds of having subsequent convictions increased for members in the control group compared to the impounded drivers (by a factor of more than 20) and for repeat offenders compared to first-time offenders (by a factor of 1.71).

3. Subsequent convictions in traffic violations included in the impoundment regulation. Table 3.9 presents the model's parameter estimates and measures of goodness of fit for predicting subsequent convictions in any traffic violations, which were included in the impoundment regulation. The negative binomial model indicated that impoundment group membership was a significant predictor of subsequent convictions, such that the odds of having subsequent convictions increased for members in the control group compared to impounded drivers (by a factor of nearly 17). The model indicated that prior convictions were also a significant predictor of subsequent convictions, such that the odds of subsequent convictions increased for repeat offenders compared to first-time offenders (by a factor of 1.85).

4. Subsequent convictions for the same traffic violation. Table 3.9 presents the model's parameter estimates and measures of goodness of fit for predicting subsequent convictions in the same traffic violations. The model indicated that both impoundment group and prior convictions were significant predictors of excess zeros, that is, of no subsequent convictions, such that the odds of having no subsequent convictions decreased for members in the control group compared to impounded drivers (by a factor of 0.08) and for repeat offenders compared to first-time offenders (by a factor of 0.24).

Discussion

The current study aimed at examining the possible deterrence effects of the impoundment regulation in Israel, using both subjective and objective measures. The subjective effect of the impoundment regulation was examined using a telephone survey administered to impounded drivers, focusing on the perceived effect of their vehicle's impoundment on their knowledge, opinions, and daily life and driving behaviors. The objective effect was examined by statistically analyzing police records data for the assessment of the specific deterrence of impoundment as evident in the subsequent involvement in traffic accidents and violations.

The telephone survey results revealed that the majority of respondents did not recognize impoundment as the set penalty for the impoundment violations list, which may indicate that although the respondents were probably aware that vehicle impoundment is a viable penal option (as their own vehicle was impounded), they did not know to which traffic violations it applied. The opinions regarding the appropriateness of the impoundment penalty tended to match the knowledge of impoundment as the set penalty: the rates of acquaintance with the penalties set by law conformed with the rates of the penalties' appropriateness, suggesting the law's acceptance may be determined in part by its repute.

The respondents viewed its effect on daily life as detrimental, and reported increased safer driving behaviors.

It is worth noting that three violations yielded both the highest knowledge scores and the highest opinion scores of the respondents, indicating a severe stance toward driving while revoked, involvement in a hit-and-run accident, and DUI. Although this may possibly indicate an agreement between the set policy and public views, the fact that more than 30% reported committing at least one DUI violation the previous year (excepting their impound violation) suggests that mere agreement and perceived severe implications do not necessarily act as a deterrent.

The police records data analyses indicated that impoundment had a differential effect across various driving behaviors, with regard to the deterrence as measured by traffic-violation convictions, that is, drivers whose vehicles were impounded committed fewer violations compared to the controls who were sanctioned by other, less severe punishments. Importantly, traffic accident records displayed no beneficial effect of impoundment on accident involvement. The lack of effect on accidents involvement contrasts with the decrease in subsequent accident involvement found in several California counties by DeYoung (1999). However, other California counties displayed such a decrease only 3 years after the implementation of the impoundment sanction (Cooper et al. 2000). A possible explanation for this is that the low probability of traffic accidents compared to that of traffic violations requires more accident cases to display statistical significance. To wit, in 2007, the Israeli traffic police recorded some 16,000 traffic accidents and approximately 1.4 million traffic violations (National Authority of Road Safety 2008). Thus, it is possible that a longer period is required for more significant effects to emerge, although it will be more difficult to control various factors that may affect crashes.

The most notable effect of impoundment compared to previous sanctions was the decreased probability for having subsequent conviction(s) in either impound violations or any traffic violation: drivers in the control group were 17–21 times more likely to be convicted again in the subsequent year. Prior convictions were also found to increase the odds for having subsequent violations, albeit less dramatically. Interestingly, drivers whose vehicle were impounded were less likely to repeat the same violation the following year: odds for having no subsequent same violations in the control group were below 10% of the odds for the impounded drivers.

The prominent effect of impoundment implies that a harsh sanction immediately after the violation may lead to a more noteworthy effect, compared to a more lenient punishment. Following behavior patterns similar to those suggested by behavioral psychology (Skinner 1970), extreme punishment measures lead to extreme repression of the punishable behavior (Azrin, Holz, and Hake 1963; Banks 1976). In addition, in a complementary fashion, a gradual increase in punishment not only decreases its effectiveness, but might also decrease that of a subsequent harsher punishment (Church 1969). Apparently, the immediate, harsh punishment of impoundment was more instrumental in the extinction of subsequent violations than the previously used sanctions.

The overall results indicate that the application of the impoundment regulation yielded positive results in regard to subsequent traffic violations, and that the sanction severity is viewed as both deterring and as a legally proportionate measure for several violations. Although other factors certainly affect traffic violation deterrence, whether measured subjectively or objectively, the finding that drivers who performed subsequent violations were almost exclusively likely to be the nonimpounded drivers displays the unique contribution of the impoundment regulation. As this effect was apparent regardless of violation type, the current findings suggest that severe punitive measures may deter the performance of various offenses. Vehicle impoundment displayed beneficial effects in different countries; these effects differed as a result of cultural and social differences, which should merit further research considerations. The efforts of both subjective and objective measurement techniques provide a uniquely comprehensive view of the effects of vehicle impoundment, by combining subjective self-reports with specific deterrence effects obtained through recorded subsequent traffic behaviors.

References

Azrin, N. H., W. C. Holz and D. F. Hake. 1963. Fixed-ratio punishment. *Journal of Experimental Analysis of Behavior* 6: 141–148.

Banks, R. K. 1976. Resistance to punishment as a function of intensity and frequency of prior punishment experience. *Learning and Motivation* 7: 551–558.

Beirness, D. J., H. M. Simpson, D. R. Mayhew and B. Jonah. 1997. The impact of administrative license suspension and vehicle impoundment for DWI in Manitoba. In *Alcohol drugs and traffic safety—T'97*, ed. C. Mercier-Guyon, 2: 919–925. Annecy, France: CERMT.

Church, R. M. 1969. Response suppression. In *Punishment and aversive behavior*, eds. B. A. Campbell, and R. M. Church, 111–156. New York: Appleton-Century-Crofts.

Cooper, D., T. Chira-Chavala and D. Gillen. 2000. *Safety and other impacts of vehicle impound enforcement*. Berkeley, CA: Institute of Transportation Studies, University of California at Berkeley.

Crosby, I. B. 1995. *Portland's assets forfeiture program: The effectiveness of vehicle seizure in reducing rearrest among "problem" drunk drivers*. Portland, OR: Reed College Public Policy Workshop.

DeYoung, D. J. 1997. An evaluation of the effectiveness of alcohol treatment, driver license actions and jail terms in reducing drunk driving recidivism in California. *Addiction* 92: 989–997.

DeYoung, D. J. 1998. *An evaluation of the specific deterrent effect of vehicle impoundment on suspended, revoked and unlicensed drivers in California*. California Department of Motor Vehicles, Sacramento, CA.

DeYoung, D. J. 1999. An evaluation of the specific deterrent effects of vehicle impoundment on suspended, revoked, and unlicensed drivers in California. *Accident Analysis and Prevention* 31: 45–53.

DeYoung, D. J. 2000. An evaluation of the general deterrent effect of vehicle impoundment on suspended and revoked drivers in California. *Journal of Safety Science* 31: 51–59.

Gebers, M. A., D. J. DeYoung and R. C. Peck. 1997. The impact of mail contact strategy on the effectiveness of driver license withdrawal. *Accident Analysis and Prevention* 29: 65–77.

Hakkert, A. S., V. Gitelman, A. Cohen, E. Doveh and T. Umansky. 2001. The evaluation of effects on driver behavior and accidents of concentrated general enforcement on interurban roads in Israel. *Accident Analysis and Prevention* 33: 43–63.

Kibria, B. G. M. 2006. Applications of some discrete regression models for count data. *Pakistan Journal of Statistics and Operation Research* 2(1): 1–16.

Kim, S. K., S. H. Myeong and Y. J. Kweon. 2011. Differences in traffic violations and at-fault crashes between license suspension and revocation. *Accident Analysis and Prevention* 43: 755–761.

Laurence, H. R., S. Simon and J. Cleary. 1996. License plate confiscation for persistent alcohol impaired drivers. *Accident Analysis and Prevention* 29: 651–665.

Liu, W. and G. Cela. 2008. Count data models in SAS, SAS global forum 2008. *Statistics and Data Analysis* 317: 1–12.

Martin, S., E. Annan and B. Forst. 1993. The special deterrent effects of a jail sanction of first-time drunk drivers: A quasi experimental study. *Accident Analysis and Prevention* 25: 561–568.

National Authority of Road Safety. 2008. *Road safety trends in Israel 1998–2007*. Jerusalem, Israel.

Rodgers, A. 1997. Effect of Minnesota's license plate impoundment law on recidivism of multiple DWI violators. *Alcohol, Drugs, and Driving* 10: 127–134.

Rosenbloom, T. and E. Eldror. 2013. Vehicle impoundment regulations as a means for reducing traffic-violations and road accidents in Israel. *Accident Analysis and Prevention* 50: 423–429.

Ross, H. R. and P. Gonzales. 1988. Effects of license revocation on drunk-driving offenders. *Accident Analysis and Prevention* 20: 379–391.

Sanderson, J. and M. Cameron. 1983. *Enforcement and accidents.* Workshop on traffic accident evaluation. Report No. 19, Monash University.

Siskind, V. 1996. Does license disqualification reduce reoffence rates? *Accident Analysis and Prevention* 28: 519–524.

Skinner, B. F. 1970. *Walden two.* Toronto: Macmillan.

Sweedler, B. and K. Stewart. 1997. Vehicle impoundment programs in California. *ICADTS Reporter* 8: 1.

Tay, R. 2003. Marginal effects of changing the vehicle mix on fatal crashes. *Journal of Transport Economy Policy* 37: 437–450.

Tay, R. 2005. The effectiveness of enforcement and publicity campaigns on serious crashes involving young male drivers: Are drink driving and speeding similar? *Accident Analysis and Prevention* 37: 922–929.

Watson, B. C. 1998. *The effectiveness of drink driving license actions, remedial programs and vehicle-based sanctions.* In: Proceedings of the 19th ARRB research conference. Department of Transport, Hobart, Australia, pp. 66–87.

Watson, B. C. and V. Siskind. 1997. *The effectiveness of license restriction for drink drivers.* In: Proceedings of the 1997 road safety research and enforcement conference. Department of Transport, Hobart, Australia.

Yu, J. and W. R. Williford. 1995. Drunk-driving recidivism: Predicting factors from arrest context and case disposition. *Journal of Studies on Alcohol* 57: 679–680.

Lean Management for Traffic Police Enforcement Planning

NICOLE ADLER
JONATHAN KORNBLUTH
MALI SHER
SHALOM HAKKERT

Contents

Introduction

Traffic police enforcement is a well-known factor in road accident reduction but the policy is costly and there are budget constraints imposed by the government. This study develops a road safety strategy using an optimization modeling approach within the operations management philosophy that increases the impact of police enforcement given the constraints on the traffic police. A case study based on this road safety strategy is analyzed over time to demonstrate the effectiveness of this approach.

Traffic police enforcement can be viewed as composed of three basic components: suppliers producing tickets (police officers and automatic cameras), office administration (handling the work stemming from the tickets), and consumers. An analysis of the system at the beginning of the study revealed that the suppliers and the office administration demonstrated diverging objectives; therefore, the products (tickets) were less effective as defined by the road safety literature. Using the terminology of production management, we show that traffic police road safety enforcement can be perceived as a manufacturing plant, where the tickets represent the raw materials. The "plant" is represented by the office administration in which the raw materials flow between the different workstations. This plant has three main customers or end users: court prosecutors who want "high quality"* tickets as evidence; general road users who are interested in reducing car accidents and offenses and improving road safety; and traffic offenders who want high service levels from the office administration. The court itself represents the equivalent of a manufacturing plant in which the traffic police system is one of its suppliers. The overall enforcement process is limited by budget and manpower. This study deals with the problem of resolving bottlenecks in the police processing of traffic tickets while assigning differential values to various types of offenses. The study analyzes the enforcement process and develops a planning model based on the concepts of Lean manufacturing in order to balance the system as a production line while maximizing the tickets issued for traffic offenses that are considered important to ensure road safety. Using a linear program, we optimize the enforcement process given the budgetary and resource constraints, identify the bottlenecks in the process, and optimize the ticket distribution system. To date, there has been no published work analyzing the traffic police enforcement system as a whole; therefore, the diverse approaches of enforcement have led to failures in the system, such as tickets not processed within the prescribed legal limits. Analyzing this system using a manufacturing plant approach, by defining suppliers, raw materials, workstations, work-in-progress, and products for different customers, we then apply Lean manufacturing concepts to this service production system. In addition, we apply linear programming to each of the Lean manufacturing stages in order to search for the optimal level of service, subject to the exogenous constraints on the system. Consequently, to the best of our knowledge, this article is the first to develop a model of road safety enforcement for the traffic police ticketing process. The models in this paper combine three domains: road safety and traffic enforcement, management theory, and operations research. The models were implemented by the Israel traffic police over 6 years (2004–2009) and, as will be demonstrated, this implementation improved both the quality of the enforcement process and the process flow.

This chapter is organized as follows: "Literature Review" is devoted to a literature review. "Description of Israeli Traffic Police Enforcement System" describes the case study of how the Israel traffic police enforcement system operated before the implementation of this study. "Lean Modeling of Ticket Production" presents the Lean ticket system. "Linear Programming Formulation" presents the linear programming formulation, details of which are presented in the appendices. "Model Implementation and Results" demonstrates an application of the results of the proposed models. Finally, conclusions and suggestions for further work are presented.

---

* "High quality" tickets are those that are either deemed important according to the law (court summonses, high fines, etc.) or those that are highly ranked by the police road safety enforcement policy (offenses related to accidents, fines related to undesirable road behavior, etc.).

Literature Review

In this section, we discuss research in the literature that is covered in this study including both Lean manufacturing (see "Lean Manufacturing Literature") and road safety and policing (see "Road Safety and Policing Literature").

Lean Manufacturing Literature

Lean production is one of the most influential contemporary manufacturing paradigms (Hines et al. 2004; Holweg 2007). It was developed at the Toyota Production System in Japan (Herron and Hicks 2008; Ohno 1988) and was influenced by the Japanese philosophy of "Lean thinking" and subsequent findings from Massachusetts Institute of Technology's International Motor Vehicle Program study (Baines et al. 2006; Smart et al. 2003; Womack et al. 1990). It has been applied to general production situations (Herron and Hicks 2008), including manufacturing and services (Baines et al. 2006; Hines et al. 2004; Jackson et al. 2008; Rubio and Corominas 2008), and the public and private sectors (Hines et al. 2004; Jackson et al. 2008; Piercy and Rich 2009; Smart et al. 2003).

The main approach within Lean production is defined as improving productivity by enabling companies to supply customer needs accurately, on time, and without waste through continuous improvement (Heizer and Render 2008; Herron and Hicks 2008). Manufacturing waste can be defined as any redundant resource application that does not add value to the product (Herron and Hicks 2008; Naylor et al. 1999; Ohno 1988; Sahoo et al. 2008; Scott et al. 2009; Womack et al. 1990). The core philosophy of Lean production applies a system-wide view of the production process to create a streamlined, high-quality finished product that meets customer needs with little or no waste. Consequently, this process encourages mutual dependency within the system by connecting all of the components, from suppliers to end customers (Lamming 1996; Rubio and Corominas 2008; Shah and Ward 2003; Smart et al. 2003).

Womack et al. (1990) and Womack and Jones (1996) identify five main concepts within the Lean manufacturing literature including *value*, which is defined with respect to products and services from the customers' perspective. The *value stream* connects the steps of the process with the goal of maximizing customer value, in turn categorizing the subprocesses into value-adding activities, nonvalue-adding activities, and necessary but nonvalue-adding activities (Sahoo et al. 2008). Additional concepts include improving the *flow* along the value stream by developing production capabilities. This concept supports the complementary goals of minimum work-in-progress and maximum value throughput. Furthermore, Womack also identifies the importance of *pull*, from the customer to the producer, in order to yield a smooth flow of the value stream by aligning production targets throughout the system with the end customers' demand, thus minimizing inventory and work-in-process. Spearman et al. (1990) compare the pull and push systems of production planning and control and conclude that the pull system is more efficient, easier to control, more robust, and more supportive of improving quality. The final concept is *perfection*, according to which strive waste is eliminated. The five concepts of Lean thinking (Womack and Jones 1996; Womack et al. 1990) are translated into the traffic police enforcement system in "Lean Modeling of Ticket Production."

Gregory (2007) and Jackson et al. (2008) define a Check–Plan–Do approach to Lean systems' continuous performance improvement. Check is an analysis of the "what" and "why" of current system performance from the customers' perspective, mapping how work flows through the system and distinguishing value work from waste. Plan is concerned with establishing the framework for eliminating waste by defining performance measures for staff and management. Do is about incrementally redesigning the system to eliminate or reduce waste wherever possible, taking into account the response of both staff and customers to the changes implemented. Check, Plan, and Do constitute a never-ending cycle designed to promote continuous improvement (Jackson et al. 2008). For an example of four consecutive applications of the Check, Plan, and Do approach, see Rivera and Chen (2007) or Rosales et al. (2009).

In applying Lean operations management principles to improve the traffic police enforcement system, we combine the methodology of the five definitions (Womack and Jones 1996; Womack et al. 1990) with continuous improvement by stages (Gregory 2007; Jackson et al. 2008; Rivera and Chen 2007). Our analysis of the traffic police enforcement system is an example of applying the Lean manufacturing methodology to a public service system with mass production (the case study produces approximately 1.5 million tickets annually) and multiple, competing road safety, police policy, and traffic court policy objectives.

Road Safety and Policing Literature

The police's main task is to reduce crime, disorder, and public fear (Weisburd and Eck 2004). In line with these tasks, police enforcement of traffic rules is one of the important contributory factors to road safety (Elvik and Vaa 2004). For example, Beenstock and Gafni (2000) found that the accident rate varies inversely with the level of police enforcement. The definition of traffic offenses as a crime is problematic. Willett (1964) provided both a legal and sociological definition of crime. From the legal aspect, even the smallest traffic offense is defined as a crime. From the sociological aspect, criminal behavior and offenses are defined as involving deliberate intent, harm to persons or property, and dishonesty. Most traffic offenses are not included in this sociological definition of crime. Stylianou (2003) focused on the perceived consequences of crime as a dimension affecting perceived seriousness. Most traffic offenses are victimless crimes with no consequences and therefore are not in the social consensus of serious offenses reflected by current laws and enforcement budgets.

In general, there are five main strategies for policing (Bayley and Shearing 1996; Crank and Giacomazzi 2007; Crank and Langworthy 1992; Harcourt 1998; Paoline and Terrill 2005; Weisburd and Eck 2004). The first strategy is the standard policing model, based on random preventative patrol vehicle assignments and rapid response to police calls for service. The second strategy is the community policing philosophy where communities are transformed from passive consumers of police protection to active coproducers of public safety by reporting offenses to the police. The third strategy is problem-oriented policing in which the police focus on specific problems and adapt their strategies to the problems identified. The fourth strategy is "hotspots" policing, according to which the police identify specific, concentrated areas of crime and then channel resources to these locations. The fifth strategy is the "broken windows," "order-maintenance," and "zero tolerance" policing, as implemented, for example, in New York City. Under this strategy, public order is achieved by aggressively enforcing all laws including minor offenses. In all of these strategies, stopping drivers (traffic stops) is an enforcement method that combines fighting crime and traffic offenses. Traffic stops are ideal situations where police officers can find drugs, witness illegal activity, or conduct random checks on people (Paoline and Terrill

2005). In addition, within the literature, there is a special focus on the location–allocation of rescue services including ambulance, fire, and police (Church et al. 2001; Curtin et al. 2005, 2010; Daskin 1982; Green and Kolesar 2004; Larson 1974; Larson and McKnew 1982; Peleg 2000; Simpson and Hancock 2009; Toregas et al. 1971; Wright et al. 2006; Yin 2006). The first major research project involving fire department deployment was the New York City Rand Project in the 1970s (Walker et al. 1979).

Traffic police use similar strategies with regard to the location and allocation of services. Enforcement programs in Australia and New Zealand, for example, have demonstrated a substantial reduction in road accident rates as a result of random police deployment (Newstead et al. 2001). The "traffic model" in Israel (Hakkert et al. 1990) ranked enforcement-stretches based on weighted historical data including the number and severity of accidents and traffic volumes. Lee et al. (2003) defined hazardous locations on the road network as "locations where risks exceeded certain preset thresholds for intervention." Statistical and geographic models have been applied to these hazardous locations analysis (see, e.g., Anderson 2009). The major factors influencing the optimal level of traffic enforcement include the costs of apprehending and convicting traffic offenders, the nature of the punishment (e.g., fines, revoking licenses, or prison terms), and the traffic offenders' responses to changes in enforcement (Becker 1968).

The main objective of traffic law enforcement is to increase road safety. This is achieved by deterring road users from committing offenses that are proven to be related to road accidents and injuries (ETSC 1999). There is a consensus that good enforcement practices should be based on accident analysis and on scientifically supported insight into enforcement effectiveness (Hakkert et al. 2001). It is also important to analyze the pattern of police officers' work with respect to both effectiveness and efficiency (Tillyer et al. 2010). International experience suggests that police operations usually succeed when applied to a limited group of violations (e.g., Leggett 1993; Noordzij and Mathijssen 1991; Vaa 1997). The European Transport Safety Council (ETSC 1999) and Elvik and Vaa (2004) identified the three key traffic offenses with a direct connection to road safety that ought to be targeted in enforcement strategies: speeding, blood alcohol concentration above the legal limit, and the use of safety belts.

Excessive speed is by far the most frequent road traffic offense. For example, in Norway, about 5% of 800,000 cars observed in 1 year violated the speed limit (Das and Robinson 2001). Both accident frequency and severity increase as driving speed increases. Average speed and variance in speed are both considered (Lave 1985; Loeb 1987). Increased speed enforcement is shown to reduce average driving speeds as well as the number of speeding offenses (Vaa 1997). Elvik and Vaa (2004), ETSC (1999), and Shin et al. (2009) summarized a metastudy of more than 16 data sets and concluded that for every 1 km/h decrease in the average speed, there is an estimated 4% reduction in the number of accidents. The cost/benefit ratio of stationary speed enforcement is between 1:3 and 1:12 depending on the parameters included, such as the cost of casualties, damage to property, and alternative costs associated with the loss of time. Taylor et al. (2000) and Cameron and Elvik (2010) summarized the relevant speed parameters connected to accidents: average speed, median speed, coefficient of variation of the speed distribution, the proportion of vehicles exceeding the speed limit, the proportion of vehicles exceeding the speed limit by more than 25 km/h, and the average speed by which drivers exceed the limit.

Driving under the influence (DUI) of alcohol is another major cause of accidents and may increase the severity of the resulting injuries. Although drunken driving is relatively infrequent compared to other traffic offenses, its effects are highly dangerous. For the European Union as a whole, roughly 3% of journeys are associated with an illegal blood alcohol level, yet approximately 30% of injured drivers have been found to be under the influence of alcohol (ETSC 1999). The key to successful enforcement strategies aimed at reducing alcohol-related casualties is to increase drivers' perceptions of the probability of detection through a lack of predictability in terms of time and place of testing. Reasonably large numbers of drivers should be tested with highly visible police operations (ETSC 1999). Enforcement methods used to raise the probability of detection include: mobile police, sobriety checkpoints, or random breath testing (Löbmann 2002). ETSC (1999) found that sobriety checkpoints by the police are effective in reducing drinking and driving, resulting in fewer fatal alcohol-related accidents. Löbmann (2002) found that mobile police and random breath testing are very effective strategies. DUI of drugs and alcohol was the main criminal behavior investigated in the literature that pertained to traffic offenses and police work. Hubicka et al. (2008) found that traffic offenses were four times more frequent among DUIs than among average drivers. Palk et al. (2007) found that 25% of police work involved alcohol-related events, mostly traffic incidents, and that these events were usually longer in duration than nonalcohol-related events.

With respect to seat belt use, the best way of currently achieving an increase in usage is through intensive, highly visible, and well-publicized enforcement. Several studies have estimated that the benefit/cost ratio of such seat belt enforcement programs is of the order of 3 or greater (ETSC 1999).

Traffic management plans generally involve setting specific measurement goals for enforcement in order to reduce road accidents (Kratooski and Das 2002). However, Hakkert et al. (2001) mentioned that the traffic police officer's daily activities have not been discussed in the academic literature and that many questions remain as to the most appropriate working practices. We will use the conclusions drawn in the road safety literature (i.e., type and amount of enforcement) as a guideline for the traffic police enforcement system.

In this study, the suggested working methods are based on a problem-oriented strategy. The traffic ticket distribution policy is based on the results described in the road safety literature. We will now continue with a description of traffic police enforcement as a "ticketing plant." Most traffic police departments throughout the world have an organized system that contains components similar to those of the Israeli police case study (i.e., manual enforcement, automatic enforcement, administration, legal experts responding to complaints, an archive, and the court system). In order to treat the process quantitatively, the situation in Israel was taken as a case study.

Description of Israeli Traffic Police Enforcement System

The Israeli traffic police enforcement system encompasses three components: suppliers, office administration, and end users (Figure 4.1). Units A and B represent the two suppliers that provide the two different inputs to the system: (A) provides tickets produced by police officers and (B) provides tickets produced from photographs taken by automatic cameras. The office administration can be represented as a manufacturing plant. The first stage in the office administration is the computer encoding of the offense data (C, D). The automatic camera input is first decoded via a computer

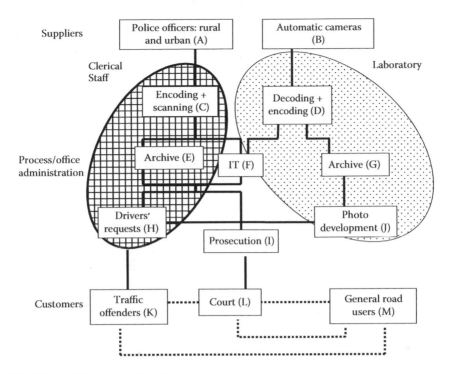

Figure 4.1 The ticket processing plant.

display, and then the laboratory staff decides whether the evidence is sufficient to proceed (D). The encoding of manual tickets requires examination of the details of the related documents and subsequent scanning of the ticket into the computer. Another group of staff is based in the archive stations (E, G). All manual tickets (A) and drivers' requests (H) are stored in the clerical archives (E), whereas camera films and developed photographs are stored in the laboratory archives (G). Both sets of archive staff are in charge of storing the material, and producing material on demand either for the prosecution as evidence to the courts (I) or per the driver's requests (H). The prosecutorial team (I) is responsible for court summonses and any criminal charges deriving from car accidents. This study only models the office administration's activities concerning ticket prosecution and does not include the prosecutorial system, which is beyond the scope of this paper. Prosecutions resulting from manual tickets derive material from archive (E), whereas those resulting from an automatic ticket derive material from archive (G) and photo development (J). The last group within the office administration is the drivers' request group (H), which is the most overloaded. Under Israeli law, a person who believes the ticket received is inaccurate or invalid is permitted by law to write a letter to the police requesting a change in the ticket type (e.g., converting a fine to a warning or a fine to a court summons), changing the ticket recipient, or canceling the ticket entirely. Other requests requiring substantial administrative support involve handling requests for discounts, monthly payments, or reproducing a lost ticket. The system's end users include the traffic courts (L), road users (M), and offenders (K). The ticket processing plant supplies the courts (L), and the flow is consequently limited by the court handling capacity. The road users (M) represent the general public whose behavior is influenced by police enforcement activities, the courts, and publicity. Traffic offenders (K) send letters to the drivers' request unit (H) and are also the accused in court.

By 2004, it became clear that the suppliers (the police officers and automatic cameras) and the office administration had diverging objectives. The suppliers produced as many tickets as possible, regardless of their road safety significance. In contrast, the office administration units, handling the work accruing from the production of these tickets, preferred to produce "quality" tickets, as defined by the traffic police headquarters protocols. Consequently, the suppliers operated as a Push system, and the number of tickets issued by the police officers (A) led to a large administrative backlog at the drivers' request unit (H). After identifying the issues, the process of reducing the backlog and reorganizing the system are described in this article. This study's aim was twofold: (1) to analyze the various components as a single plant, thereby determining the objective function of the traffic police system as a whole, and (2) to define and maximize an objective function given an exogenous budget constraint, while balancing the flow and improving the working methods, thus moving from a Push to a Pull system.

Lean Modeling of Ticket Production

A Lean model of ticket production was developed for the Israeli traffic police enforcement system based on the objectives defined in the literature. As a first step in the application of Lean modeling, we analyzed the system according to the five principles of Womack et al. (1990) and Womack and Jones (1996).

1. Identification of customer value. The customer value was identified as providing the customers with higher levels of service. The traffic police enforcement system has three end users: traffic courts, road users, and traffic offenders, each with its own customer value. Traffic courts need to receive well-prepared summonses within their handling capacity. Road users need safe roads and therefore want the police to apprehend traffic offenders, issue tickets, and deter poor driving behavior. The third end user, the traffic offenders themselves, need various procedures and requests to be handled at a reasonable service level by the office administration, for example, payments and prosecutions.

2. Management of the value stream. Police output was mapped into three groups: "value-adding" activities were identified as the police issuing quality tickets, "nonvalue-adding" activities were defined as all activities connected to fines when warning tickets were considered more appropriate, and "necessary but nonvalue-adding" activities were defined as office staff responding to drivers' requests. The aim is to concentrate on quality tickets, thus reducing fines when a warning is permitted and improving the working method at the drivers' request unit at node (H) of Figure 4.1.

3. Developing the production flow capability. Overload in the ticket processing plant departments was defined, and potentially helpful new technologies were identified, such as installing computer devices in patrol cars to permit online searches of drivers' histories, thus reducing subsequent administration at nodes (C) and (E) of Figure 4.1.

Table 4.1   Lean Management Operations

Lean Principles	Application in Traffic Enforcement Policy
1. Identification of customers' values	Higher service levels to the customers
2. Management of the value stream	Concentrating on quality tickets
3. Developing the production flow capability	Improving technology
4. "Pull" mechanisms	Determining the number and distribution of tickets
5. Reducing waste and excess	Improving working protocols

4. Pull mechanisms were identified as basing the flow and the ticket distribution on the constraints of the office administration and the end users, for example, restricting the number of court summonses according to the number of judges available.

5. Reducing waste and excess. Work-in-process was found at the drivers' request station and prosecution stations, which were reduced by introducing new protocols such as restricting the total number of tickets, in particular, tickets requiring a summons, issuing a warning instead of a fine or ticket, and introducing new technologies such as computers in the patrol cars and drivers' request scanners.

Table 4.1 summarizes the connection between the Lean manufacturing principles (Womack and Jones 1996; Womack et al. 1990) and the police enforcement strategy improvement process.

The second step in the application of Lean modeling was based on the work of Gregory (2007), which described the Lean systems as three circular steps for performance improvement: Check–Plan–Do. After the "five steps analysis," a linear program was developed to solve the Check and Plan stages, in order to determine the appropriate ticket production levels given the constraints of the process. These results were then fed back into the process for further overall improvement by increasing the value-adding components of the system at the expense of all other activities.

Linear Programming Formulation

Implementing Lean management strategies in stages was based on the general linear programming formulation for the traffic enforcement system as detailed in Appendix I. The formulation's objective function maximizes the number of tickets according to their perceived values, which may be defined in terms of, for example, financial remuneration, influence on drivers' behaviors, or the number and severity of car accidents. In our case study, the distribution of tickets was modeled via the constraints. The first set of constraints defines, at each process station (m), the maximum working hours as a budget determined by the manpower limitation and the minimum working hours, because the m process stations should not be underutilized in the decision makers' policy. Currently, these input parameters are assumingly defined exogenously as there is no option to relocate human resources or distribute budgets according to the different process stations. The second set of constraints defines the stated strategic and policing policies. These constraints rank offenses in terms of their importance with respect to traffic safety considerations. In practice, there are approximately 800 ticket types (l) that are clustered according to their

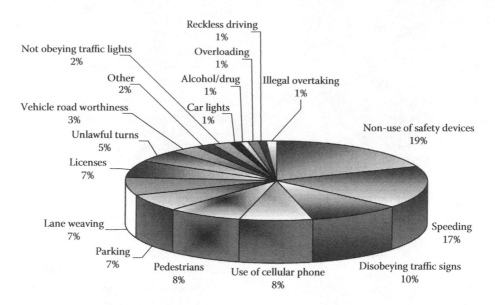

Figure 4.2 Grouping tickets according to 17 types of offenses.

characteristics. Figure 4.2 presents the grouping of the offenses (l) according to the 2007 Israeli traffic police report (g = number of groups = 17). An analysis of these groups shows that failure to apply safety devices, speeding, disobeying traffic signs, illegal use of cellular phones, and pedestrian offenses represent the largest groups (62% of the total).

An alternative type of grouping, for which $l = 2$, is achieved by differentiating between parking and nonparking (moving violation type) tickets. Figure 4.3 presents the increase in the nonparking tickets as a percentage of the total between 2000 and 2007, growing from less than 82% to 92%. This trend can be explained in two ways. First, as of 2000, the municipal bylaw authorities were given the authority to enforce parking regulations to help reduce the burden on police resources, and second, police enforcement during these years was refocused on nonparking tickets.

The third and final set of constraints instructed the police as to which groups of offenses need increased or decreased enforcement. The general linear program was applied in stages and is described in "Model Implementation and Results" and details are provided in Appendix I.

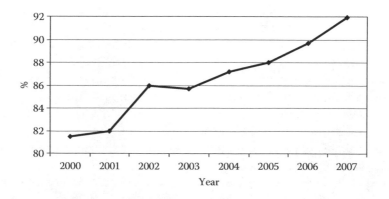

Figure 4.3 Nonparking ticketing as a percentage of total tickets over time.

Model Implementation and Results

Implementing the Lean management model in stages (see "Lean Modeling of Ticket Production") was based on results of the general linear programming formulation (see "Linear Programming Formulation" and Appendix I) for the traffic enforcement system. The Israeli case study was conducted over a 6-year period, and the results were divided into three stages: Stage 1 covers 2004–2005 (see "Office Administration Emphasized over First Period [2004–2005]"), Stage 2 covers 2006–2007 (see "Quality Tickets Emphasized over Second Period [2006–2007]"), and Stage 3 includes 2008–2009 ("Maximizing Quality Tickets in Third Period [2008–2009]"), for which 2009 represents a forecast estimate. "Results in Overview (2004–2008)" and Figure 4.4 summarize the results: before the implementation of the policy (years 2000–2004), the results achieved to date under the new policy (years 2005–2008), and the 2009 forecast.

Office Administration Emphasized over First Period (2004–2005)

The first round of the Check–Plan–Do model of the Lean production implementation (Gregory 2007; Jackson et al. 2008) occurred at the beginning of the first period, during 2004–2005. During the Check stage (end of 2004), the process stations were analyzed in order to find the maximum possible flow regardless of ticket quality or source, using a simplified linear programming formulation (without Equations 4.3 and 4.4 in Appendix I). The major bottleneck in the production flow was known to be the drivers' request unit in office administration (m = node H in Figure 4.1). For this formulation, parameters for the drivers' request unit were collected as follows: budget limitation measured in manpower working hours (b_m), processing time measured in hours (t), and the percentage of tickets entering the drivers' request unit (a_1). Table 4.2 summarizes data for the relevant parameters in the first period. More details on notations are presented in Appendix II.

The maximum flow capability was found to be 1.1 million tickets per year, implying that a maximum of approximately 260,000 drivers' requests (24% of 1.1 million) could be handled annually. In 2004, there were 426,786 drivers' requests, of which 150,000 were

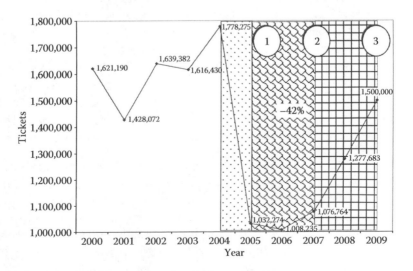

Figure 4.4 Annual ticket issuance.

Table 4.2   Model Parameter Values (First Period)

M	c_m	b_m	t_{ijm}	a_1
m_1 = drivers' requests	0	88,200[a]	0.33	24%

[a] 88,200 annual working hours are obtained by multiplying 60 workers by
   210 working days a year (excluding weekends, holidays, sick days, courses,
   vacations) by 7 net working hours a day.

Table 4.3   Changes in Ticket Issuance (2004–2005)

Groups	2004		2005	
Offenses strongly related to accidents (g_1)	47%	835,789	54%	557,428
Offenses strongly related to accident severity (g_2)	16%	284,524	17%	175,487
Aggressive behavior on the road (g_3)	5%	88,914	6%	61,936
Environmental offenses (g_4)	2%	35,566	2%	20,645
Others (g_5)	30%	533,483	21%	216,778
Total	100%	1,778,276	100%	1,032,274

backlogged. Some of these tickets from backlogged requests were eventually canceled because of the long delay in processing, thus wasting all the previous work of ticketing and processing. This sent a negative message to the public that they could avoid paying tickets were they to send in a request. In the Plan stage, it was decided to limit the total number of tickets that would be issued during 2005 to 1 million, and simultaneously move from "quantity" to "quality" tickets. The planned policy at this stage was defined as follows:

1. Raising the speed limit registered by automatic cameras, thus decreasing the number of tickets but increasing their quality by ensuring that extreme speed was caught and subsequently ticketed.
2. Increasing the number of warnings issued, as opposed to fines, thus reducing the subsequent drivers' requests.
3. Providing police officers with prioritization criteria pertaining to ticket issuance. The set of all offenses $\{l\}$ was divided into five categories (Table 4.3), where g_1 denotes offenses strongly related to accidents, such as speeding; g_2 denotes offenses strongly related to accident severity, such as failure to wear a safety belt; g_3 represents aggressive behavior on the road, such as driving on the shoulder; g_4 denotes environmental offenses, such as double parking; g_5 represents all remaining offenses. This type of clustering covers all traffic police activities because the first two categories cover car accidents, the next two categories cover criminal or inconsiderate driving behavior, and the last category refers to all other, less important offenses. The policy for 2005 was to reduce the g_5 category to the greatest extent possible.

As a result of these policy directives, there was a considerable change in the number and type of tickets issued in the Do stage of 2005. The total number of tickets dropped by 42% from approximately 1.8 million to 1 million tickets per year. This resulted in 125,000 fewer automatic camera tickets as a direct result of the speed cutoff level from priority (1) above and from a further reduction of approximately 300,000 interurban* tickets

* The interurban traffic police unit is under the direct command of the traffic police headquarters and not the districts; therefore, the Do stage was easier to implement in the interurban traffic police context.

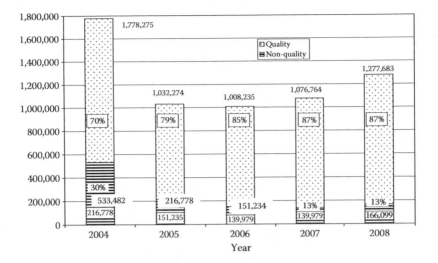

Figure 4.5 Quality tickets.

issued, by focusing on priorities (2) and (3). Furthermore, the policy to reduce the "others" group (g_5) as much as possible led to a 30% annual reduction. The policy of encouraging the production of warnings rather than fines led to approximately 40,000 warning tickets issued in 2005, which represented an increase of 1000% compared to 2004.

From 2005 onward, the tickets were recategorized into two groups with g_1'' including all quality tickets comprising g_1 to g_4, and g_2', the lower-quality tickets, previously denoted by g_5. Figure 4.5 presents the nominal number of tickets produced and the distribution between g_1' and g_2'. The quality group, g_1', increased from 70% in 2004 (prior to the new policy) to 79% in 2005.

Quality Tickets Emphasized over Second Period (2006–2007)

The second round of the Check–Plan–Do model of the Lean production implementation (Gregory 2007; Jackson et al. 2008) continued to highlight the drivers' request station owing to the continued overload despite the above-mentioned changes. In 2005, the percentage of requests from the total number of tickets issued rose to 35% compared to 24% in 2004, overloading the system by approximately 100,000 requests and exceeding the handling capabilities given the existing resources. In addition, court summonses decreased by 37% in 2005, which was not in line with the policy of increasing quality and was below court capacity assumed to be approximately 100,000 annually. Consequently, in the Plan stage for 2006–2007, the total number of tickets issued annually continued to be limited to 1 million while simultaneously moving further toward quality rather than quantity. The planned policies at this stage were defined as

1. Maintaining the higher speed threshold that the automatic cameras registered as an offense
2. Increasing the issuing of warnings as opposed to fines
3. Reinforcing police officers' priorities for issuing tickets according to quality, g_1', and within this policy, concentrating more on court summons related offenses

As a result of these policy directives, there were additional changes in the type of tick-ets issued in the Do stage. The total number of annual tickets remained about 1 million, as shown in Section 2 of Figure 4.4. However, there was a change in the proportion of tickets produced, with group g_1' high-quality tickets increasing from 79% in 2005 to 87% in 2007. A corresponding increase in warnings and court summonses, and a decrease in lower-quality tickets, in turn reduced the pressure on the back-office administration from more than 360,000 requests in 2005 to less than 250,000 in 2007.

Maximizing Quality Tickets in Third Period (2008–2009)

The third period (2008–2009) was built on the stabilized enforcement policy of years 2005–2007. The aim of the third period was to increase the total number of tickets produced according to an appropriate police-defined distribution, without requiring additional resources (Figure 4.1). In the Check stage (end of 2007), the second round of Plan–Do and the process stations (m) were analyzed in order to find the maximum possible flow given ticket quality and source. It became apparent that the number of drivers' requests in 2005 rose because the media published the new policy of issuing warnings rather than fines. As the new policy guidelines became clearer to the media and road users, the percentage of drivers' requests decreased from 35% in 2005 to 27% in 2006 and 23% in 2007, gradually falling to within the station's handling capacity.

In the Plan stage for the third period, a decision was made to no longer restrict the total number of tickets issued. The linear program, as formulated in "Linear Programming Formulation" and Appendix I, was applied in order to (1) maintain the flow within each work station's handling capacity, (2) keep the number of warnings constant, (3) continue the percentage of quality tickets at the 2007 level, and (4) increase the number of tickets issued according to the major offenses described in the road safety literature. The linear program applied in this stage is presented in Appendix II. In the data collected, we identi-fied the different percentages of tickets entering the drivers' requests unit according to the ticket production type: manual ($j = 1$) and automatic ($j = 2$). The offenses are categorized into five groups, where g_5 represents the nonquality ticket group and groups g_1–g_4 are the quality tickets divided into the main groups (g_1–g_3) and other quality offenses (g_4).

In this formulation (Appendix II), the total number of tickets issued is maximized subject to the policy considerations identified. Equation 4.3 includes three equations for separate components of the production system ($m = 1, ..., 3$). The parameter values are presented in Table 4.4.

Equation 4.8 refers to the g_5 group ("others"), and the percentage of g_5 tickets was lim-ited to an upper bound; $P_g \leq 13\%$. Equation 4.9 is composed of three equations. The policy limits for the three main groups of offenses are set in these equations covering speed-ing, nonuse of safety belts, and alcohol. The lower bound for 2008–2009 was set at 10% above the level achieved in 2007, and the upper bound was set according to budget and

Table 4.4   Model Parameter Values (Third Period)

M	c_m	b_m	t_{ijm}	a_{11m}	a_{21m}	a_{12m}	a_{22m}
m_1 = drivers' requests	0	88,200	0.33	20%	20%	30%	30%
m_2 = prosecution	0	100,000	1	100%	–	100%	–
m_3 = automatic cameras	100,000	250,000	1	–	–	100%	100%

Table 4.5   Planned Manual Ticket Distribution for 2008–2009 (in Thousands)

L	Court Summons $i = 1; j = 1$	Fine $i = 2; j = 1$	Total
g_1 = speeding	69	290	359
g_2 = safety belts	0	250	250
g_3 = alcohol	0	20	20
g_4 = other quality tickets	31	260	291
g_5 = lower-quality tickets	0	180	180
Total (i)	100	1000	1100

policy limitations. Some of the combinations were irrelevant, such as tickets for nonuse of safety belts ($l = g_2$) and tickets for excessive alcohol levels ($l = g_3$), which cannot be automatic ($j = 2$), irrespective of i. The results suggested that it was possible to return to the previous level of ticketing, that is, 1.5 million tickets annually, given the new distribution of ticket type and quality and the improved technologies, such as the online service available to patrol cars for checking a driver's past offenses. The 1.5 million tickets upper bound includes 300,000 warning tickets that previously did not exist. The various parameters for ticket distribution are as follows: (1) 1.4 million manual tickets ($j = 1$), including 300,000 warning tickets and 100,000 automatic tickets ($j = 2$). Table 4.5 shows the planned 1.1 million manual tickets distributed according to ticket group (without warning tickets). (2) 100,000 court summons based tickets ($i = 1$), all of them under manual production type ($j = 1$) and defined as quality tickets ($l = g_1 = 69\%$ and $g_4 = 31\%$ in Table 4.5), and 1.1 million fines ($i = 2$), of which 1 million are to be manually produced ($j = 1$). This solution implies that no automatic tickets are court summonses. All court summonses are produced manually, with immediate hand delivery to increase deterrence. About 180,000 fines are manual and nonquality tickets ($l = g_5$), which includes 75,000 parking tickets (Table 4.5). Alternative solutions exist because the constraints are by groups and not by individual categories. For example, in Equation 4.3, quality tickets (g_1–g_4) are constrained to be at least 87% of the total number of tickets. At this stage, there are individual limitations on each of the first three groups (g_1–g_3), but not on group g_4; therefore, tradeoffs between g_1–g_3 and g_4 are available. Another example of alternative solutions stems from the limited number of automatic tickets, in which we are free to determine the distribution between speeding (g_1) and red-light (g_4) tickets.

Results in Overview (2004–2008)

In this section, we discuss in further depth the results for the years 2004–2008 with respect to the main parameters, namely, quality tickets, drivers' requests, total and automatic ticket types. The results draw from a combination of Lean manufacturing and linear programming. As Figure 4.5 shows, the number of nonquality tickets decreased over the years (2004–2008) as a percentage of the total number of tickets issued, reaching an upper bound of 13% of the total number of tickets issued in 2008. Figure 4.6 shows that the number of drivers' requests at first increased and then decreased significantly over the time frame. Despite the substantial decrease in the total number of tickets produced between 2004 and 2005, the percentage of drivers' requests in 2005 increased to 35% of the total tickets. This

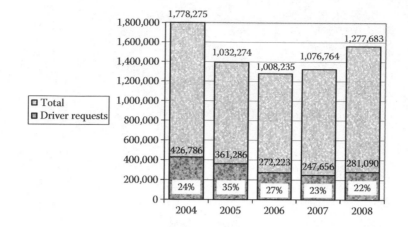

Figure 4.6 Driver requests.

was a result of the publicity given to the traffic police program without sufficiently accurate information about its implementation. From 2005 to 2008, the percentage of drivers' requests decreased from 35% to 22%. The overall number of drivers' requests rose again in 2008 because of the rise in the total number of tickets issued.

Figure 4.7 summarizes the distribution of ticket types (*i*) over the years 2004–2008. The nominal number of warning tickets rose (from 39 warnings in 2004 to around 330,000 in 2008) and the percentage of warning tickets issued, compared with total tickets issued, rose (from 0% in 2004 to 26% in 2008). The number of court summonses remained constant at around 100,000 per year because of the courts' constraints as a consumer of the traffic enforcement system's output. Consequently, there was a decreasing trend in the percentage of fines (from 93% in 2004 to 65% in 2008).

Figure 4.8 summarizes the trends in the issuance of automatic tickets. The decrease in the number of speeding tickets issued (from about 220,000 tickets in 2004 to about 80,000 tickets in 2008) is attributable to raising the speed-enforcement level. The laboratories' process station utilized this decrease to move staff from ticketing to other research and to developing other enforcement devices. We therefore recommend that there should be a maximum of 100,000 automatic tickets produced, including red-light enforcement.

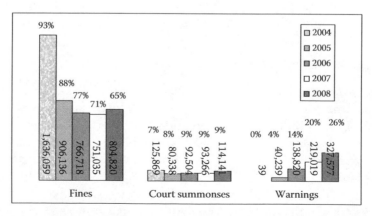

Figure 4.7 Number of tickets by type.

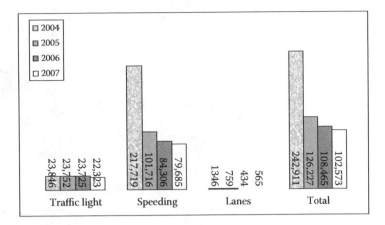

Figure 4.8 Number of automatic tickets by type.

A summary of the results shows that the effectiveness of the traffic enforcement system, according to the road safety literature, may be improved through the application of operations management and operations research modeling approaches. The products (tickets) are maximized, based on budget constraints, police policy, and road safety recommendations. According to the Lean management philosophy, these results can be further improved by additional analyses on a continual basis. The general linear programming formulation can be adapted to any change in the traffic police enforcement system, simply by changing the parameters of the budget or the decision makers' values.

Summary, Conclusions, and Further Research

This paper presents a new approach to the traffic police enforcement production system. The model developed is based on Lean manufacturing as a management theory and is implemented by operations research techniques based on the road safety literature. The models were tested using data from the Israeli traffic police. The results show that the enforcement production system (suppliers, administration, and consumers) could be improved by increasing the quality of tickets produced while maintaining a similar number of inputs. This approach is important for maximizing the benefits from the traffic police units with respect to road safety within the constraints imposed by government and society.

Until 2004, the Israeli traffic police force's enforcement system consisted of two components, each with different objectives. The first component comprised the police officers and automatic cameras, both of which produced tickets and whose joint objective was to produce as many tickets as possible. The second component was the office administration including laboratories, prosecutorial legal teams, and clerical staff, together handling the work accumulating from ticket production. After 2004, their joint objective was to produce quality tickets according to the traffic police force headquarters' decisions, mainly tickets that achieved improved levels of road safety as defined in the literature. Furthermore, the traffic police force had to abide by an exogenously set budget, and it was therefore necessary to find an optimal working method for combining these two components. This chapter outlines how the enforcement process has been analyzed. A manufacturing model based on the concepts of Lean manufacturing has been developed, and a mathematical program to balance the system has been defined while ranking offenses according to their importance with respect to road safety levels. This real life case study, drawing on the Israeli traffic police, demonstrates that a high level of enforcement can be achieved based on a preferential ranking of offense types, while ensuring that the back-office teams support the production flow. Implementing this procedure over the years 2005–2009 resulted in a steep increase in quality tickets (70% to 87%) while maintaining the same total number of tickets issued.

Further research could be directed in several directions. The proposed model could be refined to include more groups of offenses (g), such as the more serious traffic offenses of running red lights. More specific workstation details, such as the number of full-time equivalent police officers at each workstation, would allow the police force to rebalance human-resource constraints. It would also be of great interest to fully utilize the modeling approach by collecting more detailed data on the formulation parameters. For example, the U_{ijkl} values in the objective function could help guide effective police enforcement policies, enabling us to answer such questions as whether speed enforcement is best achieved by police officers or by automatic cameras. Finally, new technologies and reorganization of the traffic police system, such as upgrading the automatic cameras using digital technology and defining a single, centralized, highly automated drivers' request unit, may greatly improve the system, as we discovered through the course of this study. These changes could then be integrated into the model in order to further refine the potential output given the resources available.

Acknowledgments

The authors sincerely thank the Israeli Police Force and specifically the Traffic Police Department for providing support and data that enabled this research and its republication.

Appendix I. General Linear Program for Traffic Enforcement System

Notation

m = process stage (nodes in the ticket-processing plant (Figure 4.1)
g = number of offense groups used

$$i = \text{ticket type} = \begin{cases} 1 & \text{court summons} \\ 2 & \text{fine} \\ 3 & \text{warning} \end{cases}$$

$$j = \text{ticket production type} = \begin{cases} 1 & \text{manual} \\ 2 & \text{automatic} \end{cases}$$

$$k = \text{ticket delivery} = \begin{cases} 1 & \text{by hand} \\ 2 & \text{on vehicle's window} \\ 3 & \text{by post} \end{cases}$$

$$l = \text{type of offense} = \begin{cases} 1 & \text{speeding} \\ 2 & \text{no license} \\ . & . \\ . & . \\ 800 & . \end{cases} = \text{aggregated groups} = \begin{cases} g_1 & \text{speeding} \\ g_2 & \text{safety belts} \\ g_3 & \text{alcohol} \\ g_4 & \text{other quality tickets} \\ g_5 & \text{lower-quality tickets} \end{cases}$$

Not all combinations of i, j, k, l are possible—for example, an automatic ticket can only be delivered by post and cannot be a warning ticket, a manual ticket is generally hand delivered or placed on the vehicle's windshield, and a warning ticket or court summons cannot be delivered on the vehicle's windshield. There are approximately 2400 feasible combinations.

Data

U_{ijkl} = utility per ticket of type $ijkl$
t_{ijklm} = processing time of ticket $ijkl$ at process stage m
a_{ijklm} = percentage of tickets of type $ijkl$ entering process stage m
b_m = maximum processing time available at stage m (budget limitation)

Policy

c_m = minimum processing utilization of stage m
P_g = percentage of group g offenses out of total of all offenses $\left(\sum_g P_g \leq 1 \right)$

L_{ijkl} = lower bound on number of tickets of type $ijkl$ to be issued per year
U_{ijkl} = upper bound on number of tickets of type $ijkl$ to be issued per year

Decision Variables

X_{ijkl} = number of tickets of type $ijkl$ to be issued per year
The linear program is as follows:

$$\max \sum_{ijkl} U_{ijkl} X_{ijkl} \quad \text{s.t.} \tag{4.1}$$

$$c_m \leq \sum_{ijkl} t_{ijklm} a_{ijklm} X_{ijkl} \leq b_m \quad \forall m = \text{process stages} \tag{4.2}$$

$$\sum_{ijkl \in g} X_{ijkl} \leq P_g \sum_{ijkl} X_{ijkl} \quad \forall g \tag{4.3}$$

$$L_{ijkl} \leq X_{ijkl} \leq UP_{ijkl} \quad \forall i,j,k,l \tag{4.4}$$

$$X_{ijkl} \geq 0 \quad \forall i,j,k,l \tag{4.5}$$

The objective function (Equation 4.1) maximizes the number of tickets taking into account the utility (U_{ijkl}) of each ticket type. In this study, $U_{ijkl} = 1$ is defined for all i, j, k, and l because the utility of each type of offense is currently undetermined; for example, the importance of a fine rather than court summons or speeding enforcement by automatic camera rather than by a police officer. Instead, policy with respect to the distribution of tickets was modeled via the constraints, permitting the constraints on manpower versus capital investment to be determined exogenously.

The first set of constraints (Equation 4.2) defines the budget limitation at each process station (m). The human resources available at each process station (m) are translated into net working hours (b_m). t_{ijklm} is the length of time required to analyze ticket type $ijkl$ at process station m, and a_{ijklm} is the percentage of ticket type i, j, k, l that process station m is expected to process. In addition, the m process stations should not be underutilized; hence, minimum working hours at each station (c_m) are also defined. Equation 4.3 defines the stated strategic and policing policies. This constraint specifies the upper bound on the number of tickets of group (g) that should be ticketed as the percentage (P_g) of the total number of tickets, thus ranking the offenses in terms of their importance with respect to traffic safety considerations.

At each stage, we instruct the police as to which groups need increased or decreased enforcement according to the results of Equation 4.4, which specifies an upper and a lower bound on the number of tickets of a particular type. The minimum lower bound is zero (Equation 4.5).

Appendix II. Linear Program Model Used in Third Period

Notation (Different from Appendix I)

$$m = \text{the process stage (Figure 4.1)} = \begin{cases} m_1 & \text{drivers' requests} \\ m_2 & \text{prosecution} \\ m_3 & \text{automatic cameras} \end{cases}$$

g = number of offense groups used ($g = 5$)

$$i = \text{the ticket type} = \begin{cases} 1 & \text{court summons} \\ 2 & \text{fine} \end{cases}$$

As the number of warnings was fixed at 300,000, the third category $i = 3$ was omitted. Furthermore, there is no need for special index k (the manner in which the ticket is delivered), because automatic camera tickets are delivered by post and manual tickets are hand-delivered to the driver. (Parking tickets on the vehicle's window are a small percentage of the total and are a by-product of the nonquality tickets.)

Data (Different from Appendix I)

t_{ijm1} = processing time of ticket ij at process stage m_1 (drivers' requests)
a_{ijm1} = percentage of tickets of type ij entering process stage m_1 (drivers' requests)

Decision Variables (Different from Appendix I)

X_{ijl} = number of tickets of type ijl to be issued per year
The linear program model is

$$\max \sum_{ijl} X_{ijl} \quad \text{s.t.} \tag{4.6}$$

$$c_m \leq \sum_{ijl} t_{ijm} a_{ijm} X_{ijl} \leq b_m \quad \forall m = \text{Process stages} \tag{4.7}$$

$$\sum_{ijl \in g} X_{ijl} \leq P_g \sum_{ijl} X_{ijl} \quad \forall g_5 \tag{4.8}$$

$$\sum_{ij} L_{ijl} \leq \sum_{ij} X_{ijl} \leq \sum_{ij} U_{ijl} \quad \forall l = g_1, g_2, g_3 \tag{4.9}$$

$$X_{ijl} \geq 0 \quad \forall i,j,l \tag{4.10}$$

References

Anderson, T.K. 2009. Kernel density estimation and K-means clustering to profile road accident hotspots, *Accident Analysis and Prevention* 41(3): 359–364.

Baines, T., H. Lightfoot, G.M. Williams and R. Greenough. 2006. State-of-the-art in lean design engineering: A literature review on white collar lean. Proceedings of the Institution of Mechanical Engineers, Part B, *Journal of Engineering Manufacture* 220(9): 1539–1547.

Bayley, D.H. and C.D. Shearing. 1996. The future of policing, *Law and Society Review* 30(3): 585–606.

Becker, G.S. 1968. Crime and punishment: An economic approach, *Journal of Political Economy* 76(2): 169–217.

Beenstock, M. and D. Gafni. 2000. Globalization in road safety: Explaining the downward trend in road accident rates in a single country (Israel), *Accident Analysis and Prevention* 32(1): 71–84.

Cameron, M.H. and R. Elvik. 2010. Nilsson's power model connecting speed and road trauma: Applicability by road type and alternative models for urban roads, *Accident Analysis and Prevention* 42: 1908–1915.

Church, R., P. Sorensen and W. Corrigan. 2001. Manpower deployment in emergency services, *Fire Technology* 37: 219–234.

Crank, J.P. and A.L. Giacomazzi. 2007. Areal policing and public perceptions in a non-urban setting: One size fits one, *Policing: An International Journal of Police Strategies and Management* 30(1): 108–131.

Crank, J.P. and R. Langworthy. 1992. An institutional perspective of policing, *The Journal of Criminal Law and Criminology* 83(2): 338–363.

Curtin, K.M., K. Hayslett-McCall and F. Qiu. 2010. Determining optimal police patrol areas with maximal covering and backup covering location models. *Networks and Spatial Economics,* 10(1): 125–145.

Curtin, K.M., F. Qiu, K. Hayslett-McCall and T.M. Bray. 2005. Integrating GIS and maximal covering models to determine optimal police patrol areas. In *Geographic Information System and Crime Analysis*, eds. F. Wang, 214–235. Hershey, PA: Idea Group.

Das, D.K. and A.L. Robinson. 2001. The police in Norway: A profile, *Policing: An International Journal of Police Strategies and Management* 24(3): 330–346.

Daskin, M.S. 1982. Application of an expected covering model to emergency medical service system design, *Decision Sciences* 13(3): 416–439.

Elvik, R. and T. Vaa. 2004. *The handbook of road safety measurement.* Amsterdam: Elsevier.

European Transport Safety Council (ETSC). 1999. Police enforcement strategies to reduce traffic casualties in Europe. European Transport Safety Council.

Green, L.V. and P.J. Kolesar. 2004. Improving emergency responsiveness with management science, *Management Science* 50(8): 1001–1014.

Gregory, A.J. 2007. Target setting, lean systems and viable systems: A systems perspective on control and performance measurement, *Journal of Operational Research Society* 58: 1503–1517.

Hakkert, A.S., V. Gitelman, A. Cohen, E. Doveh and T. Umansky. 2001. The evaluation of effects on driver behavior and accidents of concentrated general enforcement on inter urban roads in Israel, *Accident Analysis and Prevention* 33: 43–63.

Hakkert, A.S., A. Yelinek and E. Efrat. 1990. *Police surveillance methods and police resource allocation models.* The International Road Safety Symposium, Denmark.

Harcourt, B.E. 1998. Reflecting on the subject: A critique of the social influence conception of deterrence, the broken windows theory, and order-maintenance policing New York style, *Michigan Law Review* 97: 292–389.

Heizer, J. and B. Render. 2008. *Operations management.* 9th edition. Upper Saddle River, NJ: Pearson, Prentice-Hall.

Herron, C. and C. Hicks. 2008. The transfer of selected lean manufacturing techniques from Japanese automotive manufacturing into general manufacturing (UK) through change agents, *Robotics and Computer-Integrated Manufacturing* 24: 524–531.

Hines, P., M. Holweg and N. Rich. 2004. Learning to evolve—A review of contemporary lean thinking, *International Journal of Operations and Production Management* 24(10): 994–1011.

Holweg, M. 2007. The genealogy of lean production, *Journal of Operations Management* 25: 420–437.

Hubicka, B., H. Laurell and H. Bergman. 2008. Criminal and alcohol problems among Swedish drunk drivers—Predictors of DUI relapse, *International Journal of Law and Psychiatry* 31: 471–478.

Jackson, M.C., N. Johnston and J. Seddon. 2008. Evaluating systems thinking in housing, *Journal of Operational Research Society* 59: 186–197.

Kratooski, P.C. and D.K. Das. 2002. Traffic policing: An international perspective, *Policing: An International Journal of Police Strategies and Management* 25(3): 619–630.

Lamming, R. 1996. Squaring lean supply with supply chain management, *International Journal of Operations and Production Management* 16(2): 183–196.

Larson, R.C. 1974. A hypercube queuing modeling for facility location and redistricting in urban emergency services, *Journal of Computers and Operations Research* 50(1): 135–145.

Larson, R.C. and M.A. McKnew. 1982. Police patrol-initiated activities within a systems queueing, *Model Management Science* 28(7): 759–774.

Lave, C.A. 1985. Speeding, coordination and the 55 mph limit, *American Economic Review* 75(5): 1159–1164.

Lee, C., B. Hellinga and F. Saccoman. 2003. Proactive freeway crash prevention using real-time traffic control, *Canadian Journal of Civil Engineering* 30(6): 1034–1041.

Leggett, L.M.W. 1993. Enforcement for road safety—Towards optimum management of resources. Paper presented at: Safely on the road to the 21th century. 19–20 October 1993. Canberra ACT Australia.

Löbmann, R. 2002. Drunk driving: Probability of detection and its perception, *Policing: An International Journal of Police Strategies and Management* 25(4): 770–788.

Loeb, P.D. 1987. The determinants of automobile fatalities—With special consideration to policy variables, *Journal of Transport Economics and Policy* 21(3): 279–287.

Naylor, J.B., M. Naim and D. Berry. 1999. Leagility: Integrating the lean and agile manufacturing paradigms in the total supply chain, *International Journal of Production Economics* 62: 107–118.

Newstead, S.V., M.H. Cameron and L.M.W. Leggett. 2001. The crash reduction effectiveness of a network-wide traffic police deployment system, *Accident Analysis and Prevention* 33: 393–406.

Noordzij, P.C. and M.P.M. Mathijssen. 1991. Police enforcement and road user behavior. In *Enforcement and Rewarding: Strategies and Effects*, eds. M.J. Koornstra, and J. Christensen, 105–107. Leidschendam, the Netherlands: SWOV.

Ohno, T. 1988. *Toyota production system: Beyond-large scale production.* Portland, OR: Productivity Press.

Palk, G., J. Davey and J. Freeman. 2007. Policing alcohol-related incidents: A study of time and prevalence, *Policing: An International Journal of Police Strategies and Management* 30(1): 82–92.

Paoline, E.A. and W. Terrill. 2005. The impact of police culture on traffic stop searches: An analysis of attitudes and behavior, *Policing: An International Journal of Police Strategies and Management* 28(3): 455–472.

Peleg, K. 2000. The effectiveness of Israel's pre-hospital emergency medical services organization. PhD thesis, Ben-Gurion University, Beer-Sheba Israel.

Piercy, N. and N. Rich. 2009. Lean transformation in the pure service environment: The case of the call service centre, *International Journal of Operations and Production Management* 29(1): 54–76.

Rivera, L. and F. Chen. 2007. Measuring the impact of lean tools on the cost–time investment of a product using cost–time profiles, *Robotics and Computer-Integrated Manufacturing* 23: 684–689.

Rosales, C.R., M.J. Fry and R. Radhakrishnan. 2009. Transfreight reduces costs and balances workload at Georgetown crossdock, *Interfaces* 39(4): 316–328.

Rubio, S. and A. Corominas. 2008. Optimal manufacturing–remanufacturing policies in a lean production environment, *Computers and Industrial Engineering* 55: 234–242.

Sahoo, A.K., N.K. Singh, R. Shankar and M.K. Tiwari. 2008. Lean philosophy: Implementation in a forging company, *International Journal of Advanced Manufacturing Technology* 36: 451–462.

Scott, B.S., A.E. Wilcock and V. Kanetkar. 2009. A survey of structured continuous improvement programs in the Canadian food sector, *Food Control* 20: 209–217.

Shah, R. and P.T. Ward. 2003. Lean manufacturing: Context, practice bundles, and performance, *Journal of Operations Management* 21: 129–149.

Shin, K., S.P. Washington and I.V. Schalkwyk. 2009. Evaluation of the Scottsdale loop 101 automated speed enforcement demonstration program, *Accident Analysis and Prevention* 41: 393–403.

Simpson, N.C. and P.G. Hancock. 2009. Fifty years of operational research and emergency response, *Journal of the Operational Research Society* 60: 126–139.

Smart, P.K., D. Tranfield, P. Deasley, R. Levene, A. Rowe and J. Corley. 2003. Integrating "lean" and "high reliability" thinking, Proceedings of the Institution of Mechanical Engineers, part B: *Journal of Engineering Manufacture* 217: 733–739.

Spearman, M.L., D.L. Woodruff and W.J. Ho. 1990. CONWIP: A pull alternative to Kanban, *International Journal of Production Research* 28: 879–894.

Stylianou, S. 2003. Measuring crime seriousness perceptions: What have we learned and what else do we want to know, *Journal of Criminal Justice* 31: 37–56.

Taylor, M.C., D.A. Lynam and A. Baruya. 2000. *The effects of drivers' speed on the frequency of road accidents.* Crowthorne: Transport Research Laboratory.

Tillyer, R., R.S. Engel and J.C. Cherkauskas. 2010. Best practices in vehicle stop data collection and analysis, *Policing: An International Journal of Police Strategies and Management* 33(1): 69–92.

Toregas, C., R. Swain, C. ReVelle and L. Bergman. 1971. The location of emergency service facilities, *Operations Research* 19: 1363–1373.

Vaa, T. 1997. Increased police enforcement: Effects on speed, *Accident Analysis and Prevention* 29: 373–385.

Walker, W., J. Chaiken and E. Ignall. 1979. *Fire department deployment analysis, The Rand Fire Project*. New York: Elsevier North-Holland.

Weisburd, D. and J.E. Eck. 2004. What can police do to reduce crime, disorder, and fear?, *Annals of the American Academy of Political and Social Science* 593: 42–65.

Willett, T.C. 1964. *Criminal on the road*. London: Tavistock Publications Limited.

Womack, J.P. and D.T. Jones. 1996. *Lean thinking*. New York: Simon & Shuster.

Womack, J.P., D.T. Jones and D. Roos. 1990. *The machine that changed the world*. Rawson Associates, New York.

Wright, P.D., M.J. Liberatore and R.L. Nydick. 2006. A survey of operations research models and applications in homeland security, *Interfaces* 36(6): 514–529.

Yin, Y. 2006. Optimal fleet allocation of freeway service patrols, *Networks and Spatial Economics* 6: 221–234.

Organizational Structure, Police Activity, and Crime[*]

ITAI ATER
YEHONATAN GIVATI
OREN RIGBI

$$5$$

Contents

Introduction

To enforce the law and prevent crime, the state must investigate crimes, adjudicate criminal cases, and house criminals upon conviction. These functions are typically undertaken, respectively, by three separate agencies: the Police, the Court, and the Prison Authority. However, these functions may be organized in a different manner. For instance, in adversarial legal systems the investigative and adjudicative functions are independent of each other, whereas in inquisitorial legal systems the Court is actively involved in investigating facts. Likewise, the investigative function and the function of housing criminal upon conviction may not be independent of each other, as in the case of military prisons, which are often operated by the military police. How do the organizational boundaries between law enforcement agencies affect their activities and crime?

[*] Reproduced from *Journal of Public Economics*, 115, Ater, I., Y. Givati and O. Rigbi, Organizational structure, police activity and crime, 62–71, Copyright 2014, with permission from Elsevier.

To address this question, we investigate the consequences of an organizational reform that transferred the responsibility for housing arrestees from the Police to the Prison Authority in Israel, thereby adjusting the organizational boundaries between the two agencies. Before the reform, arrestees were housed either at local police stations or at regional jails controlled and managed by the Police. After the reform, arrestees were no longer housed at police stations, and the control over regional jails was transferred to the Prison Authority along with the personnel working at these jails.

Theoretically, what should be the consequences of the organizational reform we investigate? We assume that the Police serves as an agent of the state, and in this agency relationship the Police is incentivized to minimize crime. It does so subject to various constraints it faces, including budgetary and managerial time constraints. The transition of responsibility for arrestees from the Police to the Prison Authority externalizes both the financial and the managerial costs of housing arrestees from the Police's perspective. It should therefore result in an increased number of arrests. Furthermore, if the Police chooses optimally which crimes to pursue, focusing first on more severe crimes and on arrestees that are more likely to be charged, then the additional arrests following the reform should be concentrated in relatively minor crimes and in arrests that are less likely to result in charges. Lastly, the increased police activity should lead to a decrease in crime. This effect should be more significant in crimes that the Police more actively pursued after the reform.

The organizational reform we investigate has particular relevance to a reform undertaken in California in October 2011. That reform, known as California's Corrections Realignment Plan, shifted responsibility from the state to counties for the custody, treatment, and supervision of individuals convicted of specified crimes. That reform was in the opposite direction to the reform we investigate, because—instead of relieving local police of the responsibility for housing arrestees—the reform in California imposed on local police an additional responsibility for some prisoners.*

In our empirical analysis, we use individual-level administrative data on the universe of arrests undertaken in Israel, as well as detailed data on reported crimes. Our empirical strategy relies on two important aspects of the organizational reform. First, the reform can be considered exogenous to police activity and crime because the decision to implement it was a direct consequence of a surprise escape of a notorious serial rapist from the hands of the Police. Second, our analysis exploits the staggered rollout of the reform across geographical regions of Israel, starting in April 2007 and ending in January 2008.

The research design and the data we use enable us to identify the effects of the reform on various measures of police activity and crime. We begin by investigating how the reform influenced the number and duration of arrests. Figure 5.1 shows the total number of arrestees before and after the control over jails was transferred from the Police to the Prison Authority, using the date of the transition in each region as time zero. The figure indicates that after the reform there was a large increase in the total number of arrestees held in custody each week. Panel data regression estimates further indicate that the increase in the number of arrestees can be decomposed into an 11% increase in the number of arrests and a 38% increase in the duration of arrests.

---

* For more details on the Californian realignment reform, see http://www.calrealignment.org, *The Economist*—http://www.economist.com/node/21555611, and *The New York Times*—http://www.nytimes .com/2011/10/09/us/california-begins-moving-prisoners.html.

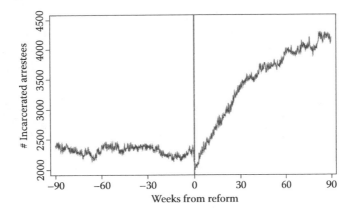

Figure 5.1 Organizational reform and number of incarcerated arrestees.

A central strength of our dataset is that it enables us to investigate the impact of the reform on a quality measure of police activity. We assess quality according to the likelihood of an arrestee being charged. This seems a natural measure of arrest quality, because arrests can be undertaken only when there is probable cause, that is, a reasonable belief that the suspect has committed a crime. Thus, the likelihood that an arrestee will be charged reflects the threshold level of probable cause that the Police sets for undertaking arrests. Our regression estimates imply a reduction of 2 percentage points in the likelihood of an arrestee being charged following the reform. Given the 11% increase in the number of arrests, back-of-the-envelope calculations suggest that individuals arrested after the reform were 20 percentage points less likely to be charged compared with individuals who were arrested before the reform. These findings are consistent with the idea that the Police pursued suspects who are less certain to be charged following the reform, and relates to the theoretical literature on the effect of public sector reforms on service quality (Hart, Shliefer, and Vishny 1997).

We also examine the effect of the reform on the severity of crimes for which arrests were undertaken. We do this in two different ways. First, we measure a crime's severity using the maximum possible prison time associated with it. Our regression estimates suggest a reduction of 6% in the average maximum possible sentence of arrestees following the reform. Given the increase of 11% in the number of arrests, back-of-the-envelope calculations suggest that, relative to the original population of arrestees, individuals arrested after the reform were arrested for crimes whose maximum possible sentence was, on average, 60% lower. Second, we look at the composition of arrests, focusing on three categories of crime that account for 80% of arrests: public order, property, and bodily harm. We find that the increased number of arrests was driven by arrests in the public order and property categories of crime, rather than in the more severe category of bodily harm. These findings are consistent with the idea that the Police pursued more minor crimes following the reform.

Our final analysis examines the impact of the reform on reported crimes. Regression estimates suggest that the reform led to a reduction of 4% in crime. Focusing on the three categories of crime mentioned above, we find that the reform led to a decrease in property and public order crimes, whereas it had no effect on bodily harm crimes. These findings lend further support to our conjecture that the reform enabled the police to pursue relatively minor crimes, whereas it had a little effect on more severe crimes. Interestingly, the reduction in crime that we document is comparable in magnitude to the effect on crime of a 10% increase in police resources, found in other studies (DiTella and Schargrodsky 2004; Draca, Machin, and Witt 2011; Evans and Owens 2007; Levitt 1997; Machin and Marie 2011).

The theoretical literature on the boundaries of the firm has established that organizational structure has important implications for economic outcomes (Grossman and Hart 1986; Williamson 1985). The empirical literature, however, has focused mostly on the determinants of integration decisions, with only a few studies examining the effects of vertical integration (see, e.g., Afendulis and Kessler 2007; Forbes and Lederman 2010; Lafontaine and Slade 2007; Mullainathan and Scharfstein 2001). In their review of the literature on vertical integration, Bresnahan and Levin (2012) write that "in a very few cases, an attempt is made to link the integration decision to economic outcomes." Studying public sector agencies is particularly important because traditional market mechanisms, such as prices and side payments, which can be used to align incentives, are usually not applicable to the public sector.

Following Becker (1968), the literature on the economics of crime has investigated how different factors affect crime, including police (e.g., Chalfin and McCrary 2013; Draca et al. 2011; Klick and Tabarrok 2005; Levitt 1996; Vollard and Hamed 2012;), incarceration (e.g., Barbarino and Mastrobuoni, 2014 ; Drago, Galbiati, and Vertova 2009; Levitt 1996), and the length of imprisonment (e.g., Abrams 2012; Kuziemko 2013; Lee and Justin 2009). Our study demonstrates that the organizational structure of law enforcement agencies should also be considered an effective policy instrument in the fight against crime.

The remainder of the paper is organized as follows. "Setting, Data, and Empirical Strategy" provides institutional background about the organizational reform, describes the data we use, and discusses our empirical strategy. In "Results," we present our results. In "Discussion" we discuss the results, and in "Conclusion" we offer concluding remarks.

Setting, Data, and Empirical Strategy

Reform in Israeli Jails

In Israel, the Prison Authority and the Police are independent national agencies operating under the Ministry of Public Security. The main duties of the Israeli Police include crime prevention, traffic control, and the maintenance of public order. The Israeli Police is responsible for investigating virtually all types of crimes, and in most cases police prosecutors decide whether to prosecute a suspect.

According to Israeli law, police officers can detain a suspect for up to 48 hours. After 48 hours, the Police must bring the arrestee to Court. At that point, if the suspect is not charged and the investigation continues, the Police may ask the Court to extend the suspect's arrest. The Court will do so if it thinks that a freed suspect is likely to interfere with the investigation, escape, or constitute a danger to the public. After the suspect is charged, the Police may ask the court that the suspect remain under arrest until the trial is completed. The Court approves such a request when the suspect is charged with a severe crime (such as drug trafficking, violent crime, crime punishable with life in prison). The Court also approves such requests if it thinks that a freed suspect is likely to interfere with the trial, influence witnesses, or constitute a danger to the public. In some cases, the arrestee is confined to house arrest instead of being sent to jail, or is released on bail.

During the years 2007 and 2008, Israel undertook a large reform in the handling of arrestees and the management of jails. Before the reform, the Police was responsible for the transportation and the housing of arrestees. Arrestees were detained either in police stations or in jails that the Police operated and controlled. The Police was also responsible for transporting arrestees from jails to courts and back. When suspects were convicted, they were moved to prisons, controlled by the Prison Authority. Under the new arrangement, the Police was no longer responsible for housing arrestees or transporting them. Jail facilities were handed over "as is" to the Prison Authority, and arrestees were no longer detained at police stations (except for a few hours). Twice a day, the Prison Authority's transportation unit would pick up new arrestees from police stations and take them to jails or to courts.

Figure 5.2 illustrates the change made by the reform. The reform did not alter the basic process that criminals go through, that is, being arrested and sent to jail, then upon conviction being sent to prison. What has changed is how the different stages of this process are divided between the Police and the Prison Authority. Before the reform, responsibility for a criminal was transferred from the Police to the Prison Authority only upon conviction. Since the reform, the transfer of responsibility occurs when an arrestee is sent to jail.

As part of the reform, all Police personnel working in jails were transferred to employment under the Prison Authority. Thus, following the reform Israeli Police manpower decreased from a total of 28,338 employees to a total of 28,049, reflecting the transition of jailers from the Police to the Prison Authority. Furthermore, the Police's budget associated with the management of jails and the handling of arrestees was fully transferred to the Prison Authority. For each region where the reform took place, the Police and the Prison Authority signed a long contract, detailing precisely the transfer of manpower, budget, facilities, and equipment from the Police to the Prison Authority. To illustrate, according to the contract for Israel's southern region, the Police committed to transferring to the Prison Authority 121 employees and the yearly budget associated with their salaries of 19.36 million NIS (New Israeli Shekels), a yearly maintenance budget of 4.35 million NIS, seven commercial vehicles and their associated yearly operational budget of 0.77 million NIS, and two trucks and their associated yearly operational budget of 0.22 million NIS. The contract went on to describe in extreme detail the equipment in each jail that the Police would hand over to the Prison Authority. For example, the contract for Israel's southern region stated that the following items (among others) would be handed over to the Prison Authority: 52 guns, 70 mattresses, 170 blankets, 50 pairs of socks, 35 prayer books, and one *shofar* (a ram's horn, used on the Jewish holiday of Rosh Hashanah).

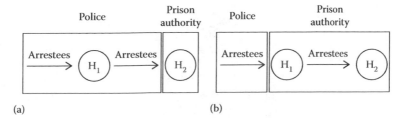

Figure 5.2 Nonintegrated (a) and integrated (b) organizational structures.

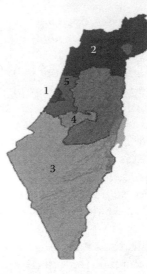

	Region	Date
1	Tel-Aviv region	04/2007
2	Northern region	06/2007
3	Southern region	09/2007
4	Jerusalem region	11/2007
5	Central region	01/2008

Figure 5.3 Police regions and timing of reform.

What led to this organizational reform? On November 24, 2006, a notorious serial rapist named Benny Sela escaped from police custody while on his way to court. Immediately after his escape a nationwide manhunt was launched, and a committee was appointed to investigate the circumstances leading to it. The committee submitted its recommendations on December 7, 2006, a day before Benny Sela was recaptured. The committee's main recommendation was the transfer of responsibility for jails and arrestees' transportation from the Police to the Prison Authority.* The idea was that unlike the Police, the Prison Authority specializes in handling the incarcerated, and therefore if it is responsible for arrestees such an escape will not occur again. That the comparative advantage of the Prison Authority in handling the incarcerated is the reason for the reform is explicitly stated in section 1(b) of each of the regional contracts between the Police and the Prison Authority noted above.

The committee also made a recommendation as to the order for the rollout of the reform in the different regions of Israel. This order was determined based on the administrative readiness of the Prison Authority in each region to accept the new responsibility for arrestees. Importantly, to the best of our knowledge no factor related to police activity was considered in determining the rollout of the reform. The Minister of Public Security adopted the committee's recommendations, and the implementation of the reform across Israel was scheduled to take place gradually throughout 2007 and early 2008. The different police regions and the timing of the reform in each region are shown in Figure 5.3. As will be further discussed in "Empirical Strategy," our identification strategy relies on this staggered rollout.

Data

We obtained from the Israeli Police full data on every arrest undertaken in Israel between September 2006 and September 2009. These data cover 153,960 arrests and 95,521 arrestees.

* The report (in Hebrew) is available at http://mops.gov.il/Documents/Publications/Reports/Yaron Committee.pdf.

Table 5.1 Descriptive Statistics

Variable	Mean	SD	10P	90P
Number of arrests	192.45	83.77	107	309
Arrest duration (days)	15.85	9.86	6.53	29.5
Maximum sentence (months)	74.45	13.73	59.95	91.92
Share indicted	0.36	0.11	0.24	0.51
Reported crimes	1041.8	326.8	558	1553

Note: All figures are at the week/region level. "Reported Crimes" refers to the number of crime files opened by the Police. SD, standard deviation.

For each arrest, we know the arresting unit, the date of arrest, and its duration (i.e., time spent in jail excluding time spent in house arrest). We also observe for each arrest the specific type of offense that led to it, and the maximum sentence that can be imposed for the offense. Additionally, we know whether the arrestee was charged after the arrest. Lastly, for each arrestee we have demographic information (age, gender, marital status, and ethnicity) as well as an anonymous identification number.

In addition to the arrest data, we also have full data on each of the nearly 834,000 crimes reported to the Police during the same period. For each crime reported, we know the date the complaint was filed, the type of crime, and the location where it was reported. The use of the number of reported crimes as a measure of crime is standard in the economic literature on crime. In Table 5.1, we present descriptive statistics of the outcome variables, constructed at the week–region level based on the individual level data.

To get a general sense of the effects of the reform on the number of arrests, on the mean duration of arrests and on the number of reported crimes, we calculated, for each region, the number of arrests, the mean duration of arrests (in days), the share of arrestees charged, and the number of reported crimes in the 90 weeks before and after the organizational reform. We then averaged these values across the five regions, using for each region the date of the organizational reform in that region as time zero. The results of the calculation, in 2-week bins, are presented in Figure 5.4. The figure shows that the organizational reform led to an increase both in the number of arrests and in their duration, and to a decrease in the share of charged arrestees and the number of reported crimes. The effect of the reform can also be graphically seen in Figure 5.5, in which we separately plot a time-series of the number of incarcerated arrestees in each region.

Empirical Strategy

We use a standard differences-in-differences research design, exploiting the gradual transfer of responsibility from the Police to the Prison Authority to study the effects of the organizational reform. Our baseline specification is as follows:

$$y_{rt} = \alpha + \beta \times \text{Post}_{rt} + \gamma_r + \delta_t + \varepsilon_{rt}, \tag{5.1}$$

where y_{rt} is the outcome variable of interest in region r in week t. The dummy Post_{rt} assumes the value one in regions and weeks in which the transfer of control over jails has already taken place. γ_r represents regional fixed effects, which control for

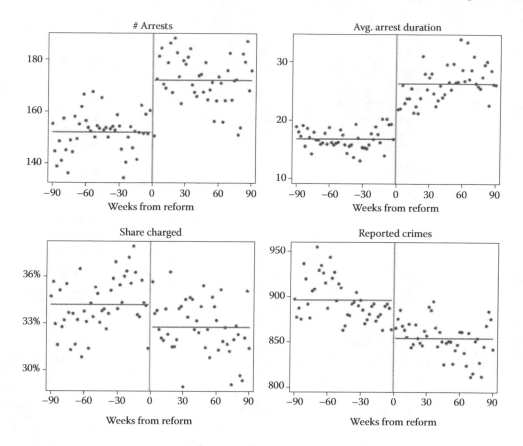

Figure 5.4 Organizational reform—number, duration, and quality of arrests and reported crimes. Note: The figure plots the number of arrests, the mean arrest duration, the share of charged arrests and the number of reported crimes. Each dot corresponds to a time period of two weeks. Week zero marks the date of reform implementation, for each region. The horizontal axis covers the 90 weeks before and after the reform. Horizontal lines represent the average values over the 90 weeks before or after the reform. Since the reform implementation date varies across regions, each dot aggregates values collected on different dates.

time-invariant differences across regions. To account for the volatility of criminal activity we also include weekly fixed effects, δ_t. We also acknowledge the possibility of criminal and police activity trends that may vary between regions by incorporating linear region-specific time trends in some of the specifications. Each observation is weighted according to the population size of its corresponding region. Finally, we account for the serial correlation in the outcome variables by clustering the error terms at the region–month level. In "Robustness," we explore alternative methods for deriving the estimates' standard errors.

This specification allows us to estimate the correlation between the implementation of the organizational reform, reflected in the variable Post$_{rt}$, and the outcome variables conditional on time and regional effects. The difference-in-difference approach implies that the impact of the reform is derived by comparing the change over time in the outcome variable in a region that has experienced the reform with the corresponding change in a region that has yet to experience the reform. For this equation to have a causal

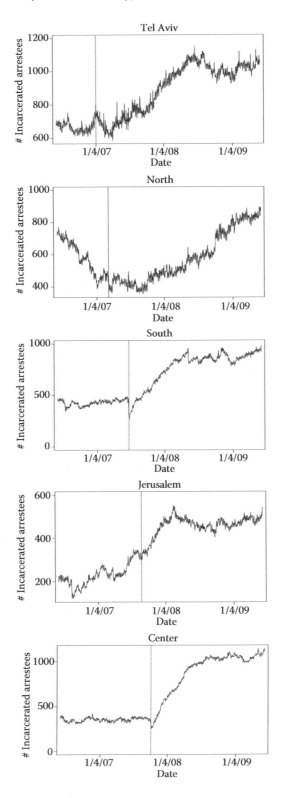

Figure 5.5 Number of incarcerated arrestees in different regions.

interpretation, the timing of the organizational reform and the order of the rollout need to be independent of unobservables that directly affect the dependent variables. Indeed, as indicated above, the decision to implement the reform and, hence, its timing were a direct consequence of the escape of a serial rapist in November 2006. Furthermore, the order in which the responsibility over jails was transferred to the Prison Authority was determined according to the administrative readiness of the Prison Authority in each region, and not based on factors relating to police activity. In "Robustness," we also conduct a formal test that validates the independence of outcomes from the order of the rollout of the reform. Thus, we do not believe that the order of the rollout constitutes a threat to the identification.

In what follows, we study the effect of the reform on four groups of outcome variables and separately also conduct the analysis for the main categories of crime:

1. Cost measures for arrests—the number of arrests and the mean arrest duration
2. Quality of arrests—the share of arrestees charged
3. Severity of arrests—the average maximum possible sentence associated with the crimes for which arrests were made, and the composition of arrests (categories of crime)
4. Crime—the number of crimes reported to the Police

Results

Number of Arrests and Mean Arrest Duration

We argue that the organizational reform externalized the costs of housing and transporting arrests from the Police to the Prison Authority. These costs include both financial and nonfinancial costs of handling arrestees (e.g., food, gasoline, hassle, and managerial time). Thus, we expect that the number and duration of arrests will increase after the reform.* As can be seen in Table 5.2, this prediction is supported by the regression analysis. In columns (1) and (2), we focus on the effect of the reform on the number of arrests in logs, without and with region-specific time trends, respectively. We find that the reform led to an increase of 11.1% or 12.6% in the average number of weekly regional arrests. Columns (3) and (4) consider the effect of the reform on arrest duration in logs, also presented without and with region-specific time trends. Our findings suggest that the reform led to a statistically significant increase of 38.5% or 23.1%, in mean arrest duration.†

Quality of Arrests

By law, the Police can arrest an individual if at the time of the arrest there is probable cause, that is, sufficient evidence to indicate that the individual has committed a crime. The Police, therefore, adopts a threshold level of probable cause above which it undertakes an arrest. A natural proxy for the threshold level that the Police adopts is the share of arrestees

---

* At the end of an arrest, the suspect is either released or charged.
† These findings suggest that following the reform, Courts more leniently approved requests for longer arrest periods. In a separate analysis, available upon request, we provide evidence that indeed requests for longer arrest periods are strongly correlated with Court decisions to approve such requests.

Table 5.2   Effect of Reform on Number and Duration of Arrests

Dependent Variable	Log (Number of Arrests)		Log (Arrest Duration)	
	(1)	(2)	(3)	(4)
Reform	0.111***	0.126***	0.385***	0.231**
	(0.0357)	(0.0349)	(0.104)	(0.102)
Week/region fixed effects	✓	✓	✓	✓
Region-specific time trends	×	✓	×	✓
R^2	0.911	0.919	0.621	0.677
Observations	785	785	785	785

Note: The unit of observation is a region–week cell. The reform variable corresponds to the dummy variable, which assumes the value one in regions and weeks in which the transfer of control over jails from the Police to the Prison Authority has already taken place. The regression includes week and regional fixed effects. Even columns also include region-specific time trends. Observations are weighted by each region's population. Standard errors are robust and clustered by region/month.

***$p < 0.01$; **$p < 0.05$.

Table 5.3   Effect of Reform on Share of Arrestees Charged and Maximum Sentence

Dependent Variable	Share Charged		Log (Maximum Sentence)	
	(1)	(2)	(3)	(4)
Reform	−0.0195**	−0.0278***	−0.0592***	−0.0635***
	(0.00845)	(0.00903)	(0.0219)	(0.0232)
Week/region fixed effects	✓	✓	✓	✓
Region-specific time trends	×	✓	×	✓
R^2	0.826	0.834	0.632	0.633
Observations	785	785	785	785

Note: The unit of observation is a region–week cell. The reform variable corresponds to the dummy variable, which assumes the value one in regions and weeks in which the transfer of control over jails from the Police to the Prison Authority has already taken place. The regression includes week and regional fixed effects. Even columns also include region-specific time trends. Observations are weighted by each region's population. Standard errors are robust and clustered by region/month.

***$p < 0.01$; **$p < 0.05$.

charged—our measure of arrest quality. How should this measure of quality be affected by the reform? Following the reform, the Police increased the number of arrests; presumably, they did so by adopting a lower probable cause threshold level. The increased number of arrests following the reform should therefore be concentrated among arrestees that are less certain to be charged, which means we expect to see a smaller share of arrestees being charged.

We calculated Equation 5.1 using the fraction of arrests that led to charges being filed in each week and region as the dependent variable. Columns (1) and (2) in Table 5.3 present the estimation results. We find that the reform led to a decrease of approximately 2 percentage points in the share of arrests leading to charges being filed, our measure for arrest quality. To obtain a better sense of the magnitude of these estimates, we performed a simple back-of-the-envelope calculation and compared the postreform population of arrestees with the prereform population. Given an 11% increase in the number of arrests, and assuming that the new population of arrestees is the cause of the change in the share of arrestees being charged, the new population of arrestees was 20 percentage points less likely to be charged compared to the original population.

Severity of Offenses and Composition of Arrests

We also examined whether the reform affected the severity of crimes that the Police pursued. Arguably, when the Police incurs lower costs of handling arrestees—as would be expected to occur owing to the reform—it may choose to pursue types of crimes that it did not pursue previously. In particular, we expect an increase in its activity toward "less important" crimes, which we measure by their severity. We used two approaches to empirically examine this conjecture.

First, we used the maximum sentence (in months) that could be imposed for each offense as a measure of crime severity. Columns (3) and (4) in Table 5.3 consider the effect of the reform on the average maximum possible sentence for arrestees in logs, without and with region-specific time trends, respectively. We find that the reform led to a decrease of approximately 6% in the average maximum possible sentence of arrestees. Back-of-the-envelope calculations suggest that the average maximum possible sentence of the postreform population of arrestees was 60% lower than that of the original population.

The second approach we used to examine the effect of the reform on the severity of crimes that the Police pursued was to distinguish between different categories of crime. We focused on three categories of crimes that accounted for 80% of arrests: public order (34%), property (30%), and bodily harm (15.5%). Whereas public order crimes (e.g., trespassing, disrupting police activity and disturbing the peace, violations of the immigration law) are relatively minor offenses, property crimes (e.g., burglary, robbery, auto theft, "theft from an auto") are more severe. Bodily harm crimes (e.g., murder, assault, and aggravated assault) are more severe than the two other categories.

Table 5.4 presents estimation results of Equation 5.1 for each of the three crime categories. The table shows the effect of the reform on the (log) number of arrests in each category. The results indicate that the reform led to an increase of 13–15.4% in the number of arrests for public order crimes and to an increase of 8.8–13.3% in the number of arrests for property crimes. The effect of the reform on arrests for bodily harm crimes is statistically indistinguishable from zero. These findings are consistent with our conjecture that the reform enabled the Police to pursue more minor crimes.

Table 5.4   Effect on Number and Duration of Arrests—by Crime Category

Dependent Variable	Public Order		Log (Number of Arrests) Property		Bodily Harm	
	(1)	(2)	(3)	(4)	(5)	(6)
Reform	0.130**	0.154***	0.0883**	0.133***	0.0146	−0.0143
	(0.0548)	(0.0533)	(0.0448)	(0.0460)	(0.0491)	(0.0497)
Week/region fixed effects	✓	✓	✓	✓	✓	✓
Region-specific	×	✓	×	✓	×	✓
R^2	0.854	0.865	0.804	0.815	0.740	0.744
Observations	785	785	785	785	785	785

Note: The unit of observation is a region–week–crime category cell. The reform variable corresponds to the dummy variable, which assumes the value one in regions and weeks in which the transfer of control over jails from the Police to the Prison Authority has already taken place. The regression includes week and regional fixed effects. Even columns also include region-specific time trends. Observations are weighted by each region's population. Standard errors are robust and clustered by region/month.

***$p < 0.01$; **$p < 0.05$.

Crime

Our final set of results examines the effect of the reform on crime rates. We report the results for the crime regressions in Table 5.5. In columns (1) and (2) we study the effect of the reform on all types of crimes, and in columns (3) to (8) we separately explore its effect on the three crime categories. The regression results suggest that the reform led to an average decrease of 2–4% in overall crime, and that this effect was mostly driven by reduction in public order and property crimes. In particular, we find that the reform led to a decrease of 1.9–4.4% in the number of public order crimes, and a decrease of 3.2–5.9% in the number of property crimes. The effect of the reform on bodily harm crimes is statistically indistinguishable from zero. These findings seem consistent with the results of our earlier analysis that indicated that the reform led to an increase in the number of arrests for public order and property crimes, but not for bodily harm crimes. The magnitude of the reduction in crime that we document is comparable to the effect of a 10% increase in police resources found in other studies on the relationship between police resources and crime (e.g., Draca et al. 2011; Evans and Owens 2007; Klick and Tabarrok 2005).

Cross-Regional Differences

Although the nature of the organizational reform was identical across regions, its actual impact could have been different. Specifically, we can expect that regions, in which more "managerial" police resources were allocated to managing jails and to the handling of arrestees, experienced a larger change in police activity following the reform. To empirically test this, we construct a reform intensity variable for each region that equals the ratio between the number of beds in jails located in the region and the total number of policemen in that region. Specifically, the range of the reform intensity variable ranges between 7 and 16.5 beds to 100 policemen. We replace the reform variable, Post, by the new variable in observations for which the reform variable has previously assumed the value 1 and then estimate Equation 5.1. Table 5.6 presents the corresponding estimation results for the five

Table 5.5 Effect of Reform on Crime

Dependent Variable	All Categories Combined		Public Order		Property		Bodily Harm	
	(1)	(2)	(3)	(4)	(5)	(6)	(7)	(8)
Reform	−0.0399***	−0.0193*	−0.0440***	−0.0189	−0.0589***	−0.0318***	0.0161	−0.0025
	(0.0118)	(0.0103)	(0.0151)	(0.0133)	(0.0134)	(0.0104)	(0.0193)	(0.0195)
Week/region fixed effects	✓	✓	✓	✓	✓	✓	✓	✓
Region-specific time trends	×	✓	×	✓	×	✓	×	✓
R^2	0.982	0.986	0.948	0.962	0.978	0.983	0.933	0.936
Observations	785	785	785	785	785	785	785	785

Note: The unit of observation in the first two columns is a region–week cell. The unit of observation in the remaining columns is a region–week–crime cell. The number of reported crimes refers to the number of crime files opened by the Police. The reform variable corresponds to the dummy variable, which assumes the value one in regions and weeks in which the transfer of control over jails from the Police to the Prison Authority has already taken place. The regression includes week and regional fixed effects. Even columns also include region-specific time trends. Standard errors are robust and clustered by region/month.

***$p < 0.01$; *$p < 0.1$.

Table 5.6 Effect of Reform by Its Intensity

Dependent Variable	Log (Number of Arrests)		Log (Arrest Duration)		Share Charged		Log (Maximum Sentence)		Log (Crime)	
	(1)	(2)	(3)	(4)	(5)	(6)	(7)	(8)	(9)	(10)
Reform Intensity	0.984***	0.952***	−1.116	0.179	−0.301***	−0.260***	−0.442**	−0.497***	−0.217**	−0.156*
	(0.260)	(0.273)	(1.019)	(0.844)	(0.0740)	(0.0735)	(0.177)	(0.182)	(0.0942)	(0.0825)
Week/region fixed effects	✓	✓	✓	✓	✓	✓	✓	✓	✓	✓
Region-specific time trends	×	✓	×	✓	×	✓	×	✓	×	✓
R^2	0.912	0.918	0.605	0.670	0.830	0.835	0.631	0.633	0.982	0.986
Observations	785	785	785	785	785	785	785	785	785	785

Note: The unit of observation is a region–week cell. The reform intensity corresponds to a variable that takes the value zero in regions and weeks before the transfer of control over jails from the Police to the Prison Authority. In the remaining regions and weeks this variable assumes the ratio between the number of beds region r jails and the total number of policemen in that region in the month before the reform was implemented. The regression includes week and regional fixed effects. Even columns also include region-specific time trends. Observations are weighted by each region's population. Standard errors are robust and clustered by region/month.

*** $p < 0.01$; ** $p < 0.05$; * $p < 0.1$.

outcome variables. The results demonstrate that for all outcome variables, except arrest duration, regions with a larger beds/policemen ratio experienced a greater response to the reform. For example, a 0.01 increase in beds/policemen ratio is associated with an increase of nearly 1% in the number of arrests. These results can at least partially explain the differences across regions observed in Figure 5.5.

Robustness

In this subsection, we present additional results that demonstrate the robustness of our findings.

First, using a difference-in-difference approach using panel data may lead to overrejection of the null hypothesis when outcome variables, such as crime and police activity measures, exhibit serial correlation (Duflo, Mullainathan, and Bertrand 2004). In this chapter, we address this concern by clustering the standard errors at the region–month level. In the Online Appendix, we also show that our results are similar when we calculate the standard errors in alternative ways, such as clustering by region; clustering by region times $Post_{rt}$; using the Moulton correction and wild bootstrap. Second, we collected monthly unemployment data and yearly data on the share of minority groups and the fraction of young men (age 18–25 years) in each region's population. These variables undergo very little variation over time, so they are nearly fully absorbed in the regional fixed effects. We verified that our results hold when these variables were included in the analysis. In addition, we verified that our findings are qualitatively unchanged even when we allow the coefficients on these background variables to vary on a yearly basis. Third, given that the analysis was based on five regions only, we verified that the results were not driven by any single region. We did so by reestimating the effects of the reform using each subset of four regions. The results presented in Table 5.7 demonstrates the robustness of our findings to the exclusion

Table 5.7   Robustness to Excluding Region

	Benchmark (All Regions Included)	Excluding Northern District	Excluding Tel Aviv District	Excluding Southern District	Excluding Center District	Excluding Jerusalem District
Log (Number of Arrests)	0.111*** (0.0357)	0.138*** (0.0443)	0.0650* (0.0357)	0.116*** (0.0395)	0.0719* (0.0423)	0.133*** (0.0383)
Log (Arrest Duration)	0.385*** (0.104)	0.418*** (0.113)	0.405*** (0.142)	0.393*** (0.115)	0.0419 (0.108)	0.530*** (0.0958)
Share Charged	−0.0195** (0.00845)	−0.0262*** (0.00941)	−0.00272 (0.0103)	−0.0198** (0.00985)	−0.0188** (0.00860)	−0.0237** (0.00928)
Log (Maximum Sentence)	−0.0592*** (0.0219)	−0.0794*** (0.0240)	−0.0144 (0.0222)	−0.0657*** (0.0246)	−0.0618*** (0.0236)	−0.0603** (0.0246)
Log (Crime)	−0.0399*** (0.0118)	−0.0488*** (0.0133)	−0.0202* (0.0114)	−0.0434*** (0.0136)	−0.0471*** (0.0180)	−0.0363*** (0.0110)

Note: The unit of observation is a region–week cell. The reform variable corresponds to the dummy variable, which assumes the value one in regions and weeks in which the transfer of control over jails from the Police to the Prison Authority has already taken place. The regression includes week and regional fixed effects. The table presents estimates of parameter β from estimating Equation 5.1. The first column is served as a benchmark that includes all five regions. Each of the remaining columns exclude the region indicated at the top of the column. Observations are weighted by each region's population. Standard errors are robust and clustered by region/month.

***$p < 0.01$; **$p < 0.05$; *$p < 0.1$.

of any single region from the analysis. Likewise, the results were also qualitatively similar when we added the West Bank region as a sixth region. We excluded this region from the main analysis because the Police's *modus operandi* in the West Bank is different from that in the other regions of the country. Fourth, we verified that the results were qualitatively the same when we normalized the dependent variables—number of arrests and number of crimes—by region population size, or alternatively when we assigned equal weights to all the regions instead of weighting them by population size.

Furthermore, we verified that the prereform crime rates and police activity measures were not associated with the order of the rollout. If, for example, the order in which the organizational reform was implemented was dictated by region-specific crime time trends, then our estimates might have captured those trends rather than the effect of the reform. To analyze this issue, we conducted a placebo test by considering a sample that started on September 1, 2006 and ended on March 31, 2007, that is, the day before the reform began to be implemented. We then reestimated our crime regression, defining a fictitious date for the implementation of the reform in each of the regions. We set a fictitious reform date in the first region in which the reform was implemented (Tel Aviv). The fictitious reform dates for the remaining regions were set to maintain the order of implementation and the relative difference in the time of implementation between regions. In this way, we reproduced the exercise as if the organizational reform had occurred during the prereform period. The results, which show a nonsignificant effect of the fictitious reform, are also presented in the Online Appendix. These results validate our empirical approach as they reveal no association between the prereform crime dynamics and the order of the organizational reform.

Finally, we tested whether the timing of the change in police activity coincided with the timing of the organizational reform. For this, we conducted a test for a structural break by estimating a series of regressions with fictitious organizational reform dates defined for every month starting from 7 months before the true implementation date of the reform up to 15 months after it. The dependent variable in each regression was the weekly number of arrests. The independent variables were a continuous week variable and its interaction with a variable indicating implementation of the organizational reform. We maintained the order of the reform among regions as well as the time difference between their implementation dates. The structural break date was defined as the date for which the regression R^2 is maximized. We find that the regression R^2s range from 0.032 to 0.077, with the largest R^2 estimated in the regression with the actual implementation dates.

Crime Displacement Effects

Our results are potentially driven by spatial displacement effects, which imply that criminal activity is diverted from regions in which the reform has been implemented into other areas where the reform has not yet taken place.[*] If spatial displacement did occur, then our

---

[*] A different type of displacement is time displacement, which implies that the criminal activity is postponed until the extra police activity levels off is not relevant to our study because of the nontransient nature of the reform we investigate. In addition, studies that exploited terror attacks to identify the effect of terror on crime (i.e., Draca et al. 2011) emphasized that correlated shocks posed a major concern with regard to identification because terror events have a dislocating impact on the economy and the population. In other words, the concern was that crime rates fell not only due to increased deployment of police forces but also because of other factors (Becker and Rubinstein 2011; Gould and Stecklov 2009). Given that we study a reform that had little effect on the general public in Israel, and in light of the direct evidence we present on arrests, we believe that this concern is not relevant to our study.

estimates for both arrests and crime rates are potentially biased downward. To test for spatial displacement effects, we focused on the 10,827 individuals who were arrested multiple times during the analyzed time frame, and were arrested at least once before April 1, 2007 (the transition date in the first region). We used the information on the first arrest (performed during the prereform period) to identify the "home" region of the repeat offender. If spatial location displacement effects are important then, conditional on being arrested again, we expected that the likelihood of being arrested in a different region during the interim period (April 1, 2007 to January 1, 2008) would be greater than the corresponding conditional probability after the completion of the rollout (after January 1, 2008). The idea is that during the interim period, the benefits from diverting efforts to other regions are higher than the benefits of doing so after the full implementation of the reform. Using this approach, however, we do not find evidence for spatial displacement. In fact, conditional on being arrested again, the likelihood of the second arrest being in a different region was higher during the postrollout period than during the interim period.*

Discussion

A question that arises with respect to our findings is whether they are mainly driven by a change that affected the Police as an organization (*top–down effect*), or whether the observed patterns were triggered by a behavioral change among individual policemen (*bottom–up effect*). In other words, the larger number of arrests may have been driven either by the lower costs of undertaking an arrest by an individual patrol officer, or alternatively by senior police officers who exploited the reform to improve the performance and efficiency of their units, resulting in more arrests.

We think that our findings reflect a top–down effect, for a few reasons. First, the analysis presented in "Cross-Regional Differences" suggests that regions in which more managerial time was allocated to jails exhibited a larger effect on police activity. Second, the fact that arrest duration increased suggests that the effect of the reform was not limited to patrol policemen, who bear the direct cost of arrest, but rather that police investigators and police prosecutors were affected as well. Third, during the investigated period and irrespective of the reform, police station commanders were also evaluated according to the total number of arrestees being charged in their precinct. In that sense, the reform helped these commanders accomplish their own and the Police's goals. Finally, police officers we spoke with noted that the direct costs of undertaking arrests for individual police officers did not necessarily decrease after the reform, mainly because the Prison Authority was procedurally much stricter than the Police when accepting arrestees. For instance, the Prison Authority requires the presence of a police officer while it conducts a thorough health checkup on each new arrestee.

Another question that we have not yet touched upon is whether the reform was desirable from a normative perspective. Although it is difficult to provide an exact welfare measure of the consequences of the reform, we believe it is still important to offer at least a rough estimate. The total annual costs of property crimes in Israel are estimated to be about $1.823 billion, and the costs of crimes which do not fall into the property and bodily

---

* An alternative approach in which we added a dummy variable equal to one in region *r* and week *t* if the reform has yet to be implemented in that region, but has already been implemented in one of region *r*'s adjacent regions, has also not supported a displacement effect.

harm crime categories is about $0.316 billion.* Thus, a reduction of nearly 6% in property crimes and 4% in public order crimes amount to a saving of roughly $115.7 million. As Figure 5.1 illustrates, following the reform the total number of arrestees increased from about 2500 to 4000. The average yearly cost of holding a prisoner in Israel, based on the Prison Authority's data, is $25,000. Thus, an increase of 1500 arrestees is associated with an increased cost of $37.5 million. Taking into account both the costs and benefits, we find that the annual net benefit of the reform is about $78 million. Furthermore, even if we focus only on the reduction in property crimes we find that the estimated net benefit of the reform is larger than $70 million dollars.

The former calculation, however, is likely imprecise in two ways. First, to estimate the cost of holding an arrestee, we used the average cost of a prisoner. As the marginal cost of holding an arrestee is likely to be significantly lower than the average cost, our assessment of the increased cost owing to the higher number of arrestees may be overstated. Second, we must also consider the cost of arrests that did not lead to charges being filed. We found that the reform led to a decrease of 2 percentage points in the share of arrests leading to charges being filed. Since after the reform, the total yearly number of arrests increased by 7300 (the weekly average regional number increased by 28); this means that in the year following the reform about 1500 individuals were arrested but not charged. Arguably, integrating into the welfare calculations the costs incurred as a result of these arrests would make the bottom line of the welfare analysis less obvious.†

Finally, our findings regarding the increased number of arrestees and the corresponding reduction in crime may suggest that the reduction in crime is a result of the incapacitation of criminals. The fact that we do not find evidence for crime displacement (see "Crime Displacement Effects") further supports incapacitation rather than deterrence. This interpretation of the results is somewhat different from those of other studies on the relationship between police and crime, which have often emphasized the deterrent role of Police (e.g., Draca et al. 2011).

Conclusion

In this chapter, we provide evidence regarding the consequences of an organizational reform in Israel that adjusted organizational boundaries between the Police and the Prison Authority. We find that the reform led to an increase in the number and duration of arrests. At the same time, the quality of arrests, measured according to the likelihood of arrestees being charged, decreased, as did the severity of offenses for which arrests were undertaken. In addition, we find that the effect of the reform on police activity also translated into significantly lower crime rates. Taken together, our results indicate that institutional details, such as organizational structure, have a substantial effect on police activity and crime, and that these effects should be taken into consideration when designing the structure of law enforcement agencies (Weisberg 2013).

* One way to integrate the welfare loss of arresting non-charged arrestees is by using the $1000 for 90 days of arrest value of freedom figure offered by Abrams and Rohlfs (2011). Using this value suggests that the total welfare cost of these arrests is in the order of $250,000, and therefore it does not change the conclusion regarding the desirability of the reform.
† See the full report (in Hebrew) at http://mops.gov.il/Documents/Publications/CrimeDamage/CrimeDamageReports/CrimeDamageReport2008.pdf.

Although we focus on law enforcement agencies, we believe that there are other settings in the public domain to which our findings might apply. In many instances, decision-makers in the public sector do not bear the costs of their decisions. Furthermore, it is important to understand the relationship between structure and performance in the public sector, not only because this relationship can shape public policy, but also because many market mechanisms that economists often propose are unlikely to apply to public sector agencies. This implies that the consequences of integration decisions within the public sector are potentially far-reaching.

Acknowledgments

We are grateful to Ran Abramitzky, Philip Cook, Daniel Chen, Raj Chetty, Liran Einav, Alon Eizenberg, Jonah Gelbach, Mark Gradstein, Oliver Hart, Justin McCrary, Dotan Persitz, Andrei Shleifer, Ron Siegel, Ity Shurtz as well as seminar participants at Harvard Labor Lunch, The Hebrew University, Tel Aviv University, University of Pennsylvania Crime, Law & Economics Workshop and Yale Law, Economics & Organization Workshop for helpful comments. We also benefited from discussions with Besora Regev and Shai Amram (Ministry of Public Security), Israel Tal, Ilan Mor (Israeli Police), and Beni Naveh (Israel Prison Authority). Eran Hoffmann and Dror Nachimov provided outstanding research assistance.

References

Abrams, D. S. 2012. Estimating the deterrent effect of incarceration using sentencing enhancements. *American Economic Journals: Applied Economics* 4(4): 32–56.

Abrams, D. and C. Rohlfs. 2011. Optimal bail and the value of freedom: Evidence from the Philadelphia bail experiment. *Economic Inquiry* 49(3) 750–770.

Afendulis, C. and D. Kessler. 2007. Tradeoffs from integrating diagnosis and treatment in markets for healthcare. *American Economic Review* 97(3): 1013–1020.

Ater, I., Y. Givati and O. Rigbi. 2014. Organizational structure, police activity and crime. *Journal of Public Economics*. 115: 62–71, with permission from Elsevier.

Barbarino, A. and G. Mastrobuoni. 2014. The incapacitation effect of incarceration: Evidence from several Italian collective pardons. *Economic Journal: Economic Policy* 6(1): 1–37.

Becker, G. 1968. Crime and punishment: An economic approach. *Journal of Political Economy* 76: 169–217.

Becker, G. S. and Y. Rubinstein. 2011. *Fear and the response to terrorism: An economic analysis.* University of Chicago mimeo.

Bresnahan, T. and J. Levin. 2012. *The handbook of organizational economics*. Princeton, NJ: Princeton University Press.

Chalfin, A. and J. McCrary. Forthcoming. Are U.S. cities underpoliced?: Theory and evidence. *The Review of Economics and Statistics*.

DiTella, R. and E. Schargrodsky. 2004. Do police reduce crime? Estimates using the allocation of police forces after a terrorist attack. *American Economic Review* 94(1): 115–133.

Draca, M., S. Machin and R. Witt. 2011. Panic on the streets of London: Police, crime, and the July 2005 terror attacks. *American Economic Review* 101: 2157–2181.

Drago, F., R. Galbiati and P. Vertova. 2009. The deterrent effects of prison: Evidence from a natural experiment. *Journal of Political Economy* 117(2): 257–280.

Duflo, E., S. Mullainathan and M. Bertrand. 2004. How much should we trust difference in differences estimates? *Quarterly Journal of Economics* 119(1): 249–275.

Evans, W. N. and E. G. Owens. 2007. COPS and crime. *Journal of Public Economics* 91:(1–2): 181–201.

Forbes, S. J. and M. Lederman. 2010. Does vertical integration affect firm performance? Evidence from the airline industry. *RAND Journal of Economics* 41(4): 765–790.

Gould, E. D. and G. Stecklov. 2009. Terror and the costs of crime. *Journal of Public Economics* 93: 1175–1188.

Grossman, S. and O. Hart. 1986. The costs and benefits of ownership: A theory of vertical and lateral integretion. *Journal of Political Economy* 94: 691–719.

Hart, O., A. Shliefer and R. W. Vishny. 1997. The proper scope of government: Theory and an application to prisons. *Quarterly Journal of Economics* 112(4): 1127–1161.

Klick, J. M. and A. Tabarrok. 2005. Using terror alert levels to estimate the effect of police on crime. *Journal of Law and Economics* 48(1): 267–280.

Kuziemko, I. 2013. How should inmates be released from prison? An assessment of parole versus fixed-sentence regimes. *Quarterly Journal of Economics* 128(1): 371–424.

Lafontaine, F. and M. E. Slade. 2007. Vertical integration and firm boundaries: The evidence. *Journal of Economic Literature* 45(3): 629–685.

Lee, D. S. and M. Justin. 2009. *The deterrence effect of prison: Dynamic theory and evidence.* Princeton, NJ: Industrial Relations Section, Princeton University.

Levitt, S. D. 1996. The effect of prison population size on crime rates: Evidence from prison overcrowding litigation. *Quarterly Journal of Economics* 111(2): 319–351.

Levitt, S. D. 1997. Using electoral cycles in police hiring to estimate the effect of police on crime. *American Economic Review* 87(3): 270–290.

Machin, S. and O. Marie. 2011. Crime and police resources: The street crime initiative. *Journal of the European Economic Association* 9(4): 678–701.

Mullainathan, S. and D. Scharfstein. 2001. Do firm boundaries matter? *American Economic Review* 91(2): 195–199.

Vollard, B. and J. Hamed. 2012. Why the police have an effect on violent crime after all: Evidence from the British crime survey. *Journal of Law and Economics* 5(4): 901–924.

Weisberg, R. 2013. Empirical criminal law scholarship and the shift to institutions. *Stanford Technology Law Review* 65: 1371–1401.

Williamson, O. E. 1985. *The economic institutions of capitalism.* New York: Free Press.

The Police and the Community

II

Police, Politics, and Culture in a Deeply Divided Society[*]

6

BADI HASISI

Contents

Introduction

A review of the academic literature in the field of police–minority relations in deeply divided societies reveals that tense relations between the minority and the police are a frequent phenomenon. One of the sources of this tension is the political and social marginality of the minority, which is most often accompanied by unbalanced and unfair policing (Brewer 1991; Brewer and Brewer 1994; Weitzer 1990, 1995). Researchers emphasize the centrality of the political variable in understanding police–minority interactions in deeply divided societies. In fact, often hovering above deeply divided democratic societies is the question of the legitimacy of the political regime in the eyes of the minority group.

The tense relations between the Arab minority in Israel and the police are common knowledge. Throughout the history of Arab–Jewish relations in Israel, this tension was sharply brought into relief in several mass political events, with the most violent example in October 2000. Prime Minister Ariel Sharon paid a visit to the Temple Mount in Jerusalem, an act perceived by the Arab minority as violating the sanctity of the Al-Aksa Mosque. The visit incited 8 days of violent riots that ended with 12 Arab citizens dead, all of them by police gunfire. This event emphasized the influence of political variables on

[*] Reproduced from Hasisi, B. 2008. Police, politics, and culture in a deeply divided society. *The Journal of Criminal Law and Criminology* 98(3): 1119–1146. With permission from Northwestern University School of Law.

minority relations with the police in Israel, and yet this is not the sole variable on which we should focus.

In deeply divided societies where divisions are also based on different ethnicities, emphasis is put on the cultural distinction between the majority and the minority. This distinction is liable to find its expression in the cultural perception of governmental institutions, including the police. The impact of cultural pluralism on police–minority relations is reinforced owing to the underrepresentation of members of the minority in the police force. The combination of these factors exacerbates the cultural disparity between the service providers—police officers who belong to the majority group—and service users—members of the minority group. We can assume that where there is greater cultural disparity between the majority and minority, there will be greater tension in minority–police relations. The Israeli-Arab minority is a native, traditional minority that differs significantly in culture from the Jewish majority, who are culturally Western oriented. This cultural distinction, and not just political variables, will be reflected in minority attitudes toward the police.

This chapter aims to evaluate the impact of political and cultural variables on minority perceptions of the police in deeply divided societies. First, I will try to illustrate the distinction between political and cultural variables and explain how making this distinction facilitates a better understanding of police–minority relations in deeply divided societies. Then I will compare the attitudes of Israeli Arabs and Jews toward the police and turn to the core of this article: an in-depth analysis of the attitudes of different Arab subgroups (Muslims, Christians, and Druze) toward the Israeli police. In so doing, I wish to elaborate on the cultural explanations for the existing tension, along with the more obvious political reasons.

Politics versus Culture

When analyzing police–minority relations, the line between political and cultural variables can become quite vague. Nevertheless, I will try to argue that there is an analytical distinction between the two variables that has significant ramifications on police–minority relations. The political aspect in police–minority relations becomes manifest when we ask the following questions: How do minority groups perceive the role of the police in the construction of the (controversial) sociopolitical order? What is the image of the police in society? What do the police represent among minority groups? Are the police there "to protect and to serve" or "to chase after and repress?" What styles of policing are practiced toward minority groups? Is it "high" or "low" policing?

Criminological and sociological scholars have tried to answer these questions by addressing the sociopolitical variables that characterize several minority groups. Many studies have pointed to the tense relations that often exist between police and minorities in various societies. There is evidence of high rates of minority arrest and incarceration, high rates of police violence toward minorities, and negative attitudes among minorities toward the police (Bayley and Mendelsohn 1969; Blauner and Blauner 1972; Decker 1981; Feagin 1991; Holdaway 2003; Kennedy 1998; Turk 1969). Furthermore, stereotypical images of minorities are prevalent among police officers. Most commonly, police view minority members as a potential criminal threat (Blalock 1967; Bobo and Hutchings 1996; Feagin 1991; Holmes 2000; Jackson 1989; Parker, Stults, and Rice 2005; Quillian and Pager 2001).

Research also shows high rates of crime among minorities. These crime rates are influenced by various social factors associated with minority status (Shaw and McKay 1942). For example, evidence shows overrepresentation of broken families, high rates of divorce, high residential density, low economic status, high levels of unemployment, and high adolescent dropout rates. These variables increase social disorganization and affect crime rates. In addition, minority populations tend to be younger and more likely to be visible in the streets (Blalock 1967; Sampson and Groves 1989). All of these factors create a supportive environment for the development of criminal behavior and, in turn, increase the contact between minorities and the police. Police officers face many obstacles in policing underclass minority neighborhoods because criminals and innocent citizens may share the same socioeconomic characteristics (Stark 1987). This, in turn, increases complaints from minority groups regarding racial profiling by the police (Weitzer et al. 2006; Withrow 2006).

Research shows that a tense and alienated relationship between police and the minority community strongly discourages police officers from enforcing criminal laws while also dissuading minorities from collaborating with police to prevent and report crime (Sung 2002). The primary complaint of minority groups is that they are simultaneously overpoliced as suspects and underpoliced as victims, which has reduced their confidence in and willingness to collaborate with the police (Blagg and Valuri 2004; Bowling 1998).

The political explanation of police–minority relations is quite common in many research studies; nevertheless, it lacks any reference to the impact of societal–cultural diversity on minority interactions and perceptions of the police. The cultural explanation of police–minority relations focuses on the impact of police organizational culture and how it affects interactions with minority groups. The pertinent questions include: How does the cultural context of police activity interact with the cultural pluralism of some minority groups? How do the cultural characteristics of the minority groups affect their perceptions of police organizational knowledge? To what extent are police officers aware of the various cultural characteristics of the different communities in society?

The cultural approach focuses on the interaction between the formal rules of the police and the subcultural values of minority groups. Some of the disparities between the majority and the minority are not merely political, but can also be attributed to cultural differences, such as language, religion, customs, family structure, informal social control, moral perceptions, and gender relations. Some cultural minorities act according to their own cultural norms and consequently may be accused of committing crimes because the legal culture of the state reflects the views of the dominant group.

Examples of such cases include bigamy, family honor murder, spousal and child abuse, parent–child suicide, acts of blood revenge, and celebratory shooting. It is reasonable to expect that the interactions of the minority with the police will reflect these cultural differences.

Some studies have claimed that the police generally represent and act in accordance with the culture of the dominant group, and this is further emphasized by the underrepresentation of minority members in the police force (Davis, Erez, and Avitabile 1998; Mazerolle, Marchetti, and Lindsay 2003). As a result, some actions taken by the police might be viewed as culturally inappropriate by traditional communities. Standard police procedure among the majority group may create unpredictable reactions in the minority community because of cultural differences.

Police–Minority Relations in a Deeply Divided Society

There is no better case that draws attention to the dominance of the political explanation in police–minority relations than the example of deeply divided societies (Brogden 1993; Della Porta 2006; Ellison and Martin 2000; McGarry and O'Leary 1999; Weitzer 1995; Whyte 1991). These are societies divided along ethnic lines where the state traditionally is affiliated with the dominant group (Lijphart 1999; Smooha and Hanf 1992; Van den Berghe 2002). Examples of these societies include Northern Ireland until 1969, Israel, Georgia, Estonia, and Latvia (Smooha and Järve 2005). The minority perceives the state as nonneutral, and this view, as a result, decreases the legitimacy of the government and police in the eyes of the minority. The minority's perception of the police is not only influenced by police actions, but also by what the police represent to the people (Weitzer 1995). Such perceived illegitimacy produces a threat to internal security, and the bulk of the state's policing resources are therefore consigned to the management of political offenses (Ellison and Smyth 2000; Weitzer 1995). This pattern affects the nature of police activities in deeply divided societies so that when policing public events, for example, the police generally practice a "zero tolerance" policy toward minority group protesters and regard their actions as political subversion against the state (Boudreau 2005; Della Porta 2006; Ellison and Martin 2000; Hinton 2006; Waddington 1994).

At the same time, the policing of nonpolitical crimes among the minority is typically less effective. This is attributable to police neglect of incidents that occur in the minority community, particularly when the crime bears no threat to the dominant group (Blalock 1967; Bowling 1998; Feagin 1991; Holmes 2000; Jackson 1989; Kent and Jacobs 2005; Mesch and Talmud 1998). Weak police performance in the minority community is also attributable to the minority group's lack of cooperation with the police. The literature shows that the main reason that minority groups in deeply divided societies tend to avoid cooperation with the police is attributable to political disagreements between majority and minority communities (McGarry and O'Leary 1999).

Ronald Weitzer, a sociologist at George Washington University, has developed a comprehensive model of the policing of deeply divided societies based on his research in Northern Ireland and Zimbabwe (Weitzer 1995). Weitzer's model describes police policies or practices as institutionally biased against members of the subordinate minority group. There is chronic overrepresentation of the dominant ethnic group in the police force, especially in the top ranks. The police tend to repress the regime's opponents, holding dual responsibility for ordinary crime control and homeland security. In the absence of effective mechanisms of accountability, the police in these countries also enjoy legal systems that provide them with great latitude in their ability to control the minority population, including with respect to the use of force (Brewer and Brewer 1994; Weitzer 1995).

The Weitzer model addresses very important political dimensions in police–minority relations in deeply divided societies, but lacks any reference to the cultural explanation. The reason might be that when Weitzer developed the model, he focused his analysis on Northern Ireland. There are few cultural dissimilarities between the Protestant majority and the Catholic minority in this country that might influence the relationship with the police. In contrast, in Israel there are marked cultural distinctions between the Arab native minority and the Jewish majority that might affect relations with the police. Arabs are part of a Mediterranean, Islamic–Arabic culture, whereas Jewish culture is often more Western oriented. These differences are manifested in various cultural expressions, including languages (Hebrew versus Arabic), religion (Jewish versus Muslim, Christian, and Druze), family structure (nuclear family versus extended family), residential patterns (urban versus rural or patrilocal), interrelations among the extended family (weak versus strong), the role of the clan as an informal social control institution (among Arabs), gender relations and segregation, and leisure patterns.

Arab society is still largely governed by traditional social structures and has not undergone radical urbanization, with a significant percentage of Arabs living in rural villages (Al-Haj 1985). Communities have preserved informal mechanisms of social control (Ginat 1997; Hasan 2002; Lia 2006). The Arab society in Israel exhibits some of the characteristics of a stateless society, especially with regard to the culture of lawlessness (toward some Israeli laws) and community self-policing (Ginat 1997; Lia 2006). The stateless characteristics of the Arab minority intensify as a result of the social and geographical segregation of Arabs and Jews in Israel (Falah 1996; Smooha and Hanf 1992). These cultural characteristics are prevalent enough to influence the relations between the minority and the police.

The cultural variable in police–minority relations is not applicable solely to deeply divided societies. It is relevant also to several Western immigrant societies—including the United States, Canada, New Zealand, and Australia—where native minorities still live in segregated communities and hold different cultural codes from the white majority, especially in terms of traditionally informal social control (Chatterjee and Elliott 2003; Forcese 1992). This makes police work a very complex task in these communities. Furthermore, several Western countries host immigrants from non-Western cultures, and some of these immigrant groups have maintained cultural codes from their homelands, even creating a Diaspora in their host countries (Chui and Regin 2005; Poole and Pogrebin 1990). The immigrants are generally unfamiliar with the culture of the host country, and their vulnerability may make them targets for abuse by criminals in the community (Abel 2006; Egharevba 2006; Holmberg and Kyvsgaard 2003; Smith 1997). These immigrants may in fact hesitate to contact the police since many come from countries or cultures that had poor relationships with the police. To sum up, in the case of native and immigrant minorities, the political variable is quite important when analyzing police–minority relations. However, we miss a significant part of the picture by ignoring the impact of cultural differences on the majority and the minority, and how these differences may affect the minority's perceptions of the police (Davis et al. 1998; Davis and Henderson 2003; Menjívar and Bejarano 2004).

Arabs in Israel: Between Political Threat and Cultural Estrangement

Arabs inside Israel's "Green Line" constitute about 17% of Israel's population, or 1.1 million people (Central Bureau of Statistics 2003, 2006). They are a native minority and part of the Palestinian nation. For more than 100 years, the Palestinian people have been engaged in a violent and ongoing national conflict with the Jewish national movement and, at a later stage, with the State of Israel. Immediately upon its establishment after the war in 1948, the State of Israel endorsed full, formal citizenship for members of the Arab minority who continued to reside in Israel. The national Palestinian identity of the Arab minority transformed them, in the eyes of the Jewish majority, into a group that was affiliated with the enemy and which possessed "dual loyalty." The solution to this threat was to enforce military rule on the minority community from 1948 to 1966. Although military rule has ended, it has not reduced the high threat perception currently held by the Jewish majority toward the Arab minority. A recent survey has shown that a majority of Israeli Jews (67%) believe that the Arab community's high birthrate endangers the state; that Arabs are intent on changing the state's Jewish character (72%); that Arabs might assist enemies of the state (78%); and that Arabs might launch a popular revolt (72%). It also showed that a majority of Israeli Jews (84%) fear Arabs because of their support of the Palestinian people and believe that most Israeli Arabs would be more loyal to a Palestinian state than to Israel (66%) (Smooha 2004).

The majority of the Israeli-Arab population lives in three geographic areas: the Galilee, the Triangle, and the Negev—areas at the periphery (and frontier) of Israeli society. Although there is an urban middle class sector, a large number of Arabs live in rural towns and villages and continue to abide by traditional forms of social organization. In fact, 90% of Israeli Arabs live in small towns populated by Arabs exclusively. Only eight cities are ethnically mixed, and these are extremely segregated residentially (Falah 1996). Such segregation is accepted by many Israelis; only a minority of Jews or Arabs express willingness to live in a mixed neighborhood (Smooha 1989).

The Arab minority is not a single homogenous group, but rather is characterized by an inner diversity that affects its relationship with the police. One of the features of this diversity is the religious–ethnic divide among Muslims, Christians, Druze, and Bedouins (Central Bureau of Statistics 2003, 2006). Ethnic distinctions among Arabs in Israel are institutionalized; for example, the State of Israel recognizes religious–ethnic divides and finances separate institutions for each of the Arab religious–ethnic groups. The subethnic distinctions of the Arab minority are not limited solely to the religious aspect, but are also manifested in the political attitudes and behaviors of the various Arab groups.

Druze have a basic difference from Muslims and Christians in their relations with the State of Israel. The Druze are an Arab ethnic group culturally. However, the Druze peoples' political identification with Palestinian national motifs is very weak, and thus they are perceived as less threatening by the Israeli state (Smooha 1993). Members of the Druze group share similar political orientations with the Jewish majority and are in fact drafted into the Israeli armed forces and the police (Frisch 1993). In light of this, we may expect that compared to other Arab subgroups, the Druze will express relatively more positive attitudes toward the police.

Although the Druze share similar political orientations with the Jewish majority, they still preserve the traditional ways of life in their segregated communities, customs that are very similar to those of the Muslim Arabs. This is quite salient in their patterns of partilocal residence, the centrality of the extended family as an informal social control mechanism, and their maintenance of social separation between the genders. These characteristics indicate that the Druze politically identify with the Jews, but culturally identify with the Muslim Arabs. In recent years, few clashes between the police and the Druze have erupted, and these mostly have stemmed from the difference between the modern and traditional cultures. In October 2007, a violent clash took place between the police and the Druze citizens of a small northern village called Pki' in. Several Druze vigilantes from the community burned some new cellular antennas that were installed in the village. The people of the village believed that the cellular antennas were responsible for the increase in cancer rates in their community. More than 200 police officers sent to arrest the vigilantes were met with harsh community resistance. The police used live ammunition and many citizens and police officers were wounded. Some of the wounded police officers were Druze. This incident emphasizes the traditional structure of Druze society in Israel and its potential conflict with law enforcement.

When addressing the population of the Christian Arabs, we face the same complexity. Because they identify strongly with the Palestinian national identity and share the Muslim Arabs' political orientation, one might assume the Christian Arabs' attitudes toward the police to be more negative. However, the lifestyle of most Christian Arabs is more Western oriented, similar to that of the Jewish population. In addition, this community is largely urban, better situated economically, and in consequence highly represented in the Israeli–Arab elite class (Sa'ar 1998). The birthrate is significantly low among Christian Arabs; it is even lower than the rate among Jews and significantly differs from that of Muslims and Druze. The practice of naming children to reflect a European–Christian heritage and the use of foreign languages in daily speech are culturally Western characteristics of the Christian Arabs. Furthermore, Christian Arabs occupy a higher class position compared to the rest of the Arab subgroups, especially in terms of educational attainment and income (Kraus and Yonay 2000; Sa'ar 1998).

Accordingly, we may conclude that the Christian Arabs are politically very close to the Muslim Arabs but culturally different from them, and from the Druze. Consequently, they still view themselves as a distinct cultural–religious minority among Arabs in Israel (Sa'ar 1998).

I have several research hypotheses for this study. I expect that the political and cultural differences within the Arab minority will create a complex picture of their perceptions toward the police. For example, I expect that the Druze will express positive attitudes toward the police in the political context. At the same time, I suspect that they will share similar (negative) attitudes to those of Muslim Arabs when community cultural codes are threatened by police practices. I also expect that Christian Arabs, similar to Muslim Arabs, will express negative attitudes toward the police in the political context, but at the same time, they will be more likely than Muslim and Druze to contact the police for assistance because of their class position and Westernized cultural orientation.

Arab–Police Relations in Israel

The Or Commission—formed to investigate the violent clashes between the police (and the Border Police) and the Israeli Arab minority in October of 2000—has noted that many Arabs do not believe that the police serve the Arab population, but are instead the "long arm" of a regime designed to control and suppress Arab political activities. At the same time, many police officers view Arabs as disloyal citizens. The police are inconsistent in enforcing ordinary criminal laws in Arab communities, a practice that leads to a degree of unchecked crime within minority communities (Comm'n 2003).

There is minimal research on police–minority relations in Israel, most of which emphasizes the negative attitudes of Israeli Arabs toward the police (Hasisi and Weitzer 2007; Rattner 1994; Weisburd, Shalev, and Amir 2002). In one poll, only 53% of Israeli Arabs felt that they should obey the police, compared to 85% of Jews (Cahanman and Tzemach 1991). Surveys conducted between 2000 and 2002 show that Arab respondents express negative attitudes toward the police (Rattner and Yagil 2002). In the 2001 poll, approximately 70% of Arabs thought that the police force was not egalitarian in its attitude toward all citizens of Israel, whereas only 35% of Jews agreed. The violent clashes between the police and Arab citizens in the October 2000 mass events significantly influenced this disparity in views. Still, even by the time of the 2002 poll, a significant majority of Arab respondents (62%) maintained their belief that the police are not egalitarian toward all citizens of Israel.

Taking into consideration the political and cultural diversity among Israeli Arabs (Muslim, Christian, and Druze), it is surprising that we could not find even one researcher who addressed the impact of this diversity on the attitudes of Arab minority subgroups toward the police. The current research is therefore quite original.

Data and Methodology

Data for this study come from a telephone survey conducted over a period of 2 weeks in March 2003 among adult Arabs and Jews over the age of 18 residing in the Israeli police force's Northern District. The Northern District ranges from the Hadera Valley (Wadi Ara) to the Lebanese border. The majority (70%) of the Israeli-Arab population lives in the Northern District, typically in communities that are highly segregated from the Jewish population.

Data were collected from a representative telephone sample drawn from locales in the Northern District with more than 1000 residents. The sample included 255 Jewish and 471 Arab respondents. The 471 Arab respondents included 328 Muslims, 77 Christians, and 66 Druze Arabs. Cluster sampling was used to ensure that each group was adequately represented in the sample, and the response rate was 40% both for Arab and Jewish respondents. Interviews were conducted both in Arabic and Hebrew by Arab or Jewish interviewers matched to the respondent's background.

Dependent Variable

In this study, two themes in citizens' attitudes toward the police were examined: trust in the police and community receptivity to contacting the police. The trust variable includes five measures in a 5-point Likert scale ranging from "strongly disagree" to "strongly agree" in regard to the following statements: "I have trust in the police"; "I have trust in the Border Police" (also known as the Border Patrol); "The police do their job fairly"; "The police work to prevent crime near my residence"; and "I would permit a member of my family to become a police officer" (Cronbach's alpha = 0.77). The receptivity variable includes four measures in a 5-point Likert scale ranging from "strongly disagree" to "strongly agree" in regard to the following statements: "Reporting criminals to the police in my view is informing on them"; "I feel that police officers are not welcome in my community"; "In the event that I become a victim of property crime, I will report the crime to the police"; and "In the event that I become a victim of violent crime, I will report the crime to the police." The receptivity variable eventually combined two items: willingness to report property crimes and willingness to report a violent crime to the police (Cronbach's alpha = 0.66).

Independent Variables

The independent variables in this study include the standard demographic factors of age, gender, and social class, with the latter measured by educational attainment. Most studies of police–citizen relations find that age is a significant predictor of attitudes toward the police, with young people more likely than older age groups to hold negative views of the police (Cahanman and Tzemach 1991). Gender and class, however, are less consistent predictors.

I suspect that the fear of crime may affect the public perception of the police (Liska, Lawrence, and Sanchirico 1982). Some studies have found that people who are fearful of crime may blame the police for the crime they fear (Baker et al. 1982; Brown and Benedict 2002). Fear of crime is measured in the present study by the following question: "To what extent are you afraid of becoming a victim of violent crime?" Responses were rated on a scale of 1 (not afraid at all) to 5 (very afraid).

A significant part of the Israeli–Arab minority holds dissident political attitudes toward the regime and rejects the Jewish identity of the state. I expect that those Arabs who express moderate attitudes toward the Israeli state will be more favorable in their perceptions of the police and more receptive to contacting the police. This variable was measured by asking Arab respondents if Israel, as a Jewish and democratic state, can guarantee equal rights to its Israeli–Arab citizens.

We know that highly controversial incidents involving the police may have an immediate and powerful effect on citizens' opinions, particularly when the incident involves members of one's own ethnic group. In Israel, it is possible that Arab communities that experienced a violent conflict with the police in October 2000 would evaluate the police negatively. Arab respondents were asked whether their community had experienced such an incident. Approximately half of our Arab respondents reported that such a clash had occurred in their community (scored 1), and the other half reported no such incident (scored 0). This variable was measured for Arab respondents only.

In a society as politicized as Israel, a person's ethnicity might be expected to influence his or her evaluations of the police. The variable of ethnicity distinguishes between Arabs and Jewish respondents, and also among Arab subgroups (Muslims, Christians, and Druze).

Analysis

I compared the attitudes and preferences of Arabs, Jews, and Arab subgroups (Muslims, Christians, and Druze) regarding the two key dimensions of police–citizen relations—trust and receptivity. Both bivariate and multivariate analyses were conducted. In the multivariate models, a linear regression analysis was performed only for the Arab respondents on each of the two indices reflecting the main dependent variables. The trust index of the police combined five items: trust in the police, trust in the Border Police, the fair performance of the police, the perception of police prevention efforts near the respondent's residence, and the likelihood of permitting a member of one's family to become a police officer. The receptivity scale combined two items: willingness to report property crimes and willingness to report a violent crime to the police.

Trust in Police

The findings in Table 6.1 show that the police are highly trusted among Jewish respondents in comparison to relatively low levels of trust among Arab respondents—59.6% and 44.8%, respectively. A significant disparity between Jews and Arabs was found in relation to trust in the Border Police—82.1% and 39.3%, respectively. Jewish respondents are more likely to evaluate the performance of the police as fair and are also more satisfied with police crime control than are Arab respondents. The data in Table 6.1 also show that Jewish respondents are more inclined than Arab respondents to permit a member of their family to join the police force.

Table 6.2 presents the attitudes of Arab subgroups (Muslims, Christians, and Druze). Findings from the table show that Druze respondents hold more positive attitudes toward

Table 6.1   Trust in Law Enforcement Institutions and Police Performance

	Percentage Agreeing Mean (Standard Deviation)	
Item	Jews ($N = 255$)	Arabs ($N = 471$)
Trust the Israel Police[a]***	59.6	44.8
	3.72 (1.10)	3.35 (1.32)
Trust the Border Police[b]***	82.1	39.3
	4.27 (0.97)	2.96 (1.60)
The police do their job fairly[c]***	54.1	32.1
	3.54 (1.12)	2.84 (1.43)
Police work to prevent crime near your residence[d]***	42.1	32.3
	3.21 (1.19)	2.93 (1.34)
You would permit a member of your family to become a police officer[e]***	60.4	47.3
	3.65 (1.55)	3.06 (1.78)

[a] The respondents were asked if they agree with the statement, "I have trust in the police." The response format was ordinal, and answers ranged from 1 to 5: 1 = strongly disagree; 5 = strongly agree.

[b] The respondents were asked if they agree with the statement, "I have trust in the Border Police." The response format was ordinal, and answers ranged from 1 to 5: 1 = strongly disagree; 5 = strongly agree.

[c] The respondents were asked if they agree with the statement, "The police do their job fairly." The response format is ordinal, and answers ranged from 1 to 5: 1 = strongly disagree; 5 = strongly agree.

[d] The respondents were asked if they agree with the statement, "The police work to prevent crime near my residence." The response format is ordinal, and answers ranged from 1 to 5: 1 = strongly disagree; 5 = strongly agree.

[e] The respondents were asked if they agree with the statement, "I would permit a member of your family to become a police officer." The response format is ordinal, and answers ranged from 1 to 5: 1 = strongly disagree; 5 = strongly agree.

Significance levels from analysis of variance: ***$p < 0.001$.

Table 6.2   Means (Standard Deviation) of Trust in Law Enforcement Institutions and Police Performance by Arab Subethnic Group

	Arab Subethnicity Percentage Agreeing Mean (Standard Deviation)		
Item	Muslims ($N = 328$)	Christians ($N = 77$)	Druze ($N = 66$)
Trust the Israel Police***	40.2	41.6	63.6
	3.25 (1.33)	3.35 (1.32)	3.74 (1.25)
Trust the Border Police***	31.4	41.7	75.8
	2.70 (1.58)	3.04 (1.60)	4.09 (1.28)
The police do their job fairly***	32.2	26	41
	2.84 (1.12)	2.84 (1.43)	3.74 (1.25)
Police work to prevent crime near your residence***	42.1	32.3	63.6
	3.21 (1.19)	2.93 (1.34)	3.74 (1.25)
You would permit a member of your family to become a police officer***	60.4	47.3	63.6
	3.65 (1.55)	3.06 (1.78)	3.74 (1.25)

Significance levels from analysis of variance: ***$p < 0.001$.

the police than do Muslim and Christian Arabs. The Druze's level of trust in the police and Border Police is very similar to that of Jewish respondents. More than Muslim and Christian Arabs, the Druze tend to evaluate the performance of the police as fair. Furthermore, the Druze are even more enthusiastic than the Jews about a member of their family joining the police (84.8%), and they significantly differ in their views on this issue from Muslim and Christian Arabs.

Receptivity to Police

A receptive relationship between the police and the community is crucial for effective police performance. Table 6.3 shows that Arab respondents are more cautious than Jewish respondents in their interaction with the police. In comparison with Jewish respondents, Arabs generally endorse the statement, "Reporting criminals to the police is like informing on them." Similar views are also shown by the response indicating that police officers are not welcome in the community. Furthermore, this dynamic is observed in the case of reporting both property and violent crimes, as Arab respondents seem to feel restricted from either reporting crimes or complaining. This constrained relationship between the police and the Arab minority may be best explained by the political variable. Similar findings were documented among nondominant groups in Northern Ireland and South Africa (Brewer and Brewer 1994; Weitzer 1995).

As noted earlier, the Druze hold similar political attitudes to those of Jews, so if the explanation for police receptivity were solely political, then I would expect the Druze to express more receptivity to the police. Findings in Table 6.4 show that this is not the case.

Table 6.3 Receptivity to Police

	Percentage Agreeing Mean (Standard Deviation)	
Item	Jews (N = 255)	Arabs (N = 471)
Reporting criminals to the police in my view is informing on them[a]***	15.7 1.87 (1.36)	31.0 2.55 (1.63)
I feel that police officers are not welcome in my community[b]***	15.8 1.82 (1.38)	34.7 2.73 (1.60)
Willingness to report property crime to the police[c]***	85.8 4.49 (1.07)	68.4 4.01 (1.40)
Willingness to report violent crime to the police[d]***	85.8 4.49 (1.07)	65.6 3.89 (1.45)

[a] The respondents were asked if they agree with the statement, "Reporting criminals to the police in my view is informing on them." The response format is ordinal, and answers ranged from 1 to 5: 1 = strongly disagree; 5 = strongly agree.

[b] The respondents were asked if they agree with the statement, "I feel that police officers are not welcome in my community." The response format is ordinal, and answers ranged from 1 to 5: 1 = strongly disagree; 5 = strongly agree.

[c] The respondents were asked if they agree with the statement, "In case you become a victim of property crime, you will report the crime to the police." The response format is ordinal and answers ranged from 1 to 5: 1 = strongly disagree; 5 = strongly agree.

[d] The respondents were asked if they agree with the statement, "In case you become a victim of violent crime, you will report the crime to the police." The response format is ordinal, and answers ranged from 1 to 5: 1 = strongly disagree; 5 = strongly agree.

Significance levels from analysis of variance: ***$p < 0.001$.

Table 6.4   Receptivity to Police by Arab Subethnic Group

	Arab Subethnicity Percentage Agreeing Mean (Standard Deviation)		
Item	Muslims (N = 328)	Christians (N = 77)	Druze (N = 66)
Reporting criminals to the police in my view is informing on them***	30.8 2.53 (1.64)	23.4 2.35 (1.53)	40.0 2.78 (1.74)
I feel that police officers are not welcome in my community***	36.8 2.83 (1.61)	32.5 2.68 (1.52)	30.8 2.42 (1.60)
Willingness to report property crime to the police***	67.7 3.97 (1.43)	83.1 4.44 (1.09)	60.6 3.73 (1.51)
Willingness to report violent crime to the police***	63.7 3.81 (1.5)	75.0 4.28 (1.18)	66.7 3.92 (1.38)

Significance levels from analysis of variance: ***$p < 0.001$.

In reality, the Druze express similar attitudes to those of Muslims in all aspects of police receptivity. They even endorse, more than Muslims, the statement that reporting criminals to the police is like informing on them (40%). Thirty percent of Druze respondents think that police officers are not welcome in their communities, and the Druze express an unwillingness, similar to that of Muslims, to report property and violent crimes to the police.

These findings suggest that the political explanation is not entirely adequate to explain the Arab minority's lack of receptivity to the police. However, it is shown that the Druze share a similar political orientation with Israeli Jews while maintaining cultural similarities with the Muslims, and this might be the explanation. The cultural explanation is also manifest when focusing on Christian Arabs' receptivity to the police. Table 6.4 shows that although Christian Arabs share a similar political orientation with Muslim Arabs (as expressed in their negative attitudes toward the police in Table 6.2), they still are significantly more willing to contact the police in the event of property and violent crimes, and in this they are more similar to Israeli Jews.

The data presented above point to differences among Arab subgroups. The Druze express positive perceptions of the police in the political context, but like Muslim Arabs, they are more restricted in their willingness to contact the police. Conversely, Christian Arabs express negative perceptions of the police in the political context, but also express positive perceptions in regard to making contact with the police. At this stage, I will first try to determine if these differences persist, independent of the influence of other variables. The survey included questions regarding the respondents' demographic attributes and other potentially relevant predictors. Second, I will try to determine what other factors, in addition to ethnic background, predict the Arab minority's perceptions of the police in Israel.

I conducted a multivariate analysis to estimate the effect of several predictors on the public's perceptions of the police. This was done in two stages. First, I used the complete survey sample including Israeli Jews as the reference category. By conditioning out this variable, I could estimate the impact of the independent variables and focus on the differences between each Arab minority group relative to Israeli Jews. Second, I estimated the model solely for the Israeli Arab minority subgroups, excluding Jewish respondents because some of the independent variables were measured only for Arab respondents—for example, endorsing the Jewish democratic state in Israel and experiencing violent clashes with the police during the October 2000 events.

In general, the police trust model in Table 6.5 is more powerful than the community receptivity model, as indicated by the adjusted R^2 figures in the models. We can see in the police trust model that education has a strong effect on predicting the public's trust in the police: the higher the education of the respondents, the lower their support of the police. This finding can be explained by the effect of education on the politicization of public awareness of police performance.

Gender has significant impact both on the trust and the receptivity model. Women tend to express more trust and be more receptive in their interaction with the police than men. One reason that Israeli women hold positive views of the police may have to do with the fact that they are more concerned than men about becoming victims of crime (Hasisi and Weitzer 2007).

Fear of crime may affect one's perceptions of the police insofar as the police are evaluated for their performance in preventing or solving crimes (Brown and Benedict 2002). The findings indicate that fear of violent victimization affects both the trust and the receptivity models; the greater the fear of crime, the higher the evaluation of the police and the greater the inclination to contact the police. As suggested above, this finding might be affected by the fact that the fear of crime is more prominent among women.

Finally, I examined the effect of Arab subethnicity in both models using Israeli Jews as the reference group. The results show that ethnic differences persist. Net of the other factors, Muslim and Christian Arabs are more likely than Druze (and Jews) to hold negative perceptions of the police in the trust model. Reviewing the receptivity model, we can see that Druze are more similar to Muslims in their restricted receptivity to the police, whereas Christian Arabs express receptive attitudes similar to those expressed by Jewish respondents in regard to contacting the police.

In the second stage, I estimated the trust and receptivity models solely for Arab respondents. In the police trust model, we can see that education has a strong effect on predicting Arab trust of the police. The higher the education of an Arab individual, the weaker their support of the police. One reason that highly educated Arabs might be critical of the

Table 6.5 Regression Estimates for Effects of Predictors on Public Perceptions of Police

Item	Trust Model $b(\beta)$	Receptivity Model $b(\beta)$
Education	−0.34 (−0.25)***	0.02 (0.03)
Gender (1 = male)	−0.60 (−0.07)**	−0.69 (−0.15)**
Fear of crime	0.31 (0.11)**	0.21 (0.14)***
Ethnicity		
Jewish (ref.)	−	−
Muslim	−4.25 (−0.48)***	−1.15 (−0.25)***
Christian	−2.68 (−0.19)***	−0.21 (−0.03)
Druze	−0.77 (−0.05)***	−1.33 (−0.17)***
R^2 (adjusted R^2)	0.22 (0.21)***	0.10 (0.09)***
N	654	712

Significance levels from analysis of variance: **$p < 0.01$; ***$p < 0.001$.

police is that they typically live not with middle-class Jews, but with poor and working-class Arabs, and therefore experience the same kind of treatment from the police (Lewin-Epstein and Semyonov 1993). Education had no significant effect on the receptivity model.

Fear of crime may affect one's perceptions of the police insofar as the police are evaluated for their performance in preventing or solving crimes (Brown and Benedict 2002). The findings indicate that fear of violent victimization affects both the trust and the receptivity models; the greater the fear of crime, the higher the evaluation of the police and the greater the inclination to contact the police.

Gender had no significant impact on the trust model, but there was some impact on the receptivity model. Arab women tend to be more receptive in their interaction with the police than Arab men. One reason that Arab women might be more receptive to contacting the police may have to do with the fact that they are more concerned than Arab men about becoming victims of crime, especially when traditional social controls in the Arab community are gender-biased (Hasan 2002; Shalhoub-Kevorkian 1999). Another reason may have to do with the negative political image of the police among Arab men, who—frequently more than Arab women—experience violent clashes with police at political events (Hasisi and Weitzer 2007).

Police–community conflict during the riots of October 2000 had a significant effect on the trust model of policing. Arabs who report that their community had experienced a violent clash with police officers are more inclined to express negative attitudes toward the police. This finding is consistent with other studies that document the effects of highly controversial policing incidents on citizens' perceptions of the police (Kaminski and Jefferis 1998; Weitzer et al. 2006). This variable has no significant effect in the case of the receptivity model (Table 6.6).

I expected that Arabs who agree that Israel, as a Jewish and democratic state, can guarantee equal rights to its Arab citizens would be more supportive of the police. This was confirmed in the two models: Arab respondents who agree with the statement express more positive attitudes toward the police and are more inclined to contact the police. The effect of this variable is, however, more salient in the (political) trust model.

Table 6.6 Regression Estimates for Effects of Predictors on Israeli-Arab Perceptions of Police

Item	Trust Model $b(\beta)$	Receptivity Model $b(\beta)$
Education	−0.46 (−0.27)***	−0.05 (−0.06)
Gender (1 = male)	−0.71 (−0.06)	−0.64 (−0.13)**
Fear of crime	0.40 (0.12)**	0.32 (0.21)***
Community–police clash (Oct. 2000)	−1.00 (−0.10)*	0.150 (−0.03)
Israeli as a Jewish democratic state can guarantee equal rights to the Israeli Arabs	1.2 (0.19)***	0.13 (0.09)*
Ethnicity		
Druze (ref.)	–	–
Muslim	−3.12 (0.27)***	0.21 (0.04)
Christian	−1.80 (−0.13)***	1.20 (0.18)**
R^2 (adjusted R^2)	0.25 (0.24)***	0.11 (0.10)
N	425	454

Significance levels from analysis of variance: *$p < 0.05$; **$p < 0.01$; ***$p < 0.001$.

Finally, I examined the effect of Arab subethnicity in both models. The results show that ethnic differences persist; net of the other factors, Muslim and Christian Arabs were more likely than Druze to hold negative perceptions of the police in the trust model. When reviewing the receptivity model, we can see that Druze are more similar to Muslims in their restricted receptivity to the police, whereas Christian Arabs express more receptive attitudes than Muslim and Druze in regard to contacting the police.

Discussion

Most of the research on police–minority relations in deeply divided societies has emphasized the political explanation, yet very little research has addressed the influence of cultural pluralism on police–community relations. In this chapter, I have tried to elaborate on the influence of cultural diversity and resistance of the Arab native minority in Israel on police performance, alongside political variables.

The major contribution of this chapter is that it sheds light on the differences within minority groups and their ramifications on police–minority relations. We usually refer to minority groups as a coherent, homogeneous group. By doing so, we may miss important distinctions within the minority group that have an effect on their relations with the police. This chapter shows that, depending on political and cultural affiliations, the Arab minority has different perceptions toward the police. Arabs who hold similar political attitudes to the Jewish majority (i.e., the Druze) expressed positive attitudes toward the police. By the same token, Arabs with a cultural similarity to the Jewish majority (i.e., the Christians) expressed a more open receptivity to the police. Both political and cultural variables contributed to a better understanding of police–minority relations in Israel.

This research can be extended to explore the relationship between police and minorities in other countries. Native-aboriginal populations reside in several Western countries, and recent studies have revealed the tense relationship between the police and the aboriginal population in these countries (Blagg and Valuri 2004). Furthermore, this research can also be extended to several Western countries who host immigrants from different cultures. Several studies have shown the tense relations between these immigrant groups and the police. This chapter suggests that a deeper analysis of the relationships between minority groups and the police should be conducted, and that researchers should be more attentive in their analysis of the differences within minority groups.

This research can also be extended to explore the relationship between the police and other social groups in Israeli society. Indeed, the Jewish population is not a homogenous group in cultural terms. For instance, ultra-Orthodox Jews are culturally distinguishable from the secular Jewish majority. Consequently, they hold significant negative attitudes toward the police (Ministry of Public Security 1999, 2001, 2002; Smith and Sharvit 2000). Further research should be directed toward analyzing police performance as perceived by ultra-Orthodox Jews, which might clarify the impact of cultural diversity on their criminal behavior and attitudes toward the police.

There are several limitations to this research that should be mentioned. Less than 25% of the statistical variance is explained in each model, and this raises the question of what factors are not taken into account and how they might affect the findings. The suggested models take into account many possible variables that have confounded other studies. Nonetheless, as in all multivariate analyses, we should be cautious in drawing conclusions

(Weisburd 2001). Future studies should even more closely specify their models of minority attitudes toward the police.

Conclusion

This chapter offers a framework for analyzing police–minority relations in deeply divided societies. In these types of societies, the regime has severe problems with its legitimacy among the minority group, which in turn affects the group's relationship with the police. Research shows that the political and cultural disparities between Arabs and Jews in Israel have reduced the trust and the willingness of Israeli Arabs to cooperate with the police. The political explanations assume that the major source of the tension between the police and the minority group stems from political variables, and in order to improve this relationship, sociopolitical reforms regarding the minority group are necessary. The cultural explanations assume that the tensions between the police and the minority group are also influenced by cultural variables, and not just sociopolitical factors. Thus, in order to improve the relationship between the minority and the police, cultural reforms are required to change the police culture both in the making of management-level and street-level decisions with respect to minority groups (Chan 1996).

The cultural and political differences between Jews and Arabs in Israel pose a challenge for police performance in the minority community. While the police are focused on law enforcement, they must also be aware of and sensitive to the cultural distinctiveness of the minority community and suitably adjust themselves to it when providing services to Arab citizens. Increased distribution of community police stations in Arab communities would create better access to police and facilitate the procedure of filing complaints. To improve Arab–police relations, a multicultural approach is needed. This approach could be put into practice by recruiting more Arab policemen and policewomen, especially non-Bedouin Muslims (Hasisi and Weitzer 2007) and, at the same time, by creating strong ties between the local political leadership and the chiefs of police stations, ties that have proven to be valuable in times of crisis (Patten 1999).

However, a multicultural approach is not without risk. A policy of cultural relativity that is too flexible in the policing of a minority group is liable to create a differential enforcement of laws and may even perpetuate criminal behaviors. I conclude that a balanced approach to police presence is necessary and that greater consideration and judgment should be exercised when enforcing the law. The complex task of policing the Arab minority in Israel must take into account the population's political and cultural composition, balancing its particular and diverse needs with the need to maintain the rule of the law.

References

Abel Jr., A. V. 2006. *Immigration and crime: Race, ethnicity, and violence.* New York: NYU Press.

Al-Haj, M. 1985. Ethnic relations in an Arab town in Israel. *Studies in Israeli Ethnicity: After the Ingathering* 76(6): 65–149.

Baker, M. H., B. C. Nienstedt, R. S. Everett and R. McCleary. 1982. Impact of a crime wave: Perceptions, fear, and confidence in the police. *Law and Society Review* 17: 319.

Bayley, D. H. and H. Mendelsohn. 1969. *Minorities and the police: Confrontation in America.* New York: Free Press.

Blagg, H. and G. Valuri. 2004. Aboriginal community patrols in Australia: Self-policing, self-determination and security. *Policing and Society* 14(4): 313–328.

Blalock, H. M. 1967. *Toward a theory of minority–group relations.* New York: John Wiley and Sons, Inc.

Blauner, R. and R. Blauner. 1972. *Racial oppression in America.* New York: Harper and Row.

Bobo, L. and V. L. Hutchings. 1996. Perceptions of racial group competition: Extending Blumer's theory of group position to a multiracial social context. *American Sociological Review* 61: 951–972.

Boudreau, V. 2005. Precarious regimes and matchup problems in the explanation of repressive policy. *Repression and Mobilization* 21: 33–57.

Bowling, B. 1998. *Violent racism: Victimization, policing, and social context.* Oxford: Clarendon Press.

Brewer, J. D. 1991. Policing in divided societies: Theorising a type of policing. *Policing and Society: An International Journal* 1(3): 179–191.

Brewer, J. D. and J. Brewer. 1994. *Black and blue: Policing in South Africa.* Oxford: Clarendon Press.

Brogden, M. 1993. *Policing for a new South Africa.* Psychology Press, London: Routledge.

Brown, B. and W. R. Benedict. 2002. Perceptions of the police: Past findings, methodological issues, conceptual issues and policy implications. *Policing: An International Journal of Police Strategies Management* 25(3): 543–580.

Cahanman, I. and T. Tzemach. 1991. *Israeli police in the eye of the public: Attitudes on selected issues.* Israel: Ministry of Police.

Central Bureau of Statistics. 2003, 2006. Annual population report, Jerusalem: Israel.

Chan, J. 1996. Changing police culture. *British Journal of Criminology* 36(1): 109–134.

Chatterjee, J. and L. Elliott. 2003. Restorative policing in Canada: The Royal Canadian Mounted Police, community justice forums, youth criminal justice act. *Police Practice and Research* 4(4): 347–359.

Chui, W. H. and I. L. Regin. 2005. Policing in a multicultural society: A Queensland case study. *Police Practice and Research* 6(3): 279–293.

Comm'n, O. 2003. The state investigative committee for the clashes between the security forces and Israeli citizens in October 2000. 1:3, 6:42.

Davis, R. C. and N. J. Henderson. 2003. Willingness to report crimes: The role of ethnic group membership and community efficacy. *Crime and Delinquency* 49(4): 564–580.

Davis, R. C., E. Erez and N. E. Avitabile. 1998. Immigrants and the criminal justice system: An exploratory study. *Violence and Victims* 13(1): 21–30.

Decker, S. H. 1981. Citizen attitudes toward the police: A review of past findings and suggestions for future policy. *Journal of Police Science and Administration* 9(1): 80–87.

Della Porta, D. 2006. *Social movements, political violence, and the state: A comparative analysis of Italy and Germany.* Cambridge: Cambridge University Press.

Egharevba, S. 2006. African immigrants' perception of police in Finland: Is it based on the discourse of race or culture? *International Journal of the Sociology of Law* 34(1): 42–63.

Ellison, G. and G. Martin. 2000. Policing, collective action and social movement theory: The case of the Northern Ireland civil rights campaign. *The British Journal of Sociology* 51(4): 681–699.

Ellison, G. and J. Smyth. 2000. *The crowned harp: Policing Northern Ireland.* London: Pluto Press.

Falah, G. 1996. Living together apart: Residential segregation in mixed Arab-Jewish cities in Israel. *Urban Studies* 33(6): 823–857.

Feagin, J. R. 1991. The continuing significance of race: Anti black discrimination in public places. *American Sociological Review* 56: 101–116.

Forcese, D. 1992. *Policing Canadian society.* Scarborough, ON: Prentice-Hall Canada.

Frisch, H. 1993. The Druze minority in the Israeli military: Traditionalizing an ethnic policing role. *Armed Forces and Society* 20(1): 51–67.

Ginat, J. 1997. *Blood revenge: Family honor, mediation and outcasting.* Brighton: Sussex Academic Press.

Hasan, M. 2002. The politics of honor: Patriarchy, the state and the murder of women in the name of family honor. *The Journal of Israeli History* 21(1–2): 1–37.

Hasisi, B. and R. Weitzer. 2007. Police relations with Arabs and Jews in Israel. *British Journal of Criminology* 47(5): 728–745.

Hinton, M. S. 2006. *The state on the streets: Police and politics in Argentina and Brazil.* London: Lynne Rienner Publishers, Inc.

Holdaway, S. 2003. Police race relations in England and Wales: Theory, policy, and practice. *Special Issue: Policing a Multicultural Society* 7: 49–74.

Holmberg, L. and B. Kyvsgaard. 2003. Are immigrants and their descendants discriminated against in the Danish criminal justice system? *Journal of Scandinavian Studies in Criminology and Crime Prevention* 4(2): 125–142.

Holmes, M. D. 2000. Minority threat and police brutality: Determinants of civil rights criminal complaints in US municipalities. *Criminology* 38(2): 343–368.

Jackson, P. I. 1989. *Minority group threat, crime, and policing: Social context and social control.* Greenwood Publishing Group.

Kaminski, R. J. and E. S. Jefferis. 1998. The effect of a violent televised arrest on public perceptions of the police: A partial test of Easton's theoretical framework. *Policing: An International Journal of Police Strategies and Management* 21(4): 683–706.

Kennedy, R. 1998. *Race, crime, and the law.* New York: Random House LLC.

Kent, S. L. and D. Jacobs. 2005. Minority threat and police strength from 1980 to 2000: A fixed effects analysis of nonlinear and interactive effects in large US cities. *Criminology* 43(3): 731–760.

Kraus, V. and Y. Yonay. 2000. The power and limits of ethno nationalism: Palestinians and eastern Jews in Israel. *The British Journal Sociology* 51(3): 525–551.

Lewin-Epstein, N. and M. Semyonov. 1993. *The Arab minority in Israel's economy: Patterns of ethnic inequality.* Boulder, CO: Westview Press.

Lia, B. 2006. *A police force without a state: A history of the Palestinian security forces in the West Bank and Gaza.* Reading, UK: Ithaca Press.

Lijphart, A. 1999. *Government forms and performance in thirty-six countries.* New Haven, CT: Yale University Press.

Liska, A. E., J. J. Lawrence and A. Sanchirico. 1982. Fear of crime as a social fact. *Social Forces* 60(3): 760–770.

Mazerolle, L., E. Marchetti and A. Lindsay. 2003. Policing the plight of indigenous Australians: Past conflicts and present challenges. *Police and Society* 7: 77–104.

McGarry, J. and B. O'Leary. 1999. *Policing Northern Ireland: Proposals for a new start.* Belfast: Blackstaff Press.

Menjívar, C. and C. Bejarano. 2004. Latino immigrants' perceptions of crime and police authorities in the United States: A case study from the Phoenix metropolitan area. *Ethnic and Racial Studies* 27(1): 120–148.

Mesch, G. S. and I. Talmud. 1998. The influence of community characteristics on police performance in a deeply divided society: The case of Israel. *Sociological Focus* 31(3): 233–248.

Ministry of Public Security. 1999, 2001, 2002. Public attitudes towards the Israeli police. Ramat Gan, State of Israel. http://www.mops.gov.il/bp.

Parker, K. F., B. J. Stults and S. K. Rice. 2005. Racial threat, concentrated disadvantage and social control: Considering the macro level sources of variation in arrests. *Criminology* 43(4): 1111–1134.

Patten, C. 1999. *A new beginning: Policing in Northern Ireland: The report of the independent commission on policing for Northern Ireland.* London: Stationery Office.

Poole, E. D. and M. R. Pogrebin. 1990. Crime and law enforcement policy in the Korean American Community. *Police Study: International Review of Police* 13: 57.

Quillian, L. and D. Pager. 2001. Black neighbors, higher crime? The role of racial stereotypes in evaluations of neighborhood crime. *American Journal of Sociology* 107(3): 717–767.

Rattner, A. 1994. The margins of justice attitudes towards the law and the legal system among Jews and Arabs in Israel. *International Journal of Public Opinion Research* 6(4): 358–370.

Rattner, A. and D. Yagil. 2002. *The culture of law: The criminal justice system in the eye of the Israeli society*. Haifa, Israel: University of Haifa Center for the Study of Crime, Law, and Society.

Sa'ar, A. 1998. Carefully on the margins: Christian Palestinians in Haifa between nation and state. *American Ethnologist* 25(2): 215–239.

Sampson, R. J. and W. B. Groves. 1989. Community structure and crime: Testing social-disorganization theory. *American Journal of Sociology* 94(4): 774–802.

Shalhoub-Kevorkian, N. 1999. Law, politics, and violence against women: A case study of Palestinians in Israel. *Law & Policy* 21(2): 189–211.

Shaw, C. R. and H. D. McKay. 1942. *Juvenile delinquency and urban areas: A study of rates of delinquents in relation to differential characteristics of local communities in American cities*. University of Chicago Press, Chicago.

Smith, D. J. 1997. Ethnic origins, crime, and criminal justice in England and Wales. *Crime and Justice* 21: 101–182.

Smith, R. and K. Sharvit. 2000. *Public attitudes towards the Israeli police: Executive summary*. Smith Consulting and Research Inc.

Smooha, S. 1989. The Arab minority in Israel: Radicalization or politicization? *Studies in Contemporary Jewry* 5: 59–88.

Smooha, S. 1993. Part of the problem or part of the solution: National security and the Arab minority. *National Security and Democracy in Israel* 39(1): 118–119.

Smooha, S. 2004. *Index of Arab–Jewish relations in Israel*. Haifa, Israel: The Jewish–Arab Center, University of Haifa.

Smooha, S. and T. Hanf. 1992. The diverse modes of conflict-regulation in deeply divided societies. *International Journal of Comparative Sociology* 33(1–2): 1–2.

Smooha, S. and P. Järve. 2005. *The fate of ethnic democracy in post-communist Europe*. Budapest: LGI Publications.

Stark, R. 1987. Deviant places: A theory of the ecology of crime. *Criminology* 25(4): 893–910.

Sung, H. 2002. *The fragmentation of policing in American cities: Toward an ecological theory of police–citizen relations*. Portsmouth, NH: Greenwood Publishing Group.

Turk, A. T. 1969. *Criminality and legal order*. Chicago: Rand McNally.

Van den Berghe, P. L. 2002. Multicultural democracy: Can it work? *Nations and Nationalism* 8(4): 433–449.

Waddington, P. A. 1994. *Liberty and order: Public order policing in a capital city*. London: Taylor & Francis.

Weisburd, D. 2001. Magic and science in multivariate sentencing models: Reflections on the limits of statistical methods. *The Israel Law Review* 35: 225.

Weisburd, D., O. Shalev and M. Amir. 2002. Community policing in Israel: Resistance and change. *Policing: An International Journal of Police Strategies and Management* 25(1): 80–109.

Weitzer, R. J. 1990. *Transforming settler states: Communal conflict and internal security in Northern Ireland and Zimbabwe*. Barkeley, CA: Univ. of California Press.

Weitzer, R. J. 1995. *Policing under fire: Ethnic conflict and police–community relations in northern Ireland*. New York: SUNY Press.

Weitzer, R. J., S. A. Tuch, A. Blumstein and D. P. Farrington. 2006. *Race and policing in America: Conflict and reform*. New York: Cambridge University Press.

Whyte, J. 1991. *Interpreting Northern Ireland*. Oxford: Oxford University Press.

Withrow, B. L. 2006. *Racial profiling: From rhetoric to reason*. Upper Saddle River, NJ: Pearson/Prentice-Hall.

Crime Victims and Attitudes toward Police
Israeli Case*

7

GALI AVIV

Contents

Introduction

Public evaluations of the police are a well-established and studied field, mainly in the United States (e.g., Frank, Smith, and Novak 2005; Gallagher et al. 2001; Wells 2007). As crime victims are the main reporters of criminal activity and those who assist in the identification and apprehension of criminals (Hickman and Simpson 2003; Hindelang and Gottfredson 1976; Maguire 1982; Shapland 1984), understanding their evaluations of the police is of great importance. Victims' attitudes have been examined using victimization surveys and public attitude surveys, revealing that victims evaluate the police more negatively than nonvictims. Moreover, their satisfaction with the police has been declining since the year 2000 (Brown and Benedict 2002; Frank et al. 2005; Maxson, Hennigan, and Sloane 2003; O'Connor 2008; Van Dijk 2011).

In Israel, although there is substantial research on public evaluations of the police (e.g., Dror-HaCohen 2009; Rattner 2009; Smith and Arian 2007; Smith and Yehezkel 2008; Yogev 2010), there is a lack of research pertaining to attitudes of crime victims. In an attempt to begin to fill this gap, this chapter examines victim evaluations of the police in Israel, and contributes to a more general understanding of victim evaluations of the police

* Reproduced from Aviv, G. 2014. Crime victims and attitudes towards the police: The Israeli case. *Police Practice and Research: An International Journal* 15(2): 115–129.

by considering a wider array of assessments than previously examined, in three important aspects of policing: performance, treatment, and trust in the police. This chapter begins with a review of victim evaluations of the police and their importance, while focusing on what is known about victim perceptions in Israel. I then turn to the study, the data, and analyses, which show that crime victims in Israel view the Israeli police more negatively than nonvictims in the three aspects of policing examined. The gap in assessments remains significant even after controlling for various sociodemographic differences between the two groups. In the discussion, I consider the implications of this finding for Israeli policing and discuss additional avenues of research that will further our understanding of victim evaluations of the police.

Public Evaluations of Police

The importance of public perceptions of the police in general, and of policing processes and outcomes in particular, has been examined extensively. Studies have found that positive evaluations and support for the police are linked to several positive outcomes, such as compliance with the law, acceptance of police decisions, and cooperation with the police (Bridenball and Jesilow 2008; Gallagher et al. 2001; National Research Council 2004; Sunshine and Tyler 2003; Tyler 1990, 2004; Tyler and Huo 2002; Wells 2007). Therefore, much research has focused on the factors that shape these perceptions, mainly sociodemographic variables, such as race, gender, education, and income (Brown and Benedict 2002; Gallagher et al. 2001; O'Connor 2008; Weitzer and Tuch 2002) as well as contact with the police (Brown and Benedict 2002; O'Connor 2008; Skogan 2006a), neighborhood characteristics, and fear of crime (Bridenball and Jesilow 2008; Brown and Benedict 2002). Studies have also examined victimization and its effects, and found significant negative effects on attitudes toward the police (Frank et al. 2005; Jesilow, Meyer, and Namazzi 1995; Maxson et al. 2003; O'Connor 2008).

In Israel, studies of public attitudes toward the police have consistently shown that the police are poorly evaluated, and are the lowest evaluated agency in the criminal justice system (Dror-HaCohen 2009; Rattner 2009; Smith and Arian 2007; Smith and Yehezkel 2008; Yogev 2010). Importantly, although these studies provide a clear picture regarding general assessments of the Israeli police, they do not shed light on evaluations of crime victims in general and in comparison to nonvictims in particular.

Victim Evaluations of Police

Crime victims have been described as the initiators of the criminal justice process, the main consumers of police services, and the main reporters of criminal activity (Shapland 1984). Because the police are the first representatives of the criminal justice system that victims encounter, the police–victim relationship is often viewed as the most important link in the criminal justice process (Hindelang and Gottfredson 1976; Zedner 2002). Moreover, without the crucial information and assistance that victims provide, the ability of the police to identify and apprehend criminals and control crime would diminish (Brandl and Horvath 1991; Hickman and Simpson 2003; Hindelang and Gottfredson 1976; Maguire 1982; Ruback and Thompson 2001; Shapland 1984; Walklate 2007).

Importantly, the mission of the police and the way it is carried out affect victim–police relations. The police were formed, in part, to protect citizens from falling victim to crime.

Therefore, experiencing a crime is experiencing failure in "civil trust" (De Greiff 2006). Victims may interpret their victimization as lack of protection, and/or feel that police ineffectiveness or neglect contributed to their victimization, which may result in declining levels of trust (Friedmann 1987; Smith and Hawkins 1973).

Research on victims' attitudes toward the police can be divided into two types of studies: victimization surveys and public attitude surveys. Over the past decades, the International Crime Victimization Survey (ICVS) has been conducted in an increasing number of countries (Van Dijk 2011). Findings from the ICVS and nation-specific surveys have consistently found that victims' evaluations of the police are lower than those of citizens who have not been victimized, and that victim satisfaction has been declining since the year 2000 (Allen et al. 2006; Flatley et al. 2010; Van Dijk 2011; Van Dijk et al. 2007).

The second type of studies, utilizing public attitude surveys, can be divided into two categories: those using victimization as one of many variables that predict evaluations of the police, and those that specifically examine crime victims. Studies of the first type have found that victimization lowers evaluations of the police (Maxson et al. 2003; O'Connor 2008). For example, a survey of Los Angeles residents tapping police performance and officer demeanor found that crime victims had lower approval ratings of the police than nonvictims (Maxson et al. 2003). Similar results were found in studies that have specifically examined crime victims. Dull and Wint (1997), for example, explored the impact of criminal victimization on fear of crime and attitudes toward the criminal justice system. They found that crime victims had more negative evaluations of police effectiveness following their victimization.

In recent years, there have been important developments concerning victims and their relationship with the criminal justice system, including the legislation of laws and acts (Herd 2010; Sebba 2000; Van Dijk 2005); new policing approaches that highlight police–community relations (National Policing Improvement Agency*; Johnson 2005; Skogan 2006b); and alternative forms of social responses to crimes, such as restorative justice (Braithwaite 1999; Sherman and Strang 2007; Van Ness and Strong 2010). However, crime victim evaluations of the police have continued to be negative in comparison to the general population (Allen et al. 2006; Brown and Benedict 2002; Flatley et al. 2010; Hinds 2009; Maxson et al. 2003; O'Connor 2008; Van Dijk 2011; Van Dijk et al. 2007).

Victims in Israel

Similar to other Western countries, the general approach toward crime victims and their role in the criminal justice system in Israel has changed. One of the most evident expressions of this change is the "Victims of Crime Rights Act" (2001; for a detailed description of the law and its development, see Sebba and Gal 2003). The law and its enforcement led to organizational changes in the Israel National Police. For example, an automated system providing victims with information regarding the progress of their complaint was developed (Pugach 2004; Shoham and Regev 2008). This system is a national and central system, which includes information uploaded by the police, the prosecution, and the prison service. Other examples are the use of victim impact statements submitted by both the victim and social workers during sentencing, which allow victims to participate in the judicial process (Pugach 2004; Shoham and Regev 2008); the implementation of different

---

* See http://cfnp.npia.police.uk/1521.aspx.

restorative justice programs* (Farkash 2002); and the establishment of rape crisis centers[†]
and new organizations that accompany and represent victims while interacting with the
authorities (e.g., the Noga Legal Center for Victims of Crime). These developments have
enhanced awareness of crime victims in Israel, improved their status in the criminal justice system, and emphasized the need to examine police–victim relations.

Nevertheless, the information supplied by victimization and public attitude surveys
in Israel does not provide a clear picture of victim evaluations of the police. Victimization
surveys have been conducted sporadically over the years, by both the Central Bureau of
Statistics (1979, 1981, 1990, 2001) and the police (Regev 2009). These surveys provide us
with findings regarding citizens' *satisfaction* with police treatment of the case at hand and
reasons for *reporting* victimization to the police; however, they do not focus on *general
evaluations* of the police, the goal of this study. For example, the 2001 victimization survey
conducted by the Central Bureau of Statistics found that 50–70% of respondents (depending on the crime) were dissatisfied with police treatment for reasons relating to the handling of their case (not treating their complaint seriously, ill treatment, lack of updates and
delayed responses to calls; Central Bureau of Statistics 2001). Furthermore, the annual
public attitude surveys conducted by the Ministry of Public Security do not specifically
examine victim evaluations or compare them to nonvictims; rather, they examine the
evaluations of those who had contact with the police, while victimization is only one of the
types of contact.

Few academic studies have examined victim evaluations of the police in Israel.
Friedmann (1987), in a study examining citizen attitudes regarding an experimental
police–community cooperation project that introduced a new police role—the Israeli
Neighborhood Police Officer, found that victimization in general negatively affected attitudes toward the police. Shoham (2000) examined battered wives' perceptions of their
encounter with police officers and found that although the majority of the women expected
police support, less than 40% felt that the officer understood their situation. Erez (2000)
found that victim satisfaction in general increased when victim impact statements were
used. These studies have either focused on specific types of policing or crimes, or on satisfaction with the criminal justice system as a whole; thus, although important, they do not
provide a clear understanding of victim evaluations of the police in general or in regard to
specific aspects of policing in particular.

To conclude, the literature on victim evaluations of the police has consistently found
that victims exhibit less support for the police than the general population. Although there
is data on public perceptions of the police in Israel, victim evaluations have yet to be examined and compared to those of nonvictims.

---

* Such as "Kedem," which conducts "Family Group Counseling" for juvenile offenders (http://www.kdm
  .org.il), and the Mosaica Center, which conducts restorative justice program for adults (http://www.mosaica
  -gishur.org.il).
† The Victim Witness Assistance Program is one of the programs offered by the rape crisis center. Regarding
  the police, they escort the victim during the process of filing a complaint and are present during police
  investigations. For more information, see http://www.1202.org.il/English/ (last viewed on February 28,
  2012).

The Study

This study utilizes a large-scale community survey carried out in 2008 (Weisburd and Jonathan-Zamir 2011). A random sample of Israelis was surveyed concerning attitudes toward the police in Israel. Nine police stations were sampled. They were not a simple random sample of the 54 police stations within the "Green Line," but rather the result of a sequential sampling method based on the threat of terrorism in the stations, as well as on ethnic diversity, crime and socioeconomic levels, and location within Israel.* It is important to note that although the sample selected is not statistically representative of the general Israeli population, the sampling frame consists of close to a third of the Israeli population (31.2%), with more than 1.7 million Israeli citizens, and has similar characteristics to those of the general Israeli population (see Appendix I).†

Respondents to the survey were presented with statements such as "I have trust in the Israeli police" and "the police perform their job well," and were asked to rank their level of agreement with the statements on a scale ranging from 1 ("strongly disagree") to 5 ("strongly agree"). Complete interviews were obtained from 3832 individuals (58% response rate).

Within the full sample ($N = 3832$), 469 respondents (12.2%) reported that they were victimized in the year prior to the survey (62.1% were victims of property crime and 15.7% were victims of violence; 72% of the victims reported their victimization to the police). When examining the main characteristics of both crime victims and nonvictims in the sample (see Table 7.1), significant differences are found on numerous characteristics. For example, 54.6% of the victim sample was male in comparison to 46.9% of nonvictim respondents. These differences may be because certain characteristics increase the risk of being victimized. For example, studies have found that young men are most at risk of being victims of violence (Goody 2005; Spalek 2006). Therefore, demographic characteristics are controlled for in subsequent analyses (see the following discussion).

This chapter reports the responses of crime victims and nonvictims to eight statements regarding the police. After comparing the responses of both groups, the results of three multivariate regression models assessing the predictors of evaluations of police performance, treatment, and trust in the police are presented.

Results

Police Performance

In past studies, "police performance" was often examined using a single statement (with the exception of O'Connor 2008 and Orr and West 2007), such as "The police perform their job well" or "The police are efficient in dealing with crime in my area of residence" (Frank et al. 2005; Myhill and Beak 2008). Unlike these studies, and based on the assumption that the use of a single statement might not be representative of subject evaluations (Myhill et al. 2011), this study examines three statements concerning the way the police perform their duties. Crime victims, in all three statements, evaluate the performance of

---

* For further information about the project and its methodology, see Weisburd and Jonathan-Zamir (2011).
† It should, however, be noted that the sample underrepresents the Arab population in Israel.

Table 7.1   Demographic Characteristics of Victim and Nonvictim Respondents

Variable	Victim	Nonvictim
	Gender	
$\chi^2 = 9.76$, $p < 0.01$	Male: 54.6%	Male: 46.9%
	Female: 45.4%	Female: 53.1%
	$N = 469$	$N = 3344$
	Ethnicity	
$\chi^2 = 0.02$, $p > 0.05$	Jewish: 90.9%	Jewish: 90.7%
	Arab: 9.1%	Arab: 9.3%
	$N = 461$	$N = 3251$
	Family Status	
$\chi^2 = 3.26$, $p > 0.05$	Married: 64.8%	Married: 69%
	Other: 35.2%	Other: 31%
	$N = 469$	$N = 3344$
	Country of Origin	
$\chi^2 = 16.05$, $p < 0.000$	Israel: 74.9%	Israel: 65.6%
	Other: 25.1%	Other: 34.4%
	$N = 466$	$N = 3330$
	Income	
$\chi^2 = 15.93$, $p < 0.000$	Less than average: 44.9%	Less than average: 47.1%
	Average: 21.2%	Average: 27.5%
	More than average: 33.9%	More than average: 25.4%
	$N = 419$	$N = 3011$
	Education	
$\chi^2 = 15.99$, $p < 0.000$	Nonacademic: 52.9%	Nonacademic: 62.5%
	Academic: 47.1%	Academic: 37.5%
	$N = 465$	$N = 3316$
	Age	
$t = 4.37$, $p < 0.000$	$M = 41.16$	$M = 44.33$
	$SD = 14.36$	$SD = 15.81$
	$N = 460$	$N = 3274$

the Israeli police less favorably than nonvictims (see Table 7.2). For example, with regard to the statement "The police are efficient in dealing with crime in my area of residence," I find that, in general, the public do not feel that the police are efficiently handling crime, with only 28.2% of nonvictims (mean [M] = 2.61, standard deviation [SD] = 1.36) agreeing/strongly agreeing with this statement (as indicated by answers 4 and 5; see Figure 7.1). At the same time, this dissatisfaction is much more prominent among victims ($M = 2.01$, $SD = 1.23$), with only 13.9% agreeing with the statement. This difference was found to be statistically significant ($t_{(3735)} = 9.72$, $p < 0.000$; medium effect* $d = 0.46$).

* The effect size chosen was the standardized mean difference (Weisburd and Britt 2002).

Table 7.2 Victim and Nonvictim Response to Statements Regarding the Police

Statement	Crime Victim % Agree + Strongly Agree	M	SD	Nonvictim % Agree + Strongly Agree	M	SD	t Test	Cohen's d
	Police Performance							
The police perform their job well	15.7	2.41	1.15	28.2	2.87	1.19	7.97***	0.39
Police presence in my neighborhood is adequate	18.7	2.25	1.30	32.1	2.71	1.44	7.08***	0.34
	Police Treatment							
The police treat citizens they encounter with respect	23.9	2.63	1.23	27.6	2.84	1.21	3.27**	0.17
The police allow citizens to express their position before they come to a decision regarding their case	16.1	2.33	1.19	26.8	2.68	1.29	5.59**	0.28
The police explain their activities well to the people they encounter	20.7	2.48	1.22	29	2.83	1.25	5.62**	0.28

**$p < 0.01$; ***$p < 0.001$.

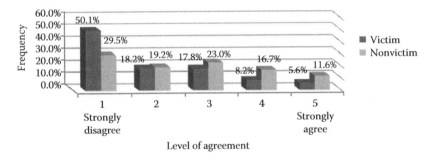

Figure 7.1 Evaluations of extent of police effectiveness in handling crime.

Police Treatment

Recent studies have begun to examine police treatment, or demeanor, as well as performance, in regard to evaluations of the police (Chaplin, Flatley, and Smith 2011; Flatley et al. 2010). Drawing from the literature on "procedural justice," four statements regarding the fairness of the processes through which the police exercise authority and make decisions were examined (see reviews by Tyler 2004, 2009). All of the statements show similar trends—victims evaluate the treatment of the police less positively than those who were not victimized (Table 7.2). For example, a quarter of nonvictims stated that the police treat citizens equally ($M = 2.56$, $SD = 1.34$; Figure 7.2), whereas only 19.8% of victims ($M = 2.28$, $SD = 1.31$) agreed with the same statement. This difference was statistically significant ($t_{(3678)} = 4.14$, $p < 0.000$; small effect $d = 0.21$).

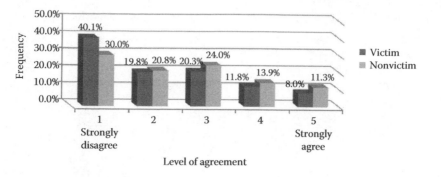

Figure 7.2 Evaluations of extent to which police treat all citizens equally.

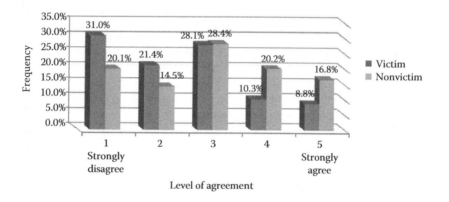

Figure 7.3 Evaluations of extent to which victims find the police to be trustworthy.

Trust in Police

A third important area of inquiry is the trustworthiness of the police. Researchers have defined a trustworthy police force as being viewed by the public as effective, fair, and as one that holds shared interests, values, and a strong commitment to the community (Jackson and Bradford 2009; Sunshine and Tyler 2003; Tyler and Huo 2002). In this survey, close to 40% of nonvictims ($M = 2.99$, $SD = 1.35$) agreed that they have trust in the police (37%; Figure 7.3). This was the case for only 19.1% of victims ($M = 2.44$, $SD = 1.27$), a difference that was found to be statistically significant ($t_{(3801)} = 8.33$, $p < 0.000$; medium effect $d = 0.42$).

Predictors of Victim Evaluations of Police

The preceding comparisons reveal that victims view the police more negatively than those who have not been victimized. However, as noted earlier, these differences could potentially be the results of other differences between the groups, such as age or gender. Thus, in order to see if they remain significant after controlling for various confounding factors,* three multivariate regression analyses were conducted.

---

* The analyses controlled for sociodemographic factors, as well as contact with the police and serving/volunteering in the Israeli police.

To formulate the dependent variables, the eight examined statements were clustered into three indexes following the above themes: police performance, police treatment, and trust in the police, as inspired by the literature on police legitimacy (Murphy, Tyler, and Curtis 2009; Reisig, Bratton, and Gertz 2007; Sunshine and Tyler 2003; Tyler 1990, 2004). Importantly, the majority of studies in the field have based their surveys on only one specific theme, with only one or two statements representing it. The studies that have examined more than one aspect have mainly combined statements into an overall variable attaining to police performance (e.g., O'Connor 2008; Orr and West 2007).

Each index was defined as a dependent variable for the regression models. Cronbach alpha (α) tests were conducted to provide an estimate of the reliability of these clusters. The police performance index was made up of the three statements representing performance mentioned earlier (see Figure 7.1 and Table 7.2; Cronbach's $\alpha = 0.78$, $N = 3690$, Range = 3–15, $M = 7.98$, $SD = 3.31$). The police treatment scale was made up of the four commonly used statements mentioned earlier (see Figure 7.2 and Table 7.2; Cronbach's $\alpha = 0.77$, $N = 3329$, Range = 4–20, $M = 10.70$, $SD = 3.94$). Trust, the third concept examined, was based on the statement "I have trust in the Israeli police." Owing to the importance of trust in the police, especially for victims, trust was analyzed although it was only represented by one statement (see, e.g., De Greiff 2006).

Table 7.3 presents the results of the multivariate regression models conducted in this study, examining the effect of victimization on evaluations of performance (Model 1), police treatment (Model 2), and trust in the police (Model 3).

As detailed in Table 7.3, all three models are statistically significant ($p < 0.01$). When examining the relative role of victimization on the dependent variables, I find that victimization is the strongest antecedent of evaluations of police performance ($\beta = -0.12$), police treatment ($\beta = -0.08$), and trust ($\beta = -0.10$), significantly and negatively impacting these evaluations. Thus, despite the numerous effects of other factors, being a crime victim remains a major predictor of attitudes toward the police, with an impact in the expected direction.

All three regression models yield low R^2 results, meaning that overall the models explain a relatively small proportion of the variance in attitudes toward the police (between 2% and 7%). This finding, however, coincides with the literature regarding the ability of sociodemographic and contact variables to explain such attitudes (Bridenball and Jesilow 2008; Gau 2010; O'Connor 2008). At the same time, as these models presented low explained variance, the specific effect of victimization on the dependent variables was of interest. To examine this effect, a block regression, in which all control variables were entered in the first block and victimization in the second, was conducted. This type of regression allows us to identify the additional effect of victimization on the three dependent variables. In all three models, victimization was found to explain a considerably large portion of this variance in comparison to other control variables. In Model 1, the adjusted R^2 for the model without the test variable was 0.05, whereas with victimization it rises to 0.07. This was also the case for Model 2, with an adjusted R^2 of 0.02 without victimization, and an adjusted R^2 of 0.03 when victimization was added. Similar results were found in Model 3 (adjusted R^2 of 0.03 without victimization and 0.04 with victimization). In all three models, we see that victimization explains 1–2% of the variance (whereas the full model explains between 2% and 7%).

Table 7.3   Ordinary Least Squares Regression Models

Variables	Model 1 Performance Index $B(\beta)$	Model 2 Treatment Index $B(\beta)$	Model 3 Trust $B(\beta)$
	Test Variable		
Victimization	−1.20 (−0.12)***	−0.98 (−0.08)***	−0.43 (−0.1)***
	Control Variables		
Experience with the Police			
Contact with the police	−0.41 (−0.06)**	−0.26 (−0.03)	−0.12 (−0.04)*
Served in the Israeli police	0.22 (0.03)	0.66 (0.07)***	0.19 (0.06)***
Volunteered in the Civil Guard	−0.17 (0.02)	0.06 (0.01)	−0.02 (−0.01)
Sociodemographic Variables			
Gender	−0.62 (−0.09)***	−0.44 (−0.05)**	−0.16 (−0.06)**
Single	0.58 (0.07)**	−0.02 (−0.00)	0.04 (0.01)
Divorced/separated/single parent	0.03 (0.00)	−0.05 (−0.00)	−0.19 (−0.04)*
Widowed	−0.04 (−0.00)	−0.09 (−0.00)	−0.24 (−0.03)
Age	−0.01 (−0.05)*	0.01 (0.02)	0.01 (0.09)***
Education	−0.12 (−0.05)**	−0.20 (−0.07)***	−0.06 (−0.06)**
Religiosity	0.17 (0.05)*	−0.01 (−0.00)	0.01 (0.01)
Income	−0.13 (−0.05)**	−0.02 (−0.01)	0.00 (0.00)
Born in Africa/Asia	−0.03 (−0.00)	−0.40 (−0.03)	0.02 (0.00)
Born in America/Europe	−0.09 (−0.01)	−0.26 (−0.02)	−0.09 (−0.02)
Born in ex-Soviet Union	0.67 (0.07)***	0.60 (0.05)*	0.16 (0.04)*
New immigrant	2.45 (0.05)**	3.61 (0.07)***	0.67 (0.04)*
Ethnicity	0.32 (0.03)	0.09 (0.01)	−0.11 (−0.02)
N	3160	2866	3248
R^2 (adjusted R^2)	0.07 (0.07)***	0.03 (0.02)***	0.04 (0.04)***

*$p < 0.05$; **$p < 0.01$; ***$p < 0.001$.

Discussion and Conclusions

Current knowledge of crime victims' evaluations of the police in Israel is limited. Surveys have consistently found that the general Israeli public evaluates the police poorly (e.g., Rattner 2009; Yogev 2010). When we add to this finding the fact that crime victims generally evaluate the police even less positively than those who were not victimized (Flatley et al. 2010; Hinds 2009; Maxson et al. 2003; O'Connor 2008), the need to specifically examine the evaluations of this subgroup in Israel intensifies.

This study reveals that respondents who stated that they were victimized in the year before the survey hold significantly lower evaluations of the police than nonvictims, with percentages of support for the police ranging from 15.7% to 23.9% among crime victims versus 25.2–37% among nonvictims, thus reinforcing findings from prior studies (Flatley et al. 2010; O'Connor 2008; Van Dijk et al. 2007). The significant negative effects of victimization on evaluations of police performance, treatment, and trust remained even after controlling for various factors that may affect evaluations of the police such as race and age. Moreover, in this sample, victimization had the strongest effect on attitudes toward the police.

The unique relationship between crime victims and the police, brought upon by their victimization and expectations from the police, may constitute an explanation for their negative evaluations. Police agencies were formed in order to protect and serve the public. For crime victims, the promise of protection was breached, thus leaving the victim with feelings of anger (Bard and Sangrey 1979; Ditton et al. 1999) and distrust (De Greiff 2006). These emotions are expected to lead to negative attitudes toward the police. Moreover, crime victims have special needs, which are expected to be met by the police and the criminal justice system more generally. Victims want and need to feel part of the process (Erez and Tontodonato 1990; Sebba 1996), and thus be informed regarding the progress of their case (Maguire 1982; Strang 2002), and to feel that they are treated with dignity and respect (Strang and Sherman 2003). When victims are not satisfied with the way they are treated and feel that these needs remain unfulfilled, their evaluations of the police may decrease accordingly.

Based on this study, it appears that the Israeli police need to pay special attention to this subgroup. They should make special efforts to improve trust and support, in order to increase both their crime-fighting ability and their overall status in the eyes of victims. This support might be achieved by focusing police training and methods of operation on crime victims and their needs, and/or by integrating professionals, such as social workers, into the police and the criminal justice system. Moreover, because the effect of victimization is not solely on the victim, but also on his/her family and close circle of friends (Rosenbaum et al. 2005), the benefit of working with crime victims is twofold—as improving policing practices and the support given to victims may improve public evaluations more generally.

Studies in recent years have found that one of the key components influencing public cooperation with the police is perceptions of police legitimacy (National Research Council 2004). Positive evaluations of police legitimacy were found to increase willingness to cooperate with and assist the police, empower them, and comply with the law (Murphy, Hinds, and Fleming 2008; National Research Council 2004; Reisig et al. 2007; Sunshine and Tyler 2003; Tyler 1990, 2004; Tyler and Huo 2002). The results of this study provide a preliminary assessment of victim evaluations of the police through the perspective of the legitimacy model. The indices "police performance" and "treatment" that were examined are similar to "police performance" and "procedural justice," which were found to be strong predictors of police legitimacy (which is partly represented by the "trust" item in this analyses; Hinds and Murphy 2007; Sunshine and Tyler 2003; Tyler 1990, 2004, 2009; Tyler and Huo 2002). Hence, the next step would be to directly examine evaluations of police legitimacy among crime victims, a subgroup that has only recently begun to be examined (Bradford 2010; Elliott, Thomas, and Ogloff 2011). In fact, recent research suggests that improving the performance of the police may assist in minimizing the gap between assessments of victims and nonvictims, and improve victim perceptions of police legitimacy (Aviv and Weisburd, in review). This finding should be translated by practitioners into police practices.

Owing to the method by which the data were gathered, this study did not include various factors that could potentially impact attitudes toward the police, such as type of contact with the police (Skogan 2006a), extent of contact (Shapland, Willmore, and Duff 1985), and type of crime (Bradford, Stanko, and Jackson 2009; Brown and Benedict 2002; Nofziger and Williams 2005; Poister and McDavid 1978; Skogan 2006a). These factors should be taken into account in future studies pertaining to victim evaluations of the police. Lastly, there has not yet been a comprehensive evaluation or examination of the effects of the recent changes in legislation, police practices, and civil society activities on victim evaluations of the police. Future studies may choose to examine differences in victim evaluations of the police before and after the developments that have occurred over the years, specifically in regard to the Victims of Crime Rights Act, its ramifications and implementation, in regard to both police behavior and victim expectations.

To conclude, in line with earlier studies, this study reveals that crime victims in Israel evaluate the police more negatively than citizens who were not victimized, even after controlling for numerous sociodemographic factors. These low assessments are worrisome, particularly given the low opinion that the general Israeli public holds for the police. The understanding that low evaluations of crime victims must be taken into account should impact on policy makers. Police practitioners invested in improving victim evaluations must develop different practices for police conduct throughout their interactions with crime victims. These practices need to deal with each of the three aspects examined in the preceding discussion.

Acknowledgments

The author thanks Professor David Weisburd for his support and enlightening comments that helped to enhance this manuscript. I also thank Tamar Berenblum and Dr. Tal Jonathan-Zamir for all their help and comments on earlier drafts. This work was supported by the United States Department of Homeland Security through the National Consortium for the Study of Terrorism and Responses to Terrorism (START) (grant number N00140510629) and the U.S. National Institute of Justice (grant number Z909601). Any opinions, findings, and conclusions or recommendations in this document are those of the author and do not necessarily reflect the views of the Department of Homeland Security or the National Institute of Justice.

Appendix I. Demographic Characteristics in the Sample and in the General Population

Variable	Israeli Population[a]	Study Sample
Ethnicity	Jews: 80%	Jews: 89.8%
	Non-Jews: 20%	Non-Jews: 10.2%
Sex	Female: 51.6%[b]	Female: 52.2%
	Male: 48.4%	Male: 47.8%
Age	Median: 45.6[c]	Median: 43.9
Socioeconomic level	Median: "Slightly above average" (self-reported)	Median: "About average" (self-reported)
Education	Median: "Academic or non-academic schooling beyond high school"[e]	Median: "Academic or non-academic schooling beyond high school"[d]

[a] Data obtained from the Israeli Central Bureau of Statistics (CBS), the Statistical Abstract for the year 2008; see http://www.cbs.gov.il.

[b] Owing to the manner in which data are reported by the CBS, these frequencies apply to citizens who are 20 years old or older.

[c] Due to the way the data is reported by the CBS, these frequencies apply to citizens who are 20 years and older. The medial was calculated from data reported categorically.

[d] Respondents were asked to rate their education on a scale of eight levels, ranging from "no education" to "PhD."

[e] Because of the way the data was reported by the CBS, this median applies to citizens who are 15 years old or older.

References

Allen, J., S. Edmonds, A. Patterson and D. Smith. 2006. *Policing and the criminal justice system, Public confidence and perceptions: Findings from the 2004/05 British Crime Survey*. Home Office Online Report 07/06.

Aviv, G. and Weisburd, D. (in review). Reducing the gap in perceptions of legitimacy of victims and non-victims: The importance of police performance.

Bard, M. and D. Sangrey. 1979. *The crime victim's book*. New York: Brunner/Mazel Publishers.

Bradford, B. 2010. The quality of police contact: Procedural justice concerns among victims of crime in London. http://ssrn.com/abstract=1596754.

Bradford, B., E.A. Stanko and J. Jackson. 2009. Using research to inform policy: The role of public attitude surveys in understanding public confidence and police contact. *Policing* 3(2): 139–148.

Braithwaite, J. 1999. Restorative justice: Assessing optimistic and pessimistic accounts. *Crime and Justice* 25: 1–127.

Brandl, S.G. and F. Horvath. 1991. Crime–victim evaluation of police investigative performance. *Journal of Criminal Justice* 19(2): 109–121.

Bridenball, B. and P. Jesilow. 2008. What matters: The formation of attitudes towards the police. *Police Quarterly* 11(2): 151–181.

Brown, B. and W.R. Benedict. 2002. Perceptions of the police: Past findings, methodological issues, conceptual issues and policy implications. *Policing: An International Journal of Police Strategies and Management* 25(3): 543–580.

Central Bureau of Statistics. 1979, 1981, 1990. Crime victims survey (Special publication number, 664, 937, 729). http://www.cbs.gov.il/reader/revaha/organiz_u.html?keywdn=332.

Central Bureau of Statistics. 2001. Crime victims survey. http://www.cbs.gov.il/publications/criminal.pdf.

Chaplin, R., J. Flatley and K. Smith. 2011. *Crime in England and Wales 2010/11—Findings from the British Crime Survey and police recorded crime*, 2nd edition. Home Office Online Report 10/11.

De Greiff, P. 2006. *The handbook of reparations*. Oxford: Oxford University Press.

Ditton, J., S. Farrall, J. Bannister, E. Gilchrist and K. Pease. 1999. Reactions to victimization: Why has anger been ignored? *Crime Prevention and Community Safety: An International Journal* 1(3): 37–54.

Dror-HaCohen, S. 2009. Attitudes towards the Israeli police force and court services: About 60% believe that the functioning of the police is not good. Press release. http://www.cbs.gov.il/reader/newhodaot/hodaa_template.html?hodaa=200919073.

Dull, R.T. and A.V.N. Wint. 1997. Criminal victimization and its effect on fear of crime and justice attitudes. *Journal of Interpersonal Violence* 12(5): 748–758.

Elliott, I., S.D.M. Thomas and J.R.P. Ogloff. 2011. Procedural justice in contacts with the police: Testing a relational model of authority in a mixed methods study. *Psychology, Public Policy, and Law* 17(4): 592–610.

Erez, E. 2000. Integrating a victim perspective in criminal justice through victim impact statement. In *Integrating a Victim Perspective within Criminal Justice International Debates*, eds. A. Crawford, and J. Goodey, 165–184. Dartmouth: Ashgate.

Erez, E. and P. Tontodonato. 1990. The effect of victim participation in sentencing on sentencing outcome. *Criminology* 28(2): 451–474.

Farkash, A. 2002. *Restorative justice in the field of criminal law*. Tel Aviv: Ministry of Justice.

Flatley, J., C. Kershaw, K. Smith, R. Chaplin and D. Moon. 2010. *Crime in England and Wales 2009/10—Findings from the British crime survey and police recorded crime*, 3rd edition. Home Office Online Report 12/10.

Frank, J., B.W. Smith and K.J. Novak. 2005. Exploring the basis of citizen's attitudes towards the police. *Police Quarterly* 8(2): 206–228.

Friedmann, R.R. 1987. Citizens' attitudes toward the police: Results from an experiment in community policing in Israel. *American Journal of Police* 60: 67–94.

Gallagher, C., E. Maguire, S. Mastrofski and R. Reisig. 2001. *The public image of the police.* Alexandria, VA: International Association of Chiefs of Police.

Gau, J.M. 2010. A longitudinal analysis of citizens' attitudes about police. *Policing: An International Journal of Police Strategies and Management* 33(2): 236–252.

Goody, J. 2005. *Victims and victimology: Research, policy and practice.* Essex, England: Pearson Education Limited.

Herd, K. 2010, February. *History and overview of rights and services for federal crime victims within the United States.* Paper presented at the 144th International Senior Seminar on the enhancement of appropriate measures for victims of crime at each stage of the criminal justice process. Tokyo, Japan.

Hickman, L.J. and S.S. Simpson. 2003. Fair treatment of preferred outcome? The impact of police behavior on victim reports of domestic violence incidents. *Law and Society Review* 37(3): 607–634.

Hindelang, M.J. and M. Gottfredson. 1976. The victim's decision not to invoke the criminal justice process. In *Criminal justice and the victim,* ed. W.F. McDonald, 57–78. Beverly Hills, CA: Sage.

Hinds, L. 2009. Public satisfaction with police: The influence of general attitudes and police–citizen encounters. *International Journal of Police Science and Management* 11(1): 54–66.

Hinds, L. and K. Murphy. 2007. Public satisfaction with police: Using procedural justice to improve police legitimacy. *The Australian and New Zealand Journal of Criminology* 40(1): 27–42.

Jackson, J. and B. Bradford. 2009. Crime, policing and social order: On the expressive nature of public confidence in policing. *The British Journal of Sociology* 60(3): 493–521.

Jesilow, P., J. Meyer and N. Namazzi. 1995. Public attitudes toward the police. *American Journal of Police* 2: 67–88.

Johnson, L. 2005. From "community" to "neighborhood" policing: Police community support officers and the "police extended family" in London. *Journal of Community and Applied Social Psychology* 15(3): 241–254.

Maguire, M. 1982. *Burglary in a dwelling: The offence, the offender and the victim.* London: Heinemann.

Maxson, C., K. Hennigan and D.C. Sloane. 2003. *Factors that influence public opinion of the police.* National Institute of Justice Research for Practice report.

Murphy, K., L. Hinds and J. Fleming. 2008. Encouraging public cooperation and support for police. *Policing and Society* 18: 55–136.

Murphy, K., T. Tyler and A. Curtis. 2009. Nurturing regulatory compliance: Is procedural justice effective when people question the legitimacy of the law? *Regulation and Governance* 3: 1–26.

Myhill, A. and K. Beak. 2008. *Public Confidence in the Police.* United Kingdom: National Policing Improvement Agency.

Myhill, A., P. Quinton, B. Bradford, A. Poole and G. Sims. 2011. It depends what you mean by "confident": Operationalizing measures of public confidence and the role of performance indicators. *Policing* 5(2): 114–124.

National Research Council. 2004. Fairness and effectiveness in policing: The evidence. The committee to review research on police policy and practices. In *Committee on law and justice, division of behavioral and social sciences and education,* eds. W. Skogan, and K. Frydl. Washington, DC: The National Academies Press.

Nofziger, S. and L.S. Williams. 2005. Perceptions of police and safety in a small town. *Police Quarterly* 8(2): 248–270.

O'Connor, C.D. 2008. Citizen attitudes toward the police in Canada. *Policing: An International Journal of Police Strategies and Management* 31(4): 578–595.

Orr, M. and D.M. West. 2007. Citizens evaluations of local police: Personal experience or symbolic attitudes? *Administration and Society* 38(6): 649–668.

Poister, T.H. and J.C. McDavid. 1978. Victims evaluations of police performance. *Journal of Criminal Justice* 6: 133–149.

Pugach, D. 2004. The victim revolution—The day after: Towards a model that recognizes individual punishment considerations. *Kiryat Hamishpat* 4: 229–268.

Rattner, A. 2009. *Legal culture: Law and the legal system in the eyes of the Israeli public.* Jerusalem: The Shasha Center for Strategic Research, Hebrew University.

Regev, B. 2009. Victimization survey 2008–2009. In *The most important in research*, ed. M. Sher, 17–28. Printed by the Israeli Police Research Department.

Reisig, M.D., J. Bratton and M.G. Gertz. 2007. The construct validity of refinement of process-based policing measures. *Criminal Justice and Behavior* 34(8): 1005–1028.

Rosenbaum, D.P., A.M. Schuck, S.K. Costello, D.F. Hawkins and M.K. Ring. 2005. Attitudes toward the police: The effects of direct and vicarious experience. *Police Quarterly* 8(3): 343–365.

Ruback, R.B. and M.P. Thompson. 2001. *Social and psychological consequences of violent victimization.* Thousand Oaks, CA: Sage Publications.

Sebba, L. 1996. *Third parties: Victims and the criminal justice system.* Columbus, Ohio: Ohio State University Press.

Sebba, L. 2000. Victim's rights and legal strategies: Israel as a case study. *Criminal Law Forum* 11: 47–100.

Sebba, L. and T. Gal. 2003. Crime victim rights in Israel. In *Shamgar book—Articles B*, eds. M. Lutsky, R. Vered, and K. Mizrahi, 157–212. Tel Aviv: Bar and Law Association.

Shapland, J. 1984. Victims, the criminal justice system and compensation. *The British Journal of Criminology* 24(2): 131–149.

Shapland, J., J. Willmore and P. Duff. 1985. *Victims in the criminal justice system.* Brookfield, VT: Gower Publishing Company.

Sherman, L. and H. Strang. 2007. *Restorative justice: The evidence.* London: The Smith Institute.

Shoham, E. 2000. The battered wife's perception of the characteristics of her encounter with the police. *International Journal of Offender Therapy and Comparative Criminology* 44(2): 242–257.

Shoham, E. and Y. Regev. 2008. The voice of a sexual assault victim in the criminal justice process. In *The supervision of sex offenders in Israel: Punishment versus treatment*, ed. E. Shoham, 203–220. Tel Aviv, Israel: Perelshtein-Ginosar Ltd.

Skogan, W.G. 2006a. Asymmetry in the impact of encounters with police. *Policing and Society* 16(2): 99–126.

Skogan, W.G. 2006b. The promise of community policing. In *Policing innovations: Contrasting perspectives*, eds. D. Weisburd, and A.A. Braga, 27–43. New York: Cambridge University Press.

Smith, P.E. and R.O. Hawkins. 1973. Victimization, types of citizen–police contacts, and attitudes toward the police. *Law and Society Review* 8: 135–152.

Smith, R. and R. Arian. 2007. *Public attitudes towards the Israeli police 2006.* Ramat Gan, Israel: Smith Consulting and Research Inc.

Smith, R. and H. Yehezkel. 2008. *Public attitudes towards the Israeli police 2007.* Ramat Gan, Israel: Smith Consulting and Research Inc.

Spalek, B. 2006. *Crime victims: Theory, policy and practice.* New York: Palgrave Macmillan.

Strang, H. 2002. *Repair or revenge: Victims and restorative justice.* Oxford: Clarendon Press.

Strang, H. and L.W. Sherman. 2003. Repairing the harm: Victims and restorative justice. *Utah Law Review* 2003(1): 15–42.

Sunshine, J. and T.R. Tyler. 2003. The role of procedural justice and legitimacy in shaping public support for policing. *Law and Society Review* 37(3): 513–548.

Tyler, T. 1990. *Why people obey the law: Procedural justice, legitimacy and compliance.* New Haven, CT: Yale University Press.

Tyler, T.R. 2004. Enhancing police legitimacy. *The Annals of the American Academy of Political and Social Science* 593(1): 84–99.

Tyler, T.R. 2009. *Legitimacy and criminal justice: The benefits of self-regulation.* Reckless/Dinitz Memorial Lecture delivered April 2, 2009 at Ohio State University.

Tyler, T.R. and Y.J. Huo. 2002. *Trust in the law: Encouraging public cooperation with the police and courts*. New York: Russell Sage Foundation.

Van Dijk, J. 2005. Benchmarking legislation on crime victims: The UN Victims Declaration of 1985. *Victims of crime and abuse of power: Festschrift in honor of Irene Mel up*. Tilburg University: United Nations Press.

Van Dijk, J. 2011. Highlights of the international crime victim's survey. In *International crime and justice*, ed. M. Natarajan, 462–470. New York: Cambridge University Press.

Van Dijk, J., J. Van Kesteren and P. Smit. 2007. *Criminal victimisation in international perspective: Key findings from the 2004–2005 ICVS and EU ICS*. The Hague: Ministry of Justice, WODC.

Van Ness, D.W. and K.H. Strong. 2010. *Restoring justice: An introduction to restorative justice*, 4th Edition. New Providence, NJ: Matthew Bender and Company, Inc.

Victims of Crime Rights Act. 2001, S.H. 1782. [in Hebrew].

Walklate, S. 2007. *Imagining the victim of crime*. Berkshire, England: Open University Press.

Weisburd, D. and S. Britt. 2002. *Statistics for criminal justice*, 2nd edition. USA: Wadsworth Publishing Company.

Weisburd, D. and T. Jonathan-Zamir. 2011. *The effects of policing terrorism on police effectiveness in crime fighting and public expectations of and attitudes toward the police: A multi-method study of the Israeli experience*. Final technical report submitted to the US National Institute of Justice (grant no. Z909601) and to the US Department of Homeland Security, the National Consortium for the Study of Terrorism and Responses to Terrorism.

Weitzer, R. and S. Tuch. 2002. Perceptions of racial profiling: Race, class, and personal experience. *Criminology* 40(2): 435–456.

Wells, W. 2007. Type of contact and evaluations of police officers: The effects of procedural justice across three types of police–citizen contacts. *Journal of Criminal Justice* 35(6): 612–621.

Yogev, D. 2010. *Public attitudes towards the Israeli police 2010*. Ministry of Public Security.

Zedner, L. 2002. Victims. In *The Oxford handbook of criminology*, 3rd edition, eds. M. Maguire, R. Morgan, and R. Reiner. Oxford, UK: Oxford University Press.

Procedural Justice, Minorities, and Religiosity*

RONI FACTOR
JUAN CARLOS CASTILLO
ARYE RATTNER

Contents

Introduction

In any society, the police represent one of the most important institutions of social control. Therefore, attitudes toward the police are a relevant indicator of how citizens perceive the legitimacy of the social order, as well as the degree of social cohesion within a society. The evaluation of such attitudes and their determinants has become a central issue in social research, and one that is particularly influenced by the concept of procedural justice (see, e.g., Cohn, White, and Sanders 2000; Lind and Tyler 1988; Thibaut and Walker 1975; Törnblom and Vermunt 2007; Tyler 1990, 2004).

Lind and Tyler's (1988) theory of procedural justice attempts to explain why people willingly comply with law enforcement authorities, even when this compliance does not necessarily seem to be in their instrumental interests. They propose that assessments of whether particular acts, including decision-making processes and procedures, are moral or just arise from internalized norms and not purely from self-interest (Tyler 1988). In accordance, willingness to comply depends on a belief that those authorities who carry out the law are legitimate—a belief that in turn relies on the perception that those authorities use just and fair procedures (Herbert 2003). The theory will be discussed further below.

* Reproduced from Factor, R., J. C. Castilo, and A. Rattner. 2014. Procedural justice, minorities, and religiosity. *Police Practice and Research: An International Journal* 15(2): 130–142.

The present research builds on the empirical approach to the procedural justice-based model of legitimacy as proposed by Sunshine and Tyler (2003b). The study has two main goals. First, we will test the replicability of Sunshine and Tyler's model in a different social setting from the original study, which was performed in the city of New York. In this regard, we will examine the applicability of some of the model's assumptions in a society with marked group cleavages, namely, Israel. Whereas Sunshine and Tyler took account of the divisions between New York's three main ethnic groups (whites, Hispanics, and African Americans), the social and political divisions between Israel's Jewish majority and Arab minority are notoriously deeper (Moore 2000; Yiftachel 1997). Second, we will look at how the perceived legitimacy of the institutions of social control (i.e., law enforcement authorities) is affected by a construct not yet examined vis-à-vis this model—namely, religiosity.

As a multicultural and multiethnic society, Israel serves as an interesting case for studying the procedural justice-based model, and in particular for exploring the effect of ethnic affiliation (minority versus majority) and religiosity on the model's main premises. Israel's Arab minority is segregated in many senses—culturally, linguistically, geographically, and economically (Moore 2000)—and members of this ethnic minority have been found to have the lowest level of support for state laws, and less supportive attitudes toward the police, relative to other social groups in Israel. Similarly, studies have found ultra-Orthodox Jews, a minority group within the Israeli Jewish majority, to have lower evaluations of the police and lower perceived obligation to obey the law compared to the majority (Hasisi and Weitzer 2007; Rattner and Yagil 2004; Rattner, Yagil, and Pedahzur 2001). Understanding the normative motivations underlying the attitudes of minority groups toward the police in a deeply divided society such as Israel may aid efforts to develop tools aimed at elevating support for the institutions of law enforcement among social or ethnic minority groups in various societies.

Procedural Justice-Based Model of Police Legitimacy

The procedural justice perspective emerged as an alternative to the so-called self-interested or instrumental perspective, according to which people's willingness to cooperate with law enforcement authorities is linked to perceptions of police performance (Sunshine and Tyler 2003a,b). According to the instrumental perspective, compliance with the police is rooted primarily in two things: (1) the principle of deterrence (i.e., the threat of sanctions that would accompany noncompliance) and (2) perceptions that the outcome of any ensuing legal process will be fair (Thibaut and Walker 1975).

Sunshine and Tyler identify three main components of the instrumental perspective: perceived risk, police performance, and distributive fairness. *Perceived risk* refers to the threat of sanctions for noncompliance. *Police performance* means that support for the police is conditioned on public perceptions of efficiency in fighting crime and reducing public disorder. Finally, *distributive fairness* has to do with how the police distribute their services across people and communities.

Sunshine and Tyler (2003a,b) argue that, although the three instrumental predictors are important, they affect people's attitudes less than *procedural fairness* does—that is, fairness in the processes by which the police make decisions about the allocation of resources, enforcement of the law, etc. Procedural fairness differs from distributive fairness in that the latter refers to outcomes, whereas the former deals with the processes that lead to those outcomes. Moreover, procedural fairness refers to fairness in specific interactions with citizens in both interpersonal treatment and in decision making. According to Sunshine and Tyler (2003a,b), the distinction between the instrumental and procedural-based perspective is crucial to understanding the legitimacy of police institutions.

Under the procedural justice-based model, support for a society's law enforcement institutions can be measured in three ways: through levels of compliance with laws and regulations; through willingness to cooperate with police activities (in actions such as reporting crimes or calling for help); and through a willingness to empower the police (i.e., to allow them greater discretion within which to act) (Sunshine and Tyler 2003b). When the police are regarded as legitimate, levels of these three indicators of support will be high.

Over the years, numerous studies have tested Sunshine and Tyler's model in various contexts and settings, with some suggesting some modifications to it (Jonathan-Zamir and Weisburd 2011; Murphy, Tyler, and Curtis 2009; Tankebe 2009). It should be noted that although empirical studies have generally supported the hypotheses derived from the model, it has been criticized for its psychometrical properties, and several variations have been found in how the original model is manifested in different countries (Hinds and Murphy 2007; Reisig, Bratton, and Gertz 2007; Tankebe 2009).

From the procedural justice-based model of legitimacy, we can generate three hypotheses. The first states that procedural justice and the three instrumental predictors (distributive fairness, police performance, and perceived risk) will be found to influence the perceived legitimacy of the police, and that procedural justice will have a greater impact than the instrumental predictors (H_1). The second hypothesis states that the perceived legitimacy of the police will be related positively to the three indicators of support for the police: compliance with the law, cooperation with police activities, and empowerment of the police (H_2). Finally, the third hypothesis posits that procedural fairness and the instrumental predictors will have a direct impact on the three indicators of support, and that procedural justice will have a greater influence on these indicators than the instrumental predictors (H_3). The model is presented in Figure 8.1, with darker lines showing the effects that are presumed to be strongest, as per H_1 and H_3.

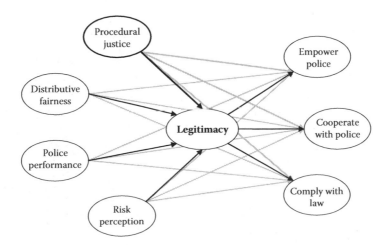

Figure 8.1 Procedural justice-based model of police legitimacy.

Minorities and Religiosity

Minorities are members of society who are defined by others as "different" in biological, cultural, behavioral, or organizational terms (Turner 1986). The segregation that tends to follow from these perceptions increases interactions among members of the minority group and so intensifies their cultural, organizational, and behavioral distinctiveness, which in turn enhances the majority's prejudices and their sense of being under threat. Growth in minority populations appears to enhance the majority's prejudices and sense of threat (Blalock 1967; Factor, Kawachi, and Williams 2011). This process is even stronger in deeply divided societies characterized by extreme polarization along ethnic lines (Hasisi and Weitzer 2007).

Studies indicate that alienation and social exclusion among minority groups may lead to reduced commitment to and compliance with the law, and to a tendency to perceive the legal culture of the majority as less than legitimate (Rattner and Yagil 2004). Indeed, there is ample evidence that members of minority groups express less trust, less confidence, and more negative attitudes about various institutions of social control than do members of the majority group (Factor, Kawachi, and Williams 2011; Hasisi and Weitzer 2007; Rattner, Yagil, and Pedahzur 2001; Sunshine and Tyler 2003b; Weitzer, Tuch and Skogan 2008). We hypothesize that such differences will be clearly present in the Israeli case, such that members of the Jewish majority will perceive the police as more legitimate and will support the police more strongly than members of Israel's Arab minority (H_4).

Sunshine and Tyler (2003b) argued that despite differences between minority and majority groups, "the psychological basis of legitimacy is similar within each group" (Sunshine and Tyler 2003b, 537). The authors found support for this assertion among New York's three main ethnic groups: whites, Hispanics, and African Americans. Yet the question remains whether this assumption holds in a society where social and political cleavages are notoriously deeper, as in Israel (Moore 2000; Yiftachel 1997). To test this assumption, we hypothesize (H_5) that the procedural justice-based model will work in a similar manner among Israeli Jews and Arabs (i.e., H_1, H_2, and H_3 will hold true for both groups).

One important issue that has received insufficient attention in the context of the procedural justice-based model is the effect of religiosity on the legitimacy of the rules and institutions of social control. Previous studies indicate that people who hold conservative religious views may give higher priority to what they regard as divine law than to rules of behavior imposed by society (Gibson and Caldeira 1996; Richards and Davison 1992). For instance, Rattner and Yagil (2004) found greater willingness to take the law into one's own hands among members of social groups with strong religious beliefs.

Thus, we add religiosity as an explanatory variable that may account for possible group differences in the Israeli context. Given the previous findings on conservative religious views described above, we propose (H_6) that highly religious individuals in both groups (i.e., Orthodox Jews and highly observant Arabs, most of whom are Muslim) will score lower on both legitimacy and support for the police than less religious individuals. However, based on previous evidence (see, e.g., Rattner and Yagil 2004), we suggest that the mechanisms in the two cases will be different: a feeling of discrimination and repression in the case of highly observant Israeli Arabs, and a perception of poor performance and effectiveness on the part of the police in the case of Orthodox Jews.

Methodology

Data

We sampled 1216 adults (809 Jews and 407 Arabs) using stratified random sampling. Probability sampling was conducted for each locality in the country, such that each locality would be represented in the final sample in proportion to the size of its population. Stratification was used in order to capture the heterogeneity of each locality in terms of religiosity and socioeconomic status. For the Jewish population, for example, we sampled groups such as the ultra-Orthodox, residents of Jewish settlements in the West Bank, secular Jews, and other subgroups in numbers equal to their proportion of the population.

We constructed our sample using the database of Israel's national phone company, which includes both landline and cellular phone numbers. Of 5962 phone numbers in the initial sample, contact was established with 3193. Complete interviews were conducted with one person aged 18 years or older in 1216 households, yielding a response rate of 38.1%, slightly above the response rate typically reported for phone surveys in Israel.

Participants were interviewed from August 2 to 27, 2009. Interviews were conducted in Hebrew or Arabic, depending on the home language of the respondent. To ensure accuracy, the questionnaire was translated into both languages using standard techniques of back-translation. In addition, we conducted a small interview-based pilot study to ensure that the items were understood similarly in both subsamples.

Variables

The survey items represented eight scales designed to tap the different aspects of the procedural justice-based legitimacy model (the items of the scales and the bivariate correlations between the scales can be obtained from the authors on request). Following Sunshine and Tyler (2003b), we used Cronbach's alpha to test the reliabilities of the scales. All the reliabilities ranged from acceptable to good except for the police empowerment scale, whose reliability was comparatively low. Nevertheless, we chose to retain this scale in the model as similar results were reported in the paper of reference ($\alpha = 0.56$). Cronbach's alpha values are shown in Table 8.1.

As represented in Figure 8.1, the three dependent variables that refer to support for the police (empowerment, cooperation, and compliance) are predicted in the model by legitimacy. At the same time, legitimacy is influenced by procedural justice and the three instrumental predictors (distributive fairness, police performance, and perceived risk).

Besides these predictive associations, we incorporate a series of control variables. The two central predictors are *group affiliation* and *degree of religiosity*. Group affiliation refers to the participant's ethnic identification with the Jewish majority or Arab minority in Israel. Degree of religiosity is measured on a 4-point scale from highly religious to not at all religious. The variables are interrelated, and so to avoid problems relating to multicollinearity, the degree of religiosity is only included in models calculated separately for Arabs and Jews. Besides group affiliation and religiosity, the model includes income, education, age, and gender as control variables. Descriptive statistics of the research variables are shown in Table 8.1.

Table 8.1   Descriptive Statistics of Main Research Variables

Variable	Range	Mean	Standard Deviation	Cronbach's α
Sex (1 = woman)	0.1	0.50	0.50	–
Age	18–88	42.03	16.38	–
Education	1–6	3.79	1.49	–
Income	1–5	2.74	1.36	–
Degree of religiosity	1–4	2.88	1.07	–
Procedural justice	1–5	3.12	0.75	0.91
Distributive fairness	1–5	2.90	0.94	0.64
Police performance	1–5	2.84	0.86	0.82
Risk perception	1–5	3.46	0.72	0.87
Legitimacy	1–5	3.38	0.76	0.87
Police empowerment	1–5	3.17	0.84	0.55
Police cooperation	1–5	3.36	0.91	0.83
Law compliance	1–5	4.57	0.59	0.64

Data Analysis

Following Sunshine and Tyler (2003b), we estimated the models with a path analysis framework using maximum likelihood with Mplus 5.0 (Muthén and Muthén 2007). Besides the fact that we aimed to replicate the original model using the same method used by its authors, path analysis by itself is especially attractive for testing the procedural justice-based model, because it enables testing all the assumptions of the model simultaneously—among other things, testing several dependent variables together—while accounting for all the variance at once. Moreover, path analysis allows for observing intermediate effects. In these respects, applying path analysis to test the research questions appears preferable to the more traditional method of executing several multivariate regressions.

We followed Sunshine and Tyler's model precisely and tested all possible paths, including direct and indirect paths. Our final models presented in the following discussion include only the significant associations, except for the correlations between the four

Table 8.2   Path Analysis of Procedural Justice-Based Model for Policing

Variable	(I) Legitimacy	(II) Police Empowerment	(III) Cooperation	(IV) Compliance
Procedural justice	0.44** (16.48)	0.27** (6.70)	0.28** (6.80)	0.07** (2.70)
Police fairness	0.07** (3.60)	0.06* (2.34)	0.11** (3.69)	– (–)
Police performance	0.19** (8.46)	0.08** (2.75)	– (–)	– (–)
Perceived risk	0.07** (2.84)	0.07* (2.19)	0.13** (3.86)	0.07** (2.90)
Legitimacy	– (–)	0.15** (4.19)	0.05 (1.39)	0.05* (2.03)
R^2	0.47	0.22	0.26	0.14

Model fit

$\chi^2 = 55.49$, $df(45)$, $p = 0.13$

CFI = 0.99, RMSEA = 0.013

Note: Maximum likelihood estimation; unstandardized coefficients; z statistics in parentheses; nondisplayed coefficients fixed to 0. CFI, comparative fit index; df, degree of freedom; RMSEA, root mean square of approximation.

*$p < 0.05$; **$p < 0.01$.

antecedents of legitimacy and the outcome variables, which were significant in most of the models but are not presented in the tables and graphs in order not to confuse our readers (the correlation between police empowerment and law compliance was not significant in the model presented in Table 8.2, and the correlation between police empowerment and police cooperation was not significant for the models presented in Figures 8.2 and 8.3).

Results

General Procedural Justice-Based Model

Table 8.2 shows the main results for the path analysis estimation of the procedural justice-based model (the parameter estimates of additional predictors can be obtained from the authors on request). Model I represents the influence of the predictors on legitimacy, whereas Models II to IV include both legitimacy and its predictors as influencing the three scales of support for the police. Some coefficients were fixed to zero to improve the fit indexes, because in an initial estimation they were not significant. Model indexes such as the comparative fit index and root mean square of approximation indicate a general good fit to the data, which means that the model works out in the Israeli sample.

In general, Model I in Table 8.2 shows that all four predictors are positively associated with legitimacy. All in all, the four predictors explain 47% of the variance of the legitimacy scale. Moreover, procedural justice has a stronger impact on legitimacy than the three instrumental predictors. Thus, the data support our first hypothesis.

Models II to IV provide partial support for our second hypothesis, dealing with the influence of legitimacy on support for the police. This is primarily attributable to the exogenous determination of police cooperation and to the design of the compliance scale. Legitimacy appears to be positively associated with empowerment of the police and compliance with the law. No significant association was found with cooperation. However, an additional analysis of the model without the control and predictor variables provides evidence for a significant effect of legitimacy on cooperation ($b = 0.11$, $p < 0.01$; these results can be obtained from the authors on request). This influence thus appears to be conditioned by exogenous predictors. In addition, the compliance scale was highly skewed and presented very low variance. For this reason, like Sunshine and Tyler (2003b), we carried out an additional analysis with a square root transformation and a logistic regression. However, this analysis did not produce any improvement in the results for the effect of legitimacy on compliance.

Our third hypothesis posited that procedural justice would have the strongest effect on the three aspects of support for the police. This is indeed the case for empowerment and cooperation (Models II to III), but in the case of the compliance scale we found a comparatively lower effect (Model IV). This finding suggests that compliance with the law is affected primarily by instrumental predictors. However, we must bear in mind the aforementioned problems with the compliance scale, and accept this result with caution. Despite the general predominance of procedural justice, which provides partial support for hypothesis 3, in general we can observe significant direct effects of the instrumental predictors, and in particular for police empowerment. Therefore, in general we can conclude that although procedural justices has primacy in determining levels of support for the police, instrumental predictors also play an important role.

To sum up the results of this first part of the analysis, we found general support for the hypotheses behind the procedural justice-based model of police legitimacy in the case of Israel. Procedural justice has a stronger impact on legitimacy compared to the instrumental predictors, legitimacy has a positive effect on support for the police, and support for the police is affected primarily by procedural justice. This replication of the model with the Israeli sample allows us to proceed confidently to the second step of this research—the analysis of differences between Israel's ethnic and religious groups.

Influence of Group Affiliation and Religiosity on Legitimacy of Police

We begin the second part of our analysis by testing for group differences in relation to the different elements that comprise the procedural justice-based model of legitimacy. Then, we apply the model separately to the two main groups (Jews and Israeli Arabs) to analyze the role of religiosity.

Table 8.3 presents the results of the path analysis comparing the Jewish and Arab ethnic groups. Here, we correlated each variable listed in the table with a binary variable that represents group affiliation (the coefficients shown in Table 8.2 are not repeated here). Several results stand out. First, members of the Israeli Arab minority perceive the police as less legitimate than do members of the Jewish majority. Consistent with this finding, members of the Arab minority also report less support for the police, in terms of cooperation with the police and compliance with the law—results that support our fourth hypothesis. Second, with regard to the predictors of legitimacy, only procedural justice does not appear to be associated with group differences. The instrumental predictors of legitimacy are all higher for the Israeli Arabs than for the Jews.

Our final hypotheses dealt with the validity of the model (H_5) and the effects of religiosity (H_6) for the Jewish and Arab populations independently. To test these hypotheses, we analyzed the procedural justice-based model separately for each population, and then analyzed all possible paths for religiosity. The statistically significant results are shown in Figures 8.2 and 8.3.

Figure 8.2 shows the results for the Jewish group. Most of the significant associations for the whole sample are also evidenced here; only compliance with the law is no longer significantly associated with legitimacy (there was no significant association for cooperation with the police in either the general model or the model for the Jewish subsample). As a consequence, the only measure of support associated with legitimacy for this subsample appears to be police empowerment. On the other hand, cooperation and compliance are directly affected by procedural justice (0.12, $p < 0.00$; 0.071, $p < 0.01$, respectively; not shown in the figure), confirming the theoretical assumptions of the procedural justice-based model. Therefore, the procedural justice scale appears to be a better predictor of support for the police in this group than legitimacy itself. This finding reveals some limitations of the model (and/or its measurement) that will be further addressed in the discussion.

Turning to the role of religiosity in the Jewish subsample, we find support for our sixth hypothesis: Greater religiosity is negatively associated with the perceived legitimacy of the police. This result is consistent with the negative effect of religiosity on perceptions of procedural justice and on cooperation with the police. On the other hand, greater religiosity is also associated with a higher perceived risk of sanctions and with greater compliance with the law.

Table 8.3   Group Differences in Procedural Justice-Based Model Scales

Group	Procedural Justice	Police Fairness	Police Performance	Perceived Risk	Legitimacy	Police Empowerment	Cooperation	Compliance
Affiliation (Ref = Jewish)								
Israeli Arab	−0.06 (−1.33)	0.31** (5.38)	0.26** (5.06)	0.29** (6.37)	−0.14** (−3.09)	0.03 (0.61)	−0.64** (−12.27)	−0.10** (−2.70)
R^2	0.04	0.03	0.07	0.11	0.46	0.22	0.25	0.14
Model fit								
$\chi^2 = 67.09$, $df(38)$, $p = 0.0.00$								
CFI = 0.99, RMSEA = 0.024								

Note: CFI, comparative fit index; *df*, degree of freedom; RMSEA, root mean square of approximation.

**$p < 0.01$.

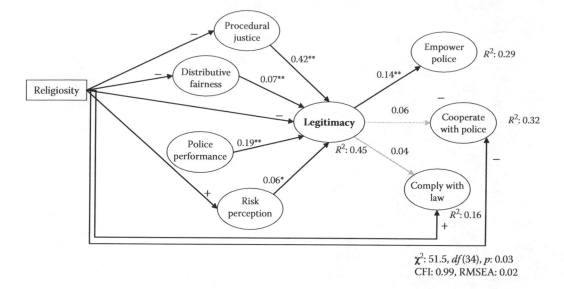

Figure 8.2 Procedural justice-based model of legitimacy in the Jewish population and the effect of religiosity.

Figure 8.3 shows the results for the Israeli Arab subsample. As the figure shows, the coefficients that were not significant for the Jewish subsample are also not significant here, and an additional relationship also loses its significance—the effect of distributive fairness on legitimacy. However, the remaining parameters of the model hold, supporting H_5. Regarding religiosity, greater religiosity among Israeli Arabs is negatively associated with perceptions of procedural justice, as in the Jewish subsample. However, in contrast to the results for the Jewish subsample, we did not find a negative direct relationship between religiosity and legitimacy, thus contradicting H_6 for this population.

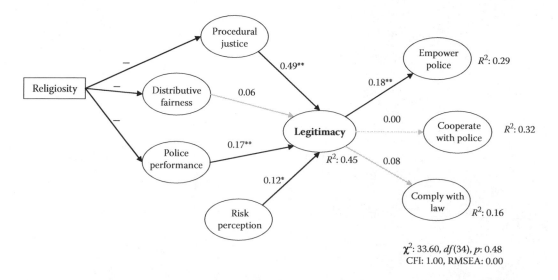

Figure 8.3 Procedural justice-based model of legitimacy in the Israeli Arab population and the effect of religiosity.

Discussion

An interesting question in the fields of criminology and social control is why people willingly comply with law enforcement authorities, even when this compliance does not necessarily serve their instrumental interests. The procedural justice-based model attempts to resolve this question by arguing that the willingness to comply depends on a belief that the institutions of law enforcement are legitimate, and that this belief relies, in turn, on a perception that the procedures followed by those institutions are fair.

In the current study, we explored the replicability of Sunshine and Tyler's (2003b) procedural justice-based model of legitimacy in a different social context with marked group cleavages. More important, we added to the original model the effect of religiosity, a dimension that, to the best of our knowledge, has not yet been examined in the context of this model. We proposed and tested six hypotheses using representative data from 809 members of Israel's Jewish majority and 407 Israeli Arabs.

Similar to other recent studies that have tested the procedural justice-based model (see, e.g., Jonathan-Zamir and Weisburd 2011; Murphy, Tyler, and Curtis 2009), we found support for the majority of our hypotheses, and we were able to replicate the model in the Israeli context. Our findings show that procedural justice has a stronger impact on the extent to which the country's law enforcement authorities are perceived as legitimate as compared with the three instrumental predictors tested (H_1). We also showed that perceived legitimacy has a positive effect on support for the police (H_2); such support is associated chiefly with procedural justice (H_3); the minority group (Israeli Arabs) regard the police as less legitimate than the majority (Jews)(H_4); the general procedural justice-based model holds for the two groups of Israeli society analyzed (H_5); and among Israeli Jews, those who are more religious tend to regard the country's rules and institutions of social control as less legitimate than do those who are less religious (H_6).

There are several important differences between our results and Sunshine and Tyler's original model. We found that legitimacy is associated with both procedural justice and the three instrumental predictors: perceived risk, distributive fairness, and performance. Therefore, we do not have enough evidence to say that legitimacy is absolutely independent of instrumental influences, at least as measured by our scale. This result is in line with that of Jonathan-Zamir and Weisburd (2011, 2), who found that "there does not seem to be a zero-sum game between 'police performance' and 'procedural justice' in predicting police legitimacy". Still, our results support one of the basic assumptions of the procedural justice model—that "procedural fairness will also be a primary influence on judgments of legitimacy when people are evaluating the police in general" (Sunshine and Tyler 2003b, p. 519).

Regarding the effect of perceived legitimacy on the three aspects of support for the police, we—like Sunshine and Tyler—found empowerment of the police to have the strongest association with legitimacy. One important difference between our findings and those of Sunshine and Tyler is that, in our case, cooperation with the police does not appear to be directly affected by legitimacy, and only once the exogenous predictors were removed were we able to replicate the original findings.

Similar to previous findings (see, e.g., Hasisi and Weitzer 2007; Rattner, Yagil, and Pedahzur 2001), our comparison between Israel's minority and majority groups shows that Israeli Arabs perceive Israel's law enforcement institutions as less legitimate than do members of the Jewish majority. They also scored lower on two measures of support for the police: cooperation with the police and compliance with the law. These distinctions were not evidenced in Sunshine and Tyler's comparative analysis of whites, Hispanics, and African Americans in New York. It can be assumed that the particular nature of Israeli society—which, as discussed above, is characterized by deep social and political cleavages—is responsible for the significant group differences exhibited in our analysis. Further studies should validate these findings in other societies experiencing similar historical and social conflicts.

A second aspect of the minority–majority comparison worthy of note is that procedural justice is the only predictor that was not affected by group differences, whereas the instrumental predictors of legitimacy were all higher for the Israeli Arabs. This means that for Israeli Arabs, the legitimacy of the state's law enforcement institutions is based comparatively more on the principle of deterrence and the perceived risk of sanctions. This is not surprising, given this group's minority status in Israel and the emotional ramifications of the Israeli–Palestinian conflict. Nevertheless, and consistent with the procedural justice theory of legitimacy, perceptions of fairness in police procedures are not only the most important predictor of legitimacy, but also appear to function independently of the instrumental predictors for minority groups. In short, for Israeli Arabs the instrumental factors that underlie the legitimacy of the police seem to be more important than for Israeli Jews, but procedural justice is not less so. It is also interesting to note that among the Jewish sample the procedural justice scale appears to be a better predictor of support for the police than legitimacy itself. One implication of these findings for policing in Israel is that Israeli law enforcement institutions should develop intervention programs aimed toward greater legitimation, mainly—according to the procedural justice-based model—through elevating the minority's perception of procedural justice.

A novel contribution of the current study is the addition of religiosity to the model. In both groups we found a negative association between religiosity and procedural justice—that is, higher religiosity is associated with lower perceptions of procedural justice. However, the effect of religiosity on legitimacy seems to differ for the minority and majority groups. In the Jewish sample, we found a negative effect of religiosity on legitimacy, meaning that Jews who are more religiously observant are likely to perceive the police as less legitimate than those who are more secular. This result is consistent with the negative association of religiosity with procedural justice and with cooperation with the police in this subsample. At the same time, among the Jews, we found a positive association between religiosity and both perceived risk of sanctions and compliance with the law, suggesting that the deterrent effect of law enforcement plays a key role in the attitudes and behavior of Israel's religious Jews toward the police. Meanwhile, in the Israeli Arab sample, we failed to find a direct negative association between religiosity and legitimacy. Thus, highly religious (ultra-Orthodox) Jews perceive the institutions of law enforcement as less legitimate than do highly religious Israeli Arabs. These findings show that attitudes and behaviors toward the police are sensitive to variables reflecting values and identity. Police and other law enforcement institutions should take this information under consideration when dealing with different segments of the population, and should seek ways to enhance perceptions of procedural justice among more religious individuals, as well as greater legitimation among highly religious Jews. Furthermore, the findings open a series of questions regarding the role played by extreme religiosity and/or extreme support for intragroup values in majority groups, and about the social mechanisms that bring highly religious Jews to perceive law enforcement institutions as less legitimate compared to highly religious Israeli Arabs—questions that call for further research.

The results of the current study should be interpreted in light of its research limitations. First, the results are based on self-reports, meaning that respondents' actual compliance or cooperation with the police is unknown. Second, we used cross-sectional data, which does not allow testing for causality. These two issues call for future studies that will test the procedural justice-based model of legitimacy with longitudinal data. Third, we did not use formal statistical analysis for testing the mediated effects. Future studies should test these mediated effects using formal statistical methods.

Finally, in order to replicate Sunshine and Tyler's original model we used the same measures of legitimacy as they used in the United States. However, legitimacy is a context-specific and culturally rich concept, meaning that personal perceptions of legitimate authority are likely to reflect the individual's culture and that culture's particular circumstances and history. Our understanding of the issues raised here would therefore benefit from a reconceptualization of legitimacy and how it is perceived in different cultures. To this end, we recommend that future studies use more recent operationalizations of the legitimacy concept, as well as suggested modifications of the original model (see, e.g., Bottoms and Tankebe 2012; Factor, Mahalel, Rafaeli, and Williams 2013; Tankebe 2013; Tyler and Jackson 2012). A similar problem exists with regard to procedural justice, which is in fact a multidimensional concept. Individuals from different backgrounds are likely to interpret the meaning of "fairness" in different ways. It is also questionable whether participants readily dissociate their assessments of procedural justice from other concepts in the model, such as police performance. Further research efforts, including the use of qualitative methods, should resolve these questions and, perhaps, uncover new measures of procedural justice.

References

Blalock, H. M. 1967. *Toward a theory of minority-group relations*. New York: Wiley.

Bottoms, A. and J. Tankebe. 2012. Beyond procedural justice: A dialogic approach to legitimacy in criminal justice. *Journal of Criminal Law and Criminology* 102(1): 119–170.

Cohn, E. S., S. O. White and J. Sanders. 2000. Distributive and procedural justice in seven nations. *Law and Human Behavior* 24(5): 553–579.

Factor, R., I. Kawachi and D. R. Williams. 2011. Understanding high risk behavior among non-dominant minorities: A social resistance framework. *Social Science and Medicine* 73(9): 1292–1301.

Factor, R., D. Mahalel, A. Rafaeli and D. R. Williams. 2013. A social resistance perspective for delinquent behavior among non-dominant minority groups. *The British Journal of Criminology* 53(5): 784–804.

Gibson, J. L. and G. A. Caldeira. 1996. The legal cultures of Europe. *Law and Society Review* 30(1): 55–85.

Hasisi, B. and R. Weitzer. 2007. Police relations with Arabs and Jews in Israel. *British Journal of Criminology* 47(5): 728–745.

Herbert, S. 2003. Trust in the law: Encouraging public cooperation with the police and courts. *Social Forces* 82(2): 840–841.

Hinds, L. and K. Murphy. 2007. Public satisfaction with police: Using procedural justice to improve police legitimacy. *Australian and New Zealand Journal of Criminology* 40(1): 27–42.

Jonathan-Zamir, T. and D. Weisburd. 2011. The effects of security threats on antecedents of police legitimacy: Findings from a quasi-experiment in Israel. *Journal of Research in Crime and Delinquency* 50(1): 3–32.

Lind, E. A. and R. R. Tyler. 1988. *The social psychology of procedural justice.* New York: Plenum Press.

Moore, D. 2000. Intolerance of "others" among Palestinian and Jewish students in Israel. *Sociological Inquiry* 70(3): 280–312.

Murphy, K., T. R. Tyler and A. Curtis. 2009. Nurturing regulatory compliance: Is procedural justice effective when people question the legitimacy of the law? *Regulation and Governance* 3(1): 1–26.

Muthén, B. and L. Muthén. 2007. *Mplus user's guide (4th ed.).* Los Angeles: Muthén and Muthén.

Rattner, A. and D. Yagil. 2004. Taking the law into one's own hands on ideological grounds. *International Journal of the Sociology of Law* 32(1): 85–102.

Rattner, A., D. Yagil and A. Pedahzur. 2001. Not bound by the law: Legal disobedience in Israeli society. *Behavioral Sciences and the Law* 19(2): 265–283.

Reisig, M. D., J. Bratton and M. G. Gertz. 2007. The construct validity and refinement of process-based policing measures. *Criminal Justice and Behavior* 34(8): 1005–1028.

Richards, P. S. and M. L. Davison. 1992. Religious bias in moral-development research—A psycho-metric investigation. *Journal for the Scientific Study of Religion* 31(4): 467–485.

Sunshine, J. and T. Tyler. 2003a. Moral solidarity, identification with the community, and the importance of procedural justice: The police as prototypical representatives of a group's moral values. *Social Psychology Quarterly* 66(2): 153–165.

Sunshine, J. and T. R. Tyler. 2003b. The role of procedural justice and legitimacy in shaping public support for policing. *Law and Society Review* 37(3): 513–547.

Tankebe, J. 2009. Public cooperation with the police in Ghana: Does procedural fairness matter? *Criminology* 47(4): 1265–1293.

Tankebe, J. 2013. Viewing things differently: The dimensions of public perceptions of police legitimacy. *Criminology* 51(1): 103–135.

Thibaut, J. W. and L. Walker. 1975. *Procedural justice: A psychological analysis.* New York: Lawrence Erlbaum Associates.

Törnblom, K. Y. and R. L. Vermunt. 2007. *Distributive and procedural justice: Research and social applications.* Aldershot: Ashgate.

Turner, J. H. 1986. Toward a unified theory of ethnic antagonism: A preliminary synthesis of three macro models. *Sociological Forum* 1: 403–427.

Tyler, T. R. 1988. What is procedural justice—Criteria used by citizens to assess the fairness of legal procedures. *Law and Society Review* 22(1): 103–135.

Tyler, T. R. 1990. *Why people obey the law.* London: Yale University Press.

Tyler, T. R. 2004. Enhancing police legitimacy. *Annals of the American Academy of Political and Social Science* 593: 84–99.

Tyler, T. R. and J. Jackson. 2012. *Future challenges in the study of legitimacy and criminal justice.* Yale Law School, Public Law Working Paper (Vol. 264). New Haven, CT: Yale University.

Weitzer, R., S. A. Tuch and W. G. Skogan. 2008. Police–community relations in a majority-black city. *Journal of Research in Crime and Delinquency* 45(4): 398–428.

Yiftachel, O. 1997. The political geography of ethnic protest: Nationalism, deprivation and regionalism among Arabs in Israel. *Transactions of the Institute of British Geographers* 22(1): 91–110.

Police Understanding of the Foundations of Their Legitimacy in the Eyes of the Public

The Case of Commanding Officers in the Israel National Police[*]

TAL JONATHAN-ZAMIR
AMIKAM HARPAZ

Contents

Introduction

The legitimacy of legal authorities has become an important area of interest in the fields of criminal justice and criminology, one that has given rise to much theoretical and empirical work. Much of this literature stems from the work of Tom Tyler and his colleagues, and uses their conceptualization of key terms such as "legitimacy" and "procedural justice" (see reviews by Bottoms and Tankebe 2012; National Research Council 2004; Tyler 2004, 2009, 2011). In this body of work, the legitimacy of an authority is typically viewed from the perspective of the citizen, who is making judgments about the entitlement of the authority and

[*] Reproduced from Jonathan-Zamir, T., and A. Harpaz. 2014. Police understanding of the foundations of their legitimacy in the eyes of the public: The case of commanding officers in the Israel National Police. *The British Journal of Criminology* 54(3): 469–489, by permission of Oxford University Press.

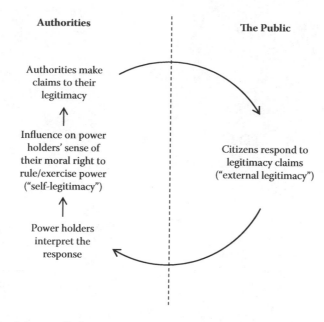

Figure 9.1 The Legitimacy dialogue.

its agents to call on the public to follow the law, cooperate with requests, accept decisions, and assist legal agents to carry out their responsibilities (Tyler 2004, 2009). Empirical studies have generally tried to identify the outcomes of legitimacy (such as citizen satisfaction, cooperation, compliance, and future law obedience) and the factors that impact legitimacy assessments (mostly focusing on procedural justice versus instrumental considerations; e.g., Hinds and Murphy 2007; Jonathan-Zamir and Weisburd 2013; Murphy, Hynds and Fleming 2008; Reisig, Bratton and Gertz 2007; Sunshine and Tyler 2003; Tyler 2001, 2004, 2009; Tyler and Fagan 2008; Tyler and Huo 2002; Tyler, Schulhofer and Huq 2010).

Recently, the field has begun developing in a number of important directions that are somewhat different from this line of work (e.g., Jonathan-Zamir, Mastrofski and Moyal forthcoming). One recent approach was set forth by Bottoms and Tankebe (2012), who have called for a "dialogic approach to legitimacy." Based on the work of Weber (1978) and Raz (2009), these authors argue that legitimacy should be viewed as an ongoing dialogue between "power holders"* and the public: authorities make claims to their legitimacy, citizens respond, and their response, in turn, impacts power holders' perceptions of their own moral right to rule and future claims to legitimacy (see Figure 9.1). Similar to earlier work, this approach acknowledges the importance of citizens' perceptions of the authority's legitimacy ("external legitimacy"; see Tankebe 2010), but it also places attention on power holders' views about their own legitimacy ("internal" or "self-legitimacy") and the cyclic nature of the interaction between them.

Viewing legitimacy as a dialogue, in turn, raises a series of important empirical questions that have, to date, received little attention. One such question concerns power holders' understanding of their external legitimacy—how do power holders think citizens view

---

* Following the terminology used by Bottoms and Tankebe (2012), we use the term "power holders" when discussing police legitimacy in the context of the "legitimacy as a dialog" approach. Clearly, there are power holders regarding the police who are not police officers (such as persons or organizations who have authority over the police). In this article, we are referring specifically to police officers when using this term.

them and their moral right to exercise power? (See third stage in Figure 9.1.) A more specific question, which is at the heart of the present study, concerns the factors that, in the eyes of the power holders, are at the core of their external legitimacy—what do power holders think makes citizens view them as legitimate? This question does not ask what the police think justifies their existence, authority, or resources. Rather, it asks what the police think citizens care about. In a democracy, this understanding is imperative to the functioning of the police because of the presumed mechanisms of accountability that flow from the police to the public. From the perspective of the dialogic approach to legitimacy, these perceptions are important because a dialogue requires understanding of the expectations of the other party. Together with other factors, power holders' understanding of the sources of their external legitimacy is expected to influence their sense of their own moral right to exercise power, the way they define goals and means, and the focus of their future claims to legitimacy, which, in turn, should impact the legitimacy citizens render to the authority.

In this chapter, we examine this question in Israel: How do Israeli commanding police officers understand the foundations of their external legitimacy? What factors do they think citizens consider when evaluating police legitimacy, and how are they prioritized? We begin with a review of the value-based approach to criminal justice as set forth by Tom Tyler and others. We then review the dialogic approach to legitimacy and the specific research question examined in this chapter. Our analysis then shows that, in contrast to the priorities of citizens (as expressed in community surveys), police officers associate their external legitimacy more with their accomplishments in fighting crime and sustaining deterrence than with the fairness of the police process. In our discussion, we consider our findings and their implications in the contexts of Israeli policing, the "legitimacy as a dialogue" approach, and legitimacy research more generally.

Police Legitimacy as the Basis for Law Obedience

The quality of "legitimacy," or public perceptions that an authority is "entitled to have its decisions and rules accepted and followed by others" (National Research Council 2004, p. 297), is often presented as one of the important possessions of police forces in democratic societies. Although the idea of legitimacy is not new (e.g., Kelman and Hamilton 1989; Weber 1978), the concept of "police legitimacy" and its significance have been highlighted in recent discussions on a "self-regulated" or "value-based" approach to criminal justice. This approach suggests that citizens' motivation to obey the law, comply and cooperate with legal authorities, and accept their decisions depends, to a large extent, on subjective views about the legitimacy of these authorities (e.g., National Research Council 2004; Sunshine and Tyler 2003; Tyler 2004, 2009, 2011; Tyler and Fagan 2008; Tyler and Huo 2002).

Tyler (2004, 2009) contrasts this approach with the traditional instrumental model, according to which compliance with the law and with the directives of its agents is obtained through threat of punishment (deterrence) and demonstrated competence in controlling crime. Tyler concludes that this model is costly, credible threat of punishment is difficult to achieve, and thus the benefits of the approach are modest (e.g., MacCoun 1993; MacKenzie 2002; Paternoster 1987, 1989). Unlike the deterrence model, the self-regulatory approach is based on internal values, namely, legitimacy, and thus compliance with the law and cooperation with legal agents become self-regulated, and as a result less dependent on sanctions or incentives provided by the authorities. Although studies demonstrate the importance of deterrence in sustaining law obedience (Nagin 2013; National Research Council 2004), empirical research also supports the propositions set forth by the "value-based" approach (e.g., Kochel, Parks and Mastrofski 2013; LaFree 1998; Mastrofski, Snipes and Supina 1996; Murphy, Hynds and Fleming 2008; Paternoster, Brame, Bachman and Sherman 1997; Reisig, Bratton and Gertz 2007; Sampson and Bartusch 1998; Sunshine and Tyler 2003; Tyler 2006; Tyler and Fagan 2008; Tyler and Huo 2002; Tyler, Schulhofer and Huq 2010; Tyler and Wakslak 2004).

Given the importance of legitimacy, the antecedents of this quality have also become an important focus of research. A major finding of such studies is that the most important predictor of police legitimacy are evaluations of procedural justice, or the fairness of the processes by which the police exercise their authority, including both fair decision making (allowing the citizens involved to express their views before decisions are made regarding their case, and making decisions in a neutral, unbiased fashion) and fair interpersonal treatment (treating the citizens involved with dignity and respect, and behaving in a way that encourages trust in the motives of the police; Hinds and Murphy 2007; National Research Council 2004; Reisig, Bratton and Gertz 2007; Tyler 2001, 2004, 2009; Tyler, Schulhofer and Huq 2010). Instrumental assessments, such as the favorability of the outcomes delivered or views regarding the ability of the police to catch rule breakers and control crime, were also found to be an important predictor of police legitimacy; however, they were generally found to be less influential than perceptions of procedural justice (Murphy, Hynds and Fleming 2008; Sunshine and Tyler 2003; Tyler 2001, 2004, 2009).

It should be noted that some cross-cultural variations were found in the relative importance of the factors predicting police legitimacy (e.g., Brockner et al. 2001; Hinds and Murphy 2007; Tankebe 2009). At the same time, a recent study carried out in Israel, our study site, revealed similar results to those found in the United States. In their survey of Israeli citizens, Jonathan-Zamir and Weisburd (2013) found that both in situations of immediate security threats and in communities facing no specific threats at the time, the most important antecedent of police legitimacy was procedural justice. Although assessments of police performance did increase in importance for the public under threat, they remained secondary to procedural justice in predicting police legitimacy in these communities (also see Factor, Castilo, and Rattner 2014).

As this review suggests, the legitimacy of the police has mostly been examined from the perspective of the citizen. This perspective is clearly important, as personal views are expected to have significant effects on citizens' behavior. At the same time, scholars have recently suggested that there may be important theoretical, empirical, and practical advantages in taking a broader view of the concept of legitimacy, one that acknowledges theoretical discussions on legitimacy within the social sciences more generally and considers legitimacy from additional standpoints, such as that of the power holder, and the interaction between the different perspectives (Bottoms and Tankebe 2012).

Legitimacy as a Dialogue and Power Holders' Understanding of the Foundations of Their External Legitimacy

Based on Weber's (1978) fundamental theorization of legitimacy and later discussions by Raz (2009), a political–legal philosopher, Bottoms and Tankebe (2012) have recently argued for a "dialogic approach to legitimacy." According to this approach, legitimacy should not be considered only from the perspective of the citizen, nor as a "single transaction" between power holders and their audience, but as a "perpetual discussion" between citizens and authorities (Bottoms and Tankebe 2012, p. 129).

These authors begin with Raz's (2009) classification of power holders, which highlights that *authorities claim legitimacy*—that is, they claim to have the right to rule or exercise power (whether or not this claim is accepted by their audience). Claiming legitimacy is precisely what differentiates "authorities" from people or groups who exert "naked power" (such as hostage takers). Bottoms and Tankebe (2012) continue with Weber's theorization of legitimacy, which highlights that authorities' claims to legitimacy are not a one-time event but are ongoing, as authorities attempt "to establish *and cultivate*" legitimacy (Weber 1978, p. 213). They conclude that rather than focusing on how legitimate authorities are perceived by citizens to be, we should be thinking about legitimacy as a "continuing relationship" (p. 129), where the authority claims to have the right to rule, the public responds, and this response, in turn, affects power holders' perceptions of their own legitimacy and subsequent claims to legitimacy.

Unlike much of the literature on legitimacy in the field of criminal justice that focuses primarily on the views of citizens, this approach places equal attention on power holders' sense of their moral right to exercise power, and the process of dialogue that shapes and forms the views of both sides (see Boulding 1967; Tankebe 2010; Weber 1978; Wrong 1979). Although the perspective of the public is clearly important, the views of the power holders are—according to this approach—at the core of authorities' claims to legitimacy and subsequent public response (Barker 2001; Bottoms and Tankebe 2012). An underlying argument is that it would be difficult to claim legitimacy and, in turn, be perceived as a legitimate authority, if the authority's agents do not view themselves as legitimate. Self-legitimacy is also viewed as critical for effective performance (Boulding 1967). It should be noted that because Weber (1978) has placed legality at the center of his legitimacy discussion, Bottoms and Tankebe (2012) argue that it is reasonable to speculate that he would have viewed legality and formality as the basis of power holders' self-legitimacy. In other words, when their positions and powers, as well as day-to-day practices, are rooted in solid formal and legal bases—power holders are expected to feel that they have the legitimate right to rule. Bottoms and Tankebe (2012) also argue, however, that this is a necessary but insufficient condition, as self-legitimacy is also highly dependent on power holders' perceptions of their legitimacy in the eyes of their audience (also see Wrong 1979).[*]

Although not stated explicitly, it is clear that as part of the legitimacy dialogue, power holders interpret and form their understanding of the audience's reaction to their legitimacy claims. This interpretation is a natural mediating step between the response authorities receive from the public and the effects of this feedback on their self-legitimacy and subsequent claims to legitimacy (see "Power-holders interpret the response" in Figure 9.1). Additionally, because Bottoms and Tankebe (2012) develop a general model, they do not elaborate on the specific type of information conveyed in each step of the legitimacy dialogue. We argue that it is reasonable to consider this dialogue not only in terms of quantity ("how much" legitimacy citizens render the authority, and, in turn, "how much" legitimacy

---

[*] Clearly, the "legitimacy dialog" and the effects of each stage are highly dependent on the political and social contexts in which the police are operating. For example, American police in the late nineteenth century are likely to have been much more concerned with the views of local political leaders than with the priorities of the public (e.g., Kelling and Moore 1988). Our study is set in the context of recent discussions of police legitimacy in the twenty-first century, on the background of community-oriented policing.

power holders feel that they have), but also in terms of the broader nature and substance of the claim (such as what citizens consider to be legitimate or which components of the authority's claim for legitimacy citizens do and do not support).

Specifically, we suggest that *one* aspect of the feedback conveyed by citizens and interpreted by the authorities includes the factors that are at the core of power holders' external legitimacy—"what makes citizens view us as legitimate?" According to the dialogic approach, this understanding is expected to have important effects on power holders' self-legitimacy, strategic choices, day-to-day behavior, and the nature of future claims to legitimacy. For example, as noted earlier, surveys have repeatedly identified procedural justice as the most important factor on which citizens judge the legitimacy of the police. If the police are aware of this, take steps to strengthen procedural justice in the behavior of officers, and believe that they have been successful in their efforts, their self-legitimacy is expected to strengthen. Moreover, in future claims to legitimacy they are likely to emphasize their focus on procedural justice, assuming that this would reinforce their external legitimacy. If, on the other hand, the police have an inaccurate understanding of citizen priorities, they may choose to emphasize aggressive crime control at the expense of procedural fairness in their work and claims to legitimacy, which may ultimately weaken their legitimacy in the eyes of the public.

The Study

The "legitimacy as a dialogue" approach is theoretical in nature, and many of the relationships suggested so far are speculative. The model does, however, set the stage for a wide range of empirical questions (some of which are highlighted by Bottoms and Tankebe 2012). In this chapter, we raise the specific question mentioned above for Israeli policing: How do Israeli police officers perceive the foundations of their legitimacy in the eyes of the public? As noted earlier, similar to numerous studies in the Western world, procedural justice was identified as the most important antecedent of external police legitimacy in Israel (Factor, Castilo and Rattner 2014; Jonathan-Zamir and Weisburd 2013). But are Israeli police officers aware of the importance of fair processes to the public, or, alternatively, do they associate citizens' evaluations of police legitimacy primarily with their accomplishments in fighting crime and creating credible risk for rule breakers?

At the outset, it is important to note that several features of the Israel National Police (INP) distinguish it from North American and some European police agencies—particularly, that it is a national, centralized police agency with significant internal security responsibilities (Ben-Porat 1988; Herzog 2001; Hovav and Amir 1979; Shadmi and Hod 1996; Weisburd, Jonathan and Perry 2009; Weisburd, Shalev and Amir 2002). This differs from the diffused, local North American policing model and the more local control of policing that can be found in some European countries such as France and Italy. Additionally, local police agencies in the United States and in many European countries began to see security problems (and particularly terrorism) as an integral part of their mission only in the recent decade (Weisburd, Jonathan and Perry 2009).

At the same time, there are important similarities between the INP and other Western police agencies. Israeli police officers are constrained and regulated by comparable legal requirements, such as clear restrictions on use of force, detention, and arrest, and are obligated to equal, nondiscriminatory treatment. Most day-to-day responsibilities and activities of local police stations, such as managing traffic, handling crime problems, and providing general services to the public, resemble those of local police agencies in other Western democracies. Finally, the INP was influenced by recent international innovations in policing, such as community policing, Compstat, and "hot spots" policing (Meniv 2013; Weisburd and Amram 2014; Weisburd, Shalev and Amir 2002). Importantly, as noted above, public expectations from the Israeli police regarding procedural fairness follow those of the United States and European countries (Jackson and Sunshine 2007; Tyler 2011). Accordingly, although every national setting has unique components, the views of the Israeli police provide an important example of police officers' understanding of the basis of their external legitimacy in a Western, democratic police agency. In our discussion later, we consider how our results may be understood in the specific context of Israeli policing and characteristics of the INP.

Sample

Our sample was selected to represent commanding officers in "field units" of the INP. Field units (in contrast to administrative or managerial departments) hold the territorial responsibility for providing day-to-day policing services to the public. They are divided hierarchically into districts, subdistricts, and local police stations (for a description of the organizational structure of the INP, see Gimshi 2007; Weisburd, Jonathan and Perry 2009). Commanding officers in field units have direct authority over street-level officers who provide regular policing services to the public, such as patrol officers, detectives, and the traffic police. These commanders have worked at the street level at earlier stages of their careers and are still very much involved in street work, either as part of their supervisory responsibilities or by providing on-the-job training to new recruits. Notably, their command position means that their views have an important impact on everyday police work, and indeed the attitudes of this group were highlighted as a critical factor in implementing procedurally just policing (see Tyler 2011).

Our overall sample of officers ($N = 290$) is made up of two major groups. The first includes 142 commanding officers (up to the rank of Commander), who were surveyed in 10 police stations (4–31 officers per station; $M = 14$) located within the five police districts in the pre-1967 border. These stations were chosen to represent large, small, rural, and urban areas of responsibility, and were stations in which the station commander agreed to cooperate with the study. In any particular station, survey forms were distributed in a regular meeting of the command staff, which most or all commanding officers are required to attend. Only a few officers in this group refused to participate in the study (response rate of 95%).

Our second group consists of 148 officers, who were, at the time of the survey, students in one of two programs at the University of Haifa. Eighty-six were relatively young officers completing their bachelor's degree as part of a special program combining academic education with the INP Commanding Officers Course. Sixty-two were experienced commanding officers, most at the rank of superintendent or above, studying for a master's degree as part of an advanced commanding officers' training programs. Police officers are selected annually for these educational programs following allocations made by the Human Resources Department of the INP, which proportionally allocates candidate positions to all field units (considering both their size and professional orientation). Within each unit, candidates are selected based on their compliance with various requirements, such as sufficient educational and training backgrounds, years in service, and recommendations. The response rate in this group was 70%.*

Although the selection of officers was not based on a randomization scheme, it includes a broad representation of the ~1500 commanding officers in the field units of the INP, from various professional backgrounds, at different stages of their careers, and from a range of locations in Israel (see Appendix I). The bias of the sample is likely toward "up and coming" officers seeking to provide leadership roles in the police; however, these are precisely the officers that are likely to play an important role in future decision making. Moreover, as detailed in the following discussion, in our main analysis we control for key individual-level variables that may affect officers' assessments of their external legitimacy, such as years of service and primary experience in the INP. We also control for the sampling group our respondents belong to.

Survey and Main Variables

The survey was carried out during the second half of 2011 and the first half of 2012, either at the specific police stations (the first group) or at the University of Haifa (the second group), using the pencil-and-paper format. The questionnaire included almost 100 questions about numerous aspects of officers' attitudes about police legitimacy, procedural justice, police effectiveness in fighting crime, deterrence in Israel, and more. Most questions were designed as statements that the officers were asked to rank according to their agreement, on a scale ranging from 1 ("strongly disagree") to 6 ("strongly agree"). Several sections of the questionnaire inquired about officers' views on their image in the eyes of the public.

The statements concerning police legitimacy, procedural justice, and police performance in the eyes of citizens as understood by the police were designed in line with previous citizen surveys on police legitimacy (e.g., Gau 2011; Reisig, Bratton and Gertz 2007; Sunshine and Tyler 2003; Tyler and Wakslak 2004), some carried out in Israel (Jonathan-Zamir and Weisburd 2013). The original statements, which were designed to measure citizens' attitudes toward the police, were revised to measure officers' views on what citizens think of them. For example, the statement "I am happy to defend the work of the NYPD when talking to my friends," which was used by Sunshine and Tyler (2003: 540) to measure trust in the police, was revised to "In my view, the average Israeli citizen is happy to defend the INP in conversations with friends." Importantly, in these sections officers were reminded multiple times that they are asked to respond not according to their own views of their organization, but according to what they believe citizens think.

Our dependent variable, the *legitimacy of the police in the eyes of the public* (as perceived by the police), was constructed by averaging seven statements tapping trust in the police, such as: "In my view, the average Israeli citizen agrees with the values that guide

---

* We attribute the difference in response rates between the two groups to the different settings in which officers were asked to participate in the study. In the first group, respondents have presumably felt more pressure to participate owing to the presence of their peers/supervisors and the strict, hierarchical nature of command at the stations. As university students in the open environment of a classroom, officers may have felt more comfortable to decline participation. Importantly, following the university ethics committee's guidelines, it was clarified to the officers in both groups that the study is being carried out by university researchers, *not* by the INP. All were assured that their participation is voluntary and anonymous, there are no sanctions for refusing to participate (or benefits for participating), and the completed questionnaires would not be available to the police.

the work of the INP" (Cronbach's $\alpha = 0.88$; $N = 284$; range: 1–6; $M = 3.38$; $SD = 0.88$). We should note that "police legitimacy" was often operationalized in community surveys as a combination of trust in the police, obligation to obey the police and the law, and sometimes affective feelings toward the police (see Hinds and Murphy 2007; Sunshine and Tyler 2003; Tyler 2004, 2009; Tyler and Fagan 2008). Because some research suggests that "trust" and "obligation to obey" may be two distinct concepts, both theoretically and empirically (see Gau 2011; Reisig, Bratton and Gertz 2007; Tankebe 2009), in our analysis we focus specifically on "trust." In doing so, we follow earlier studies on police legitimacy in Israel (Jonathan-Zamir and Weisburd 2013), which was important for comparing the views of the police to those of the public.

Our first independent variable of interest, the *fairness of police process* in the eyes of the public (procedural justice as perceived by the police), was made up of six statements including: "In my view, the average Israeli citizen believes that Israeli police officers treat those they encounter with politeness and dignity" (Cronbach's $\alpha = 0.88$; $N = 285$; range 1–6; $M = 3.69$; $SD = 0.87$). Our second independent variable of interest concerned *instrumental judgments* citizens make about the police (as perceived by police officers), including their performance in fighting crime and the level of deterrence, or "risk," they are able to sustain (see Sunshine and Tyler 2003). This scale was made up of six statements, such as: "In my view, the average Israeli citizen believes that the INP has shown many successes in handling crime over the past few years" (Cronbach's $\alpha = 0.84$; $N = 286$; range: 1–6; $M = 3.26$; $SD = 0.82$). As can be seen in Table 9.1, factor analysis using principal-axis factoring with Varimax (with Kaiser Normalization) rotation confirmed that the items indeed reflect three distinct constructs (an examination of the Kaiser–Meyer–Olkin [KMO] measure of sampling adequacy suggested that the sample was appropriate for factor analysis [KMO = 0.91]).

Findings

In light of the dialogic approach to legitimacy and our focus on officers' understanding of their public image, we found it important to first examine how well Israeli police officers think they are doing in the eyes of citizens in the three main areas of interest in this analysis: legitimacy, procedural justice, and accomplishments in solving crime and deterring offenders (instrumental considerations). We have thus compared the mean scores of the three scales using a series of paired-samples t tests (results reported in Table 9.2).

As can be seen in Table 9.2, our respondents believe that Israeli citizens would give the police the highest score in the area of procedural justice (3.69 of 6; 62 on a 0–100 metric*), followed by legitimacy (3.38 of 6; 56 on a 0–100 metric) and instrumental considerations (3.26 of 6; 54 on a 0–100 metric). The differences between the three scores were found to be statistically significant, but all three suggest that our respondents believe that the public does not evaluate the INP positively.

However, our main interest is in identifying the factors that, in the eyes of the police, are at the core of their external legitimacy. The difference between the average mean scores of procedural justice and instrumental considerations makes this analysis all the more

---

* We standardized the indices into a 0–100 metric by dividing the scale values with their upper limit and multiplying the result by 100. This was done to allow for a simple and intuitive assessment of the score.

Table 9.1   Factor Analysis Differentiating Police Legitimacy, Procedural Justice, and Instrumental Considerations (in the Eyes of Citizens as Perceived by Police)

Item	Factor 1	Factor 2	Factor 3
Police Legitimacy in the Eyes of the Public			
In my view, the average Israeli citizen…			
1. Believes that the Israel National Police (INP) makes the right decisions for the people in his/her area of residents.	0.54	–	–
2. Is proud to work with the police station in his/her area of residence.	0.61	–	–
3. Is happy to defend the INP in conversations with friends.	0.68	–	–
4. Agrees with the values that guide the work of the INP.	0.72	–	–
5. Would encourage a family member/friend who was a victim of a crime to turn to the police.	0.64	–	–
6. Believes in the INP as an organization.	0.74	–	–
7. Believes in the overall policy of the INP.	0.74	–	–
Fairness of Police Processes in the Eyes of the Public (Procedural Justice)			
In my view, the average Israeli citizen believes that…			
1. Police officers in Israel make decisions based on facts, not personal interest.	–	0.53	–
2. The police allow the people involved to express their views before making a decision in their case.	–	0.49	–
3. Israeli police officers treat those they encounter with politeness and dignity.	–	0.76	–
4. The police respect the rights of the citizens they come in contact with.	–	0.84	–
5. The INP as an organization shows concern for the well-being and quality of life of Israeli residents.	–	0.75	–
6. Officers in Israel are polite and courteous in their demeanor toward citizens on the street.	–	0.76	–
Instrumental Judgments: Police Performance and Deterrence in the Eyes of the Public			
In my view, the average Israeli citizen believes that…			
1. The INP is efficient in handling crime in his/her area of residents.	–	–	0.59
2. The INP has shown many successes in handling crime over the past few years.	–	–	0.58
3. The INP is effective in handling violent crimes in Israel.	–	–	0.73
4. The INP is effective in handling drug crimes in Israel.	–	–	0.58
5. The INP deals well with property crimes in Israel.	–	–	0.68
6. The INP solves complicated cases quickly.	–	–	0.49
Eigenvalues	7.64	2.15	1.57
Variance explained (%)	40.20	11.31	8.26

Note: $N = 275$. Only factor loadings >0.40 are displayed.

Table 9.2   Paired Samples *t* Tests

	Means	N	t	df	p
Legitimacy–procedural justice	3.39–3.69	279	−5.46	278	<0.001
Legitimacy–instrumental judgments	3.38–3.26	280	2.50	279	<0.05
Procedural justice–instrumental judgments	3.69–3.25	281	8.88	280	<0.001

intriguing—Israeli commanding police officers think they are doing somewhat better (in the eyes of the public) in exercising fair processes than in fighting crime. But do they also think procedural justice is more critical to citizens when considering police legitimacy?

In Table 9.3, we report the findings of this analysis (the correlation matrix excluding multinominal variables is reported in Appendix II). We use an ordinary least squares regression in which police legitimacy (in the eyes of the public, as viewed by the police) is the dependent variable. The predictors include our two main independent variables of interest: procedural justice and instrumental considerations, again in the eye of the public as perceived by Israeli commanding police officers. We also control for key personal characteristics that may affect officers' evaluations of their external legitimacy, such as the length and type of service in the INP (see Appendix I for descriptive statistics of control variables). We should note that three variables in our dataset—age ($N = 280$, $M = 38.24$, min–max $= 23$–56, $SD = 7.49$), years of service in the INP ($N = 279$, $M = 14.4$, min–max $= 3$–30, $SD = 6.38$), and rank ($N = 273$, ranging from 1 = Cadet to 6 = Commander)—were understandably highly correlated [age–years of service: $r(275) = 0.89$, $p < 0.001$; age–rank:

Table 9.3 External Legitimacy of the Israel National Police (INP) as Viewed by Israeli Police Officers

	B	SE	β	t
Test Variables				
Instrumental judgments	0.41	0.07	0.39***	6.12
Procedural justice	0.29	0.07	0.29***	4.46
Control Variables				
Years of service in the INP	−0.00	0.01	−0.03	−0.47
Main background				
Investigations	0.17	0.13	0.08	1.28
Intelligence	−0.06	0.14	−0.03	−0.44
Border Guard	0.38	0.17	0.15*	2.26
Traffic control	−0.28	0.23	−0.07	−1.22
Community and Civil Guard[a]	0.16	0.25	0.04	0.64
Other	0.09	0.19	0.03	0.47
Student at time of survey	0.03	0.10	0.02	0.33
Female	0.04	0.16	0.01	0.26
Single	−0.44	0.16	−0.17**	−2.74
Divorced	0.13	0.24	0.03	0.56
Living with a spouse	−0.04	0.22	−0.01	−0.17
Born outside of Israel	−0.07	0.19	−0.02	−0.35
Druze	0.10	0.21	0.03	0.49
Muslim	0.45	0.42	0.06	1.06
R^2 (Adjusted R^2)	0.40 (0.36)***	–	–	–
N	250	–	–	–

[a] The Civil Guard is an umbrella organization coordinating all voluntary citizen activity in the INP. It is the largest voluntary organization in Israel, operated by the "Police and Community" department of the INP. For more information see Weisburd, Jonathan and Perry (2009) and the INP website (www.police.gov.il).

*$p \leq 0.05$; **$p \leq 0.01$; ***$p \leq 0.001$.

$r(269) = 0.72$, $p < 0.001$; years of service–rank: $r(269) = 0.74$, $p < 0.001$]. Thus, in order to avoid multicollinearity we only included years of service in our model.

The model is statistically significant ($p < 0.001$) and explains more than one-third of the variance in officers' assessments of their external legitimacy (adjusted $R^2 = 0.36$). Tolerance levels for all variables were larger than 0.5, much higher than the commonly accepted cutoff value of 0.1 (O'Brien 2007). Additional key assumptions of normality, linearity, and homoskedasticity were tested, and no violations were detected (Cohen et al. 2003; Osborne and Waters 2002).

Table 9.3 reveals that, similar to the majority of community surveys, the two main antecedents of officers' assessments of their external legitimacy are evaluations of procedural justice and instrumental assessments about police performance (in the eyes of citizens as perceived by our responding police officers). At the same time, and in contrast to most community surveys (both in Israel and elsewhere), in which procedural justice was identified as the most important predictor of police legitimacy, in our model instrumental assessments are the strongest predictor ($\beta = 0.39$). In other words, Israeli police officers associate their legitimacy in the eyes of the public first and foremost with their ability to control crime and create credible deterrence. Their responses suggest that they also recognize the importance of the fairness of their processes; however, procedural justice is less influential than instrumental considerations in predicting external police legitimacy in our model ($\beta = 0.29$). Indeed, the model without instrumental consideration explains only 26% of the variance, compared to 36% in the full model [R^2 change $= 0.10$; F change $(1, 232) = 37.45$; $p < 0.001$], whereas in a model without procedural justice the variance explained drops by only 5% (to 31%) [R^2 change $= 0.05$; F change $(1, 232) = 19.89$; $p < 0.001$].*

We should note that two control variables showed statistically significant effects in our model: primary professional background in the Border Guard (compared to patrol) and being single (compared to married). Although these variables were not the main target of our analysis, in the following discussion we offer preliminary hypotheses about their observed effects.

Discussion

The main finding of our analysis is that Israeli commanding police officers associate their legitimacy in the eyes of the public more with their performance in fighting crime than with the fairness of their processes. These findings must be considered in conjunction with the results of recent community surveys in Israel (Factor, Castilo, and Rattner 2014; Jonathan-Zamir and Weisburd 2013), which, similar to most studies in the Western world,

---

* We also carried out the analysis for students and non-students separately. Because this separation significantly reduced the sample size in each model (students, $N = 137$; nonstudents, $N = 113$), in these analyses we only included the independent variables that showed statistically significant effects in the full model (instrumental considerations, procedural justice, primary service in the Border Guard and being single). The results were similar to the original model: in both sub-groups, instrumental considerations were the most important antecedent of officers' assessments of their external legitimacy, followed by procedural justice. Further, we analyzed the full model with interaction terms (student * procedural justice, student * instrumental considerations), which did not show significant effects. In other words, the effects of procedural justice and instrumental considerations on officers' assessments of their external legitimacy do not vary in our data by whether or not the officer was a student at the time of the survey.

reveal that Israeli citizens have the opposite priorities: they place more weight on procedural justice than on police performance when considering police legitimacy.* In this sense, our findings reveal a noteworthy gap between public priorities on the one hand, and what the police associate with their external legitimacy on the other. Such disparity may naturally lead to disappointment among the general public and to feelings of distance and alienation, which may, in turn, weaken police–community relationships.

Two control variables showed statistically significant effects in our model: primary experience in the Border Guard (compared to patrol) was found to improve assessments of external legitimacy, whereas being single (compared to married) was found to have the opposite effect. With regard to the Border Guard, the main responsibilities of this suborganization include maintaining internal security, countering terrorist threats and attacks, and securing the borderline with the Palestinian territories. Such activities, and particularly publicized successes in thwarting attacks and handling the aftermath of terrorist events, have generated much respect and appreciation for the Israeli police and improved their image among majority communities during periods of high security threats (see Jonathan 2010; Weisburd, Jonathan and Perry 2009). Thus, it is not surprising that officers who spent most of their service in the Border Guard have a more positive view of their public image. The negative effects of being single (compared to married) can be viewed as part of the more general positive influence of marriage on life satisfaction, happiness, and optimism (Gove, Hughes and Style 1983; Holt-Lunstad, Birmingham and Jones 2008; Robins and Reiger 1991), although studies in the policing context have revealed mixed findings (e.g., Brooks and Piquero 1998; Burke and Mikkelsen 2006; Malach-Pines and Keinan 2006). The effects of background characteristics on police officers' assessments of their external- and self-legitimacy clearly warrant focused analyses in future research.

Returning to our main findings, using the lens of the dialogic approach to legitimacy, we can speculate that there are several potential implications to our findings. First, because commanding officers in the INP associate their external legitimacy more with the accomplishment of instrumental goals than with procedural justice, we can expect that they would emphasize this aspect of their work in future claims to legitimacy. As community surveys suggest that this is *not* the area citizens value most, such claims are expected to have only moderate effects on the legitimacy citizens render the police, and, in turn, on the numerous desirable outcomes of police legitimacy such as law obedience, compliance, cooperation, and empowerment (e.g., Mastrofski, Snipes and Supina 1996; Murphy, Hynds and Fleming 2008; Reisig, Bratton and Gertz 2007; Sunshine and Tyler 2003; Tyler 2006; Tyler and Fagan 2008; Tyler and Huo 2002; Tyler and Wakslak 2004).

In addition, although Israeli police officers apparently think citizens place considerable value on traditional crime fighting, their assessment is that these same citizens would only give them the score of 54 in this area (on a 0–100 scale). Not only is this score unflattering, it is lower than the scores the police think the public would assign both legitimacy

---

* The analysis by Jonathan-Zamir and Weisburd (2013) shows that in Sderot, a town under severe security threats, the beta value for procedural justice was 0.49. For police performance in fighting crime, it was 0.35. In the comparison communities, which were not faced with specific security threats, the values were 0.55 and 0.24, respectively. Using path analysis, Factor et al. (2014) report the values of 0.44 for procedural justice and 0.19 for police performance as predictors of police legitimacy. These results remained consistent when differentiating between the views of Jews and Arabs—for Jews, the coefficients were 0.42 for procedural justice and 0.19 for police performance; for Arabs, they were 0.49 and 0.17, respectively. All effects were statistically significant.

and procedural justice. The belief that citizens do not think very highly of police accomplishments in fighting crime and deterring offenders, but, at the same time, care very much about crime control, is expected to weaken officers' self-legitimacy, and, in turn, the strength of their future claims to legitimacy. As noted earlier, the dialogic approach postulates that it is difficult to claim legitimacy and gain public support if the officers' own sense of legitimacy is diminished.

Our findings and their implications should also be considered in the specific context of Israeli policing. Several studies have identified a sharp and persistent drop in public trust in the Israeli police between 2002 and 2008, particularly among the majority Jewish adult population (see Hermann, Atmor, Heller and Lebel 2012; Jonathan 2010; Perry and Jonathan-Zamir 2014; Rattner 2009; Yogev 2010). Data reported by the Israel Democracy Institute in 2009 indicates that out of 24 democratic countries, the police in Israel received the fifth-lowest trust evaluations (Arian, Philippov and Knafelman 2009). More recent data from Round 5 of the European Social Survey again shows that the INP is evaluated negatively compared to other European countries (third/fourth lowest) in the areas of police effectiveness, procedural fairness, and distributive fairness (although obligation to obey the police and the law are relatively high; see Jackson, Tyler, Hough, Bradford and Mentovich 2014). Indeed, our respondents have estimated that Israeli citizens do not think very highly of the police in the three areas examined in this study, and in this sense show relatively accurate understanding of public evaluations.

At the same time, and although community surveys in Israel identified a moderate improvement in public assessments since 2009, the long downward trend has troubled high-ranking Israeli police officials, particularly given considerable accomplishments in clearing cases, lowering crime levels, and improving traffic safety during this period (see reviews by Jonathan 2010; Perry and Jonathan-Zamir 2014). Our results help shed light on this confusion and suggest that the disparity between public preferences on the one hand, and police understanding of what citizens consider and value in relation to police legitimacy on the other, may have contributed to the long drop in public support.

More generally, our findings are in line with the literature on traditional police culture, according to which police tend to see themselves predominantly as crime fighters and idealize aggressive enforcement policing, presumably as a way to deal with the ambiguity inherent in their work and gain the support of their supervisors (Cain 1973; Holdaway 1983; Paoline 2003; Smith and Gray 1985). Although the idea of an orthodox, homogeneous police culture has been questioned (e.g., Paoline, Myers and Worden 2000), we would not be surprised if future studies find similar views in other police agencies in the Western world (Loftus 2010). Nevertheless, these findings are particularly explicable in light of the unique characteristics of the INP, which is considered a highly militarized, centralized police agency, where the "professional" or "quasi-military" model of policing continues to dominate (Ben-Porat 1988; Gimshi 2007; Herzog 2001; Hovav and Amir 1979; Shadmi and Hod 1996; Weisburd, Jonathan and Perry 2009; Weisburd, Shalev and Amir 2002).

Although our findings bear important implications for Israeli policing, there are clearly contextual complexities that were not addressed in our analysis. For example, Israeli society is not homogeneous and can be viewed as made up of at least three main sectors: Jewish majority, Ultra-Orthodox Jews ("Haredim"), and Israeli Arabs. It is reasonable to assume that when asked to evaluate the views of the "average Israeli citizen," our respondents did not consider minority groups. We should note that recent research in Israel finds surprising similarities in the expectations of Jews and Israeli Arabs from the police (Hasisi and Weisburd 2014; Hasisi and Weitzer 2007). At the same time, future studies are encouraged to distinguish between different sectors of society when asking officers to evaluate their public image. It is also important to consider such views over time and in relation to political/social/economic shifts in power, which may influence the "audience" the police are most responsive to. Additional factors such as crime rates in the officer's area of service or his/her views about human nature and the exercise of coercive powers (see Muir 1977), could also help shed light on police evaluations of their external legitimacy.

As a final point, it is important to consider the broader implications of this study for the "dialogic approach to legitimacy" and legitimacy research more generally. This study highlights the authorities' interpretation stage in the legitimacy dialogue, which was only implicit in the framework articulated by Bottoms and Tankebe (2012). This stage naturally mediates between public feedback and its effects on power holders' self-legitimacy, and clearly warrants focused attention. This study also begins to identify and investigate particular aspects of the public's response to authorities' legitimacy claims, by focusing specifically on what matters to citizens when judging police legitimacy. Future studies are encouraged to continue to tease out the specific components of this feedback by addressing questions such as which parts of the authority's claims for legitimacy are accepted/rejected by the public and why.

With regard to legitimacy research more generally, surprisingly—and despite the fact that officers' views and understandings are critical for real-world policing—studies in this area have mostly addressed what citizens think. The dialogic approach to legitimacy clarifies why the views of the police cannot be ignored, and how legitimacy is formed not only in the hearts and minds of citizens, but in an ongoing interaction between the police and the public. But the next step is to empirically examine the specifics of this process. What do the police do to "claim legitimacy," and how do citizens understand and respond to such claims? What are the processes by which the police interpret the public's response, and by which mechanisms does this response impact officers' self-legitimacy? What is the nature of the relationship between the legitimacy citizens render the police and officers' self-legitimacy? In this context, it is important to keep in mind and address in future research that police officers' self-legitimacy may well be influenced by factors other than perceptions of external legitimacy, such as the formal/legal basis of their actions. Nevertheless, studying legitimacy over time as an interaction between power holders and the public has been highlighted as an important avenue for future procedural justice research (Bottoms and Tankebe 2012; Jackson, Tyler, Hough, Bradford and Mentovich 2014).

Conclusions

In this chapter we have taken the first step in exploring one particular process that takes place in the legitimacy dialogue: the understanding police form about the sources of their legitimacy in the eyes of the public. We found that in contrast to public priorities as expressed in community surveys, Israeli commanding police officers associate their external legitimacy more with accomplishments in fighting crime, bringing rule breakers to justice, and deterring potential offenders than with the fairness of the processes by which they exercise their authority. Given the dominance of crime fighting and aggressive law enforcement in classic police culture and ethos of modern policing, we suspect that our findings are not unique to Israel. Nevertheless, we are clearly not suggesting that they represent the views of police officers in other agencies or nations, and thus a major question at this juncture is what police officers in other places think. If our findings are indeed replicated in other settings, this would likely have important implications for legitimacy policing, as it would suggest that the principles of procedural justice and the value-based approach to criminal justice more generally hardly go hand in hand with popular police views, which makes the implementation of this policing style all the more challenging. Whatever the case may be, it is clearly time for researchers to broaden the study of legitimacy to the police and gain a more comprehensive understanding of the two parties participating in the legitimacy dialog.

Acknowledgments

This work was supported by a grant from British Friends of the Hebrew University to the Jerusalem Forum on Criminal Justice. The authors thank Stephen Mastrofski, David Weisburd, Justice Tankebe, and Shomron Moyal who commented on an earlier version of this paper. We also thank Maor Shay, who assisted in the data analysis.

Appendix I. Control Variables

Variable	Distribution
Years of service in the Israel National Police (INP)	$M = 14.4$; range = 3–30; $SD = 6.4$; $N = 279$
Main professional background in the INP	Patrol—30.7% (reference category)
	Investigations—22.8%
	Intelligence—14.8%
	Border Guard—13.4%
	Traffic—4.1%
	Community and Civil Guard—3.8%
	Other—7.9%
	$N = 283$
Student at time of survey?	No—49% (reference category)
	$N = 290$
Sex	Male—83.8% (reference category)
	$N = 273$
Family status	Married—74.5% (reference category)
	Single—13.4%
	Divorced—4.5%
	Living with a spouse—4.1%
	$N = 280$
Country of origin	Israel—89.7% (reference category)
	Other—6.2%
	$N = 278$
Ethnicity	Jewish—91% (reference category)
	Druze—5.2%
	Muslim—1%
	$N = 282$

Appendix II. Correlation Matrix (Pearson's *R*)

	1	2	3	4	5	6	7
1. Legitimacy	1	–	–	–	–	–	–
2. Instrumental judgments	0.55***	1	–	–	–	–	–
3. Procedural justice	0.50***	0.55***	1	–	–	–	–
4. Years of service	−0.01	−0.06	0.05	1	–	–	–
5. Student	0.03	0.08	−0.10	0.27***	1	–	–
6. Female	−0.02	−0.08	−0.04	−0.03	−0.13*	1	–
7. Born abroad	−0.03	−0.01	0.01	−0.06	0.14*	0.08	1

*$p < 0.05$; ***$p < 0.001$.

References

Arian, A., M. Philippov and A. Knafelman. 2009. *Auditing Israeli democracy, 2009: Twenty years of immigration from the Soviet Union.* Jerusalem: The Israel Democracy Institute. http://www.idi.org.il/PublicationsCatalog/Documents/BOOK_7104/Madad_2009_hebrew.pdf (accessed October 31, 2014) [In Hebrew].

Barker, R. 2001. *Legitimating identities: The self-presentation of rulers and subjects.* Cambridge, UK: Cambridge University Press.

Ben-Porat, Y. 1988. *A barrier to chaos—Decisive years in the history of the Israeli police.* Israel: Ministry of Defense (In Hebrew).

Bottoms, A. and J. Tankebe. 2012. Beyond procedural justice: A dialogic approach to legitimacy in criminal justice. *The Journal of Criminal Law and Criminology* 102: 119–170.

Boulding, K.E. 1967. The legitimacy of economics. *Economic Inquiry* 5: 299–307.

Brockner, J., G. Ackerman, J. Greenberg et al. 2001. Culture and procedural justice: The influence of power distance on reactions to voice. *Journal of Experimental Social Psychology* 37:300–315.

Brooks, L.W. and N.L. Piquero. 1998. Police stress: Does department size matter? *Policing: An International Journal of Police Strategies and Management* 21: 600–617.

Burke, R.J. and A. Mikkelsen. 2006. Burnout among Norwegian police officers: Potential antecedents and consequences. *International Journal of Stress Management* 13: 64–83.

Cain, M.E. 1973. *Society and the policeman's role.* London: Routledge.

Cohen, J., P. Cohen, G. Stephen, G. West and L.S. Aiken. 2003. *Applied multiple regression/correlation analysis for the behavioral sciences.* Mahwah, NJ: Lawrence Erlbaum Associates.

Factor, R., J. Castilo and A. Rattner. 2014. Procedural justice, minorities and religiosity. *Police Practice and Research: An International Journal, special issue: Trends in Israeli Policing: Terrorism, Community, Victimization and Crime Control.* 15(2): 130–142.

Gau, J. 2011. The convergent and discriminant validity of procedural justice and police legitimacy: An empirical test of core theoretical propositions. *Journal of Criminal Justice* 39: 489–498.

Gimshi, D. 2007. *Criminal justice system—Law enforcement in a democratic state.* Rishon Lezion: Peles Publishing (In Hebrew).

Gove, W.R., M. Hughes and C.B. Style. 1983. Does marriage have positive effects on the psychological well-being of the individual? *Journal of Health and Social Behavior* 24: 122–131.

Hasisi, B. and D. Weisburd. 2014. Policing terrorism and police–community relations: Views of the Arab minority in Israel. *Police Practice and Research: An International Journal, Special Issue: Trends in Israeli Policing: Terrorism, Community, Victimization and Crime Control.* 15(2): 158–172.

Hasisi, B. and R. Weitzer. 2007. Police relations with Arabs and Jews in Israel. *British Journal of Criminology* 47:728–745.

Hermann, T., N. Atmor, E. Heller and Y. Lebel. 2012. *The Israeli democracy index 2012*. Jerusalem: The Israel Democracy Institute (In Hebrew).

Herzog, S. 2001. Militarization and demilitarization processes in the Israeli and American police forces: Organizational and social aspects. *Policing and Society* 11: 181–208.

Hinds, L. and K. Murphy. 2007. Public satisfaction with police: Using procedural justice to improve police legitimacy. *Australian and New Zealand Journal of Criminology* 40: 27–42.

Holdaway, S. 1983. *Inside the British police: A force at work*. Oxford, UK: Blackwell.

Holt-Lunstad, J., W. Birmingham and B.Q. Jones. 2008. Is there something unique about marriage? The relative impact of marital status, relationship quality, and network social support on ambulatory blood pressure and mental health. *Annals of Behavioral Medicine* 35: 239–244.

Hovav, M. and M. Amir. 1979. Israel police: History and analysis. *Police Studies: The International Review of Police Development* 2: 5–31.

Jackson, J. and J. Sunshine. 2007. Public confidence in policing: A Neo-Durkheimian perspective. *The British Journal of Criminology* 47: 214–233.

Jackson, J., T. Tyler, M. Hough, B. Bradford and A. Mentovich. 2014. Compliance and legal authority. *The international encyclopedia of the social and behavioral sciences*. London: Elsevier.

Jonathan, T. 2010. Police involvement in counterterrorism and public attitudes towards the police in Israel: 1998–2007. *The British Journal of Criminology* 50: 748–771.

Jonathan-Zamir, T. and D. Weisburd. 2013. The effects of security threats on antecedents of police legitimacy: Findings from a quasi-experiment in Israel. *Journal of Research in Crime and Delinquency* 50: 3–32.

Jonathan-Zamir, T., S.D. Mastrofski and S. Moyal. Forthcoming. Measuring procedural justice in police–citizen encounters. *Justice Quarterly*. doi: 10.1080/07418825.2013.845677.

Kelling, G.L. and M.H. Moore. 1988. The evolving strategy of policing. *Perspectives on Policing* 4: 1–16.

Kelman, H.C. and V.L. Hamilton. 1989. *Crimes of obedience: Toward a social psychology of authority and responsibility*. New Haven, CT: Yale University Press.

Kochel, T., R.B. Parks and S.D. Mastrofski. 2013. Examining police effectiveness as a precursor to legitimacy and cooperation with police. *Justice Quarterly* 30: 895–925.

LaFree, G. 1998. *Losing legitimacy: Street crime and the decline of institutions in America*. Boulder, CO: Westview Press.

Loftus, B. 2010. Police occupational culture: Classic themes, altered times. *Policing and Society* 20:1–20.

MacCoun, R.J. 1993. Drugs and the law: A psychological analysis of drug prohibition. *Psychological Bulletin* 113: 497–512.

MacKenzie, D.L. 2002. Reducing the criminal activities of known offenders and delinquents: Crime prevention in the courts and corrections. In *Evidence-based crime prevention*, eds. L.W Sherman, D.P. Farrington, B.C. Walsh and D.L. Mackenzie, 330–404. London: Routledge.

Malach-Pines, A. and G. Keinan. 2006. Stress and burnout in Israeli border police. *International Journal of Stress Management* 13: 519–540.

Mastrofski, S.D., J.B. Snipes and A.E. Supina. 1996. Compliance on demand: The public's response to specific police requests. *Journal of Research in Crime and Delinquency* 33: 269–305.

Meniv, O. 2013. Streets of fear. *Ma'ariv*, February 1. http://www.nrg.co.il/online/54/ART2/432/927 .html (In Hebrew).

Muir, W.K. 1977. *Police: Street corner politicians*. Chicago: University of Chicago Press.

Murphy, K., L. Hynds and J. Fleming. 2008. Encouraging public cooperation and support for police. *Policing and Society* 18: 36–55.

Nagin, D. 2013. Deterrence in the twenty-first century: A review of the evidence. *Crime and Justice Annual Review*. 42(1): 199–263.

National Research Council. 2004. *Fairness and effectiveness in policing: The evidence*. Committee to review research on police policy and practices, eds. W. Skogan and K. Frydl, Committee on Law and Justice, Division of Behavioral and Social Sciences and Education. Washington, DC: The National Academies Press.

O'Brien, R.M. 2007. A caution regarding rules of thumb for variance inflation factors. *Quality & Quantity* 41: 673–690.

Osborne, J. and E. Waters. 2002. Four assumptions of multiple regression that researchers should always test. *Practical Assessment, Research & Evaluation* 8: 1–9.

Paoline, E.A. 2003. Taking stock: Toward a richer understanding of police culture. *Journal of Criminal Justice* 31:99–214.

Paoline, E.A., S. Myers and R. Worden. 2000. Police culture, individualism, and community policing: Evidence from two police departments. *Justice Quarterly* 17: 575–605.

Paternoster, R. 1987. The deterrent effect of the perceived certainty and severity of punishment: A review of the evidence and issues. *Justice Quarterly* 4: 173–217.

Paternoster, R. 1989. Decisions to participate in and desist from four types of common delinquency: Deterrence and the rational choice perspective. *Law & Society Review* 23: 7–40.

Paternoster, R., R. Brame, R. Bachman and L.W. Sherman. 1997. Do fair procedures matter? The effect of procedural justice on spouse assault. *Law and Society Review* 31: 163–204.

Perry, S. and T. Jonathan-Zamir. 2014. Lessons from empirical research on policing in Israel: Policing terrorism and police-community relationships. *Police Practice and Research: An International Journal*, 15(2): 173–187.

Rattner, A. 2009. *Legal culture: The reflection of the law and justice system in the Israeli society mirror, longitudinal study from 2000 to 2009.* Jerusalem: Sasa Center for Strategic Studies. Hebrew University of Jerusalem (In Hebrew).

Raz, J. 2009. *Between authority and interpretation.* Oxford, UK: Oxford University Press.

Reisig, M.D., J. Bratton and M.G Gertz. 2007. The construct validity and refinement of process-based policing measures. *Criminal Justice and Behavior* 34: 1005–1028.

Robins, L. and D. Reiger. 1991. *Psychiatric disorders in America.* New York: Free Press.

Sampson, R.J. and D.J. Bartusch. 1998. Legal cynicism and (subcultural?) tolerance of deviance: The neighborhood context of racial differences. *Law and Society Review* 32: 777–804.

Shadmi, A. and E. Hod. 1996. *The history of the Israel National Police, vol. A: 1948–1958 (the establishment phase).* Jerusalem, Israel: The Israel National Police (In Hebrew).

Smith, D.J. and J. Gray. 1985. *Police and people in London: The PSI report.* London: Policy Studies Institute.

Sunshine, J. and T.R. Tyler. 2003. The role of procedural justice and legitimacy in shaping public support for policing. *Law and Society Review* 37: 513–548.

Tankebe, J. 2009. Public cooperation with the police in Ghana: Does procedural fairness matter? *Criminology* 47: 1265–1293.

Tankebe, J. 2010. Identifying the correlates of police organizational commitment in Ghana. *Police Quarterly* 13: 73–91.

Tyler, T.R. 2001. Public trust and confidence in legal authorities: What do majority and minority group members want from legal authorities? *Behavioral Sciences and the Law* 19: 215–235.

Tyler, T.R. 2004. Enhancing police legitimacy. *The Annals of the American Academy of Political and Social Science* 593: 84–99.

Tyler, T.R. 2006. *Why people obey to the law.* Princetown, NJ: Princeton University Press.

Tyler, T.R. 2009. Legitimacy and criminal justice: The benefits of self-regulation. *Ohio State Journal of Criminal Law* 7: 307–359.

Tyler, T.R. 2011. Trust and legitimacy: Policing in the USA and Europe. *European Journal of Criminology* 8: 254–266.

Tyler, T.R. and J. Fagan. 2008. Legitimacy and cooperation: Why do people help the police fight crime in their communities? *Ohio State Journal of Criminal Law* 6: 231–275.

Tyler, T.R. and Y.J. Huo. 2002. *Trust in the law: Encouraging public cooperation with the police and courts.* New York: Russell-Sage Foundation.

Tyler, T.R. and C.J. Wakslak. 2004. Profiling and police legitimacy: Procedural justice, attributions of motive and acceptance of police authority. *Criminology* 42: 253–282.

Tyler, T.R., S. Schulhofer and A. Huq. 2010. Legitimacy and deterrence effects in counterterrorism policing: A study of Muslim Americans. *Law and Society Review* 44: 365–401.

Weber, M. 1978. *Economy and society: An outline of interpretive sociology.* Oakland, CA: University of California Press.

Weisburd, D. and S. Amram. 2014. The law of concentrations of crime at place: The case of Tel Aviv-Jaffa. *Police Practice and Research: An International Journal, special issue: Trends in Israeli Policing: Terrorism, Community, Victimization and Crime Control.* 15(2): 101–114.

Weisburd, D., O. Shalev and M. Amir. 2002. Community policing in Israel: Resistance and change. *Policing: An International Journal of Police Strategies & Management* 25: 80–109.

Weisburd, D., T. Jonathan and S. Perry. 2009. The Israeli model for policing terrorism: Goals, strategies, and open questions. *Criminal Justice and Behavior* 36: 1259–1278.

Wrong, D.H. 1979. *Power: Its forms, bases and uses.* London: Transaction.

Yogev, D. 2010. Public attitudes towards the Israel police. *Mahshov.* The Chief Scientist, Ministry of Public Security Jerusalem (In Hebrew).

Policing Terrorism III

Terrorist Threats and Police Performance

A Study of Israeli Communities*

10

DAVID WEISBURD
BADI HASISI
TAL JONATHAN-ZAMIR
GALI AVIV

Contents

Police forces in Western democracies have begun to see the problem of terrorism as an important part of the police function (Bayley and Weisburd 2009; International Association of Chiefs of Police 2005; National Research Council 2004; Weisburd, Jonathan, and Perry 2009). For local police agencies in some nations, this is a new problem, brought on by the recent threats of large-scale international terrorism. This is the case most dramatically in the United States, where the terrorist attacks of September 11, 2001, brought a sudden realization of the threat of global terrorism to American cities (IACP 2005; National Research Council 2004). However, for some nations such as the United Kingdom and Israel, prevention and response to terrorist threats have formed an important part of the police function for much longer (Matassa and Newburn 2003; Mulcahy 2005; Hasisi and Weisburd 2014). But even in countries that have faced terrorist threats for decades, there has been an assumption that a new "global war against terrorism" has demanded change and innovation in policing (Bamford 2004; Howard 2004; Lewis 2004).

* Reproduced from Weisburd, D., B. Hasisi, T. Jonathan, and G. Aviv. 2010. Terrorism threats and police performance: A study of Israeli communities. *The British Journal of Criminology* 50(4): 725–747, by permission of Oxford University Press.

Following this assumption, scholars and practitioners have begun to consider how the police task changes when terrorism is added to the list of concerns that local police must address (Fishman 2005; IACP 2005; Innes 2006; Kelling and Bratton 2006; Weisburd, Feucht, Hakimi, Mock, and Perry 2009; Weisburd, Jonathan, and Perry 2009). Some scholars have argued that heightened terrorism threats will naturally lead to dramatic changes in the orientation and strategies of policing. Over the past few decades, police in Western democracies have become much more concerned with local community problems. Some have termed this type of policing as "low policing," emphasizing its concentration on how the police can deal with crime, disorder, and fear in local communities (Bayley and Weisburd 2009; Brodeur 1983, 2003).

Terrorist threats are often seen as raising a strong challenge to this model of policing. Terrorism focuses police attention on "strategic" challenges that are more of a threat to the overall regime than to the communities that are directly affected. Policing strategic concerns such as terrorism is often characterized as "high policing," and police in most Western societies have emphasized response to strategic threats at one time or another (Bordua 1968; Brodeur 1983; Chapman 1970; Manning 1977). The primary tactics of the "high policing" of terrorism are covert surveillance, intelligence collection, and the clandestine disruption of terrorist plots. Bayley and Weisburd (2009) argue that "(h)igh policing differs sharply from the standard practices of normal policing because they are less transparent, less accountable, less careful with respect to human rights, and focus attention away from controlling the kinds of crime and disorder that affect the lives of individuals on a daily basis."

Although there has been much speculation about the effects of terrorism on policing in democratic societies, there has been little actual data brought to bear on how terrorist threats affect everyday policing activities. In this chapter, we provide the first systematic quantitative examination of the effects of terrorist threats on traditional police efforts to respond to crime and disorder. Our specific interest is in the impacts of terrorist threats on the ability of police to solve cases. "Solved" or "cleared" cases is a common measure of police performance, and has been examined in a large number of studies across a number of different countries (e.g., Alpert and Moore 1993; Bayley 1994; Mesch and Talmud 1998; Paré, Felson, and Quimet 2007; Reiner 1998). To examine the effect of terrorist threats on cleared cases, we take advantage of the unusually high terrorist threats in Israeli communities during the Second Intifada in Israel between 2000 and 2004. Importantly, as we illustrate in the following discussion, these threats varied considerably from community to community, and this provides perhaps a unique opportunity to examine how variations in terrorism threat levels impact on police performance in solving crimes.

We begin with a discussion of the potential impacts of terrorist threats on police performance more generally and the solving of crimes in particular. In this context, we also raise the question of whether the impacts of terrorism on police performance might be expected to differ in majority and minority communities. We are particularly concerned with the case of communities that have ethnic, religious, or national associations with groups that are associated with terrorism. We then turn to a discussion of cleared cases as a measure of police performance, and describe the Israeli context of our study and the measures we developed to assess terrorist threats. We find that the effects of terrorism vary by the type of community that is affected. Terrorist threats in primarily Jewish communities lead to lower clearance rates. In contrast, in majority Arab communities in Israel, clearance rates increase as terrorist threats increase. In our discussion, we speculate on the reasons for the differing effects, suggesting that the shift to a high policing focus changes the nature of police activities in different types of communities.

Impact of Terrorism on Police Performance

Does police attention to terrorism impact on the ability of local police agencies to address crime and disorder? Or is the policing of terrorism just another obligation of the police that can be carried out in tandem with traditional policing responsibilities? Indeed, there is some evidence that the policing of terrorism can lead to more effective prevention of crime. In an Israeli study of the impacts of closures and other antiterrorism efforts during the Second Intifada, Herzog (2003) found that vehicle thefts in Israel declined significantly. In this case, and perhaps others, heightened surveillance regarding terrorism and related efforts to restrain movements of terrorists can lead to crime control gains.

Such unintended consequences of crime prevention activities are not exceptional. For example, in a program that sought to reduce prostitution in an area in North London, Matthews (1990) found not only a decline in prostitution and cruising, but also reductions in a range of serious crimes, such as burglary and auto thefts. This "diffusion of benefits" (Clarke and Weisburd 1994) has been identified in numerous studies examining crime prevention programs (see review by Clarke 2005). More generally, increased surveillance of police in specific areas as a means of preventing terrorism might be expected to deter other crime and disorder problems. Such heightened surveillance might also be expected to increase the ability of police to identify and capture suspects, thus increasing the performance of the police in solving conventional crimes.

But there are many reasons to suspect that terrorist threats might impair the ability of the police to respond to crime problems. As we noted above, policing terrorism is likely to lead to an approach to policing that follows a "high policing" model. This model can change the orientation of policing from "service" to "suspicion" and is likely to lead to a change in the relationship of the police to the communities that they serve (Bayley and Weisburd 2009; Hasisi, Alpert, and Flynn 2009). This change, in turn, might impact on the ability of the police to gain information about crime from the community, and thus might hinder their efforts to prevent or solve crimes.

It might also be the case that the addition of terrorism to the list of police responsibilities will divert the police away from more traditional crime and disorder functions. Policing is often a "zero sum game." Police agency budgets are not necessarily increased when the police are given new responsibilities. In such cases, we might expect that the police will simply have fewer resources to devote to the prevention and solving of crimes, and thus police performance in these areas will decline. Hasisi, Alpert, and Flynn (2009) have noted that as the police devote more and more time and effort to perfecting counterterrorism strategies and tactics, they tend to spend less time on problem solving and relationship building in the community. In this sense, terrorist threats may divert attention from more mundane everyday police activities.

Moreover, given the priority of terrorist threats when they are present, it would seem reasonable to assume that antiterrorism functions would have precedence over many traditional policing activities. In the Montgomery County sniper case in the United States that placed the police on high alert for weeks, the Montgomery County police department temporarily shut down many policing units in order to focus on the critical terrorist threat that was faced. This included the policing not only of less serious crimes such as burglaries, but also the rape response unit (University of Maryland Symposium 2003*). Terrorist threats are deeply felt by communities, and when terrorism is present, there is great pressure on the police to solve this community problem. As one police manager in Montgomery County responded when asked whether the sniper incident had led to the reduction of community policing functions: "We were doing community policing, because focusing on the sniper threat is what the community wanted us to do."

Bayley and Weisburd (2009) also point to the attractiveness of "high policing" in contrast to traditional crime control or "low policing" obligations. Antiterrorism and homeland security activities appear to have particular salience and status for police. When community policing was promoted in the 1980s and 1990s, police resisted taking on its community-engaged and servicing functions, preferring to rely on higher status preventive patrolling and criminal investigation (Braga and Weisburd 2006; Weisburd and McElroy 1988; Weisburd, Shalev, and Amir 2002). Similarly, Bayley and Weisburd (2009) argue that there will be a tendency for the police to prefer homeland security-related "high policing" over traditional low policing functions. This same tension was noted by Skolnick (1993) in regard to the "war on drugs" and the subsequent tendency of police to pursue drug-related arrests.

Our discussion so far suggests that the relationship between terrorist threats and police performance in solving crimes is complex. Although there is good reason to suspect that police attention to terrorism will take away from their concern with local crime and disorder problems, heightened surveillance as part of counterterrorism strategies might unintentionally lead to preventing and solving crimes.

The picture becomes even more complex when we consider possible differences in the impacts of terrorism on majority and minority communities. If, for example, minority communities have ethnic, religious, or national ties to groups from which terrorism emerges, the police may consider those communities as high risk and may increase surveillance and control (Hasisi, Alpert, and Flynn 2009; Hasisi and Weisburd 2014). Such surveillance and control, moreover, might not be seen by such communities as representing an improvement in the quality of local policing. Indeed, such increases in police activities in minority communities have often been viewed by the communities themselves as a case of their being unfairly profiled by the police as "the enemy within" (Henderson, Ortiz, Sugie, and Miller 2006; Innes 2006; Khashu, Busch, Latif, and Levy 2005; Thacher 2005).

The police, in this context, may have contradictory goals and programs directed at these minority groups. In the United Kingdom, for example, there has been a growing effort to develop intelligence and surveillance of Muslim minorities, especially given the involvement of radical local groups in terrorist events (Innes 2006). At the same time, the police initiated innovative programs to educate the public and prevent violence against Muslim communities after specific terrorist attacks (Henderson, Ortiz, Sugie, and Miller 2006; Innes 2006; Thacher 2005). Whatever the specific response of police agencies in different countries, it is likely that the police will emphasize high policing activities of

---

* This symposium of police executives from the Washington, DC, tri-state area took place at the University of Maryland, College Park, on May 9, 2003, and was organized by the Department of Criminology and Criminal Justice, Police Research Group.

surveillance and intelligence gathering in local communities that are seen as linked in some way to terrorist threats.

Again, the emphasis on surveillance and intelligence gathering might lead to greater effectiveness in preventing and solving crimes. However, the use of high policing tactics may at the same time lead to an alienation of the police from the public, and thus cut the police off from critical information on crime and disorder in local communities. Previous research has shown that community cooperation is a key factor in successful crime investigations (Sampson, Raudenbush, and Earls 1997). Accordingly, here—as in majority communities—without systematic data it is difficult to come to a clear conclusion regarding how terrorist threats will affect police performance.

Clearance Rates and Police Performance

The ability of police to solve crime is often assessed by measuring the rate of "cleared" or "solved" cases (Alpert and Moore 1993; Bayley 1994; Mesch and Talmud 1998; Paré, Felson, and Quimet 2007; Reiner 1998). Crime clearance is calculated on the basis of crimes rather than offenders. For example, if five offenders are involved in a violent assault toward one victim and are all arrested and charged, then this is counted as one case cleared. Alternatively, if only one of the five is identified and charged while the other four remain unidentified and go free, this also counts as one case cleared. The clearance rate is generally measured by the number of cleared cases divided by the total number of cases opened by the police for a specific period. Clearance rates measure the extent to which the police are able to link suspects to the crimes that are investigated by the police.

Clearance rates are generally viewed as providing more objective and reliable measurement of police performance than alternative indicators, such as crime rates, arrest rates, public attitudes toward the police, and fear of crime (Davenport 1999; Paré, Felson, and Quimet 2007; Reiner 1998). Crime rates summarize all cases opened by the police and are generally seen as a better indicator of "police workload" than "police performance." Although some recent police innovations such as Compstat have used changes in crime rates as an indicator of police performance (Weisburd, Mastrofski, McNally, Greenspan, and Willis 2003), it is generally recognized that crime rates are affected by many social and economic factors outside of the control of the police (Maguire and Uchida 2000; Mastrofski 1999).

Arrest rates provide a more direct measure of police performance and have been used by several scholars to determine police performance (Black 1971; Sherman and Smith 1992; Smith and Visher 1981). Nonetheless, a simple accounting of arrest rates is likely to be strongly influenced by the number of reported crimes. Higher crime areas may have more arrests in this context, irrespective of the "quality" of police performance. In turn, because single police investigations may lead to one or multiple arrests, arrests as a measure of police performance is confounded by the nature of the crimes investigated. Numerous problems have also been identified with using public perception of the police and fear of crime as an indication of police performance. Naturally, public attitudes are subjective and do not always reflect the "real" picture of police performance. They may, for example, be highly influenced by biased media coverage (Leishman and Mason 2003).

Clearance rates have an advantage of focusing directly on the activities of the police. Because clearance rates take the ratio of the number of crimes solved to the number of crimes reported, it accounts for the differing rates of crime in different jurisdictions. Also, its focus on "crimes" rather than arrests means that it is linked directly to police investigations rather than specific offenders. At the same time, although clearance rates have many advantages over other indicators of police performance, a number of scholars have raised questions about the reliability and validity of clearance rates (e.g., Bayley 1993; Brodeur 1998; Hoover 1996; Loveday 1999; Maguire 1997; Reiner 1992, 1998).

One problem relates to the difficulty of comparing clearance rates across police agencies. There are often significant differences between jurisdictions in how clearance rates are defined, thus making it difficult to make comparative statements about police performance across jurisdictions. For example, a crime may be defined as cleared if a suspect is charged, if a suspect is arrested even if there is no charge, or if a likely suspect is identified but no charge or arrest is made. In this context, clearance rates provide a problematic measure of police performance across police agencies.

However, problems have also been noted in using clearance rates within single jurisdictions. The fact that clearance rates are often used by police agencies as a measure of police performance places significant pressure on commanders in specific geographic areas to increase their clearance rates. Not surprisingly, a number of scholars have pointed to manipulation of clearance rates in police agencies by recording offenses in a way that flatters police performance (see Cordner 1989; Gill 1987; Loveday 1999; Maguire 1997; Reiner 1992, 1998; Walker 1992). In this regard, some scholars have distinguished what they define as *primary* versus *secondary* clearance by the police (Bayley 1994; Black 1972; Loveday 2000). Primary clearance refers to a direct police field activity, whereas secondary clearance refers to an arrested suspect who helps the police to clear old offenses, not necessarily those he or she is currently charged for. Skolnick (1966) noted almost half a century ago that the police could easily manipulate clearance rates by offering reductions in present charged offenses in exchange for help in clearing other cases.

Despite these limitations, clearance rates remain one of the most commonly used measures for assessing police performance (Paré, Felson, and Quimet 2007). It is a particularly reliable measure when a large number of police jurisdictions following similar procedures, and under a single command structure are compared, as is the case in the analyses below.

The Study

Our study focuses on Israeli communities during the so-called Second Intifada between 2000 and 2004. Although Israel has, for many years, experienced relatively high threats of terrorism, this period was distinguished by the largest number of attacks and civilian casualties since the State's founding in 1948. More than 160 terrorist events were recorded during this period, with more than 4000 casualties and almost 600 deaths. Unlike the United States, where one very large terrorist attack has dominated public perceptions of terrorism, during the Second Intifada terrorism was almost a daily occurrence in Israeli communities.

We examine 257 Israeli communities within the "Green Line" or Israel's border before the 1967 Israeli Arab War. The 257 communities represent the universe of Israeli cities and towns with more than 1000 residents. We chose not to examine jurisdictions smaller than this because we thought that the number of crimes found would likely be too low to allow for robust analysis of clearance rates. We examine only communities within the "Green

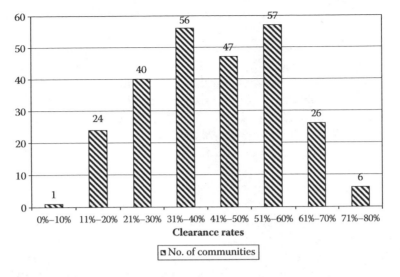

Figure 10.1 Clearance rates in Israeli communities.

Line" because the Israeli National Police (INP) have sole jurisdiction for matters of crime and homeland security in these areas. Data on clearance rates in every city/town in Israel for the years 2000–2004 were obtained from the INP. A case is defined as cleared when, by the end of the investigation, at least one suspect was identified as responsible for the crime committed.

Offenses included in police reporting of clearance rates in Israel reflect traditional crime and disorder categories, such as property crimes, sexual offenses, drug offenses, and violent crimes.* However, it is important to note that security-related offenses within the Green Line are classified according to traditional crime categories and are not specifically identified. Accordingly, an arrest of suspects involved in a terrorist attack would be likely to lead to a charge for a traditional violent crime offense. Although such events are very rare relative to the incidence of more traditional crimes and thus unlikely to impact on the overall number of crime incidents, it may be that certain types of incidents, such as those generated as a result of arrests during violent protests, would have a more meaningful effect on the statistics we examine. In our discussion, we consider in more detail the potential implications of these security-related offenses for our findings.

Figure 10.1 shows a histogram of clearance rates across the 257 communities that were studied. As is apparent, clearance rates vary considerably with a few communities having clearance rates below 20%, and some having clearance rates as high as 71–81%. Not surprisingly, the communities with unusually low clearance rates have very high proportions of reported property crime, whereas communities with very high clearance rates have few property crimes proportionally and high numbers of violent crimes.† In Israel, only 13% of property crimes are solved, whereas the clearance rate is 78% for violent crimes (see Annual Reports of the Israeli Police; for similar findings in the United States, see Cordner

---

* For a complete list of specific crimes included, see the Israeli Police Annual Reports, available from http://www.police.gov.il/meida_laezrach/pirsomim/Pages/statistika.aspx.
† For example, in the two communities with the lowest clearance rates, Michmoret and Kfar-Vitkin, property crimes make up more than 80% of all reported crimes to the police. In the two highest clearance rate communities, Bsama and Ajar, property crimes make up less than 20% of the total opened cases.

1989). The mean clearance rate across the communities is 43%, which is very close to the median reported.

The key question in our study is how threats of terrorism impact on clearance rates in local communities. We began with the assumption that the key factor in this regard was not the direct impact of terrorist threats on communities but the impact that such threats would have on police jurisdictions with responsibilities for those communities. The INP within the Green Line is divided into five large police districts: Northern, Tel Aviv, Central, Jerusalem, and Southern. Each District ("Machoz") is again divided into two to four subdistricts ("Merchav"), and within the subdistricts are the local police stations. Allocation of police resources to specific communities is made at the level of the 52 police stations in Israel, which can be seen as analogous to local police departments in the United States or the United Kingdom. We thought that the terrorist threats that are faced by these "police stations" provide the best indicator of how terrorism affects the allocation of police resources. When terrorist threats impact a particular community within a station, it is the responsibility of the station commander to make the key decisions as to how specific resources, such as police officers, will be allocated to the specific community.

Accordingly, we measured threats of terrorism at the station level, and not the community level.* We defined terrorism at the outset by identifying three main measures: (1) the number of terror attacks targeting civilians, (2) the number of individuals wounded by these attacks, and (3) the number of fatalities. We thought that these three variables assessed both the threat of terrorism as indicated by the frequency of terrorist events, and its impacts, at least as indicated by personal injuries within the stations examined. In discussions with Israeli police officials, they recommended that we add a fourth variable to our measure of terrorism, the proximity of the police station to the border with the Palestinian territories. They argued that proximity to the Palestinian territories was a significant factor in the overall threat that a police station faced, not only because attacks generally originated from those areas, but also because a station close to the border would have to allocate greater resources to prevent infiltrations and ensure the safety of local communities.

Data on the number of attacks, deaths, and injuries was obtained from the National Security Studies Center at the University of Haifa,[†] as well as from official sources such as the Prime Minister's Office[‡] and the Israeli Ministry of Foreign Affairs.[§] Data on the distance from the border with the Palestinian territories was measured using electronic interactive maps.[¶] A station's proximity to the border was determined according to the shortest distance between the border and the community closest to the border within the specific station.

Each of the four threat indicators was transformed into an ordinal variable ranging from 0 (no attacks/no deaths/no injured/large distance from the Palestinian territories) to 3 (large number of attacks/large number of deaths/large number of injuries/short distance from the Palestinian territories). The values that fall within each category were determined by examining the distribution of the data and using natural braking points (see Appendix I). Lastly, for each police station the categories were added up so as to create an

---

[*] We also measured threats at the community level and estimated similar models to those reported here. As we expected the impact of threat at the community level on clearance rates was much less stable and weaker than that found below.
[†] See http://nssc.haifa.ac.il/.
[‡] See http://www.pmo.gov.il/PMOEng/Communication/IsraelUnderAttack/attlist.htm?Page=1.
[§] See http://mfa.gov.il/MFA.
[¶] See http://www.mapa.co.il/general/searchresult_locked.asp.

overall "terrorism threat" level, ranging from 0 (very low threat) to 12 (very high threat). We assessed the internal consistency of the scale by using Cronbach's alpha, a coefficient that measures how well items within a scale measure a single latent construct. Alpha levels of 0.70 and above are generally considered to represent strong scales (Carmines and Zeller 1979; DeVillis 1991; Nunnaly 1978). The Cronbach alpha value for our threat scale is 0.86.

The distribution of the terrorist threat variable is presented in Figure 10.2. As can be seen, there is considerable variability on this measure. As we noted earlier, this provides a unique opportunity to examine how variability in terrorist threats impact on police performance in terms of clearance rates in local communities.

As noted earlier, we thought at the outset that there may be important differences in the effects of terrorist threats on majority and minority communities, especially when such communities are linked ethnically, religiously, or nationally to groups that are associated with terrorist threats. Israel includes a large Arab minority of almost 20% of the national population. Although the Israeli Arab population includes a number of different religious and ethnic groups, including large numbers of Christians and Druze, the dominant ethnic Arab group is Muslims, who make up almost 83% of the Arab population in Israel. Israeli Arabs are Israeli citizens, but have strong ethnic, national, and religious ties to Arabs in the Palestinian territories from which most terrorist attacks originated.

Data on the number of residents in each community as well as their ethnicity (Arab/Jewish) was obtained from the INP. In part because of the nature of the development of Jewish and Arab settlements before the establishment of the State of Israel, Arab and Jewish communities in Israel are often geographically distinct (Mesch and Talmud 1998). Development of communities after the state's establishment has followed this pattern, with surveys in Israel showing that both Arabs and Jews have preference for ethnically distinct communities (Smooha 1989). Only eight cities and towns in our sample included what might be considered mixed populations of Jews and Arabs. All of these communities are predominantly Jewish, with Arab minorities ranging between 4% and 33%. Given the overall distribution of communities, we divided our sample into predominantly Jewish ($N = 165$) and predominantly Arab communities ($N = 92$; for a similar approach in regard to analyzing clearance rates, see Mesch and Talmud 1998).

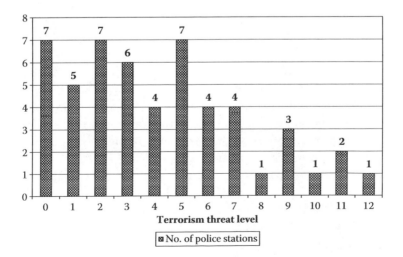

Figure 10.2 Terrorism threat levels faced by police stations.

Control Variables

Although our main interest is in examining the impacts of terrorism on clearance rates, we recognized at the outset that terrorist threats may be confounded with other measures that have been found to be related to clearance rates. Accordingly, in developing our statistical models, we sought to control for factors that have been identified as important in understanding clearance rates in other studies. We identify those factors and how they are measured in our study below, and report the correlation matrix for these variables and threat and community type in Table 10.1.

Other studies have found that police workload strongly affects clearance rates (Bayley 1994; Sullivan 1985; also see review by Paré, Felson and Quimet 2007). The fewer cases the police handle (in relation to the population size), the higher the clearance rate reported. Accordingly, data on the yearly number of criminal cases opened in each community during the years 2000–2004 was obtained from the Israeli Police, and the yearly average of criminal cases per 1000 residents was calculated.

The influence of the number of sworn officers on clearance rates from previous studies is mixed (Cameron 1987; Eck and Maguire 2000; Levitt 1997). Cordner's (1989) analysis of police performance in Maryland found that in metropolitan areas, higher numbers of sworn officers increased the clearance rate, whereas in nonmetropolitan areas higher numbers of sworn officers decreased the clearance rate. Consulting with Israeli police officials, we were told that the absolute number of officers per station has not changed significantly in recent years. To measure police strength, we use data from the most recent year that we could obtain such data, which was 2007, although we recognize that this measure may not reflect fully police strength during the period examined.

Additionally, the type of case investigated has also been found to impact strongly on clearance rates (Cordner 1989; Mesch and Talmud 1998; Paré, Felson, and Quimet 2007). The police may be more responsive to some offenses than others, or, alternatively, particular types of crime may be generally easier to solve. Thus, the more "solvable" investigations the police engage in, the more likely we are to witness higher clearance rates (Cordner, 1989; Paré, Felson, and Quimet 2007). For example, as we noted above, clearance rates for violent crimes are relatively high, possibly because police emphasize the investigation of such crimes because of their severity, or because the personal interaction involved may ease the identification of the offender (Mesch and Talmud 1998; Paré, Felson, and Quimet 2007). Additionally, offenses cleared upon detection, such as numerous drug offenses, have high clearance rates. At the same time, property offenses are rarely solved (Cordner 1989; Mesch and Talmud 1998; Paré, Felson, and Quimet 2007; also see yearly reports of the Israeli Police*). In this regard, we again obtained data from the Israeli Police on the number of investigations opened during the years 2000–2004 in each community, for different types of crime, including property offenses, violence, sex offenses, and drug crimes. We then calculated the percentage of cases opened for each of the four types of crime out of all cases opened, for each community separately.

The sociodemographic characteristics of communities have also been identified as a factor that influences clearance rates (Borg and Parker 2001; Crank 1990; Liska and Chamlin 1984; Litwin 2004; Mesch and Talmud 1998; Miller and Bryant 1993; Paré, Felson, and Quimet 2007; Smith 1986; Sullivan 1985). We considered two main community

---

* Available from http://www.police.gov.il/meida_laezrach/pirsomim/Pages/statistika.aspx.

Table 10.1 Correlation Matrix

	Clearance Rates	Threat Level Faced by Station	Community Type (Jewish/Arab)	Population Size	Percent of Property Cases Out of All Cases Opened	Percent of Violence Cases Out of All Cases Opened	Percent of Sex Cases Out of All Cases Opened	Percent of Drug Cases Out of All Cases Opened	Community Socioeconomic Level	Cases Opened per 1000 Residents	No. of Officers per 1000 Residents
Clearance rates											
Threat level faced by station	-0.23***	–									
Community type (Jewish/Arab)	0.70***	-0.15*	–								
Population size	-0.13*	0.19**	-0.18**	–							
Percent of property cases out of all cases opened	-0.91***	0.20**	-0.77***	0.14*	–						
Percent of violence cases out of all cases opened	0.69***	-0.19**	0.74***	-0.09	-0.77***	–					
Percent of sex cases out of all cases opened	-0.13*	0.07	-0.28***	-0.01	0.01	0.05	–				
Percent of drug cases out of all cases opened	0.37***	-0.21**	-0.04	-0.04	-0.27***	-0.01	0.05	–			
Community socioeconomic level	-0.65***	0.18**	-0.73***	0.10	0.70***	-0.70***	0.10	-0.06	–		
Cases opened per 1000 residents	-0.41***	0.15*	-0.46***	0.17**	0.48***	-0.43***	-0.05	0.14*	0.38***	–	
No. of officers per 1000 residents	-0.07	-0.23***	-0.15*	-0.07	0.08	-0.10	0.08	-0.01	0.13*	0.05	–

*$p < 0.05$; **$p < 0.01$; ***$p < 0.001$.

characteristics in our analysis beyond community type: size and socioeconomic status. With regard to size, it has been argued that clearance rates should be higher in smaller communities where residents are likely to have stronger connections to each other and the police (Cordner 1989; Mesch and Talmud 1998; Paré, Felson, and Quimet 2007), although the evidence for this hypothesis is mixed (see review by Paré, Felson, and Quimet 2007). Similarly, studies of the relationship between socioeconomic status of communities and clearance rates have not provided a clear picture (see Borg and Parker 2001; Crank 1990; Liska and Chamlin 1984; Litwin 2004; Miller and Bryant 1993; Paré, Felson, and Quimet 2007; Smith 1986; Sullivan 1985). Despite the mixed outcomes regarding these factors, we thought it important to consider demographic characteristics in our models.

Data on the population size of each community was obtained from the Israeli Police. Information regarding the socioeconomic status of each community was obtained from the Israeli Central Bureau of Statistics (CBS). The CBS has created a socioeconomic scale, ranging from 1 to 198, which takes into account various community characteristics such as financial resources, living conditions, and level of education. The scale was created by rank-ordering all communities with a population of more than 2000 according to their socioeconomic status, and assigning each community a score consistent with its rank. A total of 64 communities in our sample had a population of less than 2000, and were thus not included in the ranking procedure. As we did not want to lose almost one-quarter of the sample because of missing data, we decided to create a score for each of these 64 communities based on the average socioeconomic level of the other communities of the same ethnicity (Jewish/Arab) in the district in which the community was found. Recognizing the possible biases that this approach might bring to our overall models, we also ran our analyses excluding the socioeconomic variable altogether. The results were found to be very similar for all the main variables (see Appendix II).

Model and Findings

In Table 10.2, we present the main findings of our analysis. We use an ordinary least squares regression in which overall clearance rates for each community is the dependent variable. Each of the control variables is included in both models presented, as is our terrorism threat variable and the community type variable. In model 1, we present the model including the main effects of terrorism threat and community type. In model 2, we include an interaction term for terrorism threat by community type.* This is our main model of interest because it allows us to identify whether the effect of terrorist threats on stations impacts on predominantly Arab and predominantly Jewish communities differently. Both models evidence very high R^2 values (0.86; 0.87), suggesting that overall the models are doing a good job explaining the variability in clearance of cases across Israeli communities.

Although the addition of an interaction term is likely to add model instability because of potential multicollinearity (see Weisburd and Britt 2007), and this might be expected to be accented in a model in which the overall level of variance explained is very high, the

---

* The interaction term was created by recoding community type to (1) for predominantly Jewish communities and (2) for predominantly Arab communities, and then multiplying this by level of terrorist threat. We found that this coding better fit the functional form of the data than using a 0 and 1 split of the community type variable.

Table 10.2   Main Findings with and without an Interaction Term

Variables	Model 1 $B(\beta)$	Model 2 $B(\beta)$
Terrorism threat level of police station	−0.03 (−0.01)	−1.02 (−0.24)**
Ethnicity of community (Jewish/Arab)	−1.30 (−0.04)	−4.17 (−0.13)*
Interaction: Ethnicity of community × Terrorism threat level of station	–	0.70 (0.24)**
Population size	−0.00 (−0.00)	−0.00 (0.01)
Percent of property investigations out of all cases opened	−0.79 (−0.80)***	−0.78 (−0.80)***
Percent of violence investigations out of all cases opened	0.13 (0.07)	0.14 (0.07)
Percent of sex investigations out of all cases opened	−2.22 (−0.14)***	−2.22 (−0.14)***
Percent of drug investigations out of all cases opened	0.50 (0.15)***	0.49 (0.15)***
Socioeconomic status of community	−0.01 (−0.04)	−0.01 (−0.03)
Files opened per 1000 residents	−0.01 (−0.02)	−0.01 (−0.02)
No. of police officers per 1000 residents	0.20 (0.01)	−0.03 (−0.00)
R^2 (adjusted R^2)	0.86 (0.86)	0.87 (0.86)
N	257	257

$*p < 0.05; **p < 0.01; ***p < 0.001.$

indications in this study are that the interaction term increases the overall stability and strength of the model.* The effects of the control variables are very similar in both models, suggesting that the introduction of an interaction term did not create significant instability in the model estimated. The major difference between model 1 and model 2 is that the factors included in the interaction term became stronger and statistically significant.

Model 2 suggests that there is both an overall main effect of terrorism threat and community type in our data, as well as an additional interaction effect. On average, controlling for the other variables in the model, community type has a significant and strong effect on clearance rates. All else being equal, Arab communities in our sample have about a 4% lower rate of case clearance than predominantly Jewish communities. Terrorism threat, in turn, has on average a negative and significant effect on clearance rates.† However, these

---

* We examined overall multicollinearity for the model using tolerance statistics. Three measures—Community Type, Percent of Property Cases, and Percent of Violence cases—all had tolerance levels of between 0.20 and 0.29. Although these are relatively low tolerance levels, tolerance levels of 0.20 and above are generally considered acceptable (Weisburd and Britt 2007). The main issue in this case is whether the coefficients are unstable. We examined the models including and excluding these specific factors and found the coefficients of the variables remained relatively stable across specifications. We also note that the main coefficients have relatively high levels of statistical significance, which suggests that multicollinearity is not a major factor in the models. The addition of an interaction term as noted is likely to increase multicollinearity, but the results here suggest that the term is adding to the correct specification of the model.

† We recognize that the fact that communities are "nested" in the station level threat variable may impact upon estimates of the standard error for this measure. At the same time, the number of communities that are found within any particular police station is relatively small. There is also significant heterogeneity in the specific number of communities found within the stations. In such cases, corrections for clustering or nesting of data may lead to misleading results (Nichols and Schaffer 2007). At the same time, the clustering observed in our data is not considerable and would be expected to have relatively small impacts on the standard errors and thus significance statistics. The fact that our main measures in model 2 are all strongly significant suggests that we are not unfairly interpreting these statistics.

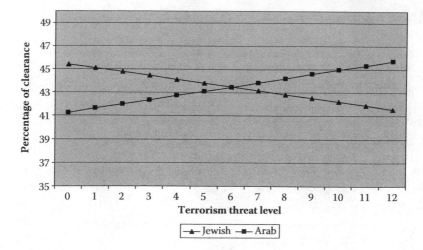

Figure 10.3 Terrorism threats and clearance rates in predominantly Jewish/Arab communities.

effects cannot be interpreted fully without examining the influence of the interaction term, which is also statistically significant.

In Figure 10.3, we illustrate the relationship suggested by our model between terrorist threats at police stations, and crime clearance rates in communities, conditional on the community type. It is not possible to visualize this relationship with actual data because of the confounding effect of other variables. For example, predominantly Jewish communities in Israel are likely to have relatively high reported rates of property crime, and predominantly Arab communities have a much higher proportion of violent crimes relative to all cases opened. Given the very dominant impact of crime type on clearance rates (see model 2), it would accordingly be misleading to represent the relationships between terrorist threats and clearance rates without taking this factor into account. In Figure 10.3, we present the relationship between terrorist threats and clearance rates for predominantly Arab and Jewish communities separately, based on parameter estimates in model 2 for terrorist threat, community type, and the interaction term, holding all control variables at their mean value.[*]

The relationship observed is a very interesting one. As indicated by our model, when terrorist threats are very low (and other variables are controlled for), Arab communities have about a 4% lower rate of solved cases than predominantly Jewish communities. It is important to remember that this estimate takes into account the types of cases that are brought within these communities, suggesting that there is a clearance rate gap that is not explained by the type of cases or other variables we examine. But importantly, as the level of terrorist threats at the stations increase, the rates of cases cleared moves in different directions. For predominantly Jewish communities, there is a general downward spiral consistent with the view that concern with terrorism reduces the effectiveness of the police in responding to ordinary crime. For Arab communities, the relationship is reversed with overall clearance rates increasing strongly as terrorist threats increase.

---

[*] We first estimated the regression equation. Then, we placed the mean values of all variables in the equation, except for terrorism threat, city type (predominantly Jewish/Arab), and the interaction term. Lastly, we calculated the equation 26 times: 13 times for Jewish communities with all possible threat values (0–12), and 13 times for Arab communities, again with all possible threat values.

Discussion

Our data appear to confirm contradictory hypotheses regarding the effects of terrorist threats on police performance, as measured by clearance rates. On the one hand, for the majority of the communities we study, defined as predominantly Jewish communities, heightened terrorist threats lead to declining clearance rates. But we also find that terrorist threats have the opposite impact on Arab communities in Israel. What explains these variant findings and how do they relate to our overall understanding of the relationship between terrorist threats and police performance?

The declining performance of police in predominantly Jewish communities in which stations face heightened terrorist threats seems straightforward to us. There are likely to be significant opportunity costs in police investment of major resources in homeland security functions at the local level. Assuming an unlimited supply of resources for the police, it might be possible to predict little impact of policing terrorism on other police functions. However, the INP did not receive any major increase in its budget during the period of the Second Palestinian Intifada (see Atad 2001; Nahoom-Halevi 2005; also see the budget of the Ministry of Public Security Israel 2007*).[†]

In turn, Fishman (2005) identifies a direct link between declining police service in Israel and the Second Intifada. Drawing from discussions with ranking police commanders, social scientists, legal scholars, and representatives from the community, he notes that the diversion of resources to homeland security functions was seen to inhibit the development of advanced data systems, technologies, and efforts to enhance the professionalism and skills of Israeli police officers. Fishman also reports that limited resources, combined with the numerous tasks of normal and homeland security policing, were seen to result in officer fatigue, a degradation in the quality of service provided to the public, and ultimately more crime (Fishman 2005).

The prioritization of homeland security activities, moreover, likely affected the ability of police agencies to provide "normal" police services in Israeli communities during the Second Intifada. For example, after a terrorist attack (or even in the process of preventing an attack), many officers from different units, including administrative staff, are called to stop their routine activities and attend the scene (see Weisburd, Jonathan, and Perry 2009). Everything that is not considered urgent is pushed aside. Many of the issues that trouble local communities may not be viewed as "urgent" in this context, and attention to

---

* Available online from: http://www.mof.gov.il/budget2007/docs/302.pdf [In Hebrew].

[†] In this regard, our finding that police resources (as measured by number of police officers per 1000 residents) did not have a statistically significant effect in the model is particularly interesting. If resources are a key issue then why did this measure not have a more meaningful impact? One explanation is simply that a basic level of resources was available in all stations as would be expected in a national policing agency as opposed to locally financed agencies. In turn, studies do not suggest that small increases in police officer strength have important impacts on police effectiveness (see Weisburd and Eck 2004). Moreover, our argument is focused on the allocation of such resources within stations and not on the absolute level of resources. We hypothesize that police resources within a station were shifted away from traditional crime and disorder functions within primarily Jewish communities during times of high terrorist threats. Such shifting of resources would be expected to negatively impact upon police performance as measured by closed cases. Finally, we think that caution should be used in drawing strong conclusions from our measure of police resources. As we noted earlier, we were only able to gain data from 2007. Although police sources told us that police strength in the stations had not changed greatly since the time of the Second Intifada, we have no hard data on this issue and there may have been large short term changes in police allocations at that time.

these problems is delayed or terminated altogether. A similar process, as we noted earlier, was observed in Montgomery County in 2002 when police forces were trying to identify and capture a sniper responsible for a series of fatal shootings (University of Maryland Symposium 2003*).

Finally, as we noted at the outset, there may be a potential danger of the attractiveness of "high policing" in contrast to traditional crime control or "low-policing" obligations. Antiterrorism and homeland security activities appear to have particular salience and status for police (Bayley and Weisburd 2009).

Although these factors provide an explanation for the decline in police performance in solving crimes in predominantly Jewish communities, the question remains why we find the opposite effect in Arab communities in Israel. We cannot simply conclude that a zero sum game of resources leads to lower clearance rates, if they increase in Arab communities. Nor can we assume that police attentions will be drawn to terrorism as opposed to ordinary crime if we find the reverse in Arab communities, at least as measured by clearance rates.

At the same time, if we return to the distinction we made earlier between "high" and "low" policing and its possible relationship to terrorist threats, it is possible to understand the very different effects we observe in our data for predominantly Arab and Jewish communities. We argued earlier that terrorist threats are likely to lead to greater emphasis on high policing strategies and goals. This means as well that low policing may have greater emphasis when terrorist threats are lower.

We think in this regard that it is particularly interesting in our data that police performance in solving crimes is significantly higher in predominantly Jewish communities (as contrasted with predominantly Arab communities) when terrorist threats are low, after controlling for other possible confounding variables. This reality is consistent with other studies in Israel that have noted that police allocation of resources to Arab communities, and police service in those communities is at a lower level on average than in majority Jewish communities (Hasisi 2005). This "neglect" of minority communities more generally has been noted in a number of studies of policing in other countries (Black 1976; Hawkins 1987; LaFree 1989; Liska and Chamlin 1984). More generally, we might assume that the relative disadvantage of Arab communities re clearance rates in ordinary times reflects the status quo when police are focusing on low-policing duties.

Why then do clearance rates increase when terrorist threats are high? One way to clarify this impact is by considering the effect of the threat that minorities are perceived to bring toward majority communities (Blalock 1967; Feagin 1991; Holmes 2000; Jackson 1989; Parker, Stults, and Rice 2005). Jacobs and Helms (1999) argue that the majority's threat perception of the minority group plays a very important role in the allocation of police and other governmental social control. When the majority is threatened, it is likely to increase surveillance in minority communities. Although surveys have long suggested that Israeli Jews perceive Israeli Arabs as representing a potential threat to the State, it is certainly the case that the majority Jewish community in Israel began to see the threat of Arab minority as growing during the Second Intifada (Smooha 2004). Such perceptions were reinforced by large-scale Arab rioting in Israel at the beginning of this period

---

* This symposium of police executives from the Washington, DC, tri-state area took place at the University of Maryland, College Park, on May 9, 2003, and was organized by the Department of Criminology and Criminal Justice, Police Research Group.

(Hasisi 2005; Hasisi and Weitzer 2007), and isolated examples of Arab citizens who aided Palestinian terrorists (Hasisi, Alpert, and Flynn 2009). The response of the police to the riots in October 2000 that led to 12 Israeli Arabs and one Palestinian national being killed was strongly criticized in a later government report (Or Commission 2003). Nonetheless, the response itself suggests the extent to which the Israeli police perceived the Arab minority as a threat during this period.

The reality of the physical proximity and social connections between Israeli Arabs and Arabs in the Palestinian Territories certainly reinforced these perceptions. It would not be surprising for Israeli police to focus greater attention in Arab towns and villages that might provide cover for Palestinian terrorists infiltrating to areas within the Israeli Green Line. The greater attention in these towns and villages, in turn, likely led to fewer police resources in predominantly Jewish communities. But the allocation of resources itself may not explain the increasing rates of case clearance observed.

One explanation for higher clearance rates may be that the police view ordinary crime investigations as a method of gaining intelligence about terrorism. In this sense, crime investigations become a high policing function where the goal is not necessarily to solve crimes but to identify suspects who can provide information on potential terrorist activities. Such a strategy has been noted by Kelling and Bratton (2006), who argue that the Israeli police see ordinary crime investigations as a means for gaining strategic intelligence on terrorism. We might speculate that heightened surveillance in Arab communities, combined with a police orientation that sees the solving of crime as a method of gaining information on terrorism, is an important part of the explanation of the relatively higher rates of solving cases found as terrorist threats increase in Arab communities. However, the fact that the Israeli police do not distinguish security-related offenses means as well that some part of the effect we observe may be the result of investigations for offenses that cannot be simply classified as ordinary crimes. Large numbers of arrests in violent protests, for example, would increase clearance rates in communities, although such arrests certainly do not suggest that police performance in solving ordinary crimes has improved. We think this is related more broadly to an emphasis on high policing, but we think it is important to note that the higher clearance rates we observe in Arab communities is likely due in part to the prosecution of security-related crimes themselves.

Moreover, one should be cautious in defining a "terrorism dividend" in police performance in minority communities in Israel as a result of heightened terrorist threats. As we noted earlier, increases in surveillance in minority communities have often been viewed by the communities themselves as a case of their being unfairly profiled by the police as "the enemy within" (Henderson, Ortiz, Sugie, and Miller 2006; Innes 2006; Khashu, Busch, Latif, and Levy 2005; Thacher 2005). In a survey conducted during the Second Intifada, 43% of the Arab respondents thought that the police treated them as a "security threat" (Hasisi and Weitzer 2007). A more recent survey conducted by Hasisi and Weisburd 2014) suggests that both Arab and Jewish Israelis believe that police concern with terrorism impacts negatively on the crime control function. About half of Arab Israelis, and a similar proportion of Jewish Israelis, agreed that the "police explain failure in handling crime by the fact that they are busy fighting terrorism." In turn, slightly over half of Israel Arabs surveyed argued that policing terrorism had a negative effect on police community relations. This was true for only about a third of Jewish respondents.

Conclusions

Taking advantage of the very high rates of terrorism in Israel during the Second Intifada, and the particular structure of Jewish and Arab communities in Israel, we were able to examine how police performance as measured by solved cases is affected by terrorist threats. Our study suggests two distinct causal mechanisms, one in predominantly Jewish communities and the other in predominantly Arab communities. Both mechanisms are explained by the shift of local police agencies to high policing strategies (see Bayley and Weisburd 2009), and both suggest the salience of terrorism in its effects on traditional policing responsibilities.

We find that heightened terrorist threats decrease the performance of police in solving cases in predominantly Jewish communities. This is consistent with the position that a shift in focus of police agencies to strategic threats such as terrorism will naturally lead to a diminution of attention to normal crime fighting. Such high policing draws police attention and resources away from crime investigations. But in predominantly Arab communities high policing led to the opposite effect. Increased terrorist threats in the stations in which Arab communities are found leads to higher clearance rates. In this case, we speculate that this is because police surveillance increased in such communities.

We think our findings have broader implications for understanding the relationship between terrorism and police performance, and suggest some caution as local police agencies are pushed to take on counterterrorism functions. Terrorism is likely overall to reduce police effectiveness in solving crimes. This is a main implication of our finding. But the effect of terrorism is likely to vary, and in communities that are seen as associated religiously, nationally, or ethnically with terrorist groups police effectiveness in solving crimes is likely to increase. Importantly, this is not necessarily an indication of increased police service in such communities, and indeed may develop from heightened surveillance and suspicion regarding people who live in such communities.

We recognize that there are many limitations in drawing conclusions from our data and generalizing to other places and contexts. The Israeli situation is unique in many ways, and indeed the very high rates of terrorism and strong differentiation between Arab and Jewish communities provided an opportunity to examine these questions in ways that would be difficult in most other Western democracies. Our findings show a complex relationship between terrorist threats and police performance. That relationship may differ in other settings. Nonetheless, our data suggest the importance of examining such issues carefully, as many police agencies begin to see combating terrorism as an important part of the police function.

Acknowledgments

This work was supported by the United States Department of Homeland Security through the National Consortium for the Study of Terrorism and Responses to Terrorism (START) (grant number N00140510629) and the U.S. National Institute of Justice (grant number Z909601). Any opinions, findings, and conclusions or recommendations in this document are those of the authors and do not necessarily reflect the views of the Department of Homeland Security or the National Institute of Justice.

Appendix I. Categories of Threat Variables at Station Level

		Category			
		0 (Low Threat)	1	2	3 (High Threat)
No. of attacks	Range	0	1–4	5–10	11 and above
	N	21	19	8	3
No. of injured	Range	0	1–62	63–138	139 and above
	N	25	16	4	6
No. of death	Range	0	1–11	12–42	43 and above
	N	24	17	7	3
Distance from border (km)	Range	50 and above	21–49	6–20	1–5
	N	8	9	19	15

Appendix II. Regression without SES Variable

Variables	$B(\beta)$
Terrorism threat level of police station	−1.05 (−0.24)**
Ethnicity of community (Jewish/Arab)	−3.85 (−0.12)*
Interaction: Ethnicity of community × Terrorism threat level of station	0.72 (0.25)**
Population size	0.00 (0.01)
Percent of property investigations out of all cases opened	−0.79 (−0.81)***
Percent of violence investigations out of all cases opened	0.16 (0.08)
Percent of sex investigations out of all cases opened	−2.22 (−0.14)***
Percent of drug investigations out of all cases opened	0.49 (0.15)***
Files opened per 1000 residents	−0.01 (−0.02)
No. of police officers per 1000 residents	−0.05 (−0.00)
R^2 (adjusted R^2)	0.87 (0.86)
N	257

*$p < 0.05$; **$p < 0.01$; ***$p < 0.001$.

References

Alpert, G. and M. Moore. 1993. Measuring police performance in the new paradigm of policing. In *Performance measures for the criminal justice system*, ed. J. Wilson, 109–142. Washington, DC: U.S. Department of Justice.

Atad, A. 2001. The police demands a 1.8 million shekel increase in budget. *Yediot Aharonot* [In Hebrew], September 10. http://www.ynet.co.il/articles/0,7340,L-1103849,00.html.

Bamford, B. 2004. The United Kingdom's "war against terrorism." *Terrorism and Political Violence* 16:737–756.

Bayley, D. 1993. Back from Wonderland, or toward the rational use of police resources. In *Thinking about police resources*, ed. A.N. Doob, 1–34. Toronto, Canada: University of Toronto, Centre of Criminology.

Bayley, D. 1994. *Police for the future*. New York: Oxford University Press.

Bayley, D. and D. Weisburd. 2009. Cops and Spooks: The role of the police in counterterrorism. In *To protect and to serve: Policing in an age of terrorism*, eds. D. Weisburd, T. Feucht, I. Hakimi, L. Mock, and S. Perry, 81–101. New York: Springer.

Black, D. 1971. The social organization of arrest. *Stanford Law Review* 23:1087–1111.

Black, D. 1972. The boundaries of legal sociology. *Yale Law Journal* 81:1086–1100.

Black, D. 1976. *The behavior of law.* New York: Academic Press.

Blalock, M.B. 1967. *Toward a theory of minority-group relations.* New York: John Wiley & Sons, Inc.

Bordua, D. 1968. Police. In *International encyclopedia of the social sciences,* ed. D.L. Sills, 174–181. New York: Macmillan.

Borg, M.J. and K.F. Parker. 2001. Mobilizing law in urban areas: The social structure of homicide clearance rates. *Law and Society Review* 35:435–466.

Braga, A.A. and D. Weisburd. 2006. Problem-oriented policing: The disconnect between principles and practice. In *Police innovation: Contrasting perspectives,* eds. D. Weisburd and A. A. Braga, 133–152. Cambridge, UK: Cambridge University Press.

Brodeur, J.P. 1983. High and low policing: Remarks about the policing of political activities. *Social Problems* 30:507–520.

Brodeur, J.P. 1998. *How to recognize good policing: Problems and issues.* Thousand Oaks, CA: Sage Publications.

Brodeur, J.P. 2003. Democracy and secrecy: The French intelligence community. In *Democracy, law and society,* eds. J.P. Brodeur, P. Gill, and D. Tollborg, 19–23. Aldershot, UK: Ashgate Publishing Ltd.

Cameron, S. 1987. A disaggregated study of police clear-up rates for England and Wales. *Journal of Behavioral Economics* 16:1–18.

Carmines, E. and R. Zeller. 1979. *Reliability and validity assessments.* Newbury Park, CA: Sage.

Chapman, B. 1970. *Police state.* New York: Praeger.

Clarke, R.V. 2005. Seven misconceptions of situational crime prevention. In *Handbook of crime prevention and community safety,* ed. N. Tilley, 39–70. Cullompton, Devon, UK: Willan Publishing.

Clarke, R.V. and D. Weisburd. 1994. Diffusion of crime control benefits: Observations on the reverse of displacement. In *Crime prevention studies,* vol 2, ed. R.V Clarke, 165–183. Monsey, NY: Criminal Justice Press.

Cordner, G.W. 1989. Police agency size and investigative effectiveness. *Journal of Criminal Justice* 17:145–155.

Crank, P.J. 1990. The influence of environmental and organizational factors on police styles in urban and rural environments. *Journal of Research in Crime and Delinquency* 27:166–189.

Davenport, D.R. 1999. Environmental constraints and organizational outcomes: Modeling communities of municipal police departments. *Police Quarterly* 2:174–200.

DeVillis, R.F. 1991. *Scale development: Theory and applications.* Newbury Park, CA: Sage.

Eck, J.E. and E.R. Maguire. 2000. Have changes in policing reduced violent crime? An assessment of the evidence. In *The crime drop in America,* eds. A. Blumstein and J. Wallman, 207–265. Cambridge, UK: Cambridge University Press.

Feagin, J.R. 1991. The continuing significance of race: Anti-black discrimination in public places. *American Sociological Review* 56:101–116.

Fishman, G. 2005. *Balanced police action between terror and maintaining public order: A summary of an era and challenges for coming years.* Jerusalem, Israel: The Israel Democracy Institute. [In Hebrew].

Gill, P. 1987. Clearing up crime: The big "Con." *Journal of Law and Society* 14:254–265.

Hasisi, B. 2005. *Policing and citizenship in a deeply-divided society: Police–minority relations in Israel.* PhD dissertation, University of Haifa, Israel.

Hasisi, B. and D. Weisburd. 2014. Policing Terrorism and Police-Community Relations: Views of the Arab minority in Israel. *Police Practice and Research* 15(2):158–172.

Hasisi, B. and R. Weitzer. 2007. Police relations with Arabs and Jews in Israel. *British Journal of Criminology* 47:728–745.

Hasisi, B., G.P. Alpert, and D. Flynn. 2009. The impacts of policing terrorism on society: Lessons from Israel and the U.S. In *To protect and to serve: Policing in an age of terrorism,* eds. D. Weisburd, T. Feucht, I. Hakimi, L. Mock, and S. Perry, 177–203. New York: Springer.

Hawkins, D.F. 1987. Beyond anomalies: Rethinking the conflict perspective on race and criminal punishment. *Social Forces* 65:719–745.

Henderson, N.J., C.W. Ortiz, N.F. Sugie, and J. Miller. 2006. *Law enforcement and Arab American community relations after September 11th, 2001: Engagement in a time of uncertainty.* New York: Vera Institute of Justice.

Herzog, S. 2003. Border closures as a reliable method for the measurement of Palestinian involvement in crime in Israel: A quasi-experimental analysis. *International Journal of Comparative Criminology* 3:18–41.

Holmes, M.D. 2000. Minority threat and police brutality: Determinants of civil rights criminal complaints in U.S. municipalities. *Criminology* 38:343–367.

Hoover, L.T. 1996. *Quantifying quality in policing.* Washington: Police Executive Research Forum.

Howard, P. 2004. *Hard won lessons: How police fight terrorism in the United Kingdom.* New York: Manhattan Institute. http://www.manhattan-institute.org/pdf/scr_01.pdf (accessed January 10, 2007).

Innes, M. 2006. Policing uncertainty: Countering terror through community intelligence and democratic policing. *The Annals of the American Academy of Political and Social Science* 605:222–241.

International Association of Chiefs of Police. 2005. *Post 9-11 policing: The crime-control-homeland security paradigm—Taking command of new realities.* Alexandria, VA: International Association of Chiefs of Police.

Jackson, P.I. 1989. *Minority group threat, crime, and policing: Social context and social control.* New York: Praeger.

Jacobs, D. and R. Helms. 1999. Collective outbursts, politics and punitive resources: Toward a political sociology of spending on social control. *Social Forces* 77:1497–1524.

Kelling, G.L. and W.J. Bratton. 2006. *Policing terrorism.* New York: Manhattan Institute. http://www.manhattan-institute.org/html/cb_43.htm (accessed December 2007).

Khashu, A., R. Busch, Z. Latif, and F. Levy. 2005. *Building strong police–immigrant community relations: Lessons from a New York City project.* New York: Vera Institute of Justice.

LaFree G. 1989. *Rape and criminal justice: The social construction of sexual assault.* Belmont, CA: Wadsworth.

Leishman, F. and P. Mason. 2003. *Policing and the media: Facts, fictions and factions.* Cullompton, Devon, UK: Willan Press.

Levitt, S. 1997. Using electoral cycles in police hiring to estimate the effect of police on crime. *American Economic Review* 87:270–290.

Lewis, L. 2004. *Speech: Terrorism–Policing the unknown.* http://www.homeoffice.gov.uk/docs3/speech_policefed.html (accessed January 10, 2007).

Liska, A. and M. Chamlin. 1984. Social structure and crime control among macro-social units. *American Journal of Sociology* 90:383–395.

Litwin, K.J. 2004. A multilevel multivariate analysis of factors affecting homicide clearances. *Journal of Research in Crime and Delinquency* 41:327–351.

Loveday, B. 1999. The impact of performance culture on criminal justice agencies. *International Journal of the Sociology of Law* 27:351–377.

Loveday, B. 2000. Managing crime: Police use of crime data as an indicator of effectiveness. *International Journal of the Sociology of Law* 28:215–237.

Maguire, E.R. and C.D. Uchida. 2000. Measurement and explanation in the comparative study of American police organizations. In *Criminal justice 2000: Vol 4. Measurement and analysis of crime and justice,* ed. D. Duffee, 491–558. Washington, DC: National Institute of Justice.

Maguire, M. 1997. Crime statistics, patterns and trends: Changing perspectives. In *The Oxford Handbook of criminology,* eds. M. Maguire, R. Morgan, and R. Reiner. Oxford: Oxford University Press.

Manning, P. 1977. *Police work.* Cambridge, MA: MIT Press.

Mastrofski, S.D. 1999. *Policing for people. Ideas in American policing.* Washington, DC: Police Foundation.

Matassa, M. and T. Newburn. 2003. Policing and terrorism. In *Handbook of policing*, ed. T. Newburn, 467–500. Cullompton, Devon, UK: Willan.

Matthews, R. 1990. Developing more effective strategies for curbing prostitution. *Security Journal* 1:182–187.

Mesch, G.S. and I. Talmud. 1998. The influence of community characteristics on police performance in a deeply divided society: The case of Israel. *Sociological Focus* 31:233–248.

Miller, M. and K. Bryant. 1993. Predicting police behavior: Ecology, class, and autonomy. *American Journal of Criminal Justice* 18:133–151.

Mulcahy, A. 2005. The "other" lessons from Ireland? Policing, political violence and policy transfer. *European Journal of Criminology* 2:185–209.

Nahoom-Halevi, R. 2005. The state comptroller: The police have lost deterrence. *MSN News*. [In Hebrew], March 9. Accessed September 25, 2007. http://news.msn.co.il/news/Internal/Internal/200503/20050308202900.html.

National Research Council. 2004. *Fairness and effectiveness in policing: The evidence.* Committee to review research on police policy and practices, ed. W. Skogan and K. Frydl, Committee on Law and Justice, Division of Behavioral and Social Sciences and Education. Washington, DC: The National Academies Press.

Nichols, A. and M. Schaffer. 2007. *Clustered errors in Stata.* College Station, TX: Mimeo.

Nunnaly, J. 1978. *Psychometric theory.* New York: McGraw-Hill.

Or Commission. 2003. *Report of the state commission of inquiry to investigate the clashes between the security forces and Israeli citizens in October 2000: Volume 2.* Jerusalem: Government Printing Press. [In Hebrew].

Paré, P.P., R.B. Felson, and M. Quimet. 2007. Community variation in crime clearance: A multilevel analysis with comments on assessing police performance. *Journal of Quantitative Criminology* 23:243–258.

Parker, K., B.J. Stults, and S. Rice. 2005. Racial threat, concentrated disadvantage and social control: Considering macro level sources of variation in arrests. *Criminology* 43:1111–1135.

Reiner, R. 1992. *The politics of the police.* Hemel Hempstead, UK: Harvester Wheatsheaf.

Reiner, R. 1998. Process or product? Problem of assessing individual police performance. In *How to recognize good policing: Problems and issues*, ed. J.P. Brodeur, 55–72. Thousand Oaks, CA: Sage.

Sampson, R.J., S.W. Raudenbush, and F. Earls. 1997. Neighborhoods and violent crime. *Science* 277:918–924.

Sherman, L.W. and D.A. Smith. 1992. Crime, punishment and stake in conformity: Legal and informal control of domestic violence. *American Sociological Review* 57:680–690.

Skolnick, J. 1966. *Justice without trial: Law enforcement in democratic society.* New York: John Wiley & Sons, Inc.

Skolnick, J. 1993. Justice without trial revisited. In *Problems of law, order, and community*, eds. D. Weisburd and C. Uchida, 190–207. New York: Springer-Verlag.

Smith, D. 1986. The neighborhood context of police behavior. In *Crime and justice*, vol 8, eds. A. Reiss and M. Tonry, 313–341. Chicago: University of Chicago Press.

Smith, D.A. and C.A. Visher. 1981. Street-level justice: Situational determinants of police arrest decisions. *Social Problem* 29:167–177.

Smooha, S. 1989. *Arabs and Jews in Israel. Vol. 1: Conflicting and shared attitudes in a divided society.* London: Westview Press.

Smooha, S. 2004. *Index of Arab–Jewish relations in Israel.* Haifa, Israel: The Jewish–Arab Center, University of Haifa.

Sullivan, P.S. 1985. *Determinants of crime and clearance rates for seven index crimes.* Washington, DC: US Department of Justice, National Institute of Justice.

Thacher, D. 2005. The local role in homeland security. *Law and Society Review* 39:635–676.

Walker, M.A. 1992. Do we need a clear-up rate? *Policing and Society* 2:293–306.

Weisburd, D. and C. Britt. 2007. *Statistics in criminal justice*, Third Edition. New York: Springer Verlag.

Weisburd, D. and J. Eck. 2004. What can the police do to reduce crime, disorder and fear? *Annals of the American Academy of Social and Political Sciences* 593:42–65.

Weisburd, D. and J. McElroy. 1988. Enacting the CPO role: Findings from the New York City pilot program in community policing. In *Community based policing: Rhetoric or reality*, eds. J. Greene and S. Mastrofski, 89–101. New York: Praeger.

Weisburd, D., T. Feucht, I. Hakimi, L. Mock, and S. Perry. 2009. *To protect and to serve: Policing in an age of terrorism*. New York: Springer.

Weisburd, D., T. Jonathan, and S. Perry. 2009. The Israeli Model for Policing Terrorism: Goals, Strategies and Open Questions. *Criminal Justice and Behavior* 36(12):1259–1278.

Weisburd, D., S. Mastrofski, A. McNally, R. Greenspan, and J. Willis. 2003. Reforming to preserve: Compstat and strategic problem solving in American policing. *Criminology and Public Policy* 2:421–456.

Weisburd, D., O. Shalev, and M. Amir. 2002. Community policing in Israel: Resistance and change. *Policing: An International Journal of Police Strategies and Management* 25:80–109.

Police Legitimacy under the Spotlight
Media Coverage of Police Performance in the Face of High Terrorism Threat*

REVITAL SELA-SHAYOVITZ

Contents

Introduction

Periods of external security threats highlight the important role of police legitimacy, as legitimacy is a key antecedent in the public's willingness to cooperate and obey police directives (Sunshine and Tyler 2003; Tyler 2001, 2004). Indeed, in times of terrorist attacks legitimacy becomes even more crucial because of the multiple responsibilities of the police in counterterrorism and routine activities (Bayley and Weisburd 2009).

Another aspect is related to the powerful impact of the media on police legitimacy. News coverage of the police has a central role in sustaining legitimacy, although coverage can also undermine public trust and decrease legitimacy (Altheide 1985; Gallagher, Maguire, Mastrofski and Reisig 2001; Lawrence 2000; Loader and Mulcahy 2003; Lovall 2001;

* Reproduced from Sela-Shayovitz, R. 2014. Police legitimacy under the spotlight: Media coverage of police performance in the face of a high terrorism threat. *Journal of Experimental Criminology.* doi 10.1007 /s11292-014-9213-8, with kind permission of Springer Science+Business Media.

Surette 2001; Tyler 2004; Weitzer 2002). To date, the majority of studies have focused on the effect of the coverage of police misconduct cases on public attitude toward the police (Chermak, McGarrell and Gruenewald 2006; Weitzer 2004; Weitzer and Tuch 2004). This chapter aims to contribute to the existing literature by extending the focus to the effect of terrorism threat on the media framing of police legitimacy.

The current study focuses on the Second Intifada in Israel, which is a unique period in Israeli history.* This period is significantly different because it was marked by intensive, random, and extremely brutal attacks that transformed civilian life into a battlefront (Cromer 2006). During this particular period, between September 2000 (the outbreak of the Intifada) and December 2007, 187 suicide bombings took place in various locations all over Israel and 552 terrorists were arrested on their way to commit suicide bombings (Israel Security Agency 2009). Moreover, these activities led to the largest number of civilian casualties in Israeli terrorism history—more than 4000 wounded and almost 600 fatalities (Weisburd, Jonathan and Perry 2009). However, this period is also exceptional because terrorist acts received such massive media exposure. In view of these circumstances, this period provides a unique opportunity for the purpose of the study.

By way of introduction, and in order to elucidate the theoretical frameworks of the research, I begin by reviewing the literature on police legitimacy and policing terrorism. I also elaborate on the media coverage of police and the framing of terrorism. Subsequently, I delineate the methodology, which was based on a quasi-experimental, interrupted time-series design. The examination reveals that terrorism threat was significantly and positively related to police legitimacy. After the outbreak of the Second Intifada, there was a significant increase in the framing of police legitimacy. However, after the decrease in terrorism threat, the positive coverage of the police significantly declined. Finally, I discuss the findings, while drawing attention to the broader implications for understanding the role of the media in framing police legitimacy.

Police Legitimacy and Policing Terrorism

There has been a growing corpus of literature on the role of police legitimacy in facilitating public law-abiding behavior over the past decades (Loader 1997; Loader and Mulcahy 2003; Sunshine and Tyler 2003; Tyler 1990). The process-based model (Sunshine and Tyler 2003; Tyler 1990, 2004) identified two core elements as predictors of police legitimacy: people's sense of obligation to obey the police and public trust and confidence in the police (Sunshine and Tyler 2003; Tyler 1990, 2004; Tyler, Schulhofer and Huq 2010; Tyler and Huo 2002; Tyler and Smith 1997). According to this model, when people perceive the police as legitimate and place trust in them, they are more willing to obey the law and police directives. Legitimacy of the olice is linked to two additional key elements: the evaluation of procedural-justice processes as fair and assessments of police performance as effective. Based on the process-based model assumption, individuals will view the police as more legitimate

---

* The term *Intifada* refers to the violent Palestinian uprisings against the Israeli occupation of the West Bank and Gaza Strip, both of which have been under Israeli military control since 1967. The First Intifada lasted for approximately 5 years, from 1987 to 1993. The Second Intifada began in September 2000 but the final date is controversial. Some scholars consider the ending in 2005, following the decline in terrorist attacks, and others perceive the end in 2007 after signing a "wanted terrorists" agreement.

if they perceive that the application of procedural-justice processes is fair (i.e., reasonable, unbiased, and objective), and that police treat citizens with dignity and respect (Sunshine and Tyler 2003; Tyler 2004). Furthermore, if the police are perceived as effective in fighting crime, this will increase the public's view of police legitimacy (Sampson, Raudenbush and Earls 1997; Sunshine and Tyler 2003; Tyler 2004). Although both key elements—fairness of procedural-justice processes and effectiveness of police performance—are essential for legitimacy, there is a strong support for the assumption that the procedural-justice process is the primary factor shaping legitimacy, whereas police performance was found to be the second most important factor (Jonathan-Zamir and Weisburd 2011).

Although there is a growing number of studies relying on Sunshine and Tyler (2003) model, some scholars remain skeptical about this concept (Reisig and Lloyd 2009; Tankebe 2009). Recent studies have found that the obligation to obey the police was not significantly associated with legitimacy, whereas trust in the police predicted both compliance and cooperation (Reisig, Bratton and Gertz 2007). Consequently, some scholars use only public trust measures as proxies for legitimacy (Reisig, Bratton and Gertz 2007). Similarly, evaluations of procedural-justice processes are not consistently associated with legitimacy (Reisig and Mesko 2009), and were also correlated with a variety of beneficial outcomes, such as satisfaction with the police and acceptance of police decisions (Reisig and Chandek 2001; Tyler and Fagan 2006; Tyler and Huo 2002). Thus, the process-based model is controversial, and police legitimacy can be operationalized in different ways.

Yet, during periods of security threat, such as the danger of a severe terrorism attack, the roles of police performance and procedural-justice processes might change in maintaining legitimacy. In this context, research suggests that during this type of threat, the public's evaluation is more focused on the effectiveness of police performance and less concerned with the fairness of procedural-justice processes (Deutsch 1990; Nagata 1993; Sullivan, Piereson and Marcus 1982). Indeed, in the counterterrorism era that followed the 9/11 terror attack, evaluations of police performance directly shaped police empowerment; however, procedural justice was the key antecedent of legitimacy both before and after this major terror attack (Sunshine and Tyler 2003). In much the same way, during the decade that included the intense terrorism threats of the Second Intifada, patterns of trust in police seemed to reflect police performance more than the evaluations of procedural justice (Jonathan 2010). However, a recent study indicates that although evaluations of performance effectiveness significantly rise under security threats, this factor remains second in importance, whereas procedural justice is found to be the primary factor in determining legitimacy (Jonathan-Zamir and Weisburd 2011).

In a similar vein, an analysis of the attitudes of Muslim Americans with respect to cooperation in antiterror policing efforts strongly supports the assumption that procedural justice is the primary factor shaping police legitimacy (Tyler, Schulhofer and Huq 2010). Thus, it can be suggested that in a situation involving a security threat, police performance becomes more important, although the role of procedural justice is still primary in maintaining legitimacy (Jonathan-Zamir and Weisburd 2011; Tyler, Schulhofer and Huq 2010). The discussion in the following paragraphs elaborates on the effect of counterterrorism policing on police legitimacy.

Scholars have defined counterterrorism policing as "high policing," which focuses on strategic issues at the macro level within the prevention paradigm (Bayley and Weisburd 2009; Brodeur 1983; McCulloch and Pickering 2005; O'Reilly and Ellison 2006). High policing in counterterrorism primarily consists of strategies, such as surveillance, gathering covert intelligence, and the disruption of terrorist plots (Bayley and Weisburd 2009;

Hasisi, Alpert and Flynn 2009). However, terrorist attacks occur at the local level, and therefore raise the necessity of cooperation between macro and micro levels.

Two opposing theoretical hypotheses have been offered regarding the impact of security threats on police legitimacy. The first hypothesis assumes that an external security threat may lead to increased police legitimacy (Jonathan 2010). This perspective is based both on the cohesion hypothesis and the "Rally Effect." The cohesion hypothesis argues that an external threat has a strengthening effect on the internal cohesion of a society (Coser 1956; Selye 1956; Simmel 1955). In much the same vein, the Rally Effect indicates how the impact of a security threat may increase the legitimacy of a government. However, as the external threat diminishes or lasts longer than expected, approval ratings decrease and return to preemergency levels (Mueller 1970, 1973; Sigelman and Conover 1981). Studies demonstrate that in the wake of security threats, the legitimacy of governmental institutions increases (Jonathan 2010; Norpoth 1991; Parker 1995). For example, during times of intense terrorism in the Second Intifada, there was an increase in the Jewish public's positive evaluations of the police (Jonathan 2010).

The opposite hypothesis contends that during periods of heightened terrorism, police legitimacy may decrease because counterterrorism may reduce the police's competence in controlling crime and providing services to the community (Fishman 2005; Jonathan 2010; Weisburd, Jonathan and Perry 2009; Weisburd, Hasisi, Jonathan and Aviv 2010). Studies have confirmed this contention and show that during the first years of the Second Intifada, there was an increase in crime rates and a decrease in solving cases among Jewish communities (Fishman 2005; Weisburd, Jonathan and Perry 2009). Yet, the intensification of police surveillance may also lead to a prevention of conventional crimes. Findings indicate that during the Second Intifada crime clearance rates in Arab communities were higher (Weisburd, Jonathan and Perry 2009), and there was a significant decline in vehicle thefts during this period (Herzog 2003).

Another argument is that counterterrorism strategies are less transparent and less concerned with the infringements of human rights, and consequently police legitimacy may decrease (Bayley and Weisburd 2009; Sidel 2004; Thacher 2005; Wilkinson 2001). Indeed, following the 9/11 events, counterterrorism often became a justification for undermining civil liberties and human rights, and as a consequence led to public disapproval (McCulloch and Pickering 2009).

Police Legitimacy and Media

Mass media are a key arena through which police legitimacy is reshaped. The media work as a mechanism of regulation and compliance in covering the police, which urges police accountability and in turn contributes to legitimacy (Chermak and Weiss 2005; Ericsson 1991). As Reiner (1985, p. 139) notes, "the existence of the media as apparently independent, impartial and ever-vigilant watchdogs over state agencies on behalf of the public interest is conducive to the legitimization of these apparatuses."

The tendency of the media to focus on police work derives from the perception that the police represent rule-governed order and symbolize the state's moral authority (Ericsson 1991). Furthermore, the police force is the most visible organization of the criminal justice system, and therefore the burdens of crime and social control issues tend to fall disproportionately within their mandate (Chermak and Weiss 2005). Consequently, the police organization will predominantly focus on controlling its professional image in the public view, because the media can considerably become a detriment to legitimacy (Altheide 1985; Lawrence 2000; Lovall 2001; Surette 2001).

Even a single high-profile event of police misconduct in the media can dramatically undermine public trust and police legitimacy (Chermak, McGarrell and Gruenewald 2006; Weitzer 2002). Findings indicate that following well-publicized incidents of misconduct cases, there was an immediate and dramatic increase in public disapproval of the police that persisted for a long time (Sunshine and Tyler 2003; Weitzer 2002). Similarly, heavily publicized cases of corruption and abuse of rights in Britain have considerably damaged police legitimacy (Loader and Mulcahy 2003; Reiner 2000).

News media mainly focus on a specific crime or crime trends, and the implicit message is the inability of the police to catch offenders (Gallagher, Maguire, Mastrofski and Reisig 2001). Furthermore, police performance is frequently portrayed as ineffective and incompetent, except for some cases in which the media profile policing as highly professional (Lawrence 2000; Surette 1998). News coverage also tends to concentrate on a few sensational cases in tabloid-style journalism, which in turn has a negative impact that leads to the public's loss of confidence in the police (Fox and Van Sickel 2001).

Still, police organizations have increasingly acknowledged that the media provide a good opportunity for manipulating coverage in order to sustain police legitimacy (Chermak and Weiss 2005; Ericsson 1991). For example, media exposure of procedural impropriety problems and corruption in police work can generate a process of regulation and reform, which in turn reinforces legitimacy (Ericsson 1991). Having delineated the theoretical frameworks on counterterrorism policing and the relationship between the media and police legitimacy, the following discussion elaborates on the role of the media in framing terrorist attacks.

Framing Terrorist Attacks

There is considerable debate about the role of the media in framing terrorism threats. News reports provide terrorist attacks with meaning by reconstructing them within a social and political context that can be understood in a simple and coherent manner (Norris, Marion and Montague 2003; Weimann and Winn 1994). However, not all terrorism events receive news coverage. The media tend to ignore some of them, whereas terrorist attacks that result in a high death toll or in significant destruction will produce significant amounts of coverage (Chermak, McGarrell and Gruenewald 2006; Kern, Just and Norris 2003; Nacos 2002).

Several studies have sought to explore the role of the media during wartime on the Rally Effect. Findings clearly demonstrate that in the face of a security threat, the media reshape the public's positive attitude toward government institutions (Bennett 1990; Livingston 1994; Philo and Berry 2004; Ruigrok and Van Atteveldt 2007; Ryan 2004; Schlesinger 1991). For example, CNN's massive coverage of the Gulf crisis in 1990–1991 relied heavily on official sources and reshaped public approval of U.S. policy by providing justifications for a military response (Livingston 1994).

Furthermore, immediately after the 9/11 attacks, editorials from the 10 largest newspapers in the United States reflected Bush's policy of "war on terror" and refrained from reporting criticizing voices or discussing the moral and practical implications of military intervention (Ryan 2004). Moreover, news framing creates networks of associations among ideas, images, and symbols—such as "war" and "homeland security"—that stimulate public support for the government (Entman 2003). Additionally, American media coverage tended to be more patriotic after the 9/11 events in comparison to other countries that suffered from terrorism, such as Britain (Ruigrok and Van Atteveldt 2007).

Similarly, during the first years of the Second Intifada, press editorials adopted the official point of view, emphasized ideas and symbols of security, and consequently contributed to the public's approval of government policy (Dor 2001, 2004; Korn 2004). However, as the terrorism threat became protracted, a process of routinization developed in the framing of terrorism and the media reassumed the traditional framing (Liebes and Kampf 2007).

In summary, the heightened terrorism threat during the Second Intifada had an immense impact on Israeli society. Furthermore, this period strongly affected the activities of the Israel Police, which basically shouldered the responsibility for maintaining public safety. Yet, there is considerable debate regarding counterterrorism policing and the impact of the security threat on the legitimacy of the police, as mentioned above. From the media aspect, there has been a growing corpus of literature on framing terrorism and the role of the media in the Rally Effect during wartime. However, coverage of police work during times of terrorism has been largely neglected. Furthermore, although the literature highlights the media's role in reshaping police legitimacy, there has been a lack of insight into how the media frame legitimacy. This study attempts to fill this gap by analyzing the effect of security threats on the press coverage of police legitimacy.

In this context, it is important to note that during the Second Intifada, journalists were at the forefront of events, and consequently police work received the greatest media attention. Therefore, this period provides a unique opportunity for the purpose of the study.

Method

This study was based on the "natural experiment" conditions created by the Second Intifada period and was designed as a field quasi-experiment (Cook and Campbell 1979). The research model focused on a restricted pre-Intifada period (January 1998–August 2000), and on the duration of the Second Intifada, that is, from September 2000 to December 2007. The analysis of police legitimacy in the media was based on the framework of Sunshine and Tyler (2003). However, it seems that depictions of the obligation to obey the police only infrequently appeared in articles that formed the database (3.2%). It may, therefore, be assumed that cases of obeying the police are not newsworthy. Thus, the current study used measures of trust in the police as proxies for legitimacy. This strategy is based on previous findings, which indicated that the obligation to obey the police was not significantly associated with legitimacy, whereas trust in police significantly related to legitimacy (Reisig, Bratton and Gertz 2007).

Furthermore, because the procedural-justice process includes two main elements (interpersonal treatment and application of procedural justice), the study analyzed these elements separately in order to verify whether there were differences in news coverage. Accordingly, the coverage of police legitimacy was examined via the following indicators: trust in police, police performance, police interpersonal treatment of citizens, and application of procedural justice.

Yet, one of the main threats to internal validity was the possibility that factors other than the variables under investigation may have influenced the dependent variable, namely, trust in police as covered in the press (see Cook and Campbell 1979, p. 211). For example, it is possible that an increase in crime rates may have influenced the coverage of police legitimacy. Thus, by including crime rates as control variables, it will help us understand whether fluctuations in legitimacy were due to changes in crime rates or due to the security threat.

Another concern was related to the possibility that the actual effectiveness of police performance may have influenced the coverage of legitimacy. Therefore, the model also included crime clearance rates as control variables. It should be noted that clearance rates are a common measurement of police performance and have been examined previously in different countries (e.g., Bayley 1994; Mesch and Talmud 1998; Reiner 1998; Weisburd, Jonathan and Perry 2009). The measurement of clearance rates is generally calculated by the number of cleared cases divided by the total number of cases opened by the police during a specific time frame. Scholars have indicated that the clearance rates indicator (rather than other variables such as crime rates or arrest rates) has several advantages in assessing police performance (Reiner 1998; Weisburd, Jonathan and Perry 2009). First, measures of clearance rates focus directly on police activities. Because it evaluates the ratio of the number of crimes solved to the number of crimes reported, it accounts for differing rates of crime in different jurisdictions. Furthermore, this indicator is related directly to police investigations rather than to specific offenders, because it focuses on the felony and not on the arrest (Weisburd, Jonathan and Perry 2009). In the preliminary analysis, the study focused on terrorist attack trends during the period of study. Figure 11.1 presents the patterns of suicide bomber attacks, the consequent number of injuries, and the death toll.

As can be seen, before the Second Intifada the terrorism threat was relatively very low. However, after the outbreak of the Intifada (September 2000), there was a dramatic increase in the number of terrorist attacks, and the consequent number of injuries and death toll also increased. This surge of terrorism reached a peak in 2002 and continued to be high in 2003. However, in subsequent years there was a sharp decline in terrorism. Similarly, the number of injuries and death toll resulting from terrorist attacks considerably decreased

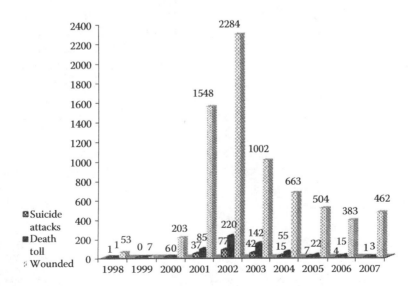

Figure 11.1 Suicide bomber terrorist attacks, number of injuries, and death toll in Israel (1998–2007). Note: Number of terrorist attacks and death tolls were provided by the Israeli Ministry of Defense.

(Israel Security Agency 2009). Therefore, the study can be divided into three periods: before the Second Intifada (January 1998–September 2000), the period of the highest levels of terrorism threat (October 2000–December 2003), and the period with a decline in terrorism (January 2004–December 2007).

Data

The articles were drawn from three major dailies in Israel—*Yedi'ot Aharonot*, *Ma'ariv*, and *Ha'aretz*—from January 1, 1998, to December 31, 2007. These newspapers are privately owned and represent the general public opinion in Israel (Dor 2005; Sela-Shayovitz 2007). By choosing different sources, we ensured a broader range of police coverage, and at the same time addressed the selection bias (Earl, Martin, McCarthy and Soule 2004). Furthermore, it allowed us to analyze coverage processes from a wide array of "voices," which increased the external validity (Babbie 2001). Additionally, to capture a fuller range of events, articles for all the issues were collected using two types of retrieval: electronic archives search and hard copies of the press (e.g., the electronic search was liable to miss some of the events that were framed in unusual ways). The search yielded 24,990 articles for the study period.

The sample was stratified by month for the 10-year period and included 2600 articles. This procedure involved randomly selecting articles from each stratum, for different weeks of the month and for different days of the week. Furthermore, in order to increase the representativeness of the sample, the strategy included picking 21 articles per month, that is, seven articles for each newspaper.*

Yet, there are several limitations worth noting. One of the main concerns in studying content changes across longer periods is the efficiency of sampling for inference (Riffe, Lacy and Fico 2005). In this context, studies have shown that constructed week sampling is more efficient for analyzing daily newspapers (Lacy, Riffe, Stoddard, Martin and Chang 2000; Riffe, Aust and Lacy 1993; Riffe, Lacy and Fico 2005). However, it seems that this strategy is less appropriate for the current study, as Israeli papers are flexible and can vary significantly in their coverage because of the security situation. Indeed, during the Intifada period, the media coverage varied considerably because of the terrorism threat (Dor 2004).† Thus, it seems that stratified sampling is more suitable for the purpose of this study.

Furthermore, a possible limitation with the use of random sampling relates to the validity of the sample. In other words, there is a possibility that in some months the articles might be inadequate in representing the coverage of police legitimacy. However, sampling a relatively large proportion of articles from each stratum and for different days of the week improves the representativeness of the sample and reduces the potential for bias. Moreover, because this period was characterized by a huge number of terrorist attacks, it seems that this procedure permitted a reasonable representation for the purpose of the study.

Another concern is related to the possibility that there was an increase in the extent of reporting about police during the Intifada, which might affect the nature of coverage.

---

* In months with 31 days, 22 articles were selected. The additional articles were randomly selected from weeks that were not covered by the random selection process in order to improve the representativeness of the sample.
† In the wake of intensive terrorist attacks, press coverage is liable to change in several aspects such as the construction of news headlines (e.g., rhetorical, hyperbole, emotional overstatement, melodramatization), the length of news articles, topics covered in the articles, and the visuals accompanying the news article, namely, the headline colors and images in the photographs and the numbers of photographs accompanying the news items (Dor 2004; Sela-Shayovitz 2007).

Thus, to further scrutinize and make valid inferences, we checked the temporal patterns of the number of reports about the police. The findings indicate that no significant changes were found in the amount of articles covering the police, although in the wake of terrorist attacks the size of news reports frequently increased, as previously mentioned. However, because the materials included different types of articles (news items, editorials, columns, etc.), the potential for bias was reduced, and a broader perspective of the nature of reporting was also ensured. Despite these concerns, these data still provide a comprehensive assessment of the media coverage of police legitimacy.

Coding Procedure

The coding procedure was conducted in two stages. Initially, a pilot content analysis was conducted on 60 articles (not part of the sample) to identify items in the articles referring to police legitimacy. The coders (the author and research assistant) received criteria for police legitimacy and participated in practice sessions before they began their actual work. The coding unit was a combination of headlines and article. In this context, it is important to note that even though the main purpose of newspaper headlines is to attract readers with a minimum of words, they also play a fundamental role in contributing to the social construction of reality (Dor 2004, 2005). Then, in the second stage, based on agreement among coders, several changes were made in the categories.

To guarantee a high degree of reliability of the coding process, the research analysis was based on general coding guidelines commonly accepted in content analysis (Krippendoff 2004).*

Intercoder reliability was assessed using Cohen's kappa coefficient in two stages. First, after the practice sessions, the reliability of each of the variables was quite high with kappa values ranging from 0.73 to 1.0; the average kappa value was 0.91. Finally, after the coding process was completed, the reliability of the full sample shows that the range of agreement was from 0.68 to 0.94, and the average coefficient was 0.83. In general, kappa values exceeding 0.80 indicate a high level of agreement (Landis and Koch 1977).

Measures and Variables

As mentioned earlier, four indicators were associated with police legitimacy: trust in police, police performance, police interpersonal treatment, and the evaluation of procedural-justice processes as fair. These monthly indicators were measured by using different items that appeared in the articles and reflected positive and negative views of the police. It should be noted that in the same article there could be some items that reflected a positive view and other items that presented a negative view. In addition, there were articles with no items related to legitimacy.

The procedure for each of the indicators was the same and was carried out in two stages. First, monthly items that fell within the indicator categories were identified according to

---

* The general guidelines for coding relate to maintaining the following requirements: employ pilot content analysis, indicate clear instructions for coding, use skilled coders and engage in practice sessions, code independently, use clear criteria, and use a single classification principle to strive for an accurate reflection of research objectivity. By using these guidelines, the reliability of the coding process increases (Krippendoff 2004).

their positive or negative view. Appendix I elaborates the details of items used to evaluate each of the indicators and provides several examples of items from the newspapers. Second, the indicator was constructed by defining a "negative weight," denoted by N (the sum of all negative view items in the month), and a "positive weight," denoted by P (the sum of all the positive items in the month). Accordingly, the indicator was determined using the following weighted mean formula: $(P - N)/(P + N)$. Finally, this index was an ordinal variable ranging from -1 (negative opinion of the police) to $+1$ (positive view of the police) with 0 (neutral or balance) in between.

This technique of measurement has both strengths and weaknesses. The weakness is that different items were scored equally, although there might, in fact, be differences between them (e.g., quotations of citizens vs. those of government ministers; varied strategies of reporting such as censorious, sarcastic, rhetorical, or emotional overstatement; length of the item; location in the paper; visuals accompanying the articles). Although these differences may have an effect on the way police legitimacy is perceived in the press, it is difficult to achieve an accurate and objective score because some of these aspects have multiple meanings and may lead to subjective interpretations of the data. Furthermore, these features of newspaper coverage are more suitable for a qualitative analysis. Therefore, these aspects were not examined in the current study. However, the strength of the current technique of measurement is that it allows us to take into account varied views of police in each of the articles and at the same time—by scoring the items equally—it allows an objective examination of the coverage of police legitimacy. The following paragraphs present the variables.

Dependent Variable

Trust in Police—This variable was operationalized as an index consisting of six items that include positive statements made by citizens or government ministers (e.g., "I trust the police") and comparable items with negative statements (e.g., "I don't trust the police").* The Cronbach alpha coefficient, which was used for assessing internal consistency, was 0.70.

Independent Variables

Police Performance—The newspaper coverage of this variable was assessed using six items of positive views on police performance (e.g., "The police are fighting crime effectively") and similar items with negative views on performance (e.g., "The police failed to fight crime effectively"). Cronbach's alpha for this indicator was 0.72.

Interpersonal Treatment—This variable was operationalized on the basis of six items that included items with positive statements made by citizens (e.g., "Police treated citizens with dignity and respect") and comparable items with negative views (e.g., "Police treatment was not respectful"). Cronbach's alpha for this scale was 0.70.

Procedural-Justice Processes—The reporting of the application of procedural-justice processes was measured using six items that included positive statements (e.g., "The police's decision was just and based upon facts") and items with negative views (e.g., "Police decisions were racially biased"). Cronbach's alpha for this scale was 0.69.

* As mentioned before, further details on the items of legitimacy indicators are provided in Appendix I.

The Second Intifada—The analysis of the terrorism threat was based on terrorism patterns (Figure 11.1). Accordingly, this variable consisted of three periods: the pre-Intifada period (January 1998–September 2000); the first period of the Intifada—involving the highest terrorism threat (October 2000–December 2003); the second period of the Intifada—the decline in terrorism threat (January 2004–December 2007), which was the comparison group.

Control Variables

Monthly Crime Rates—Four variables were used to measure crime rates: public order offenses, murder felonies, drug offenses, and sex offenses. One of the basic assumptions of the study was that fluctuations in the rates of these felonies may have affected the newspaper coverage of police legitimacy. This assumption was also based on the relatively high frequency of the press coverage of these felonies. Thus, including crime rates in the model would allow us to assess whether trends in the profiling of police legitimacy were attributable to changes in crime rates. Data were provided by the official statistics of the Israel Police.

Monthly Crime Clearance Rates—Crime clearance rates related to the same offenses as crime rates (e.g., public order, murder, drug, and sex offenses). This variable was constructed in the model in order to examine whether the police's actual performance had an effect on the coverage of legitimacy, as mentioned previously. Data for crime clearance were provided by the official statistics of the Israel Police. The descriptive statistics of the study variables are provided in Table 11.1.

Table 11.1 Descriptive Statistics of Coverage of Police Legitimacy

Variables	Mean	SD	N
Police Indicators[a]			
Trust in police	−0.18	0.65	860 (33.1)
Performance of the police	0.08	0.64	1875 (72.1)
Interpersonal treatment	−0.42	0.71	697 (26.8)
Procedural-justice processes	−0.08	0.8	741 (28.5)
Crime Rates[b]			
Public order offenses	765.39	202.89	91,846
Drug offenses	388.85	46.16	48,662
Sex offenses	50.95	8.02	6114
Murder	4.17	1.28	500
Clearance Rates			
Public order offenses	595.05	114.54	71,406
Drug offenses	261.26	40.78	31,323
Sex offenses	14.85	16.87	1782
Murder	3.2	1.28	384

[a] Frequency of police indicators in the articles (percentages in parentheses).
[b] Figures of crime rates and clearance rates were standardized to rates per 1,000,000 population.

Figures 11.2 and 11.3 present the trends in the newspaper coverage of police legitimacy indicators (trust in police, police performance, police interpersonal treatment, and procedural-justice processes).

Inspection of Figure 11.2 reveals that the news coverage of police legitimacy indicators shows generally similar trends over the study period. Before the Second Intifada (1998–2000), there was a decline in the coverage of public trust in the police and the evaluation of procedural-justice processes as fair. However, in 2001, accompanying the surge

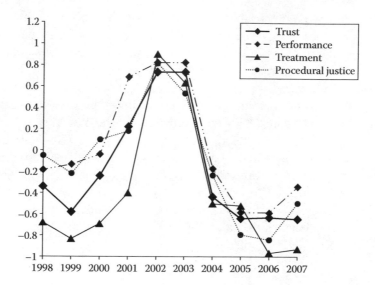

Figure 11.2 Terrorism threat and media coverage of police legitimacy (1998–2007).

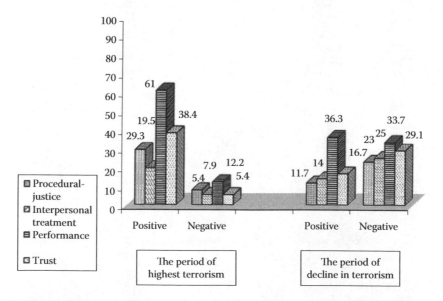

Figure 11.3 Media coverage of positive and negative views of police legitimacy during the Second Intifada (in percentages). The period of highest terrorism: October 2000–December 2003; the period of the decline in terrorism: January 2004–December 2007.

of terrorism, there was a dramatic increase in the media coverage associated with police legitimacy. This reached a peak in 2002 and remained at a high level throughout 2003. In the subsequent period there was a sharp decline in the framing of legitimacy. There was a relatively moderate rise following 2005 in the coverage of police performance and in the application of procedural-justice processes. Yet, the coverage of trust in police and interpersonal treatment remained low.

Figure 11.3 presents the frequency of positive and negative views of legitimacy in two periods: the period with the highest levels of terrorism threat (October 2000–December 2003) and the period with a decline in terrorism (January 2004–December 2007). As can be seen, during the period of the highest levels of terrorism, the newspapers frequently emphasized more positive views of the police than during the period of reduced terrorism. This trend appeared in the coverage of the four indicators: trust in police (38.4% vs. 16.7%), police performance (61% vs. 36.3%), interpersonal treatment (19.5% vs. 14%), and procedural-justice processes (29.3% vs. 11.7%). Conversely, negative views of police were reported more often during times of decreased terrorism in comparison to the period of intensive terrorism: trust in police (29.1% vs. 5.4%), police performance (33.7% vs. 12.2%), interpersonal treatment (25% vs. 5.4%), and procedural-justice processes (23% vs. 7.9%). Similarly, during the time of the highest levels of terrorism, police performance was mentioned much more often than other elements associated with police legitimacy.

Analytical Strategies

In the first step, we fitted a regression model and checked the autocorrelation function and partial autocorrelation function for the raw series and the Ljung–Box Q statistics to assess the adequacy of the model (see Box and Jenkins 1976; Box, Jenkins and Reinsel 1994). Results indicate that the correlations of the residuals were not significant. Furthermore, no indication of multicollinearity was found between the variables.

Then, based on these results, a series of ordinary least squares regression models were conducted to determine the effect of the Second Intifada and the indicators associated with police legitimacy, namely police performance, interpersonal treatment and procedural justice on trust in police. Accordingly, the first model assesses only the effect of the Second Intifada; the second model considered the intifada variables with police performance, interpersonal treatment and procedural justice; and in the last model the crime rates and clearance rates (control variables) were entered. Table 11.2 presents the results of the regression models coefficients for trust in the police.

Results

The findings of model 1 in Table 11.2 indicate that the pre-Intifada period and the first period of the Intifada were positively associated with trust in police. Thus, levels of trust in the police were higher during these periods than the second part of the Intifada, when terrorism threat declined. Yet, the regression coefficient of the first period of the Intifada ($\beta = 0.77$, $p = 0.0$) is much larger than that in the pre-Intifada period ($\beta = 0.14$, $p = 0.10$), and when comparing the regression coefficients of the two Intifada variables across the models, we find that only the first period of the Intifada had a significant effect on trust

Table 11.2 Summary of Regression Models Coefficients for Police Legitimacy in Media Coverage

	Trust in Police					
	Model 1		Model 2		Model 3	
Variables	β	(SE)	β	(SE)	β	(SE)
Security Situation						
Intifada A	0.14*	(0.10)	0.05	(0.07)	0.28	(0.23)
Intifada B	0.77**	(0.09)	0.26*	(0.14)	0.43*	(0.21)
Legitimacy Indicators						
Performance of the police	–		0.27**	(0.08)	0.26*	(0.09)
Interpersonal treatment	–		0.28**	(0.07)	0.22*	(0.08)
Procedural-justice processes	–		0.12	(0.06)	0.12	(0.06)
Crime Rates						
Public order	–		–		0.15	(4.06)
Murder	–		–		−0.02	(14.17)
Drug	–		–		−0.02	(56.06)
Sex	–		–		−0.18	(22.37)
Clearance Rates						
Public order	–		–		0.17	(6.68)
Murder	–		–		−0.00	(66.32)
Drug	–		–		−0.00	(16.41)
Sex	–		–		−0.10	(16.67)
N	120		120		120	
R^2 value	0.52		0.67		0.69	

Note: Standardized coefficients: standard errors are in parentheses: Intifada A—value 1 = pre-Intifada period (January 1998–September 2000); value 0 = otherwise; Intifada B—value 1= first period of the Intifada (October 2000–December 2003); value 0 = otherwise.
*$p < 0.05$; **$p < 0.01$.

in police (see models 2 and 3). These results confirm the hypothesis that levels of high terrorism threat plays a significant role in predicting the coverage of trust in the police. As mention above, model 2 considered the effects of the Intifada variables and the indicators associated with police legitimacy. The results show that police performance and interpersonal treatment were significantly and positively related to trust in police ($\beta = 0.27$, $p = 0.08$ and $\beta = 0.28$, $p = 0.07$, respectively). In contrast, no significant effect was found for procedural justice on trust in police. These suggest that at a time of security threat the coverage of police performance and interpersonal treatment plays a larger role than procedural justice in predicting the framing of trust in police. Furthermore, the findings of model 3 confirm the hypothesis that police performance and interpersonal treatment play a significantly role in predicting trust in police in the media. However, no significant effect was found for crime and clearance rates (see model 3). These data, therefore, suggest that media framing of trust in police is not affected by trends of crime or the actual effectiveness of police performance.

Discussion and Conclusions

This study utilized the unique opportunity provided by the Second Intifada to examine whether the threat of terrorism affects the media framing of police legitimacy. At a time like the present, when many countries are required to deal with terrorism threats, this theme is particularly pertinent. Several findings were specifically noteworthy.

First, the first period of the Second Intifada was found to have a significant and positive effect on the coverage of police legitimacy. Following the outbreak of the Second Intifada, there was a significant increase in the media portrayals of public trust and confidence in the police. These results confirm the hypothesis that periods with high levels of terrorism threat plays a significant role in media shaping of police legitimacy. Moreover, the findings show that police performance and interpersonal treatment play a significantly larger role in predicting legitimacy than procedural justice. Recently, it was found that public evaluations of procedural justice remain the primary antecedent of legitimacy during time of security threat. However, the researchers have noted that under extreme existential threat, procedural justice may become less important in predicting legitimacy (Jonathan-Zamir and Weisburd 2011). Indeed, during these times the public is more concerned about the effectiveness of performance rather than the fairness of procedural justice (Nagata 1993; Tyler and Huo 2002). Thus, it may be assumed that news editors are attentive to people's concerns, and consequently the role of performance and procedural-justice processes become stronger in maintaining legitimacy. Moreover, it is also feasible that the coverage is not accurately reflected in public evaluations of legitimacy, as different factors and agencies (e.g., police organizations, politicians, and social groups) can be involved in the way the media is framing the police.

Nevertheless, the findings show that the media did not remain favorable toward the police for long. Following the decrease in terrorism-related events (the second period of the Intifada), the coverage highly emphasized negative views of the police. Moreover, levels of trust in police were significantly lower during the second period of the Intifada in comparison to the pre-Intifada period and the first period with highest terrorism threat.

These trends in the coverage of police legitimacy are compatible with the Rally Effect hypothesis. Previous studies have shown that at times of a high security threat, the media play an important role in the Rally Effect by reshaping the legitimacy of the government and fostering public approval (Livingston 1994; Ruigrok and Van Atteveldt 2007; Ryan 2004).

Furthermore, conceptually situated within the *patriotism* approach (Entman 2003; Hetherington and Nelson 2003; Ryan 2004), it may be assumed that in the wake of a terrorism threat the media tend to be more patriotic and consequently foster police legitimacy. This assumption is based on the fact that Israeli police forces were in the forefront of the battle against terrorist attacks. Hence, by underscoring the effectiveness of the police's counterterrorism efforts in the press, and even by portraying them in some cases as heroic, the media contributes to the enhancement of legitimacy as reflected in the press.

It is also feasible that the increase in coverage of legitimacy resulted from the tendency of journalists during terrorist attacks to rely on police sources, which draws attention to police successes. In this regard, previous studies have shown that during the first period of the Intifada, press editorials tended to adopt the official point of view provided

by the government (Dor 2004; Korn 2004). However, as terrorism began to decline, journalists rigorously scrutinized and emphasized police failures, which eroded legitimacy.
For example, the exposure of the Parinyan brothers' misconduct case* by the media at
the time gained prominent publication and generated significant upheaval in the police.
Consequently, it led to the resignation of the inspector general of the police and other
senior officers. Thus, it seems that the media resumed its traditional role as "watchdog"
of police work.

Second, it seems that trends in the framing of legitimacy were generally consistent
with a prior study, which indicated that Israeli Jewish public evaluations of police were
influenced by levels of terrorism threat (Jonathan 2010). It may be assumed that there was
a reciprocal flow of influence between public opinion and the media: positive public attitudes toward the police affected the way in which the media profiled the police, and simultaneously the positive coverage of police reinforced public approval. However, in light of
the concept that the media are a key arena in which legitimacy is reshaped (Chermak and
Weiss 2005; Ericsson 1991), it may be suggested that newspaper coverage had a strong
impact on crystallizing public approval. Findings confirmed this hypothesis and show
that the media play a significant role in shaping public opinion of the police (Gallagher,
Maguire, Mastrofski and Reisig 2001) as well as essentially contribute to the Rally Effect
(Ruigrok and Van Atteveldt 2007; Ryan 2004).

Third, police legitimacy has been mainly examined via public survey studies. With
this in mind, it was argued that using alternative methodologies would help us gain a
deeper understanding of this concept (Reisig, Bratton and Gertz 2007). Thus, the current
study provides a new insight into the process-based model (Sunshine and Tyler 2003; Tyler
2004). In light of the debate regarding the role of procedural justice (Reisig, Bratton and
Gertz 2007; Reisig and Mesko 2009), the study provides a new insight into the importance
of police performance and procedural justice in media shaping legitimacy under conditions of high terrorism threats.

The current study, of course, is not without its limitations. Despite consistent variations
in the police legitimacy before and during the Second Intifada, it is difficult to attribute all
of the variations exclusively to the impact of the security threat on media coverage. The
abovementioned explanations regarding the impact of the levels of terrorism threat on the
media framing of legitimacy clearly indicate that further research is required. Expanding
the analysis to the relationship between police legitimacy and variables such as the government view of the police and police spokespeople's strategies will enhance existing knowledge in the field.

Acknowledgments

I thank the anonymous reviewers, Professor David Weisburd, and Dr. Tal Jonathan-Zamir
for their insightful and helpful comments on earlier drafts of this paper.

---

* The Parinyan brothers' case relates to the involvement of senior police officers in organized crime in
  Israel. Consequently, a commission of inquiry appointed by the Israeli government published a report,
  which harshly criticized the police and led to the resignation of the inspector general and other senior
  police officers.

Appendix I. Legitimacy Indicators

The following items were identified as fit with respect to each one of the indicators, including positive and negative opinions (in parentheses). Furthermore, several examples from the newspapers are provided below for each of the indicators.

Trust in Police
1. I trust the police (I don't trust the police).
2. I have confidence that the police are doing their job well (I don't have confidence in the police).
3. I think that police constables are generally honest (I think that police constables are generally dishonest).
4. I believe that the police will succeed in dealing well with these assignments (I don't believe that the police will succeed in dealing with these assignments).
5. The police can be trusted to make the right decisions (The police failed to make the right decisions).
6. Police constables act within the law (Police constables exceed their authority).

Examples from the newspapers regarding trust in the police

a. "Minister of Internal Security, Avi Dichter: 'I trust the police. The police in Israel are responsible and professional enough and if there were mistakes they will be investigated and corrected.'" *Ha'aretz*, October 31, 2007.
b. "Prime Minister Sharon pledged his full support to the police [before the disengagement operation] and said: 'I trust the police that they will perform the assignment in a good and professional manner. You [the] officers: Don't be deterred by any threat and by those who threaten you.'" *Yedi'ot Aharonot*, May 17, 2005.
c. "The decision to dismiss Major General Moshe Mizrahi, head of the Investigations Division in the police, is a courageous decision, based on the report of the State Comptroller and Attorney General, and in this way it reinforces rules of proper administration and restores the public's trust in the police." *Yedi'ot Aharonot*, November 22, 2004.
d. "Survey: 40% of the public feel distrust toward the police. Public trust in the police is constantly eroding—only 14% of the public have great trust in the police." *Ha'aretz*, February 20, 2007.
e. "A concerned citizen: 'I don't believe that the police are capable of taking care of everything. Citizens are tired of waiting for the police to stop handling security issues and find time to deal with ordinary crimes.'" *Ma'ariv*, May 15, 2005.
f. "'Minister of Internal Security Avi Dichter's latest series of appointments indicates the minister's distrust of the police organization and senior command,' senior police officers stated last night." *Ma'ariv*, October 7, 2005.

Police Performance
1. The police are fighting crime effectively (The police failed to fight crime effectively).
2. The police responded quickly to people calling for help (The police did not respond rapidly to a call for help).

3. The police succeeded in solving criminal investigations (The police failed to solve criminal investigations).
4. The police succeeded in counterterrorism policing tasks, such as arresting terrorists on their way to commit a suicide attack (The police failed in arresting terrorists on their way to committing suicide).
5. Police efforts led to a decline in crime rates (The police failed to control crime rates).
6. The police are doing a good job in providing services to the community (The police fail to provide services to the community).

Examples from the newspapers of police performance

a. "Police confronted a double challenge and did excellent police work during the disengagement in view of all those who could have been harmed by the evacuation." *Ma'ariv*, August 26, 2005.
b. "The police investigation succeeded in leading to the arrest of 17 suspected drug traffickers in a massive operation that lasted seven months." *Ma'ariv*, December 28, 2003.
c. "Police constables prevented the attack with their own bodies: Three constables overpowered a suicide bomber carrying a huge explosive." *Yedi'ot Aharonot*, July 12, 2001.
d. "A police officer's alertness prevented a severe explosion yesterday: The police officer suspected a young man who was sweating profusely along the Jerusalem border and had him arrested. The terrorist was going to blow himself up in the city center." *Yedi'ot Aharonot*, July 18, 2006.
e. "The police report of 2003: Mounting crime. Police figures show that the sharpest increase in the last six years was 4.2% in reported crime rates." *Yedi'ot Aharonot*, February 15, 2004.
f. "Violence is raging, crime is rampant, corruption is on the rise. Why did this happen to us? Where are the police? Is the situation really worse than ever?" *Yedi'ot Aharonot*, June 10, 2005.

Interpersonal Treatment
1. The police treat citizens with respect and dignity (Police treatment was degrading or disrespectful).
2. The police respected people's rights (Police treatment was a violation of human rights).
3. The police treat everyone equally (Police treatment was racially biased).
4. The police tried to help citizens with their problems (Police constables didn't provide assistance to citizens).
5. The police treat people's complaints seriously (The police ignore people's complaints).
6. Police treatment was appropriate (Police treatment was inappropriate).

Examples from the newspapers for interpersonal treatment

a. "The rape victim, A, said that the attitude of the police investigators was polite but firm: 'They asked all the difficult questions, but waited patiently and sensitively until I was able to answer.'" *Ma'ariv*, November 5, 2006.

b. "A survey in 2006 commissioned by the police found a discrepancy between the public's attitude to a police constable and its attitude to the police in general: While the public considers the police constable a courteous and polite person, it still shows dissatisfaction with the police system as a whole." *Yedi'ot Aharonot*, February 6, 2007.

c. "Att. Eitan Ben-David: 'The police were courteous and fair. I went down to the patrol car without handcuffs even though I know they have to put handcuffs on suspects.'" *Yedi'ot Aharonot*, May 16, 2003.

d. "You can't shoot a Druze man who is no less loyal to the country than a Jew. In a Jewish settlement this [kind of] thing would not happen." *Yedi'ot Aharonot*, November 2, 2007.

e. "The victim is punished twice: The victims are subjected to a humiliating treatment by the police and are not considered a 'party' in the trial." *Yedi'ot Aharonot*, October 18, 2004.

f. "The sister of the murder victim: 'We went to the police station; we stood and waited for help and almost nobody paid attention to us. The attitude of the police was humiliating. They simply refused to acknowledge us and they referred us to the Kfar Saba police.'" *Ma'ariv*, December 16, 1998.

Procedural-Justice Processes

1. The police's decision was just and based on facts (The police's decision was not just or was not based on facts).

2. The police's decision was not racially biased (The police's decision was racially biased).

3. The police constables gave an explanation for their actions (No explanations were given for police actions).

4. The police applied the law consistently to different people (The police applied the rules differently toward minorities).

5. The police applied the rules accurately (The police did not apply the rules accurately).

6. The police consider people's opinions in their decisions (The police ignored the people's point of view in their decisions).

Examples from the newspapers for procedural-justice processes

a. "Judge Yehudit Tzur: 'I won't be exaggerating if I say that police investigators in this case acted with remarkable sensitivity…while ensuring that a fair, businesslike and proper investigation be conducted.'" *Yedi'ot Aharonot*, November 29, 2001.

b. "The court concluded that police proceeding in the arrest of Ze'ev Rosenstein was fair. The police investigation was conducted professionally and in accordance with existing procedures." *Ma'ariv*, December 31, 2005.

c. "Commander of the Sharon region: 'The police acted properly and in accordance with existing procedures in these cases [missing person]" *Yedi'ot Aharonot*, December 16, 1998.

d. "State Comptroller Micha Lindenstrauss found serious faults in the police's functioning and established that some of the faults came from improper organizational culture and inobservance of procedures and regulations as required." *Ha'aretz*, April 11, 2011.

e.   "The difficult questions [are]: 'Why didn't the police know in advance that the residents of Pki'in were prepared for such a violent struggle? Why did the police dispatch such a large force in order to arrest just 17 suspects? Why did they shoot at the residents using live ammunition? Why did they enter the praying area which is holy to the Druze?'" *Yedi'ot Aharonot*, October 31, 2007.

f.   "Head of the Police Internal Investigations Department Eran Shendar: 'I definitely think that police are not telling the truth when asked about their fellow constables. I saw police standing in the hall and coordinating testimonies in public.'" *Yedi'ot Aharonot*, October 15, 1999.

References

Altheide, D. L. 1985. *Media power*. Beverly Hills, CA: Sage Publications.

Babbie, E. R. 2001. *The practice of social research*. Belmont, CA: Wadsworth Thomson Learning.

Bayley, D. H. 1994. *Police for the future*. New York: Oxford University Press.

Bayley, D. and D. Weisburd. 2009. Cops and spooks: The role of the police in counterterrorism. In *To protect and to serve: Policing in an age of terrorism*, eds. D. Weisburd, T. Feucht, I. Hakimi, L. Mock and S. Perry, 81–101. New York: Springer.

Bennett, L. W. 1990. Toward a theory of press–state relations in the United States. *Journal of Communication* 40: 103–125.

Box, G. E. P. and G. M. Jenkins. 1976. *Time series analysis: Forecasting and control*. San Francisco, Holden-Day.

Box, G. E. P., G. M. Jenkins and G. C. Reinsel. 1994. *Time series analysis: Forecasting and control*. Englewood Cliffs, NJ: Prentice Hall.

Brodeur, J. P. 1983. High and low policing: Remarks about the policing of political activities. *Social Problems* 30: 507–520.

Chermak, S. and T. A. Weiss. 2005. Maintaining legitimacy using external communication strategies: An analysis of police–media relations. *Journal of Criminal Justice* 33: 501–512.

Chermak, S., E. McGarrell and J. Gruenewald. 2006. Media coverage of police misconduct and attitudes toward police. *Policing: An International Journal of Policing & Strategies* 29: 261–281.

Cook, T. D. and D. T. Campbell. 1979. *Quasi-experimentation: Design and analysis for field settings*. Chicago: Rand McNally.

Coser, L. A. 1956. *The functions of social conflict*. New York: Free Press.

Cromer, G. 2006. Analogies to terror: The construction of social problems in Israel during the Intifada Al Aqsa. *Terrorism and Political Violence* 18: 389–98.

Deutsch, M. 1990. Psychological roots of moral exclusion. *Journal of Social Issues* 46: 21–25.

Dor, D. 2001. *Newspaper under the influence*. Tel Aviv, Israel: Babel [in Hebrew].

Dor, D. 2004. *Intifada hits the headlines: How the Israeli press misreported the outbreak of the second Palestinian uprising*. Bloomington, IN: Indiana University Press.

Dor, D. 2005. *The suppression of guilt: The Israeli media and the reoccupation of the West Bank*. London: Pluto Press.

Earl, J., A. Martin, J. D. McCarthy and S. A. Soule. 2004. The use of newspapers data in the study of collective action. *Annual Review of Sociology* 30: 65–80.

Entman, R. M. 2003. Cascading activation: Contesting the White House's frame after 9/11. *Political Communication* 20: 415–432.

Entman, R. M. 2004. *Projections of power: Framing news, public opinion, and US foreign policy*. Chicago: University of Chicago Press.

Ericsson, R. V. 1991. Mass media, crime, law, and justice: An institutional approach. *The British Journal of Criminology* 31: 219–249.

Fishman, G. 2005. *Balanced police action between terror and maintaining public order: A summary of an era and challenges for coming years.* Israel: The Israel Democracy Institute [in Hebrew].

Fox, R. L. and R. W. Van Sickel. 2001. *Tabloid justice: Criminal justice in an age of media frenzy.* Boulder, CO: Lynne Rienner Publishers.

Gallagher, C., E. Maguire, S. Mastrofski and M. Reisig. 2001. *The public image of the police: Final report to the international association of chiefs of police.* Manassas, VA: George Mason University, Administration of Justice Program.

Hasisi, B., G. P. Alpert and D. Flynn. 2009. The impacts of policing terrorism on society: Lessons from Israel and the U.S. In *To protect and to serve: Policing in an age of terrorism*, eds. D. Weisburd, T. Feucht, I. Hakimi, L. Mock and S. Perry, 177–203. New York: Springer.

Herzog, S. 2003. Border closures as a reliable method for the measurement of Palestinian involvement in crime in Israel: A quasi-experimental analysis. *International Journal of Comparative Criminology* 3: 18–41.

Hetherington, M. J. and M. Nelson. 2003. Anatomy of a rally effect: George W. Bush and the war on terrorism. *Political Science & Politics* 36: 37–42.

Israel Security Agency. 2009. The distribution of deaths from Palestinian terrorism in the current conflict, and in comparison with the preceding decade. Retrieved December 31, 2009 http://www.shabak.gov.il/publications/Pages/default.aspx (in Hebrew).

Jonathan, T. 2010. Police involvement in counterterrorism and public attitudes toward the police in Israel: 1998–2007. *British Journal of Criminology* 50: 748–771.

Jonathan-Zamir, T. and D. Weisburd. 2011. The effects of security threats on antecedents of police legitimacy: Findings from a quasi-experiment in Israel. *Journal of Research in Crime & Delinquency* 1–30.

Kern, M., M. Just and P. Norris, P. 2003. The lessons of framing terrorism. In *Framing terrorism*, eds. P. Norris, M. Kern, and M. Just, 281–302. London: Routledge.

Korn, A. 2004. Reporting Palestinian casualties in the Israeli press: The case of Ha'aretz and the Intifada. *Journalism Studies* 5: 247–262.

Krippendoff, K. 2004. Reliability in content analysis. *Human Communication Research* 30: 411–433.

Lacy, S., D. Riffe, S. Stoddard, H. Martin and K. Chang. 2000. Sample size for newspaper content analysis in multi-year studies. *Journalism & Mass Communication Quarterly* 78: 836–845.

Landis, J. R. and G. G. Koch. 1977. The measurement of observer agreement for categorical data. *Biometrics* 33: 159–174.

Lawrence, R. 2000. *The politics of force.* Berkley, CA: University of California Press.

Liebes, T. and Z. Kampf. 2007. Routinizing terror: Media coverage and public practices in Israel, 2000–2005. *The Harvard International Journal of Politics* 12: 108–116.

Livingston, S. 1994. *The terrorism spectacle.* Boulder, CO: Westview Press.

Loader, I. 1997. Policing and the social: Questions of symbolic power. *British Journal of Sociology* 48: 1–18.

Loader, I. and A. Mulcahy. 2003. *Policing and the condition of England: Memory, politics and culture.* Oxford, UK: Oxford University Press.

Lovall, J. S. 2001. Police performances: Media power and impression management in contemporary policing. Unpublished doctoral dissertation. Newark, NJ: The State University of Rutgers.

McCulloch, J. and S. Pickering. 2005. Suppressing the financing of terrorism: Proliferating state crime, eroding censure and extending Neo-Colonialism. *British Journal of Criminology* 45: 470–486.

McCulloch, J. and S. Pickering. 2009. Pre-crime and counter-terrorism imagining future crime in the "war of terror." *British Journal of Criminology* 49: 628–645.

Mesch, G. S. and I. Talmud. 1998. The influence of community characteristics on police performance in a deeply divided society: The case of Israel. *Sociological Focus* 31: 233–248.

Mueller, J. E. 1970. Presidential popularity from Truman to Johnson. *American Political Science Review* 64: 18–34.

Mueller, J. E. 1973. *War, presidents and public opinion.* New York: Wiley.

Nacos, B. L. 2002. *Mass-mediated terrorism: The central role of the media in terrorism and counter-terrorism.* Lanham, MD: Rowman & Littlefield.

Nagata, D. 1993. *Legacy of injustice.* New York: Plenum.

Norpoth, H. 1991. The popularity of the Thatcher government: A matter of war and economy. In *Economics and politics: The calculus of support,* eds. H. Norpoth, M. S. Lewis-Beck and J. D. Lafay, 141–161. Ann Arbor, MI: University of Michigan Press.

Norris, P., J. Marion and K. Montague. 2003. *Framing terrorism: Understanding terrorist threats and mass media.* New York: Routledge.

O'Reilly, C. and G. Ellison. 2006. Eye spy private high: Re-conceptualizing high policing theory. *British Journal of Criminology* 46: 641–660.

Parker, S. L. 1995. Toward an Understanding of 'Rally' Effects: Public Opinion in the Persian Gulf War. *Public Opinion,* 59(4): 526–546.

Philo, G. and M. Berry. 2004. *Bad news from Israel.* London: Pluto Press.

Reiner, R. 1985. *The politics of the police.* New York: St. Martin's Press.

Reiner, R. 1998. Process or product? Problem of assessing individual police performance. In *How to recognize good policing: Problems and issues,* ed. J.P. Brodeur, 55–72. Thousand Oaks, CA: Sage.

Reiner, R. 2000. *The Politics of the police.* Oxford, UK: Oxford University Press.

Reisig, M. D. and M. Chandek. 2001. The effects of expectancy disconfirmation on outcome satisfaction in police–citizen encounters. *Policing: An International Journal of Police Strategies & Management* 24: 88–99.

Reisig, M. D. and C. Lloyd. 2009. Procedural justice, police legitimacy, and helping the police fight crime. Results from a survey of Jamaican adolescents. *Police Quarterly* 12: 41–62.

Reisig, M. D. and G. M. Mesko. 2009. Procedural justice, legitimacy, and prisoner misconduct. *Psychology, Crime & Law* 15: 41–59.

Reisig, M., J. Bratton and M. Gertz. 2007. The construct validity and refinement of process-based policing measures. *Criminal Justice & Behavior* 34: 1005–1028.

Riffe, D., C. F. Aust and S. R. Lacy. 1993. The effectiveness of random, consecutive day and constructed week samples in newspaper content analysis. *Journalism Quarterly* 70: 133–139.

Riffe, D., S. Lacy and F. G. Fico. 2005. *Analyzing media messages: Using quantitative content analysis in research.* Mahwah, NJ: Lawrence Erlbaum Associates.

Ruigrok, N. and V. Van Atteveldt. 2007. *Global angling with a local angle: How US, British and Dutch newspapers frame global and local terrorist attacks.* Charleston, SC: Booksurge Publishers.

Ryan, M. 2004. Framing the war against terrorism: US newspaper editorials and military action in Iraq. *Gazette* 66: 363–382.

Sampson, R. J., S. W. Raudenbush and F. Earls. 1997. Neighborhoods and violent crime: A multilevel study of collective efficacy. *Science* 277: 918–924.

Schlesinger, P. 1991. *Media, state and nation: Political violence and collective identities.* London: Sage.

Sela-Shayovitz, R. 2007. Female suicide bombers: Israeli newspaper reporting and the public construction. *Criminal Justice Studies* 20: 197–215.

Selye, H. 1956. *The stress of life.* New York: McGraw-Hill.

Sidel, M. 2004. *More secure, less free? Antiterrorism policy and civil liberties after September 11.* Ann Arbor, MI: University of Michigan Press.

Sigelman, L. and P. J. Conover. 1981. The dynamics of presidential support during international conflict situations. *Political Behavior* 3: 303–318.

Simmel, G. 1955. *Conflict and the web of group affiliations.* New York: Free Press.

Sullivan, J., J. Piereson and G. E. Marcus. 1982. *Political tolerance and American democracy.* Chicago: University of Chicago Press.

Sunshine, J. and T. R. Tyler. 2003. The role of procedural justice and legitimacy in shaping public support for policing. *Law & Society Review* 37: 513–548.

Surette, R. 1998. Some unpopular thoughts about popular culture. In *Popular culture, crime and justice*, eds. F. Bailey and D. Hale, xiv–xxiv. Belmont, CA: Wadsworth.

Surette, R. 2001. Public information officers: The civilianization of a criminal justice profession. *Journal of Criminal Justice* 29: 107–117.

Tankebe, J. 2009. Public cooperation with the police in Ghana: Does procedural fairness matter? *Criminology* 47: 1265–1293.

Thacher, D. 2005. The local role in homeland security. *Law & Society Review* 39: 635–676.

Tyler, T. R. 1990. *Why people obey the law.* New Haven, CT: Yale University Press.

Tyler, T. R. 2001. Public trust and confidence in legal authorities: What do majority and minority group members want from legal authorities? *Behavioral Sciences & the Law* 19: 215–235.

Tyler, T. R. 2004. Enhancing police legitimacy. *The Annals of the American Academy of Political & Social Science* 593: 593–608.

Tyler, T. and J. Fagan. 2006. *Legitimacy and cooperation: Why do people help the police fight crime in their communities?* Public Law & Legal Theory Working Paper Group. New York: Columbia Law School.

Tyler, T. R. and Y. J. Huo. 2002. *Trust in the law.* New York: Russell Sage.

Tyler, T. R. and H. J. Smith. 1997. Social justice and social movements. In *Handbook of social psychology*, eds. D. T. Gilbert, S. Fiske and G. Gardner, 595–633. New York: Addison-Wesley.

Tyler, T., S. Schulhofer and A. Z. Huq. 2010. Legitimacy and deterrence effects in counterterrorism policing: A study of Muslim Americans. *Law & Society Review* 44: 365–401.

Weimann, G. and C. Winn. 1994. *The theater of terror: Mass media and international terrorism.* London: Longman.

Weisburd, D., B. Hasisi, T. Jonathan and G. Aviv. 2010. Terrorist threats and police performance: A study of Israeli communities. *British Journal of Criminology* 50: 725–547.

Weisburd, D., T. Jonathan and S. Perry. 2009. The Israeli model for policing terrorism: Goals, strategies and open questions. *Criminal Justice & Behavior* 36: 1259–1278.

Weitzer, R. 2002. Perceptions of racial profiling: Race, class, and personal experience. *Criminology* 40: 435–456.

Weitzer, R. 2004. Reforming the police: Racial differences in public support for change. *Criminology* 42: 391–416.

Weitzer, R. and S. A. Tuch. 2004. Race and perceptions of police misconduct. *Social Problems* 51: 305–325.

Wilkinson, P. 2001. *Terrorism versus democracy: The liberal state response.* London: Frank Cass Publishers.

Policing Terrorism and Police–Community Relations
Views of Arab Minority in Israel*

BADI HASISI
DAVID WEISBURD

Contents

Introduction

Research on police over the past three decades has been focused primarily on questions of crime and disorder, and community. However, since the 9/11 terrorist attack, the United States and other Western countries have been challenged by a new set of responsibilities for policing, which are likely to require changes in police strategies and organization (Bayley and Weisburd 2009; International Association of Chiefs of Police 2005; National Research Council 2004). Although several studies have been written on the policing of terrorism in recent years, we still know very little about the impact of policing terrorism on society, and more specifically on minority groups.

* Reproduced from Hasisi, B., and D. Weisburd. 2014. Policing terrorism and police-community relations: Views of the Arab minority in Israel. *Police Practice and Research: An International Journal* 15(2):158–172.

Several studies have emphasized the tense relationship that often exists between the police and minority groups (Weitzer and Tuch 2006); however, the discussion of minority perceptions of the police takes a new turn when we analyze police involvement in counterterrorism. This discussion has unique patterns with regard to certain kinds of minority groups who have an affiliation to the source of threat from terror. The phenomenon of minority groups that are affiliated with a hostile external political element has been documented in several countries (Horowitz 2001). After the 9/11 terror attacks, American Muslims felt that they were profiled by the police and other agencies of homeland security, especially by airport security, as constituting a threat to homeland security (Arab American Institute Foundation 2001; Hasisi, Alpert and Flynn 2009; Hasisi and Weisburd 2011; Thacher 2005; Tyler, Schulhofer and Huq 2010).

Similar complaints were also raised by British Muslims after the terror attacks in London in July 2005. Prime Minister Tony Blair even warned against blaming all Muslims for the terror attacks.* This demonstrates that minorities with an external affinity to a country (the homeland) or culture with which the country where they currently reside is at violent conflict (i.e., terror attacks) are liable to generate an image of an "enemy within." This image creates significant challenges to the relationship of the minority group with the police, especially when the latter is involved in counterterror missions.

The purpose of the current study is to give an overview of Arab and Jewish attitudes in Israel toward the involvement of the police in counterterror missions. Israel has a tragic history of terrorism. Since its establishment, the State of Israel has been exposed to widespread terrorism, perpetrated primarily by Palestinians and Arabs from the region. The phenomenon of Palestinian suicide terrorism emerged in the beginning of the 1990s, and increased significantly during the years 2001–2002 (Second Intifada), causing the deaths of hundreds of Israeli civilians (Hasisi, Alpert and Flynn 2009; Jonathan 2010; Jonathan and Weisburd 2010). In 1974, the Israeli police was given the authority to handle threats to homeland security. Over the years, dealing with terrorism has become one of the main missions of the Israeli police; however, this role (policing terrorism) became particularly salient during the Second Intifada.

Israel also finds itself in a situation where its largest Arab minority group has an ethnic and national affiliation to the source of threat to homeland security (the Palestinian people and the neighboring Arab countries). Over the years, the involvement of Israeli Arabs in terrorism was quite rare; however, during the Second Intifada, a significant rise in their involvement in terrorism was observed. One can assume that Jewish and Arab attitudes toward the policing of terrorism would be very different, with Jews being much more positive and Arabs seeing the issue of terrorism and counterterrorism as part of the more general conflict between Arabs and Jews in Israel. Social surveys show that Jews and Arabs hold different views in many aspects of life, especially with regard to political identity and perceptions of state apparatus. While a majority of Israeli Arabs view their national identity as Palestinian, Israeli Jews view this same identity as the identity of the enemy and view it as a risk to homeland security.

The main purpose of the current study is to give an overview of Arab and Jewish attitudes in Israel toward the involvement of the police in counterterror missions. We will focus our analysis on three main areas: *first*, we analyze how the public views the impact of policing terrorism on police routine performance; *second*, we analyze public perceptions

---

* British Prime Minister Tony Blair stated: "We know that these people acted in the name of Islam. But we also know that the vast majority of Muslims both here and abroad are decent and law-abiding people who abhor this kind of terrorism every bit as much as we do" (http://news.bbc.co.uk/2/hi/uk_news/4661059.stm).

of how police involvement in counterterrorism missions affects police–community relations; and *third*, we examine the willingness of Israeli Arabs and Jews to collaborate with the police in two areas: reporting terror threats and reporting crime. Some of these questions have been already studied in Israel with regard to the Jewish majority community. Jonathan and Weisburd (2010) have found that Israeli Jews see policing terrorism as damaging the relationship between the police and the public, yet we still do not know how the attitudes of the Israeli Arab minority differs from the Jewish majority.

The study is based on telephone survey that was conducted in December 2008. Our findings indicate that although there are significant differences between the attitudes of Arabs and Jews, those differences are often not large; and overall, Jews and Arabs share many common beliefs about terrorism and its implications. There is, in this sense, more consensus than would be expected. However, the results also indicate that Israeli Arabs were much more concerned about the social ramifications of police involvement in counterterrorism and the impact it might have on the relationship of the police with the Arab minority.

Policing Terror and Minorities

The policing of terrorism impacts differently on different kinds of social groups. For instance, minority groups with an affiliation to the source of the terrorist threat (e.g., Arab-Americans, British Muslims, or Israeli Arabs) add international implications to local law enforcement that are liable to impinge significantly on police–community relations (Hasisi, Alpert and Flynn 2009; Henderson, Ortiz, Sugie and Miller 2006; Thacher 2005; Tyler, Schulhofer and Huq 2010). Members of Muslim American communities generally express a strong allegiance to America and very little support for terrorism or terrorists however, Tyler, Schulhofer and Huq (2010) argue that "...cultural or religious ties between these communities (i.e., Muslim American) and contexts from which anti-American terrorism is emerging (e.g., Afghanistan, Pakistan, the Gulf States, Somalia) mean that Muslim American communities have become a focus for anti-terror policing efforts in the United States" (Tyler, Schulhofer and Huq 2010, p. 366). In Israel, in recent years, many social surveys have shown that the Jewish majority holds significant negative perceptions of the Arab minority, especially that they fear that this minority might collaborate with the enemy and pose a threat to the homeland security of the state of Israel (Hasisi 2005; Smooha 2004; The Israeli Democracy Institute 2010).

These minority groups might be profiled by the police as "enemies within," justifying the use of oppressive measures against them, which in turn may harm the relationship between the police and the minority community (Hasisi 2008; Thacher 2005; Tyler, Schulhofer and Huq 2010). This is likely to jeopardize the community's trust and confidence in the police, that is, not seeing police as legitimate soldiers in the war against terrorism; this means that community members will deem the police illegitimate and will hesitate to call upon their services or cooperate with them in fighting and preventing crime (Thacher 2005; Tyler, Schulhofer and Huq 2010).

As mentioned above, prior studies have indicated that minority views of the police tend to be negative when compared to the attitudes of the majority (Hasisi and Weitzer 2007; Weitzer and Tuch 2006). We assume that this will worsen when we consider the attitudes of minority groups on issues of policing terrorism, especially when the minority group has ethnic or national ties with the source of the threat from terror (i.e., Arab Americans,

British Muslims, Israeli Arabs) (Hasisi, Alpert and Flynn 2009; Nguyen 2005; Rabasa et al. 2014; Tyler, Schulhofer and Huq 2010). These negative attitudes toward policing terrorism can be partly explained by the minority understanding that these kinds of practices will be mainly targeted at them (Brodeur 1983). This, in turn, raises concerns of racial and ethnic profiling with regard to policing terror among the minority groups.

Arab Minority in Israel

The Arabs in Israel are those who remained after the 1948 Israeli War for Independence with the neighboring Arab countries. They constitute about 20% of the population. They are a native minority and generally view themselves as part of the Palestinian nation (Ghanem 2001; Smooha 2004).* Immediately upon its establishment after the war in 1948, the State of Israel endorsed citizenship for members of the Arab minority who continued to reside in Israel. However, the national Palestinian identity of the Arab minority and the specific situation after the war led to concern regarding the possible security threats that might emanate from the Arab communities in Israel (Hasisi 2005; Ozacy-Lazar 1998).

Israeli Arab Palestinian identity raises suspicions among the Jewish majority that it entails either dual loyalty (to Israel and to the Palestinian cause) or full sympathy with Israel's enemies. The results of a public survey, for example, show that an overwhelming majority of Israeli Jews believed that Israeli Arabs might assist enemies of the state; that Israeli Arabs might launch a popular revolt; that they feared Israeli Arabs because of their support of the Palestinian people; and that they believed that most Israeli Arabs would be more loyal to a Palestinian state than to Israel (Smooha 2004). One might speculate that these perceptions would be diffused among the national security agencies in Israel (Police, Army, and the Secret Service), especially when some Israeli Arabs were suspected of collaborating with Palestinian terrorists during the Second Intifada (The Meir Amit Intelligence and Terrorism Information Center 2005).

Similar to other minorities, the Israeli Arabs are overrepresented in different stages of the Israeli criminal justice system. Israeli Arabs (age 19 and above) are about three times more likely to be involved in violent crimes when compared to Jews in the same age category (Rattner and Fishman 2009: 27).† Israeli Arabs are also overrepresented in the offense of attacking police officers (more than double), which might reflect the tense relationship between the police and the Arab community (Hasisi 2005). Data from the Israeli Prison Service show that although Israeli Arabs are about 20% of the population, they constitute about 45% of the inmate population in Israeli prisons (Volk 2011). These numbers clearly show that Israeli Arabs are overrepresented in the criminal justice system in Israel, and it is important to raise this fact while analyzing Israeli Arab attitudes toward the police. The focus of the current study is to examine how the Arab minority views the involvement of the police in counterterrorism and its ramifications on police–community relations.

---

* There are also marked sociodemographic distinctions between Arabs and Jews in Israel, such as age, income, education level, gender, and marital status (Hyder 2008). For instance, we know that the Israeli Arab minority is much younger and poorer on average than the Jewish majority. Data also indicate that the Israeli Arab population has lower educational achievements than Israeli Jews (Weisblay 2006). See http://www.knesset.gov.il/mmm/data/pdf/m01585.pdf.

† http://weblaw.haifa.ac.il/he/Research/ResearchCenters/SocietyAndCrime/cls%20publications/%D7 %93%D7%95%D7%97%20%D7%9E%D7%97%D7%A7%D7%A8%20%D7%90%D7%9C%D7%99%D7 %9E%D7%95%D7%AA.pdf.

The Study

To understand the views of the Israeli public toward the involvement of police in missions of counterterrorism, a survey was carried out in nine police districts in Israel. In choosing the nine stations, we did not intend to gain a simply random sample of the 54 police stations within the "Green Line" (Israel's 1967 boundaries). Rather, we used a sequential sampling method that was based on the threat of terrorism in the districts, and ethnic diversity there, and as well as variability in crime levels, socioeconomic status, and geographic location. In this context, the sample selected for this survey is not statistically representative of the general Israeli population. At the same time, it does provide a broad view of the Israeli Jewish population, with a sampling frame of more than 1.7 million Jewish citizens, covering almost a third of the Jewish population in Israel, and 80,000 Arab citizens, covering about 7% of the Arab population in Israel. Moreover, when examining the characteristics of the respondents, we find that they are generally congruent with those of the general population in Israel, both for Jews and Arabs (see Appendix I).

Between 421 and 441 individuals from each police district were interviewed (3832 interviews altogether). Within each district, respondents were proportionally sampled from all communities so as to represent that district. Within each city/town, respondents were selected randomly. Each police district included between 1 and 17 cities/towns, bringing the total number of communities that were eventually part of our sample to 59.

A random telephone survey was carried out between October and December 2008 by the Statistics Counseling Unit at the University of Haifa, covering approximately 85% of households in Israel (CBS 2008*). Out of 6645 calls, complete interviews were obtained from 3832 individuals, resulting in a response rate of 58%. The survey was carried out in Hebrew, Arabic, and Russian. Our final sample was composed of 3832 individuals, which included 90.6% Jewish respondents and 9.1% Arab respondents.[†] The percentage of Arabs in our survey is much lower than the general population statistics (about 20%) because our sampling procedures led us to oversample districts with high rates of terrorist attacks. Such districts are more likely to have high percentages of Jewish residents. The Arabs in Israel are not a homogenous group: there are important subgroups—Muslims, Christians, Druze, and Bedouins. However, our Arab sample is drawn primarily from the Muslim community—95%. Thus, attitudes of "Israeli Arabs" in our survey represent primarily the Arab Muslim population in Israel. In recent years, studies in Israel and in other Western countries have concluded that Muslim Arabs have the most sensitive relationship with the police with regard to the mission of policing terrorism. This became even more salient after 9/11 and the London attacks (Hasisi, Alpert and Flynn 2009; Tyler, Schulhofer and Huq 2010).

Survey Questions

Our study aims to analyze the attitudes of majority and minority Israelis on issues related to the role of the police in counterterrorism. Our hypothesis is that the Jewish respondents will hold much more positive attitudes when compared with the Arab respondents on issues related to the involvement of police in counterterrorism.

---

* http://www.cbs.gov.il/reader/newhodaot/hodaa_template.html?hodaa=200811082.
[†] The remaining 0.3% were composed of non-Arab Christians who mainly immigrated from the Former Soviet Union.

To analyze public attitudes toward policing terrorism, we identified three main areas: *police performance, police–citizen relations,* and *public cooperation with the police*. In the area of *police performance,* we asked our respondents to what degree they agree that: (1) dealing with terrorism is one of the main responsibilities of the Israeli police; (2) policing terrorism hampers the police's other duties, such as dealing with property crime, violence, drugs, and traffic. The respondents were asked to rank their agreement with statements from 1 to 5 (1 = strongly disagree; 5 = strongly agree). In the area of *police–citizen relations,* we asked our respondents to what degree they agree that: (1) when the police fight terrorism they gain respect; (2) policing terrorism negatively affects police–citizen relationships; (3) police activities in fighting terrorism impair their relationship with the Israeli-Arab population. The respondents were asked to rank their agreement with statements from 1 to 5 (1 = strongly disagree; 5 = strongly agree). In the area of *public collaboration with the police,* we asked our respondents: (1) how likely it is that they would call the police if they encountered a suspicious object; (2) how likely it is that they would call the police if they witnessed a crime. The respondents were asked to rank their willingness to report to the police from 1 to 5 (1 = highly unlikely; 5 = highly likely).

Results

We organized our results following the three main themes: (1) *police performance,* (2) *police–citizen relations,* and (3) *public cooperation with the police*. In every area, we compared the perceptions of Arabs and Jews. However, we are faced with a specific statistical problem at the outset. Are the relationships observed attributable to ethnic differences, or might they be the result of differences in social background characteristics of Arabs and Jews in Israel? This question is important because there are marked social and demographic distinctions between Arabs and Jews in Israel, such as age, income, education, gender, and marital status (Hyder 2008). For example, The Israeli Arab minority is much younger and poorer on average than the Jewish majority (see Appendix I). We use multivariate analysis to examine whether differences observed between Arabs and Jews are persistent after we control for sociodemographic factors. Our survey included questions regarding respondents' demographic attributes and other potentially relevant predictors. We chose five main background variables: gender, marital status (single), age, education, and religiosity. It is important to emphasize that use of the multivariate analysis is devoted to support the descriptive findings and to demonstrate if ethnicity still plays a significant role after controlling for sociodemographic variables.*

Policing Terror and Police Performance

Table 12.1 shows that 55% of the overall sample endorsed the statement that dealing with terrorism is one of the main responsibilities of the Israeli police. These findings show that

---

* We report findings here from ordinary least squares (OLS) regression results, primarily because the intervals in the dependent measures in our analysis can be seen as equivalent. Nonetheless, we recognize that they also can be viewed as ordinal measures. Accordingly, we estimated (and report in Appendix III) the findings using ordinal regression. As illustrated in the appendix, the results are very similar to those found in the linear OLS regressions.

Table 12.1 Percentage of Public Attitudes toward Police Performance and Involvement in Counterterrorism by Ethnicity

% Agree and Strongly Agree	General Population	Jews	Arabs
Dealing with terrorism is one of the main responsibilities of the Israeli Police	55	56	48
Policing terrorism hampers the police's other duties, such as dealing with property crimes, violence, drugs, and traffic	64	66	54

our Israeli public sample understands the major role that the police play in preventing and responding to terrorism. Comparing the attitudes of Israeli Arabs and Israeli Jews, we find a small but significant difference in our sample, where Israeli Jews tend to be more positive than Israeli Arabs (56% and 48%, respectively). Using Cohen's d as an indication of the variability, the size was 0.16—which indicates that this is a small effect size.[*] The multivariate analysis showed similar results (see Appendices II and III).[†] This finding (the small difference) might be explained by the fact that this question reflects an objective evaluation by the respondent that dealing with terror is one of the main responsibilities of the police, without expressing a positive or negative evaluation of the ramifications of police involvement in counterterrorism.

Some police scholars argue that police involvement in fighting terrorism has ramifications on its classic performance (i.e., handling property crime, violence, drugs, traffic) (Bayley and Weisburd 2009; Weisburd, Hasisi, Jonathan and Aviv 2010). Our findings in Table 12.1 show that about 64% of the Israeli public sample agree with the "zero sum game" (or "short blanket") hypothesis, that policing terrorism hampers the police's other duties such as dealing with property crime, violence, drugs, and traffic offenses. However, when we compared the attitudes of Arabs and Jews, we found again a small but significant difference in our sample.[‡] Whereas 66% of the Israeli Jews endorsed this statement, only 54% of the Israeli Arabs did so. Using Cohen's d as an indication of the variability, the size was 0.25. The multivariate analysis showed similar results.[§]

This gap might be explained by the nature of policing terrorism and the different effects it has on majority and minority communities in Israel. Several studies in recent years have shown that Israeli Arabs tend to evaluate police performance as poor and accuse the police of neglecting the needs of the Arab community (Abraham Fund Initiative 2010; Hasisi 2005; Hasisi and Weitzer 2007). One can argue that given the baseline of low expectations of the police, the Arab minority is less concerned than the Jewish majority that the mobilization of police resources will affect the enforcement of classic crimes. Furthermore, the explanation of this gab might be that Israeli Jews are more likely than Israeli Arabs to see the tradeoff between ordinary and counterterrorism policing because the latter receive ex ante less policing and do not see much change when mobilization of police resources take place (Hasisi 2008).

Another explanation might be related to the different consequences of policing terrorism on Arab and Jewish communities. A recent study in Israel has shown that although

[*] $t(3721) = 2.512$, [*]$p < 0.05$, Cohen's $d = 0.160$.
[†] We used an effect size calculator to estimate the d from a standardized regression coefficient. The unstandardized coefficient of ethnicity is $\beta = -0.038$, and the effect size is -0.130 (see Appendix II). See http://gemini.gmu.edu/cebcp/EffectSizeCalculator/d/standardized-regression-coefficient.html.
[‡] $t(3698) = 4.043$, $p < 0.05$, Cohen's $d = 0.250$.
[§] We used an effect size calculator to estimate the d from a standardized regression coefficient. The unstandardized coefficient of ethnicity is $\beta = -0.034$, and the effect size is -0.117 (see Appendix II).

Table 12.2   Percentage of Public Attitudes toward Social Ramifications of Police
Involvement in Counterterrorism by Ethnicity

% Agree and Strongly Agree	General Population	Jews	Arabs
When the police fight terrorism they gain respect	69	70	52
Policing terrorism negatively affects police–citizen relationships	36	34	51
Police activities in fighting terrorism impair its relationship with the Israeli-Arab population	44	43	58

an increased threat of terror in the jurisdiction of a Jewish police station decreased its
performance in fighting classic crimes, an opposite effect was detected in police stations
that served the Arab communities, meaning that the increased threat of terror within the
jurisdiction of Arab police stations increased police performance in fighting classic crimes
(Weisburd, Hasisi, Jonathan, and Aviv 2010).

Policing Terrorism and Police–Community Relations

We assumed that Israeli police involvement in policing terrorism has several effects on the
public. One of the questions that we were interested in answering is what happens to police
prestige when it handles terrorism. The findings in Table 12.2 show that about 69% of our
Israeli public sample agrees that when the police fight terrorism, they gain respect. This finding indicates how valuable police work in fighting terrorism is to the Israeli public. Terror
events receive wide media coverage and the public is exposed to the role that the police take in
handling terror scenes (Weisburd, Hasisi, Jonathan and Aviv 2010). However, when we compared Israeli Arabs and Israeli Jews, we found larger differences in attitudes in our sample.
Whereas 70% of the Israeli Jews endorsed this statement, only 52% of the Israeli Arabs agreed
with it.[*] Using Cohen's d as an indication of the variability, the size was 0.37—which indicates
that this is a small to moderate size effect. The multivariate analysis showed similar results.[†]

Several studies in Israel have pointed to the fact that the Israeli police gain more respect
during terror attacks, although this effect was mainly detected among the Jewish majority
(Jonathan 2010; Jonathan and Weisburd 2010). Most of the terror attacks were directed
toward Israeli Jewish communities, and the police was viewed by the Israeli public as one
of the major first response agencies. In Israel, the Army (Israel Defense Force [IDF]) and
the General Security Services (GSS-SHABAK) enjoy significant legitimacy among citizens,
especially the Jewish majority, mainly because of their role in saving lives and protecting
the state from serious security threats. Police involvement in counterterrorism may have
a similar effect to the performance of the IDF and the GSS. A survey conducted by the
National Security Study Center, University of Haifa (2002) showed that, whereas 86% of
Jewish respondents expressed trust in the GSS, only 38% of Arab respondents expressed
the same trust.[‡] One can argue that when the Israeli police act similar to the GSS, it gains
more popularity among the Jewish citizens than among the Arabs.

[*] $t(3705) = 5.925$, $p < 0.05$, Cohen's $d = 0.370$.
[†] We used an effect size calculator to estimate the d from a standardized regression coefficient. The
unstandardized coefficient of ethnicity is $\beta = -0.115$, and the effect size is 0.398 (see Appendix II).
[‡] See http://nssc.haifa.ac.il/files/herzellia2020022a.ppt.

We were also interested to know how the Israeli public views the ramifications of policing terrorism on police–community relationship. Table 12.2 shows that only 36% of the Israeli public in our sample thought that policing terrorism negatively affects police–citizen relationships. Again, when we compared Arabs and Jews, we found a moderate and statistically significant difference in our sample: whereas only 34% of the Israeli Jews endorsed this statement, among Arabs a majority of 51% endorsed it.[*] Using Cohen's *d* as an indication of the variability, the size was −0.36—which indicates that this is a small-medium size.[†] This finding indicates that Israeli Arabs are more concerned by the negative consequences of police involvement in counterterrorism on the relationship between the police and the community. These concerns might be explained by the notion that practices of policing terrorism will be much more salient and frequent toward the Arab community.

Although the former question on the ramifications of policing terrorism on police–citizen relations was very general, we chose to ask a specific question on the ramifications of policing terrorism on Israeli Arabs' relationship with the police. Table 12.2 shows that about 44% of the Israeli public in our sample endorse the statement that police activities in fighting terrorism impair its relationship with the Israeli-Arab population. This shows that the Israeli public in our sample believes that there are specific consequences of policing terrorism on the relationship of the Israeli Arab community with the police. As expected, a significant disparity was also found when we compared Arabs and Jews in the sample; whereas only 43% of Jews endorsed this statement, the majority (58%) of Arab respondents endorsed the same statement.[‡] Using Cohen's *d*, this difference has an effect size of 0.33, which is again small to moderate. The multivariate analysis showed similar results.[§] Both Israeli Jews and Israeli Arabs are aware of the risk that police involvement in counterterrorism may jeopardize its relationship with Israeli Arab citizens; yet, these concerns were much more salient among the Israeli Arab respondents.

Policing Terrorism and Public Cooperation with Police

A receptive relationship between the community and the police is crucial for police performance. Every police force needs the help of the public in order to carry out its missions; this is also true in the case of counterterrorism. Police legitimacy plays a major role in predicting the level of public collaboration with the police. This was also found to be true in the area of policing terrorism in Israel (Jonathan and Weisburd 2010), and more recently among the American Muslim community (Tyler, Schulhofer and Huq 2010). We asked the respondents in our sample to report how likely it was that they would call the police if they witnessed terror threats or ordinary crime threats. Hasisi, Alpert and Flynn (2009) have shown that the Israeli public is very attentive to terror threats and is inclined to report such threats by calling the police emergency number. The public usually reports suspect persons, suspect objects, and suspect cars to the police. In our survey, we asked the respondents about their willingness to

---

[*] $t(3585) = -6.08$, $p < 0.05$, Cohen's $d = -0.360$.
[†] The multivariate analysis showed similar results. We used effect size calculator to estimate the d from a standardized regression coefficient. The unstandardized coefficient of ethnicity is $\beta = 0.120$, and the effect size is 0.415 (see Appendix II).
[‡] $t(3559) = -5.58$, $p < 0.05$, Cohen's $d = -0.330$.
[§] We used an effect size calculator to estimate the d from a standardized regression coefficient. The unstandardized coefficient of ethnicity is $\beta = 0.129$, and the effect size is 0.447 (see Appendix II).

Table 12.3   Percentage of Public Willingness to Help Police Fight Terrorism and Crime by Ethnicity

% Likely and Highly Likely	General Population	Jews	Arabs
How likely is it that you would call the police if you encountered a suspicious object or witnessed a crime?	89	90.5	72
How likely is it that you would call the police if you witnessed a crime?	72	70.1	50.6

report to the police if they encountered a suspicious object. We also asked them how likely it was that they would report to the police if they witnessed an ordinary crime.

Table 12.3 represents public willingness to report terror and crime threats in Israel. Our results show that about 89% of the Israeli public in our sample would call the police if they encountered a suspicious object, compared with 72% that would call the police if they encountered a crime threat. This finding shows that the Israeli public in our sample is more attentive to terror threats than crime threats. We might speculate as well that the public is more confident that their report will be taken more seriously by the police in the case of a terror threat than when reporting a crime threat. However, our concern in this paper is mainly directed to the comparison between Jewish and Arab respondents in Israel. Our data show that the Jewish respondents in our sample are more willing than the Arab respondents to report suspicious objects to the police (90.5% and 72%, respectively).* But the difference is surprisingly small, especially when considering the tension between the police and Arabs reported in public surveys (Abraham Fund Initiative 2010; Hasisi and Weitzer 2007) and the fact that there are among Israeli Arabs many salient political barriers to contacting the police in issues related to terror and homeland security (Hasisi, 2005; Hasisi, Alpert and Flynn 2009). Importantly, the gap in reporting crime is similar, perhaps reflecting that there is more consensus between Arabs and Jews regarding cooperation in response to terrorist threats than is ordinarily assumed. Table 12.3 also shows a gap between Arabs and Jews with regard to reporting crime threats: Israeli Arabs expressed less willingness to report a crime threat compared with Israeli Jews in the sample (50.6% and 70.1%, respectively).†

Conclusions

The main hypothesis of the current study is that Jewish respondents will hold more positive attitudes when compared with Arab respondents on issues related to the involvement of police in counterterrorism. This hypothesis was supported in our study. Indeed, Israeli Jews tend to recognize more directly the importance of the role of the police in handling terrorism, and are more willing to attribute social prestige to the police for involvement in this area of homeland security. As for the Arab respondents, our study showed that they are more concerned with the ramifications of police involvement in counterterrorism

* $t(3795) = 7.97$, $p < 0.05$, Cohen's $d = 0.530$. The multivariate analysis showed similar results. We used effect size calculator to estimate the d from a standardized regression coefficient. The unstandardized coefficient of ethnicity is $\beta = -0.162$ and the effect size is -0.564 (see Appendix II).
† $t(3771) = 8.48$, $p < 0.05$, Cohen's $d = 0.511$. The multivariate analysis showed similar results. We used effect size calculator to estimate the d from a standardized regression coefficient. The unstandardized coefficient of ethnicity is $\beta = -0.138$ and the effect size is -0.479 (see Appendix II).

on police–citizen relations and, more specifically, on police–Arab relations. As we would expect, there are significant differences between the views of each community.

Although these differences are noteworthy, they were in general smaller than we expected at the outset. Overall, both Israeli Jews and Israeli Arabs in our sample recognized the central role that the police play in dealing with terrorism and they (Arabs and Jews) express high levels of willingness to cooperate with the police. Although there are differences, these differences are often not large. The question is, why?

Perhaps one reason is that the problem of terrorism affects everyone. Despite much residential segregation in Israel with Jews and Arabs often living in primarily Jewish or Arab communities, there is also much more integration than many people realize. Jews and Arabs use many of the same public facilities (e.g., transportation, malls, and cinemas) and accordingly are both subject to potential attacks. Another reason might be the Arab awareness that terror attacks jeopardize the status of Israeli Arabs and harm their relationship with the state and more precisely with the police.

Our study indicates that the Israeli public is aware of the social costs of police involvement in counterterrorism. One-third of the respondents in our sample thought that police involvement in counterterrorism negatively affects police–citizen relations. These concerns might be based on Bayley and Weisburd's argument that when the police increase their involvement in counterterrorism missions, the orientation of the police might change from being service-oriented to becoming the "Big Brother," who regards citizens as suspects to be watched (Bayley and Weisburd 2009). These concerns become more salient when comparing Jewish and Arab attitudes. We find that Arabs are much more concerned than Jews about police–citizen relations following the involvement of the police in counterterrorism.

These concerns are even more pronounced when we asked our respondents more specifically about the effects of policing terrorism on the relationship of the police with the Arab minority. Our findings show that a significant part of the Israeli public in our sample is aware of the sensitive position of Israeli Arabs with the police, especially when the latter is involved in counterterror assignments. However, as expected, these concerns were much more salient among the Israeli Arab respondents.

The implications of policing terrorism are different for Jews and Arabs, especially in terms of likelihood of being involved in terror activity, and thus it is not surprising that there are significant differences between the groups with regard to the ramifications of policing terrorism on police–community relations. Our study suggests that despite such differences, there is a significant degree of consensus among both Arabs and Jews regarding the importance of the policing function, and its possible negative implications for police/minority relations and traditional service and crime control functions of the police.

Acknowledgments

This study was supported by the Science and Technology directorate of the U.S. Department of Homeland Security under Grant Award Numbers N00140510629 and 2008-ST-061-ST0004, made to the National Consortium for the Study of Terrorism and Responses to Terrorism (START, www.start.umd.edu), and by the U.S. National Institute of Justice under Grant Number Z909601. The views and conclusions contained in this document are those of the authors and should not be interpreted as necessarily representing the official policies, either expressed or implied, of the U.S. Department of Homeland Security, START, or the National Institute of Justice.

Appendix I. Demographic Characteristics of Respondents and General Population in Israel by Ethnicity

	Jewish Respondents	Jewish Population in Israel	Arab Respondents	Arab Population in Israel[a]
Gender	Female: 51.8% Male: 48.2%	Female: 51.8%[b] Male: 48.2%	Female: 56% Male: 44%	Female: 49.4% Male: 50.6.2%
Age	Median: 44	Median: 42.3[c]	Median: 36	Median: 32.3
Education	Median: "Non-academic education beyond high school"[d]	Median: 12.8 years of education[e]	Median: "Non-academic education beyond high school"	Median: 11.1 years of education
Income	Median: "About average"[f]	Median: within the 6th decile[g]	Median: "Less than average"	Median: within the 4th decile

Source: Data obtained from the Israeli Central Bureau of Statistics, the Statistical Abstract of Israel for the year 2008; see www.cbs.gov.il.

[a] We focused the analysis on Muslim Arabs when data were available.

[b] Because of the way the data were reported by the CBS, these frequencies apply to Israeli citizens who are 20 years old or older.

[c] Because of the way the data were reported by the CBS, these results apply to the population of Jewish citizens who are 20 years old or older. The median was calculated from data reported categorically.

[d] Respondents were asked to state their education on a scale of eight levels, ranging from "no education" to "PhD."

[e] Because of the way the data were reported by the CBS, this median applies to the population of Jewish citizens who are 15 years old or older.

[f] Respondents were told that the average gross monthly income per household in Israel is about 12,000 NIS and were asked to state their level of income in relation to these results: much less than average/a little less than average/about average/a little above average/much above average.

[g] The CBS reports income data in deciles.

Appendix II. OLS and Ordinal Regression Models by Ethnicity, after Controlling for Sociodemographic Variables

	1 b (SE) β	2 b (SE) β	3 b (SE) β	4 b (SE) β	5 b (SE) β	6 b (SE) β	7 b (SE) β
	Dealing with terrorism is one of the main responsibilities of the Israeli police	Policing terrorism hampers the police's other duties	When the police fight terrorism they gain respect	Policing terrorism negatively affects police–citizen relationships	Police activities in fighting terrorism impair their relationship with the Israeli-Arab population	Willingness to report suspicious objects	Willingness to report crime
OLS regression							
Arab (Jew = 0)	−0.183 (−0.082)* −0.038	−0.158 (0.080)* −0.034	−0.500 (0.074)*** −0.115	0.576 (0.083)*** 0.120	0.630 (0.085)*** 0.129	−0.546 (0.055)*** −0.162	−0.65 (0.081)*** −0.138

Note: Standard error in parenthesis. Level of significance: *$p < 0.05$; ***$p < 0.001$. OLS, ordinary least squares.

Appendix III. Ordinal Regression Models by Ethnicity, after Controlling for Sociodemographic Variables

	1 b (SE)	2 b (SE)	3 b (SE)	4 b (SE)	5 b (SE)	6 b (SE)	7 b (SE)
	Dealing with terrorism is one of the main responsibilities of the Israeli police	Policing terrorism hampers the police's other duties	When the police fight terrorism they gain respect	Policing terrorism negatively affects police–citizen relationships	Police activities in fighting terrorism impair their relationship with the Israeli-Arab population	Willingness to report suspicious objects	Willingness to report crime
Ordinal regression							
Arab (Jew = 0)	−0.195 (0.108)*	−0.224 (0.108)*	−0.644 (−0.108)***	0.816 (0.109)***	0.923 (0.109)***	−1.04 (0.123)***	−0.45 (0.115)***

Note: Standard error in parenthesis. Level of significance: *$p < 0.05$; ***$p < 0.001$.

References

Abraham Fund Initiative. 2010. *The Police and the Arab society in Israel: Trends, issues and recommendations.* [Hebrew]. http://www.abrahamfund.org/img/upload/0/0_3051.pdf.

Arab American Institute Foundation. 2001. Arab American attitudes and the September 11 attacks. Washington, DC: Author.

Bayley, D. and D. Weisburd. 2009. Cops and spooks: The role of the police in counterterrorism. In *To protect and to serve: Policing in an age of terrorism*, eds. D. Weisburd, T.E. Feucht, I. Hakimi, L.F. Mock and S. Perry, 81–101. New York: Springer.

Brodeur, J.-P. 1983. High and low policing: Remarks about the policing of political activities. *Social Problems* 30:507–520.

CBS. 2008. Press release: 60th Independence Day. Israeli Bureau of Statistics (Hebrew).

Ghanem, A. 2001. The Palestinian-Arab minority in Israel, 1948–2000: A political study. Albany, NY: State University of New York Press.

Hasisi, B. 2005. *Policing and citizenship in a deeply-divided society: Police–minority relations in Israel.* PhD dissertation, University of Haifa, Haifa, Israel.

Hasisi, B. 2008. Police, politics and culture in a deeply divided society. *The Journal of Criminal Law and Criminology* 98:1119–1146.

Hasisi, B. and D. Weisburd. 2011. Going beyond ascribed identities: The importance of procedural justice in airport security screening in Israel. *Law and Society Review*, 45:867–892.

Hasisi, B. and R. Weitzer. 2007. Police relations with Arabs and Jews in Israel. *British Journal of Criminology* 47:728–745.

Hasisi, B., G.P. Alpert and D. Flynn. 2009. The impacts of policing terrorism on society: Lessons from Israel and the U.S. In *To protect and to serve: Policing in an age of terrorism*, eds. D. Weisburd, T.E. Feucht, I. Hakimi, L.F. Mock and S. Perry, 177–203. New York: Springer.

Henderson, N., C.W. Ortiz, N.F. Sugie and J. Miller. 2006. Law enforcement and Arab American community relations after September 11, 2001: *Technical report.* New York: Vera Institute of Justice.

Horowitz, D.L. 2001. The deadly ethnic riots. Berkeley, CA: University of California Press.

Hyder, A. 2008. The Arab society in Israel: Population, society and economy. Jerusalem: Van Leer Institute.

International Association of Chiefs of Police. 2005. *Post 9–11 policing: The crime-control–home-land security paradigm—Taking command of new realities.* Alexandria, VA: International Association of Chiefs of Police.

Jonathan, T. 2010. Police involvement in counterterrorism and public attitudes towards the police in Israel: 1998–2007. *The British Journal of Criminology* 50:748–771.

Jonathan, T. and D. Weisburd. 2010. How do majority communities view the potential costs of policing terrorism?: Findings from a community survey in Israel. *Policing: A Journal of Policy and Practice*, 4:169–181.

National Research Council. 2004. *Fairness and effectiveness in policing: The evidence.* Committee to review research on police policy and practices, eds. W. Skogan and K. Frydl, Committee on Law and 3, Division of Behavioral and Social Sciences and Education. Washington, DC: The National Academies Press.

Nguyen, T. 2005. *We are all suspects now: Untold stories from immigrant communities after 9/11.* Boston: Beacon Press.

Ozacy-Lazar, S. 1998. Security and Israel's Arab minority. In *Security concern: Insights from the Israeli experience*, eds. D. Bar-Tal, D. Jacobson and A. Klieman. *Contemporary studies in sociology* 17:347–69, Stanford, CT: JAI Press.

Rabasa, A., C. Benard, P. Chalk et al. 2014. *The Muslim world after 9/11.* Santa Monica, CA: RAND.

Rattner, A. and G. Fishman. 2009. *Micro and macro analysis of violence in Israel.* Report submitted to the Ministry of Science (Grant No. 3-2557).

Smooha, S. 2004. *Index of Arab–Jewish relations in Israel.* The Jewish–Arab Center, University of Haifa, Haifa, Israel.

Thacher, D. 2005. The local role in homeland security. *Law and Society Review* 39:635–676.

The Israeli Democracy Institute. 2010. *The Israeli democracy index: Democratic values in practice*, IDI, Jerusalem.

The Meir Amit Intelligence and Terrorism Information Center (MLM). 2005. *Israeli Arabs' involvement in terror activity.* Research Center for Intelligence and Terror. http://www.terrorism-info.org.il/malam_multimedia/html/final/sp/pa_t/i_a.html (accessed November 9, 2014) (Hebrew).

Tyler, T., S. Schulhofer and A. Huq. 2010. Legitimacy and deterrence effect in counterterrorism Policing: A study of Muslim Americans. *Law and Society Review* 44:365–401.

Volk, D. 2011. The characteristics of the inmates in Israeli prisons. Paper presented at the Hebrew University Jerusalem, Israel, December 26, 2011.

Weisblay, E. 2006. Equal opportunities in education: From the nursery school to the university. A report that was submitted to the committee of 'Children's' Rights'. *The Israeli Parliament* (in Hebrew).

Weisburd, D., B. Hasisi, T. Jonathan and G. Aviv. 2010. Terrorism threats and police performance: A study of Israeli communities. *The British Journal of Criminology* 50:725–47.

Weitzer, R. and S. Tuch. 2006. *Race and policing in America: Conflict and reform.* Cambridge, UK: Cambridge University Press.

How Has the Israel National Police Perceived Its Role in Counterterrorism and Potential Outcomes? A Qualitative Analysis of Annual Police Reports*

13

TAL JONATHAN-ZAMIR
GALI AVIV

Contents

* Reproduced from Jonathan-Zamir, T., and G. Aviv. 2014. How has the Israel National Police perceived its role in counterterrorism and the potential outcomes? A qualitative analysis of annual police reports. *Police Practice and Research: An International Journal* 15(2):143–157.

Introduction

Since the terror attack of September 11, 2001, police forces in the democratic world have become significantly more aware of potential terrorist threats and increased their involvement in counterterrorism (Bayley and Weisburd 2009; International Association of Chiefs of Police 2005; National Research Council 2004). Counterterrorism was a relatively new role for local police agencies in countries such as the United States and not necessarily perceived as natural (IACP 2005; Weisburd, Jonathan, and Perry 2009), and thus, along with the rise in policing terrorism, police scholars and practitioners have begun to debate, speculate on, and investigate the effects that this unique responsibility may have on the performance of the police, their role in society, and their relationship with the public (e.g., Fishman 2005; Lyons 2002; Murray 2005; Thacher 2005; Weisburd, Feucht, Hakimi, Mock, and Perry 2009; Weisburd, Jonathan, and Perry 2009).

Despite the growing interest, we are unaware of studies that have considered how the potential outcomes of policing terrorism are viewed by the *police* and how police perceive and experience their counterterrorism responsibilities. Do they view counterterrorism as a natural extension of their "classic" duties, or, alternatively, as a major diversion? How do police agencies view the effects of policing terrorism on their crime control and order maintenance responsibilities? Do police believe that involvement in counterterrorism impacts their relationship with the public, and, if so, how?

In this chapter, we address these questions within the Israeli context, using the Annual Reports issued by the Israel National Police (INP) during three periods that are particularly relevant to the context of policing terrorism. We begin with a review of the potential outcomes of policing terrorism as identified in the literature. We continue with a description of our data source, its advantages and limitations, and the analytic approach we have taken. We then present our findings, which suggest interesting differences between the three examined periods in the extent to which focusing on counterterrorism was perceived as a major reform and shift in priorities. Our analysis also suggests that in all three periods the INP acknowledged the positive effects of policing terrorism on police–community relationships, but only some of the potentially negative outcomes. In our discussion, we compare the perceptions of the INP to previous discussions in the literature and to the views of Israeli citizens (as evidenced in community surveys), and speculate on what may account for the differences between the three periods.

What Are the Potential Outcomes of Policing Terrorism?

Over the past decade, corresponding with increased police involvement in counterterrorism in many Western democracies, policing scholars and practitioners have begun to consider the potential, unintended outcomes of policing terrorism. One major concern raised pertains to the ability of local police to adequately address their "classic" responsibilities while being extensively involved in countering terrorism, not only because police resources, including time, manpower, and funds are limited, but also because the urgency associated with terrorism threats may well result in counterterrorist activities taking priority over classic responsibilities. Thus, it has been suggested that policing terrorism is likely to come at the expense of fighting crime, enforcing traffic regulations, and addressing other issues that are troubling local communities (Bayley and Weisburd 2009; Fishman

2005; Hasisi, Alpert, and Flynn 2009; Weisburd, Jonathan, and Perry 2009). Empirical support for this argument may be found in an analysis of clearance rates in Israel between 2000 and 2004 (Weisburd, Hasisi, Jonathan, and Aviv 2010), which revealed that in majority Jewish communities, as terrorism threats increased, the percentage of cases where an offender was identified ("cleared cases") decreased. In other words, when terrorism threats were high, police performance in solving crime weakened in these communities.[*]

A second central concern relates to the potential effects of police involvement in security matters on the way the police view their goals and roles in society and the manner by which they interact with the public. For example, Bayley and Weisburd (2009) have argued that extensive homeland security responsibilities may change the dominant style of policing from "low" to "high" (Brodeur 1983, 2007). The focus of high policing is on macro- rather than micro-level problems. Its methods are characterized by covert tactics such as surveillance and intelligence gathering, which are often less transparent and accountable and associated with violations of human rights and procedural justice. Thus, high policing may change the orientation of the police from providing service and viewing citizens as clients, to controlling the public and viewing citizens as suspects (Bayley and Weisburd 2009; also see Braga and Weisburd 2006; Fishman 2005; Hasisi, Alpert, and Flynn 2009; Lyons 2002; Mastrofski 2006; Murray 2005; Thacher 2005; Weisburd, Jonathan, and Perry 2009). Such concerns were often raised specifically in the context of minority Arab or Muslim communities (Hasisi 2005; Henderson, Ortiz, Sugie, and Miller 2006; Thacher 2005).

At the same time, it has also been suggested that policing terrorism may *improve* the relationship between the police and majority communities (see Fishman 2005; Weisburd, Jonathan, and Perry 2009). As reviewed by Jonathan (2010a), police involvement in the "prestigious" security realm may increase their status and reputation. Rapid counterterrorism responses may encourage public evaluations of efficiency and professionalism, and, moreover, in specific periods when terrorism threats are the problem citizens find most troubling, by engaging in counterterrorism the police may be perceived as highly attentive to local needs and concerns. Lastly, policing terrorism may encourage contact and collaboration between the police and community organizations and individuals, which may, in turn, strengthen police–community partnerships. Indeed, Jonathan (2010a) recently found that when faced with the terrorism threats of the Second Intifada, public evaluations of the Israeli police improved, but only for a limited time. Once threat levels began to drop, public support dropped as well. This author suggests that both of the processes mentioned above may be taking place, one in the short term and the other in the long term.

Following these debates and limited empirical evidence, some researchers have shifted attention to the question of public awareness: does the public consider the potential, unintended implications of policing terrorism? Research suggests that some potential outcomes were indeed recognized by community members. For example, Henderson, Ortiz, Sugie, and Miller (2006) found that since September 11, 2001, Arab Americans have experienced heightened levels of suspicion, often taking the form of policies and practices such as registration requirements, racial profiling, and detention and deportation, which caused great concerns among members of these communities. Interestingly, a recent survey carried out in Israel revealed that majority Jewish communities are also aware of some of the potential negative outcomes of extensive police involvement in counterterrorism. Jonathan and

---

[*] The opposite effect was found in Arab communities; for further details, see Weisburd, Hasisi, Jonathan, and Aviv 2010.

Weisburd (2010) found that many survey respondents believed that policing terrorism negatively affects the relationship between the Israeli police and the public, particularly with Arab communities. Respondents also expressed strong agreement with the notion that policing terrorism in Israel comes at the expense of other police responsibilities, such as fighting crime and enforcing traffic regulations. Similar views were expressed by minority Arab Israelis (Hasisi and Weisburd, 2014).

A question that remains understudied, however, concerns the perspective of the *police*. Do the police believe that focusing on security hampers efforts to control crime? Do they feel that they receive less, or alternatively more, public support when they engage in counterterrorism? More generally, do the police perceive counterterrorism as an intrinsic role for them, or have they experienced the integration of security obligations as a major reform?* The police are the ones striving to implement "classic policing" with "counterterrorism policing" in the field and thus their views are of great value. The perspective of the police is particularly important in relation to that of the public, as different understandings of roles, priorities, and outcomes may suggest a gap in expectations, which may impact both external and self-police legitimacy as part of the "legitimacy dialogue" (see Bottoms and Tankebe 2012). The views of the police also bear important policy implications, as awareness of a potentially negative outcome is the first necessary step in addressing it.

The Study

Israel as a Research Setting

In the following analysis, we use the case of the INP. As discussed by Weisburd, Jonathan, and Perry (2009), there are similarities—but also important differences—between the INP and police forces in other Western democracies. Unlike many local police agencies in the Western world that began to see terrorism as a priority only in the recent decade, the INP has been assigned with "internal security" responsibilities as early as 1974. Additionally, the terrorism threats faced by the state of Israel since its establishment appear to have been stronger and more persistent than security threats in many Western democracies. Although these two features make the Israeli case somewhat unique, they also make the examination of our research questions possible, and—as argued by Weisburd, Jonathan, and Perry (2009)—make the Israeli case a fruitful one for examining various aspects of policing terrorism.

Accordingly, our preliminary hypotheses were developed within the Israeli context. As a result of the unique history of the INP, we suspected that this police force would perceive its security-oriented roles as a natural extension of classic policing. The INP has always been involved in general security, a feature that may be traced back to several sources, including the foundation of the INP as a corps in the Israel Defense Forces (IDF; the Israeli Army) during the War of Independence, based on the structure and legal framework of the British Mandate Police; the strong link between security and

---

* Although some studies have examined the views of the police regarding counterterrorism and homeland security (e.g., Davis et al. 2004; Donnermeyer 2002; Foster and Cordner 2005; Stewart and Morris 2009), they have generally inquired about assessments of risk, preparedness, organizational changes since 9/11, and the extent to which homeland security had become the dominant policing strategy, not overall experiences and perceptions of implications.

crime threats in Israel at the time; and the ongoing security threats faced by the State of Israel since its establishment (Gimshi 2007; Hod 2004; Shadmi and Hod 1996). Second, we suspected that the INP would show little consideration for the possible implications of extensive involvement in counterterrorism. The fear, vulnerability, and urgency associated with such threats, as well as a strong sense of mission in an ongoing fight for a "righteous cause," were expected to push aside long-term considerations of potential, unintended outcomes (see Jonathan and Weisburd 2010; Weisburd, Jonathan, and Perry 2009). Clearly, different hypotheses could be developed in other countries such as the United States, where local policing has evolved in a very different context and much emphasis is placed on localized services and high-quality interpersonal treatment (e.g., National Research Council 2004).

Analysis of INP Annual Reports

We address the above questions through an analysis of the Annual Reports issued every year by the INP. These reports are publicly available (online* or in libraries), and provide a description of the objectives and activities of the INP in any given year. The reports follow a generally consistent format that includes an introduction by the Commissioner, chapters describing the activities of the different police units, and aggregated statistics.

It is important to clarify from the outset that although these reports provide a good data source for our purposes, we recognize their limitations. Because these reports are publicly available, we expect that their potential impact on public opinion has been considered and steps were taken to portray the INP favorably (see Manning 1997). Sensitive or classified information was, in all likelihood, banned from the reports. The length and depth of these reports vary from year to year, whereby recent reports are generally more succinct and appear to provide more "facts" at the expense of broad perceptions and contemplations. Finally, it is reasonable to assume that these reports provide a better representation of the views of the acting Commissioner and top leaders of the INP (or the official position of this organization) than those of lower-ranking officers, and in this sense should be viewed as organizational presentations (Manning 1997). In our discussion, we consider how these features may have impacted specific findings. At the same time, we view these reports as an important data source. Publicly available information about policing terrorism in Israel is scarce, and these reports provide a unique opportunity to study this area. These reports also allow us to examine changes in perceptions over time and in relation to varying threat levels, which would have been difficult to accomplish using a single wave of surveys or interviews.

In our analysis, we chose to focus on three specific periods in the history of the INP where its counterterrorism role had become particularly salient: the official assignment of the INP with counterterrorism (or "internal security") responsibilities, and the first and the second Palestinian Intifada (or "uprising"). For each period, we begin our analysis 2 years before the event and end 2 years after its conclusion. Our approach in analyzing the 27 reports that fall within these periods was to thoroughly read all chapters and extract any type of information related to counterterrorism, such as descriptions of strategies, activities, quantitative data, or general discussions. This information included, for example,

* See http://www.police.gov.il/meida_laezrach/pirsomim/Pages/statistika.aspx.

descriptions of the activities of the Border Guard,* data on terror attacks, and general discussions about prioritization and allocation of resources. At the second stage, we reread and assessed the extracted sections, searching specifically for narratives or descriptions that concerned either the perceived *implications* of counterterrorism obligations or *general perceptions* of this role. The relevant sections were then organized according to the themes emerging from the data, for each period separately. This process was separately carried out by both authors, and any disagreements were discussed and resolved. In the following sections, we present our findings followed by an integrative discussion.[†]

Period I: Assignment of the INP with Counterterrorism Responsibilities

"Internal Security" as a Major Reform and Top Priority

Historical accounts reveal that the INP has been involved in security-oriented tasks since its establishment in 1948 (Gimshi 2007; Hod 2004; Shadmi and Hod 1996). This feature of Israeli policing is clearly articulated in the Annual Police Reports from 1972 and 1973. In 1974, after a particularly horrific terror attack in the town of "Ma'alot" and a more general rise in terrorism subsequent to the "Yom Kipor" war, the Israeli government formally assigned the INP with "internal security" responsibilities within the "Green Line" (the pre-1967 border). Despite the familiarity of the INP with security problems, scholars have argued that this assignment demanded major reforms from the police on the conceptual, organizational, and strategic levels (Gimshi 2007; Hod 2004). The Police Annual Reports from the years following the new assignment support these arguments:

> Such reorganization of the [police] system requires changes that are above and beyond shifting the boundaries between units, moving tasks from department to department, or changing the administrative structure and positions. This reorganization required transformations in patterns of thinking and evaluating on all the working levels—on the operational and administrative, and even on the personal level. (INP Annual Report, 1974:7)

One of the themes clearly emerging from the reports following the assignment of the INP with counterterrorism responsibilities is the significance of this role and its conceptualization as the top priority, often at the expense of other obligations. For example, in the report from 1974 the Commissioner states:

> The immediate effect of the change was felt to a great extent in the breadth of its (the INP's) activities and the nature of the roles performed. Internal security received the top priority, sometimes at the expense of other important duties in the realm of police services that are provided to the public. (INP Annual Report, 1974:3)

---

* The operational and professional arm of the INP in matters of internal security and combating terrorism; see http://www.police.gov.il/mehozot/mishmarHagvol/Pages/default.aspx.
† While special efforts were taken to translate the Hebrew quotes as accurately as possible, minor revisions were inevitable. In some quotes additional words were inserted for clarification. As a result of space limitations we were forced to limit the number of quotes used as examples; additional examples from the original text are available from the authors.

The Civil Guard as an Important Vehicle for Fostering Police–Community Relationships

As detailed earlier, there may be important effects of police involvement in counterterrorism on the relationship between the police and the public. When considering these effects in the Israeli context, scholars have devoted much attention to the Civil Guard. The Civil Guard is the largest voluntary organization in Israel, officially established by the government under the auspices of the INP in 1974 in an attempt to institutionalize private initiatives to patrol and secure local neighborhoods.* Scholars have suggested that, in addition to substantial support in terms of manpower, over the years the Civil Guard has made important contributions to the relationship between the police and the public (Friedmann 1992; Weisburd, Jonathan, and Perry 2009; Weisburd, Shalev, and Amir 2002). The reports from this period suggest that the INP has indeed recognized these positive outcomes:

> In addition to the regular-statutory tasks the police (INP) has handled over the year, its responsibility was extended to [include] the issue of internal security, following the increased activities of terrorist organizations. In the background of this activity, a new, important communication channel between the police and the public was born, through which the public got to know the police organization up-close, its roles, its problems and even its dilemmas. Thus, positive contacts with numerous citizens increased, including with teenagers who volunteer in the Civil Guard. (INP Annual Report, 1974:96)

Period II: The First Palestinian Intifada

Counterterrorism as a Major Transition and Shift in Priorities (1988–1989), Followed by Reconciliation with the Dual Role (1990–1995)

The first Palestinian uprising ("First Intifada") began toward the end of 1987 in the Gaza Strip, Judea, and Samaria, and officially ended in 1993 with the Oslo Accords. Although the Israeli Army (IDF) played the major role in responding to the uprising in the Palestinian territories, the INP placed much emphasis on internal security within the pre-1967 borders, particularly in Jerusalem and in Israeli-Arab communities (mainly in the north of Israel), as they were considered sensitive areas and in risk of mass disturbances and violent protests owing to solidarity with the Palestinian uprising (Hod 2004; Shalev 1990; also see the website of the INP[†]).

In the reports from the 2 years preceding the outbreak of the First Intifada (1985–1986), we found evidence of police involvement in counterterrorism (e.g., INP Annual Report 1986, p. 12). However, we also found strong indications that *other* issues, particularly fighting crime, were the focus of Israeli policing (e.g., INP Annual Report 1985: 5,14). Thus, it is not surprising that after the outbreak of the First Intifada in late 1987, the INP experienced the renewed emphasis on security matters as a major transition, as expressed in the Commissioner's comments:

---

* See the website of the Civil Guard: http://www.police.gov.il/mehozot/agafKehila/Pages/historia.aspx#2.
† See http://www.police.gov.il/mehozot/agafAME/education_history_legacy/history/Pages/history1985-1990.aspx.

This reality, which forced the INP to focus its attention on maintaining public order and internal security, suggests a major shift in police activities in comparison to previous years. While up to this year the police had carried out its mission of maintaining public safety and internal security while carrying out its main task—fighting crime, starting from this year (1988) it had had to invest its resources first and foremost in carrying out tasks of public safety and internal security, and only while doing so, it also dealt with its main role—fighting crime. (INP Annual Report, 1988:8)

Moreover, similar to the first period examined, immediately after the outbreak of the First Intifada (1988–1989) we again find indications that not only did the INP place counterterrorism at the top of its priorities, but that this focus affected the ability of the police to carry out other duties. Limited resources are also mentioned in this context:

The mass disturbances events...forced the police to place the maintenance of internal security at the top of the priorities list. The cut in the ongoing budget of the police and partial funding of the expenses resulting from the events of the Intifada, forced the police to absorb part of these expenses at the cost of its regular budget, and prepare without an increase in resources to providing adequate response to the needs of the field, while hampering the level of service [provided] to the citizen. (INP Annual Report, 1989:7)

However, in subsequent years (1990–1995), it appears that the INP had reconciled with its dual role. Counterterrorism tasks are now being mentioned alongside crime control, and, what is more, it appears that the police are gradually beginning to argue that they are capable of performing well in both domains:

Fighting crime is the essence of the classic police, as defined in Section 3 of the Police Command...the present situation in Israel, [which] cannot be ignored, demands diverting the attention of the police from its classic tasks to internal security tasks. The Investigations Division is obligated today to maintain the balance and the efficient and professional division of resources between classic policing and security needs. (INP Annual Report, 1995:7)

The Significance of the Civil Guard to Police–Community Relationships

The only identifiable link between policing terrorism (or "internal security") and police–community relations in the reports from this period can be found in discussions about the Civil Guard. As noted above, the Civil Guard was established for the purpose of organizing citizen efforts to assist in internal security, and indeed the reports confirm that volunteers mostly operated in this area (e.g., INP Annual Report 1985, p. 15). The reports also stress the importance of the Civil Guard in developing and nurturing the relationship between the police and the public:

Operating volunteers and utilizing their assistance is one of the important foundations of police community relations, since volunteers are a link in the relationship between the police and the community, and together with the police they form a unified frontier for fighting "shoulder to shoulder" toward a mutual goal—improving the quality of life in the community. (INP Annual Report, 1985:28)

Period III: The Second Palestinian Intifada

The second Palestinian uprising (or Second Intifada) began in September 2000, and terrorism threats generally returned to pre-Intifada levels by 2006.* Although this confrontation between Israel and the Palestinian Authorities took numerous forms (Shay and Schweitzer 2001), it was mostly characterized by an unprecedented wave of multicasualty suicide bombing attacks within the pre-1967 border, which is considered the longest and most costly in terms of human lives (Erlich 2006). Thus, this period demanded significant responses from the INP, including major efforts in thwarting terror attacks and handling scenes of attacks that had already occurred.

Ongoing Reconciliation and Acceptance of the Dual Role

In the years preceding the outbreak of the Second Intifada (1998–1999), we found clear indications that the INP had focused on crime control (e.g., INP Annual Report 1998, p. 65). At the same time, these reports clarify that not only was counterterrorism not neglected, but that both crime control and counterterrorism were perceived as inherent police responsibilities. Unlike the previous periods where this acceptance emerged only *after* terrorism threats became a priority, here we find what appears to be a long-term internalization of this dual role:

> The main objective that the INP has set for itself for the year of 1998 was to create a new organizational balance between the two realms of its responsibility—'classic' police tasks on the one hand, and its responsibility for internal security on the other. (INP Annual Report, 1998:3)

Moreover, in contrast to the two earlier periods, here we *did not* find statements suggesting that the high-threat situation resulted in a major shift in focus or priorities, or that focusing on counterterrorism hampered efforts to control crime. Alternatively, it is frequently claimed that despite the severe security situation, and through special efforts, the police were able to perform well in both domains, as expressed in the Commissioner's introduction to the 2003 Annual Report (p. 3), titled *Law Enforcement in an Age of Terrorism*:

> Despite the numerous difficulties, we have made special efforts and accelerated the war against crime, particularly the war against organized crime.... The uncompromising war against terrorism, alongside the persistent war on crime, and particularly organized crime, were handled with devotion and determination.... We did not give up on training the units, on operational preparedness, on strategic thinking and on service to the citizen.... The personal security of the citizen and providing quality service were a main component in our activities, and we insisted on upholding this objective, regardless of other difficulties. (INP Annual Report, 2003:3)

---

* See terrorism data on the website of the Israeli Ministry of Foreign Affairs, http://www.mfa.gov.il; and the Global Terrorism Database of the START Center: http://www.start.umd.edu/gtd.

Lack of Resources

Although we did not find explicit statements that focusing on counterterrorism came at the expense of fighting crime, we did find frequent mentions that the INP perceived its budget to be insufficient. Although the INP did receive some additional resources in the period of the Second Intifada (see Annual Police Report from 2001 and from 2003),* the reports suggest that they were not perceived to be enough for the numerous tasks:

> Today we are in the process of political developments and major decisions, which concern our very existence. These are accompanied by a wave of terrorism and violence, which generate a cloudy and painful atmosphere. Alongside these, the INP is in a constant state of lack of resources and means in relation to the tasks it is required to perform. (INP Annual Report, 2000:4)

Pride and Grief

Another consistent theme emerging from the reports of this period is *pride and satisfaction* with accomplishments in counterterrorism, often in conjunction with *grief* over colleagues who have lost their lives while trying to prevent terrorist attacks:

> The un-compromising war on terrorism has collected a heavy and unprecedented toll this year...police officers have stopped terrorists at the price of their lives, like the officer, who by stopping a booby-trapped car with a terrorist in it has prevented a terror attack in Jerusalem and paid with his life, or the patrol policewomen, who was called to a scene of a shootings terror attack and was shot by the terrorist. The alertness of the traffic policemen has brought about the identification of the booby-trapped car. For stopping the vehicle he paid with his life. Another patrol officer hit a terrorist, but was eventually stabbed and died. (INP Annual Report, 2002:3)

Positive Impact on Police–Community Relationships

The Annual Police Reports from the years of the Second Intifada indicate two perceived effects of the security situation on the relationship between the police and the public. First, the high level of terrorism threats encouraged many citizens to volunteer and join the Civil Guard:

> The security situation, together with publicity efforts and the professional preparation of the Division of Community and Civil Guard have conveyed public assistance to the police. Over the passing year 38,243 volunteers were recruited, which is an unprecedented increase. (INP Annual Report, 2002:3)

The second effect takes the form of public sympathy toward the police as a result of appreciation of their extremely difficult working conditions and extensive efforts to protect human lives:

---

* For the budgets of the INP between 2000 and 2010, see the website of the Israeli Ministry of Public Security (in Hebrew): http://www.mops.gov.il/BP/About+MOPS/Budget/.

Stretching of the "organs" (units, resources) was almost to the edge of our abilities, in the difficult security, social and economic reality. A situation where traffic police fight terrorists; a situation where working excessive shifts has become a daily routine; a situation where [police] stations are having a hard time operating without the assistance of volunteers, have brought about wide public sympathy and fruitful cooperation with institutions and authorities who volunteered to assist. The unified frontier of the police and the public contributed to firm standing and social strength, which enable [living] a normal life in an un-normal reality. (INP Annual Report, 2002:3)

Discussion

How has the INP perceived its counterterrorism role and its implications over the years? In line with historical accounts (e.g., Gimshi 2007), the INP Annual Reports reveal that this organization has always been involved in security tasks, even before its official assignment with internal security responsibilities and in years when terrorism threats were relatively low. This feature of Israeli policing was recognized by majority and minority communities in Israel (Hasisi and Weisburd 2014; Jonathan and Weisburd 2010), and is not surprising given the diverse and ongoing security threats faced by the State of Israel since its establishment. Nevertheless, the reports also show that there is variability in the extent of police investment in this domain—when terrorism threats were relatively low, "classic" policing became the primary focus of police work.

The analysis of the reports from the first two periods reveals that despite ongoing occupation with security issues, both the official assignment of the INP with internal security responsibilities and the outbreak of the First Palestinian Intifada were perceived as a major transition, which—in addition to logistic adjustments—required changes in the organizational state-of-mind, from a police agency mostly focused on "classic" policing, to one that is highly security-oriented. This finding, which contradicts our preliminary hypothesis, suggests that even in the tense Israeli situation, counterterrorism was not always perceived as a "natural" role for the police. As argued by Bayley and Weisburd (2009) in the context of American policing, although the police have traditionally been first responders to emergencies such as natural disasters or major accidents, it was not obvious that they ought to take part in covert activities such as intelligence collection or interdiction of terrorist plots. In the first two periods, and particularly in the reports from the "First Intifada," we also find repeated statements that as terrorism threats increased, counterterrorism became the top priority for the INP, often at the expense of its classic responsibilities. This finding is in line with concerns voiced by policing scholars and practitioners and recent empirical evidence (see Bayley and Weisburd 2009; Fishman 2005; Hasisi, Alpert, and Flynn 2009; Weisburd, Feucht, Hakimi, Mock, and Perry 2009; Weisburd, Jonathan, and Perry 2009).

However, a different picture emerges from the reports of the third period. In line with our preliminary hypothesis, in the years of the "Second Palestinian Intifada," we *did not* find indications that the INP perceived the high threat period as a major transition in its overall outlook or priorities. Indeed, the reports from the 2 years preceding the outbreak of the "Second Intifada" clarify that despite the focus on crime control, the INP had accepted the notion that it is a dual-purpose police force, charged with both classic policing and counterterrorism. This acknowledgment was also found in earlier periods; however, there it appears to have developed only *after* the INP was forced to make counterterrorism a priority. It may be the case that over the years, and particularly after the First Palestinian Intifada, the Israeli police developed long-term acceptance of their dual role, perhaps as a result of a tradition that had gradually evolved since 1974, resources (money, manpower etc.) received from the government specifically for the task of combating terrorism.

Along the same lines, and unlike earlier periods, in the reports from the years of the Second Intifada we *did not* find arguments suggesting that crime control could not be performed well because of extensive investments in counterterrorism. Internal security *is not* mentioned as the top priority, and, what is more, efforts are taken to argue that the police are performing well in both domains.* These perceptions are in sharp contrast with the views of Israeli citizens—a recent survey revealed that 66.3% of the non-Ultraortho-dox Jewish respondents and 54% of Israeli Arabs "agreed" or "strongly agreed" that "han-dling terrorism threats hampers other police duties, such as property crimes, violence, drugs and traffic" (Hasisi and Weisburd 2014; Jonathan and Weisburd 2010). These reports do, however, include complaints about shortage of resources in relation to the extent of tasks required, which may be a different way of stating that it is not feasible to perform well in both tasks during periods of intense terrorism threats, at least not without a major budget increase. Other sources (e.g., Fishman 2005) also indicate that the leaders of the INP were aware of the price paid in the realm of crime control during the Second Intifada.† Then why not make clear statements about this in the reports, as in earlier periods?

We suspect that not only did the top leaders of the INP view it as their responsibility to address both crime and security problems regardless of the intense terrorist threats, but that the public and perhaps the government expected them to do so as well. In 2004, in response to requests for additional resources, Prime Minister Ariel Sharon replied: "No crying and no wailing and no arguments that it can't be done."‡ In his speech, he emphasized that the requirements from the INP are not about to change, and the police are expected to be creative and perform well in all their areas of responsibility within the existing budget. Thus, explicitly stating in publicly available reports that crime control has suffered as a result of focusing on counterterrorism would have likely resulted in harsh public and government criticism, which police leaders most likely tried to avoid.

Despite the lack of resources, it appears that the Israeli police do believe that they have done everything in their power to handle terrorism threats well, even if it required improvising, working long shifts, or attempting to stop terrorists without the appropriate training or equipment. A sense of pride and accomplishment thus appears from the reports of the Second Intifada, although it is interwoven with grief because of the particularly dif-ficult situation and the loss of police officers' lives.

Pertaining to police–community relations, positive outcomes of policing terrorism are explicitly mentioned in the reports. In the first two periods, they are linked to the Civil Guard, as a result of its major role in bringing the police and the community closer together, increasing positive interactions, opening mutual communication channels, and helping the public better understand the police—a finding that supports observations made by police scholars (Friedmann 1992; Weisburd, Shalev, and Amir 2002). In the third

---

* Similar, though somewhat weaker, trends were also found in the later years of our second period of examination.
† Public statements about this issue were also made by the Police Commissioner at the time of the Intifada; see http://www.ynet.co.il/articles/0,7340,L-3305187,00.html [in Hebrew].
‡ See http://news.nana10.co.il/Article/?ArticleID=106337 [in Hebrew].

period, we read of public sympathy toward the police as a result of their efforts and sacrifices in handling terrorism threats.

Notably, and in line with our preliminary hypotheses, we did not find explicit statements in any of the three periods suggesting acknowledgment of the potential *negative* effects of policing terrorism on police–community relations. Indeed, in the first and second periods, when stating that focusing on internal security impended performance in crime control, it may be understood that the police are considering a potential loss of public trust as a result of inadequate performance. At the same time, we found no evidence suggesting that the top leaders of the INP have considered potential changes in the nature and character of Israeli policing in the direction of high policing, which, as reviewed earlier, may distance the police from the public and impend efforts to implement community-policing programs or a broad service-oriented approach (see Bayley and Weisburd 2009; Hasisi, Alpert, and Flynn 2009; Lyons 2002; Mastrofski 2006; Murray 2005; Thacher 2005).

This finding could perhaps be attributed to the military culture that is firmly rooted in the organization and philosophy of the INP (e.g., Ben-Porat 1988; Gamson and Yuchtman 1977; Herzog 2001; Hovav and Amir 1979; Shadmi and Hod 1996; Weisburd, Shalev, and Amir 2002; also see review by Shalev 2003). Thus, it may be that such potential implications were not contemplated because the INP already considered itself a semimilitary organization, or because a change in that direction was not necessarily perceived as negative. Importantly, as discussed by Jonathan (2010b), public trust in the Israeli police has dropped significantly between 2002 and 2009, whereas police performance in numerous domains improved. We suspect that disregard for the potential negative effects of policing terrorism on police–community relations may provide partial explanation for this trend. Notably, more than one-third (34.9%) of the non-Ultraorthodox Jewish respondents and 51.3% of Arab respondents to the survey mentioned above "agreed" or "strongly agreed" that "dealing with terrorism negatively affects the relationship between the police and the public" (Hasisi and Weisburd 2014; Jonathan and Weisburd 2010).

Additionally, although clearly recognized by both majority and minority communities in Israel (Hasisi and Weisburd 2014; Jonathan and Weisburd 2010), we did not find evidence suggesting that the INP considered the potential negative effects of its counterterrorism roles on its relationship with Israeli-Arab communities. Scholars have often argued that the majority community in Israel perceives Israeli Arabs as a potential security threat, particularly in periods of increased terrorism threats and tension around the Israeli–Palestinian conflict (Hasisi 2005; Hasisi, Alpert, and Flynn 2009; Hasisi and Weitzer 2007; Smooha 2004), which may explain why relationships with Arab communities were not contemplated. It may also be that the acuteness and urgency associated with terrorism threats resulted in police focus on short-term goals—that is, eliminating the threat and minimizing damage, whereas considerations of long-term relationships with Arab communities were temporarily postponed. Lastly, it may be that these potential outcomes were indeed considered by police officials but not mentioned in the reports because of the sensitivity of the matter.

Conclusions

The annual reports issued by the INP suggest that the top leaders of this agency have recognized and chose to present some implications of the INP's role in counterterrorism. The reports express concerns about the effects of extensive investment in internal security on the INP's ability to handle crime problems, although more so in earlier than in later years. Israeli police officials also believe that counterterrorism tasks improve police–community relationships, particularly through working together with Civil Guard volunteers (in earlier periods), or as a result of public sympathy for police efforts (in more recent periods). At the same time, and contrary to Israeli citizens, they did not appear to acknowledge that "internal security" tasks may contribute to a more military style of policing, which may ultimately jeopardize public trust. Moreover, the potential effects of policing terrorism on the relationships between the police and Israeli Arab communities did not appear to be considered.

Understanding police views about the implications of policing terrorism is particularly important. A gap between police and public perceptions suggests a mismatch in expectations, which may hinder public trust in the police and police legitimacy, both in their own eyes (self-legitimacy) and in the eyes of community members (external legitimacy; see Bottoms and Tankebe 2012). Additionally, the way the police understand their role in counterterrorism and its outcomes is expected to impact strategic planning, prioritization, allocation of internal resources, and daily activities. Although focusing on counterterrorism may not be a matter of choice for the police, particularly in situations of extreme, immediate threat, considering and acknowledging the potential, unintended outcomes of this unique role is a necessary first step in addressing them in ways that would maximize the positive outcomes while minimizing ones that are undesirable.

Acknowledgments

This study was supported by the Science and Technology directorate of the U.S. Department of Homeland Security under Grant Award Numbers N00140510629 and 2008-ST-061-ST0004, made to the National Consortium for the Study of Terrorism and Responses to Terrorism (START, http://www.start.umd.edu), and by the U.S. National Institute of Justice under Grant Number Z909601. The views and conclusions contained in this document are those of the authors and should not be interpreted as necessarily representing the official policies, either expressed or implied, of the U.S. Department of Homeland Security, START, or the National Institute of Justice.

References

Bayley, D. and D. Weisburd. 2009. Cops and spooks: The role of the police in counterterrorism. In *To protect and to serve: Policing in an age of terrorism*, eds. D. Weisburd, T. Feucht, I. Hakimi, M. Lois, and S. Perry, 81–99. New York: Springer.

Ben-Porat, Y. 1988. *A barrier to chaos—Decisive years in the history of the Israeli Police*. Israel: Ministry of Defense. [In Hebrew].

Bottoms, A. and J. Tankebe. 2012. Beyond procedural justice: A dialogic approach to legitimacy in criminal justice. *The Journal of Criminal Law and Criminology* 102:119–170.

Braga, A. A. and D. Weisburd. 2006. Conclusion: Police innovation and the future of policing. In *Police innovation: Contrasting perspectives*, eds. D. Weisburd, and A. A. Braga, 339–352. Cambridge, UK: Cambridge University Press.

Brodeur, J. P. 1983. High and low policing: Remarks about the policing of political activities. *Social Problems* 30:507–520.

Brodeur, J. P. 2007. High and low policing in post-9/11 times. *Policing* 1:25–37.

Davis, L. M., G. Ridgeway, J. Pace et al. 2004. *When terrorism hits home: How prepared are state and local law enforcement?* Santa Monica, CA: RAND.

Donnermeyer, J. F. 2002. Local preparedness for terrorism: A view from law enforcement. *Police Practice and Research* 3:347–360.

Erlich, R. 2006. *The battle for the hearts and minds: The ongoing Israeli–Palestinian confrontation as a case study.* Israel: Intelligence and Terrorism Information Center at the Center for Special Studies. http://www.intelligence.org.il (accessed November 3, 2014).

Fishman, G. 2005. *Balanced police action between terror and maintaining public order: A summary of an era and challenges for coming years.* Jerusalem: The Israel Democracy Institute. [In Hebrew].

Foster, C. and G. Cordner. 2005. *The impact of terrorism on state law enforcement: Adjusting to new roles and changing conditions.* Washington, DC: National Institute of Justice.

Friedmann, R. R. 1992. *Community policing: Comparative perspectives and prospects.* New York: St. Martin's Press.

Gamson, W. A. and E. Yuchtman. 1977. Police and society in Israel. In *Police and society*, ed. D. H. Bayley, 195–218. Beverly Hills, CA: Sage Publications.

Gimshi, D. 2007. *Criminal justice: Law enforcement in democracy.* Rishon Le-Zion, Israel: Peles Publishers. [In Hebrew].

Hasisi, B. 2005. *Policing and citizenship in a deeply-divided society: Police–minority relations in Israel.* PhD dissertation, University of Haifa, Haifa, Israel. [In Hebrew].

Hasisi, B. and D. Weisburd. 2014. Policing terrorism and police–community relations: Views of the Arab minority in Israel. *Police Practice and Research: An International Journal* 15(2):158–172.

Hasisi, B. and R. Weitzer. 2007. Police relations with Arabs and Jews in Israel. *British Journal of Criminology* 47:728–745.

Hasisi, B., G. Alpert and D. Flynn. 2009. The impacts of policing terrorism on society: Lessons from Israel and the U.S. In *To protect and to serve: Policing in an age of terrorism*, eds. D. Weisburd, T. Feucht, I. Hakimi, M. Lois, and S. Perry, 177–202. New York: Springer.

Henderson, N. J., C. W. Ortiz, N. F. Sugie and J. Miller. 2006. *Law enforcement and Arab American community relations after September 11, 2001: Technical report.* New York: Vera Institute of Justice.

Herzog, S. 2001. Militarization and demilitarization processes in the Israeli and American police forces: Organizational and social aspects. *Policing and Society* 11:181–208.

Hod, E. 2004. *Eras in the development of the Israel National Police.* Jerusalem: Yovel Publishing. [In Hebrew].

Hovav, M. and M. Amir. 1979. Israel police: History and analysis. *Police Studies* 2:5–31.

International Association of Chiefs of Police. 2005. *Post 9-11 policing: The crime-control–homeland security paradigm—Taking command of new realities.* Alexandria, VA: International Association of Chiefs of Police.

Jonathan, T. 2010a. Police involvement in counterterrorism and public attitudes towards the police in Israel: 1998–2007. *The British Journal of Criminology* 50:748–771.

Jonathan, T. 2010b. *The effects of security threats and the policing of terrorism on public attitudes towards the police: The case of majority communities in Israel.* PhD dissertation, Hebrew University of Jerusalem, Jerusalem.

Jonathan, T. and D. Weisburd. 2010. How do majority communities view the potential costs of policing terrorism? Findings from a community survey in Israel. *Policing: A Journal of Policy and Practice* 4:169–181.

Lyons, W. 2002. Partnerships, information and public safety: Community policing in a time of terror. *Policing: An International Journal of Police Strategies and Management* 25:530–542.

Manning, P. K. 1997. *Police work: The social organization of policing.* Prospect Heights, IL: Waveland Press.

Mastrofski, S. D. 2006. Community policing: A skeptical view. In *Police innovation: Contrasting perspectives*, eds. D. Weisburd, and A. A. Braga, 44–73. New York: Cambridge University Press.

Murray, J. 2005. Policing terrorism: A threat to community policing or just a shift in priorities? *Police Practice and Research* 6:347–361.

National Research Council. 2004. *Fairness and effectiveness in policing: The evidence.* Committee to review research on police policy and practices, eds. W. Skogan and K. Frydl, Committee on Law and Justice, Division of Behavioral and Social Sciences and Education. Washington, DC: The National Academies Press.

Shadmi, A. and E. Hod. 1996. *The history of the Israel National Police, vol. A: 1948–1958 (The establishment phase).* Jerusalem, Israel: Israel National Police. [In Hebrew].

Shalev, A. 1990. *The Intifada: The reasons, the characteristics and the implications.* Tel Aviv: Papyrus. [In Hebrew].

Shalev, O. 2003. *Organizational change in Israel National Police toward community policing: New era in control of police?* PhD dissertation, Hebrew University, Jerusalem. [In Hebrew].

Shay, S. and Y. Schweitzer. 2001. *The Al-Aqsa Intifada—Palestinian-Israeli confrontation.* Herzliya, Israel: International Institute for Counter-Terrorism. http://www.ict.org.il/Articles/tabid/66 /Articlsid/60/currentpage/24/Default.aspx.

Smooha, S. 2004. *Index of Arab–Jewish relations in Israel.* Haifa, Israel: Jewish–Arab Center, University of Haifa.

Stewart, D. M. and R. G. Morris. 2009. A new era of policing? An examination of Texas police chiefs' perceptions of homeland security. *Criminal Justice Policy Review* 20:290–309.

Thacher, D. 2005. The local role in homeland security. *Law and Society Review* 39:635–676.

Weisburd, D., T. Feucht, I. Hakimi, L. F. Mock and S. Perry. 2009. *To protect and to serve: Policing in an age of terrorism.* New York: Springer.

Weisburd, D., B. Hasisi, T. Jonathan and G. Aviv. 2010. Terrorism threats and police performance: A study of Israeli communities. *The British Journal of Criminology* 50:725–747.

Weisburd, D., T. Jonathan and S. Perry. 2009. The Israeli model for policing terrorism: Goals, strategies and open questions. *Criminal Justice and Behavior* 36:1259–1278.

Weisburd, D., O. Shalev and M. Amir. 2002. Community policing in Israel: Resistance and change. *Policing: An International Journal of Police Strategies and Management* 25:80–109.

Lessons from Empirical Research on Policing in Israel

Policing Terrorism and Police–Community Relationships*

14

SIMON PERRY
TAL JONATHAN-ZAMIR

Contents

Introduction

What do we know about policing in Israel? What lessons, based on empirical research, can be drawn from the experience of the Israel National Police (INP)? Israel has the potential to serve as a fascinating research laboratory for studying policing in a polarized, democratic society. The police in Israel have a special role because of the unique security situation, ethnic diversity, and significant political, religious, and cultural differences and tensions. At the same time, Israel is a democratic country where the police are obligated to protect civil rights and are restrained and regulated by law, and where an independent Supreme Court plays a dominant role. In turn, relying on empirical evidence when formulating policy and practice is expected to increase police effectiveness and to improve their relationships with the communities they serve (Bayley 1994; Sherman 1998; Weisburd and Braga 2006; Weisburd and Neyroud 2011; Welsh 2006).

    The goal of this chapter is to review recent empirical studies on policing in Israel in the areas of policing terrorism and police–community relationships, and to derive insights for better policing in Israel and other democratic societies. The first topic was chosen because of the unique experience of the INP with counterterrorism. Whereas the police in many Western democracies have begun to see terrorism as an acute problem and an integral part of their mission only in the recent decade, the INP has almost 40 years of experience in this

* Reproduced from Perry, S., and T. Jonathan-Zamir. 2014. Lessons from empirical research on policing in Israel: Policing terrorism and police–community relationships. *Police Practice and Research: An International Journal* 15(2): 173–187.

area. Indeed, interest in the Israeli model for policing terrorism has given rise to two large-scale research projects (Weisburd, Feucht, Hakimi, Mock, and Perry 2009; Weisburd and Jonathan-Zamir 2011). The topic of police–community relationships has figured prominently in discussions on policing in recent decades, particularly in the context of community policing (e.g., Corder 1999; Kelling and Moore 1988; Mastrofski 2006; Skogan 2006) and police legitimacy (e.g., National Research Council 2004; Schulhofer, Tyler, and Huq 2011; Tyler 2004, 2009, 2011; Tyler and Jackson 2012). This matter requires particular attention in Israel, where public trust in the police has significantly dropped since 2002 (e.g., Rattner 2009). Importantly, concerns about trust and confidence in the criminal justice system are not unique to Israel (e.g., Samkin, Allen, and Wallace 2010; Sherman 2002; Tyler 2011).

In our search, we focused primarily on academic publications from the past decade related to policing in Israel. We have also reviewed, when available, studies commissioned by the Israeli Ministry of Public Security (which is responsible for the INP), studies conducted by research units in the INP, and unpublished manuscripts such as doctoral dissertations. Our review includes 23 quantitative and qualitative empirical studies published in either Hebrew or English (the complete list of studies including their goals, methods, findings, and conclusions is available from the authors). Our starting point is that of "evidence-based policy" (see Sherman 1998; Weisburd and Neyroud 2011), and thus literature that does not present original empirical work is not reviewed, but is frequently used to provide context and discuss the results of the empirical studies.

We continue this introduction with general background on the INP. The subsequent sections summarize the studies we have reviewed. In the Discussion and Conclusions sections, we take a broad perspective and discuss the empirical literature and its implications as a whole. Our review suggests that studies on policing terrorism have mostly centered on the unintended outcomes of this police role, whereas studies on police–community relationships provide probable explanations for the long decline in public support. Notably, these two themes are not mutually exclusive. Numerous studies are related to both, and, as we discuss below, the relationship between the police and citizens cannot be understood in isolation from the unique security situation in Israel and the counterterrorism role of the INP.

INP

The INP is Israel's national police force. It was founded with the state of Israel in 1948, originally as a brigade in the Israel Defense Force (IDF; the Israeli Army).* Its initial organizational structure and practices were based on the model of the British Mandate Police, a colonial–military police force. Organizational, philosophical, and strategic changes have taken place over the years, although it is often argued that the INP has retained its strong, centralized, semimilitary orientation (Ben-Porat 1988; Gamson and Yuchtman 1977; Gimshi 2007; Herzog 2001; Hovav and Amir 1979; Shadmi and Hod 1996; Shalev 2003; Weisburd, Shalev, and Amir 2002).

Today, the INP is divided into seven districts, each divided into two to four subdistricts comprising several police stations. This geographical organization also represents

---

* This section is based on Weisburd, Jonathan, and Perry (2009). See this article for more details on the history, structure, mission, and practices of the INP.

the hierarchy of command, supervised by the Commissioner who is appointed by the government based on the recommendation of the Minister of Public Security. The National Police Headquarters, located in Jerusalem, directly commands additional national police units, such as the National Unit for Organized and International Crime. The INP employs about 28,000 sworn officers in two main suborganizations. About two-thirds make up the "regular" police force, often termed the "Blue Police." The rest comprise the "Border Guard," a quasi-military body serving primarily as the operational and professional arm of the police for matters of internal security and the combating of terrorism. It also plays a role in traditional police activities. The units of the Border Guard are subordinated to the respective territorial commanders of the Blue Police. Border Guard officers are recruited primarily as part of the national military draft.

The responsibilities of the INP, as defined by law, include preventing crime, investigating and clearing crime, identifying offenders and bringing them to justice, supervising and controlling traffic, maintaining public order and safety, and maintaining "internal security." This last responsibility was assigned to the INP in 1974, following the rise in Palestinian terrorism and one major terror attack. The security situation in 1974 also led to the establishment of the Civil Guard, the largest voluntary organization in Israel, whose estimated 75,000 volunteers assist police units in all areas of responsibility.

Despite the differences (mostly structural) between the INP and police agencies in other Western democracies, there are important similarities. By law the INP is constrained from abusing its authority over citizens, and is required to provide equal treatment irrespective of ethnicity, religion, or national origin. Unlike most police forces in democracies, the INP is not directly accountable to the wider public. There are, however, several institutions that oversee and regulate its activities: the Ministry of Public Security, a department within the Ministry of Justice responsible for investigating illegal police behavior; the National Ombudsman; the court system led by the Supreme Court of Justice; and the media, which extensively covers police activities. The responsibilities of the INP and the Israeli context are unique to the extent that they enable the examination of questions that would be difficult to study elsewhere, particularly in the area of counterterrorism. At the same time, policing in Israel is similar enough to law enforcement in other democratic societies in terms of legal restraints and supervision to allow for careful generalization of the findings. For this purpose, as well as for drawing local conclusions, in the next two sections we review recent empirical evidence on policing terrorism and police–community relationships in Israel.

Policing Terrorism in Israel

Although policing terrorism has become a central responsibility for police in Western democracies, evidence-based models are scarce (Bayley and Weisburd 2009; International Association of Chiefs of Police 2005; Weisburd, Jonathan, and Perry 2009). As argued by Weisburd, Jonathan, and Perry (2009), the ongoing security threats in Israel, along with the fact that the INP has been responsible for counterterrorism since 1974, provide a natural laboratory for studying police responses to terrorism and their outcomes. These authors describe the Israeli model for policing terrorism and raise a series of research questions. Following their preliminary review, several important studies on policing terrorism have been conducted in Israel.

As a starting point, there has been much guesswork about the unintended effects of policing terrorism on traditional policing functions, but little empirical research to guide decision making (IACP 2005; Innes 2006; Kelling and Bratton 2006; Weisburd, Feucht, Hakimi, Mock, and Perry 2009). This is a critical question because the additional responsibility of counterterrorism was naturally expected to hamper the quality of classic law enforcement services. Clearance of police case files is an important indicator of police performance in solving crime, and was thus analyzed by Weisburd, Hasisi, Jonathan, and Aviv (2010). These authors found that heightened terrorist threats reduce clearance rates in predominantly Jewish communities, a finding that is not surprising given the expected shift in the attention and resources of the police. In contrast, in predominantly Arab communities, a rise in terrorist threats was found to increase clearance rates, indicating better performance in solving crime. The authors attribute this finding to increased surveillance in these communities during high threat periods, because they are often perceived to be linked to the source of terrorism threat. Thus, this "improvement" is not expected to be viewed positively by community members.

The unique position of Israeli-Arabs, especially during periods of high terrorism threats, calls for a particular examination of this population. Hasisi and Weisburd (in this book) analyzed the attitudes of Israeli Arabs toward the counterterrorism function of the INP. Their findings reveal that this sector is more concerned than Jewish citizens about the consequences of policing terrorism in terms of police–community relationships. At the same time, differences in attitudes between Jews and Arabs were generally small, and many shared beliefs were identified. For example, both acknowledge the central role that the police play in dealing with terrorism and both express willingness to cooperate with the police in this context. These authors attribute the similarities in perceptions to the fact that terrorism threatens everyone. Additionally, Israeli Arabs may recognize that terror attacks jeopardize their status and hamper their relationship with the state and the police.

No less important, police involvement in counterterrorism may have implications for the relationship between the police and majority communities. Jonathan (2010) utilized annual surveys initiated by the Israeli Ministry of Public Security to examine changes in attitudes of Jewish adults in Israel toward the police between 1998 and 2007, a decade that included the high threat period of the second Palestinian uprising ("Intifada"). The analysis showed that public attitudes toward the INP have generally weakened, except for an episodic and statistically significant improvement in 2002, the height of the terrorism threat. The author attributes this peak to internal cohesion in the face of an external threat and to the way the police handled the situation. However, the peak in support was short-lived; evaluations dropped along with the terrorism threats, eventually reaching lower levels than those measured at the beginning of the decade. The author concludes that there are both short- and long-term implications for police focus on counterterrorism.

These findings naturally lead to questions about how majority communities view the counterterrorism role of the INP. In a subsequent study, Jonathan and Weisburd (2010) examined the views of the general Jewish population in Israel about the potential consequences of policing terrorism. Their findings reveal that majority communities are very much aware of the costs of policing terrorism in numerous areas, including police performance in fighting crime and police–community relationships, particularly with regard to the Arab minority. The authors conclude that in the face of immediate threat, majority Jewish communities still expect the police to address "classic" concerns and to exercise fair processes.

Still focusing on majority communities, Jonathan-Zamir and Weisburd (2013) examined the relationship between the mission of policing terrorism and police legitimacy. Based on the legitimacy model (e.g., Tyler 2004, 2009), they compared the relative importance of police performance and procedural justice for citizens in circumstances of severe security threats (in Sderot, a town in close proximity to the Gaza Strip and thus under constant security threats), to the situations of "no threat" (in other Israeli communities not suffering from specific security problems). Their findings reveal that under threat, the importance of police performance in predicting police legitimacy increased for the public, but the importance of procedural justice *did not* decline. Moreover, procedural justice remained the primary antecedent of police legitimacy. These findings highlight that despite the hardships citizens face in periods of intense security threats, majority communities still care more about the fairness of police treatment than about police accomplishments when considering police legitimacy.

In light of the interesting perspectives of minority and majority communities, Jonathan-Zamir and Aviv (in this book) shifted attention to the perspective of the *police*, as reflected in the annual reports issued by the INP. Their analysis reveals that in certain high-threat periods, the INP has given top priority to its counterterrorism responsibilities. In some years, the reports show recognition that this focus came at the expense of "traditional" policing such as crime control. The INP has shown recognition of some negative outcomes of policing terrorism (such as in the area of crime control), but not of others (potential shift to "high policing" and its ramifications for the relationship between the police and the public, particularly the Arab sector).

Another important aspect of the INP's dual mission of both "classic" and counterterrorism policing is its impact on the police officers themselves. In two studies, Pines and Keinan (2003a,b) used surveys to examine stress and burnout among both Border Guard and "regular" ("Blue") police officers in the INP. Their findings indicate that in the Border Guard, the top causes of stress were low wages; work overload; and shortage of weapons, vehicles, and manpower. Most interviewees reported reasonable satisfaction with their job, which—according to the authors—could be explained by their perception of their work as extremely important. Pertaining to the "Blue Police," the authors found that stress factors included low wages, unfair treatment by superiors, heavy workload, and lack of means and resources. About a quarter of respondents reported that they have suffered from posttraumatic symptoms as a result of their involvement in handling terror attacks or car accidents. At the same time, 70% expressed satisfaction with police work and 81% felt that their work is important and makes a difference.

Taken together, these findings show that focusing police attention on counterterrorism comes with a price. Although there may be short-term benefits for the police such as a temporary wave of public support and officers' sense of pride and accomplishment, there appear to be long-term costs, particularly in terms of the ability of the police to address crime problems and their relationship with the public, especially with the Arab sector. And the public is not blind to these costs. Both Arabs and Jews in Israel recognize, in a surprisingly similar fashion, many of the potential negative outcomes of police focus on counterterrorism. Some of these costs, however, appear to be lacking from police discussions. Finally, these studies suggest that even in situations of intense security threats, although citizens obviously want the police to provide security, they still expect them to exercise their authority in a fair manner.

Police–Community Relationships in Israel

The importance of the relationship between the police and the public is well documented (e.g., National Research Council 2004; Skogan 2006; Tyler 2004, 2009). The police cannot prevent and solve crime, maintain order, and address various community problems without the cooperation of the public, and indeed much of the research on policing in Israel addresses the relationship between the INP and Israeli citizens, both majority and minority. In this section, we summarize what we have learned about police–community relationships in Israel.

Community Policing in Israel

Like many other police agencies in Western democracies, the INP has tried to improve its relations with the public by means of community policing. The implementation process of this initiative was studied by Weisburd, Shalev, and Amir (2002) over a period of 3 years, using observations, interviews with both police and citizens, and community surveys. These authors found that specific changes were indeed made, including the establishment of "service centers" for citizens, the development of closer collaborations with city councils, and the implementation of specific problem-oriented interventions. At the same time, community policing had no observed effects on the everyday activities of officers, and the implementation process gradually weakened over the years of the study, suggesting that the broad idea of community policing was not effectively adopted. The authors identify three factors responsible for this outcome: rapid implementation, resistance within the INP to the demands of community policing, particularly to decentralization, and lack of organizational commitment to the program. The authors argue that these obstacles are not unique to Israel; however, several characteristics of the INP, such as its commitment to a semimilitary, centralized command structure, made the implementation of community policing in Israel all the more challenging.

A subsequent study focused specifically on the work of the Community Policing Centers (CPCs)* (Ofek 2004). The author identified several problems with the operation of the centers, including only moderate involvement of the community in the development and implementation of policing programs, weak data collection on local crime trends, and Center Commanders often being on duty in the "mother station" at the expense of their jobs at the CPC. At the same time, he also found that most CPCs were highly familiar with their area and provided a variety of services to local residents. Citizens who received services at the centers were generally pleased, as were other community representatives. Ofek concludes that the mere presence of a CPC was viewed positively by local residents, community representatives, and commanders at the "mother stations." In a related study using Participatory Action Research, Geva and Shem-Tov (2002) focused specifically on four new centers set up in 1998 in a particular city. Their findings revealed that community representatives expected the centers to be proactive and to address not only "typical" crime (e.g., theft, burglary, and drug abuse), but also problems that affect their quality of

---

* A community policing center is a remote endpoint of a police station, operated by police officers and volunteers as part of the Israeli community policing model. Its goals include providing services to the local population, solving problems, reducing crime, handling conflicts, and running local prevention programs.

life, including vandalism, noise, and traffic jams. These authors also found that community representatives were eager to collaborate with the police.

Taking a different approach, Harpaz (2008) studied the relationship between the implementation of community policing and police prejudice against minorities (Arabs and ultra-Orthodox Jews). He found that systematic implementation and strict monitoring of community policing leads to a reduction in police prejudice. He argues, however, that the difficulty lies in the tension between the principles of community policing, particularly the reliance on public cooperation, and the values characterizing the dominant police culture in Israel.

Overall, these findings suggest that the INP has implemented a modest version of community policing at best. Weisburd, Shalev, and Amir (2002, p. 103) point to the "overall resistance of the organizational culture of the Israeli police to structural changes suggested by community policing." They explain that community policing, particularly as originally envisioned in Israel, places much emphasis on the autonomy, flexibility, and authority of street-level officers. They found strong resistance to this approach, which they link to high commitment to the military style of management that emphasizes the role of the commanders, and tight control and supervision. Shadmi (2001), a radical criminologist, has argued that the INP has always been "the police of the state" rather than "the police of the people," and that social, political, and organizational changes are needed to push toward police transformation with an emphasis on community policing.

Public Attitudes toward the INP

Several years after the initiative to implement community policing in Israel, Rattner (2009) began a study on the legal culture in Israel. He examined public attitudes toward the criminal justice system between 2000 and 2009, focusing on issues such as fairness, equality, and trust. His surveys show the effects of group affiliation, social context, and historical events on public attitudes toward the police. Importantly, these surveys also reveal significant problems with public trust in the police. Overall, the INP was trusted less and perceived to be less fair and neutral than the court system and the Supreme Court. For most sectors of Israeli society, perceptions of fairness, equality, and trust have weakened over the years. For example, only 19% of the general Jewish population expressed confidence in the police in 2009, compared with 32% in 2000. The trust of West Bank settlers and ultra-Orthodox Jews was found to be even lower: In 2009, 14% of ultra-Orthodox and settlers expressed trust in the INP, compared with 16% and 26%, respectively, in 2000. Interestingly, the highest levels of trust were found among the Arab population: 23% in 2009 compared to 25% in 2000.

Rattner's findings are consistent with annual surveys carried out by the Israeli Ministry of Public Security* (e.g., Smith and Arian 2007; Smith and Yehezkel 2008; Yogev 2010), which show that, overall, Israeli citizens evaluate the police poorly. The crisis in trust is also clearly expressed in Aviv's study of crime victims (in this book). Aviv used data from a large-scale community survey conducted in Israel in 2008, of which 12.3% were victimized

---

* These reports are not reviewed individually in this article. Complete details on survey methods, periods and samples are available in the work of Jonathan (2010). Surveys from some years (including summaries in English) are available online: http://mops.gov.il/English/ResearchAndDevelopmentENG /RnDProjects/Pages/PublicAttitude.aspx.

in the year before the survey. Her analysis showed that not only does the general public evaluate the Israeli police negatively, but crime victims' assessments of the INP are even weaker in three substantial areas: police performance, treatment, and trust.

Tying the study of public attitudes to the legitimacy model (Tyler 2004, 2009), Factor, Castilo, and Rattner (in this book) examined the predictors and outcomes of police legitimacy in Israel, replicating the seminal study by Sunshine and Tyler (2003). Their analysis of 1216 Israeli adults revealed that, similar to studies from the United States, perceived legitimacy has a positive effect on support for the police, and procedural justice has a stronger effect on perceived legitimacy than instrumental considerations (distributive fairness, police performance, and perceived risk). Their findings highlight the relevance of the model to the Israeli context and the critical importance of fair processes to Israeli citizens.

Police–Minority Relations in Israel

Numerous studies have shown tense relations between police and minorities in divided societies (Hasisi 2009), including high rates of mistreatment and incarceration, and, in turn, negative attitudes toward the police. This is especially true in situations of terrorist threats, which lead to amplified control over minorities perceived to be linked to the source of the threat. Such treatment is often viewed by these communities as discriminatory and illegitimate (Henderson, Ortiz, Sugie, and Miller 2006; Innes 2006; Khashu, Busch, Latif, and Levy 2005; Thacher 2005; Weisburd, Feucht, Hakimi, Mock, and Perry 2009). Thus, as in many Western democracies, the relationship between the police and minorities in Israel requires special attention.

Following the initiative of the Israeli Ministry of Public Security, Santo and Ali (2008) surveyed a representative sample of Israeli Arabs (excluding Druze) on their views of the INP. The findings revealed that this population perceives police conduct as discriminatory, hostile, and forceful. For example, the police were perceived to be less willing to take action when victims are Arabs than when they are Jews. Their study reinforced Hasisi and Weitzer's (2007) findings that minority Arabs are consistently more critical of the police than Jews. A subsequent study by Ben Porat and Yuval (2009) further showed low levels of confidence in the police among Arabs, which were attributed to perceptions that they were both overpoliced outside of their communities and underpoliced within Arab villages. This study also showed that Arabs wanted the police to be more aware and sensitive to their unique needs.

But is the Arab minority homogeneous? Hasisi (2008a) found that both Druze and Muslims exhibited lack of willingness to be in contact with the police when police practices threaten their cultural values. At the same time, according to Hasisi and Weitzer (2007), the political views of Druze are similar to those of the Jewish majority, and accordingly they are less critical of the police than Muslims (Hasisi 2008a). Similarly, Weitzer and Hasisi's (2008) findings show that Druze are more sympathetic to the state and the police than other Arab minorities, especially Muslims.

The generally negative attitudes of Israeli Arabs toward the INP are not surprising when viewed in light of Hasisi's (2010) findings, which show inadequate allocation of police resources to Arab communities. Hasisi argues that little police presence and insufficient services ("underpolicing") have, over the years, created distance and alienation among Israeli Arabs, which have contributed to hostility toward law enforcement and the laws of the state more generally. Hasisi's findings are consistent with research in other countries; however, interestingly, the gap between the attitudes of Jews and Arabs in Israel is smaller than those between polarized groups in other deeply divided societies. Hasisi and Weitzer (2007) suggest that this may be attributed to lower levels of trust that the Jewish majority has in the police compared to what might be expected from the literature on deeply divided societies. Israeli Arabs are also somewhat less critical of the police compared, for example, to the Catholic minority in Northern Ireland before the "Good Friday" agreement.

What can be done to improve police–minority relations in Israel? It has been argued that the underrepresentation of Arabs, especially non-Bedouin Muslims, in the INP contributes to alienation (Hasisi 2010; Weitzer and Hasisi 2008). Weitzer and Hasisi (2008) examined the assumption that ethnic diversification in the INP would improve police relations with Israeli Arabs, either because it would improve the overall treatment of Arabs or because of its symbolic value. They found, however, that only one-third of Arab respondents expressed preference for Arab officers in their communities. Moreover, more than 50% felt that it would *not* be acceptable for a family member to join the police. However, attitudes varied: 85% of Druze would endorse a family member joining the police compared to only 36% of Muslims. The authors suggest that addressing cultural differences when working with minority communities may be more important than the representation of minorities within the police force. Interestingly, Ben Porat and Yuval (2009) found much more support for the recruitment of Arabs to the INP as well as more willingness to join the police.

With regard to the potential effects of community policing on the relationship between the police and Israeli Arabs, Al-Krenawi and Tubo (2002) found in two case studies that community policing models based on cooperation between local police and community representatives contributed to more positive views of the police by Arab citizens. At the same time, Ben Porat and Yuval (2009) found that Arabs perceive community policing as ineffective, because it does not, in their view, address their unique needs.

Overall, these studies suggest that the Arab minority in Israel does not view the INP positively, although views vary across Arab sectors and are not as negative as one might expect (also see Rattner 2009). Nevertheless, police conduct is generally viewed as discriminatory, hostile and forceful, disrespectful in terms of culture norms, and inadequate in terms of policing services. Findings regarding the effects of recruiting more Arab police officers and utilizing community-policing models are mixed. All the same, Ben Porat and Yuval (2009) stress that Israeli Arabs are not willing to give up policing services altogether, and seek reforms that will improve their relationship with the INP.

However, Arabs are not the only minority group in Israel. In a unique study, Goren (2009a) focused on the ultra-Orthodox population ("Haredim") in a specific city in Israel. She carried out in-depth interviews with police officers, community representatives, officials working with the ultra-Orthodox sector, rabbis, and victims of crime. Her findings reveal that this group suffers from violent offenses, juvenile delinquency, and domestic violence as much as do secular Jews. However, crimes in the ultra-Orthodox sector are generally not reported to the police and mostly handled within the community. She attributes this trend to the presence of informal social control mechanisms, lack of confidence in the police, fear of criminal records, and concern about exposing community problems. Clearly, there is a need for more research on the relationship between the police and this unique community.

Discussion and Conclusions

In this chapter, we have reviewed recent empirical research on policing terrorism and police–community relationships in Israel, with the goal of drawing lessons for both the INP and police agencies in other democratic societies. Our review suggests that studies on the first topic mostly focus on the implications of police involvement in counterterrorism. Viewed as a whole, they suggest that shifting police resources to counterterrorism comes with a price. In Israel, policing terrorism came at the expense of addressing local crime in Jewish communities, a side effect recognized by citizens as well as by the INP. Policing terrorism also appears to have complex effects on public attitudes. In the short term, the police receive overwhelming support, probably in large part because of the tendency for internal cohesion in the face of an external threat. Officers also share this sense of unity and pride. In the long run, it appears that both majority and minority citizens begin to recognize the price. They believe that they are receiving inadequate services in terms of crime control, and that police officers are becoming more militaristic and hostile, especially toward Arab citizens. Public support subsequently drops. We are not arguing, however, that this trend should be viewed as moral justification for the drop in public support. Although the studies reviewed indeed suggest that carrying out both "classic" and counterterrorism policing is challenging, and although the police may be forced to focus on counterterrorism in certain periods, acknowledging the risks and taking steps to address them is expected to mitigate the potential negative outcomes. We should note in this context that even under threat citizens view fairness in police treatment as the top priority. The risks that are associated with "high policing" suggest that when fighting terrorism, the police should pay even more attention to issues of fairness.

What do we still need to know about policing terrorism in Israel? None of the empirical studies identified for this review focused on the effectiveness of specific strategies. For example, we know little about the best approaches to thwart an attack or the most efficient way of responding to an attack once it had occurred. Such studies are understandably scarce (Lum, Haberfeld, Fachner, and Lieberman 2009), given the sensitivity of this type of information. Nevertheless, as in any area of policing, the police can be most effective and efficient when they focus their resources on strategies and tactics that have been found to be successful (Weisburd and Neyroud 2011).

Our choice to focus on the relationship between the Israeli police and the public as the second theme for this review was guided, in large part, by the long downward trend in public trust in the police, which was indeed evident in the studies reviewed. Research on the minority-Arab population also shows tense relationships with the police. We should note that we do not think it is reasonable to attribute the problems with public trust to factors that are unrelated to police conduct or are outside police control. For example, in contrast to common arguments about lack of manpower, Goren (2009b) shows that the officer/citizen ratio in Israel is about average compared to Organisation for Economic Co-operation and Development countries. Based on the empirical literature, we argue that public assessments of the INP are directly linked to trends in Israeli policing.

First, the themes of policing terrorism and police–community relationships cannot be viewed in isolation. The studies examining the effects of policing terrorism on police–community relationships suggest that the drop in public support is at least partly the result of an excessive focus on counterterrorism, which, over time, came at the expense of crime control and service orientation, and weakened the relationship between the police and Israeli-Arabs. Indeed, much has been written in recent years on the potential effects of assigning a police force in a democracy with "high policing" tasks such as counterterrorism, which are less transparent and accountable, and may change the orientation of the police from viewing citizens as clients to be served to viewing them as suspects to be watched (e.g., Bayley and Weisburd 2009).

The importance of the nature of interpersonal treatment provided by the police is emphasized in the studies reviewed. Both studies using the legitimacy framework (Factor, Castilo, and Rattner in this book; Jonathan-Zamir and Weisburd 2013) clearly show that, similar to findings from the United States and other Western democracies, the factor most important to Israeli citizens when assessing police legitimacy is procedural justice—that is, the fairness of the processes by which the police exercise their authority. These evaluations were found to be more influential than assessments of the outcomes of policing. Such findings strongly suggest that the drop in public trust (which is a central component of police legitimacy as defined in this model) is attributable, in large part, to the public not viewing police processes as fair—that is, processes that enable participation; show neutrality, transparency and respect; and exhibit trustworthy motives (Tyler 2004, 2009). It is reasonable to suspect that the counterterrorism role of the INP has made it difficult to adopt such a policing style.

Research findings regarding Israel's modest implementation of community policing further reinforce these propositions. Community policing encourages involving the public in the identification of the problems that should be addressed and their potential solutions; viewing the police role as broader than merely enforcing the criminal law; and using a problem-solving approach rather than simply responding to specific calls for service (see Corder 1999; Kelling and Moore 1988; Mastrofski 2006; Skogan 2006). These principles, in turn, are expected to increase public satisfaction and police legitimacy (Gill, Weisburd, Bennett, Telep, and Vitter in progress; Rix, Joshua, Maguire, and Morton 2009). Thus, it is not surprising that in Israel we find both weak implementation of community policing and low public trust.

In sum, the findings reviewed above suggest that the drop in public trust in the INP is, in large part, the result of inadequate police treatment on the interpersonal level, or—put differently—too little procedural justice in police behavior. This hypothesis could have been generated simply on the basis of the legitimacy model as tested in other countries, but it is clearly stronger when based on empirical research from Israel. Similar to findings from other Western democracies, the critical importance given to procedural justice was found among Israeli citizens. The militaristic orientation that often comes with the role of counterterrorism, as well as weak implementation of community policing principles, have presumably contributed to the disregard for procedural justice in Israeli policing.

To conclude, we should note that while we chose to focus this review on policing terrorism and police–community relationships, important empirical studies were carried out in Israel in other areas of policing, such as crime concentration in micro places (Weisburd and Amram in this book); the economic behavior of the heroin market and the "rational criminal" (Perry 2004); the rational behavior of white-collar criminals (Regev 2008); deterrence strategies (Feinmeser 2009; Yonay, Zamir, and Levin 2009); public order and crowd control (Carmeli and Yamin 2005; Hasisi 2008b); police use of force (Carmeli and Shamir 2000; Herzog 2000); and police treatment of violence against women (Shoham

2000; Shoham and Regev 2000). Thus, given its potential to serve as a fascinating laboratory for the study of policing, we call for a broad, systematic review of policing studies carried out in Israel to date (see Farrington, Weisburd, and Gill 2011).

References

Al-Krenawi, A. and N. Tubo. 2002. Sharing cultural intermediaries in traditional arbiters of police intervention and social workers in Arab society in Israel. *Police and Society* 6:33–72. [In Hebrew].

Aviv, G. In this book. Crime victims and attitudes towards the police—The Israeli case study.

Bayley, D. 1994. *Police for the future*. New york: Oxford University Press.

Bayley, D. and D. Weisburd. 2009. Cops and spooks: The role of police in counter terrorism. In *To protect and to serve: Policing in an age of terrorism*, eds. D. Weisburd, T. E. Feucht, I. Hakimi, L. F. Mock and S. Perry, 81–99. New York: Springer.

Ben Porat, G. and P. Yuval. 2009. Police and Arab society in Israel: Attitudes, expectations and needs. In *The Essence of the research: Studies and surveys of literature in the work of the Israel Police*. Jerusalem: Israel Police, Strategic Research Department and Statistics. [In Hebrew].

Ben-Porat, Y. 1988. *A barrier to chaos—Decisive years in the history of the Israeli police*. Israel: Ministry of Defense. [In Hebrew].

Braga, A. and D. Weisburd. 2006. Conclusion: Police innovation and the future of policing. In *Police innovation: Contrasting perspectives*, eds. D. Weisburd and A. Brega, 339–352. Cambridge, UK: Cambridge University Press.

Carmeli, A. and N. Shamir. 2000. *Police violence against citizens: Research report*. Jerusalem: The Chief Scientist, Ministry of Public Security. [In Hebrew].

Carmeli, A. and A. Yamin. 2005. *Mass events and public order*. Jerusalem: The Chief Scientist, Ministry of Public Security. [In Hebrew].

Corder, G. 1999. Elements of community policing. In *Policing perspectives: An anthology*, eds. L. K. Gaines and G. Corder, 137–149. Los Angeles: Roxbury.

Factor, R., J. Castilo and A. Rattner. Chapter 8 in the present book. Procedural justice, minorities, and religiosity.

Farrington, D. P., D. Weisburd and C. E. Gill. 2011. The Campbell collaboration crime and justice group: A decade of progress. In *Routledge handbook of international criminology*, eds. C. J. Smith, S. X. Zhang and R. Barberet, 53–63. New York: Routledge.

Feinmeser, E. 2009. *Effectiveness in providing warning statements, the essence of the research: Studies and surveys of literature in the work of the Israel Police*. Jerusalem: Israel Police, Strategic Research Department and Statistics. [In Hebrew].

Gamson, W. A. and E. Yuchtman. 1977. Police and society in Israel. In *Police and society*, ed. D. H. Bayley, 195–218. Beverly Hills, CA: Sage Publications.

Geva, R. and O. Shem-Tov. 2002. Setting up community policing centers: Participatory action research in decentralized policing services. *Police Practice and Research* 3:189–200.

Gill, C. E., D. Weisburd, T. Bennett, C. W. Telep and Z. Vitter. In progress. Community-oriented policing to reduce crime, disorder, and fear and increase legitimacy and citizen satisfaction in neighborhoods. Campbell Collaboration Systematic Review.

Gimshi, D. 2007. *Criminal justice system—Law enforcement in a democratic state*. Rishon Lezion, Israel: Peles Publishing.

Goren, T. 2009a. Violence in the ultra religious sector and an examination of the relationship with the police. *The essence of the research: Studies and surveys of literature in the work of the Israel Police*. Jerusalem: Israel Police, Strategic research Department and Statistics. [In Hebrew].

Goren, T. 2009b. Rate of police officers per 1000 Residents in Israel—An international comparison. *The essence of the research: Studies and surveys of literature in the work of the Israel Police*. Jerusalem: Israel Police, Strategic Research Department and Statistics. [In Hebrew].

Harpaz, A. 2008. *Community policing and police attitudes toward minority communities in Israel: Contact with the communities and changing prejudice.* Unpublished PhD dissertation, Haifa University, Israel.

Hasisi, B. 2008a. Police, politics, and culture in a deeply-divided society. *The Journal of Criminal Law & Criminology* 98:1119–1145.

Hasisi, B. 2008b. Policing the 'enemy within': Protest policing and perceived threat in times of conflict. *Jerusalem criminal justice study group working paper no. 21—Working paper series.* Jerusalem: Hebrew University.

Hasisi, B. 2009. Policing minorities in a deeply divided society. In *Plurality and citizenship in Israel—Moving beyond the Jewish/Palestinian civil divide,* eds. D. Avnon and Y. Benziman, 152–170. New York: Routledge.

Hasisi, B. 2010. Policing minorities in a deeply divided society, police performance and presence in Israel, In: Aunun Dan and Benziman Yontam, *Plurality and Citizenship in Israel, Moving Beyond the Jewish/Palestinian Civil Divide,* 152–170. Routledge.

Hasisi, B. and D. Weisburd. In this book. Policing terrorism and police–community relations: Views of the Arab minority in Israel.

Hasisi, B. and R. Weitzer. 2007. Police relations with Arabs and Jews in Israel. *British Journal of Criminology* 47:728–745.

Hasisi, B., G. Alpert and D. Flynn. 2009. The impacts of policing terrorism on society: Lessons from Israel and the U.S. In *To protect and to serve: Policing in an age of terrorism,* eds. D. Weisburd, T. Feucht, I. Hakimi, M. Lois and S. Perry, 177–202. New York: Springer.

Henderson, N. J., C. W. Ortiz, N. F. Sugie and J. Miller. 2006. *Law enforcement and Arab American community relations after September 11th, 2001: Engagement in a time of uncertainty.* New York: Vera Institute of Justice.

Herzog, S. 2000. Is there a distinct profile of police officers accused of violence? The Israeli Case. *Journal of Criminal Justice* 28:457–471.

Herzog, S. 2001. Militarization and demilitarization processes in the Israeli and American police forces: Organizational and social aspects. *Policing and Society* 11:181–208.

Hinds, L. and K. Murphy. 2007. Public satisfaction with police: Using procedural justice to improve police legitimacy. *Australian and New Zealand Journal of Criminology* 40:27–42.

Hovav, M. and M. Amir. 1979. Israel police: History and analysis. *Police Studies: The International Review of Police Development* 2:5–31.

Innes, M. 2006. Policing uncertainty: Countering terror through community intelligence and democratic policing. *Annals of the American Academy of Political and Social Science* 605:222–241.

International Association of Chiefs of Police. 2005. *Post 9-11 policing: The crime control–Homeland Security paradigm—Taking command of new realities.* Alexandria, VA: International Association of Chiefs of Police.

Jonathan, T. 2010. Police involvement in counterterrorism and public attitudes towards the police in Israel: 1998–2007. *The British Journal of Criminology* 50:748–771.

Jonathan, T. and D. Weisburd. 2010. How do majority communities view the potential costs of policing terrorism? Findings from a community survey in Israel. *Policing: A Journal of Policy and Practice* 4:169–181.

Jonathan-Zamir, T. and G. Aviv. In this book. How have the Israel national police perceived its role in counter terrorism and the potential outcomes? A qualitative analysis of annual police reports. *Police Practice and Research: An International Journal.*

Jonathan-Zamir, T. and D. Weisburd. 2013. The effects of security threats on antecedents of police legitimacy: Findings from a quasi-experiment in Israel. *Journal of Research in Crime and Delinquency* 50:3–32.

Kelling, G. L. and W. J. Bratton. 2006. Policing terrorism. New York: Manhattan Institute for Policy Research. http://www.manhattan-institute.org/pdf/scr_01.pdf (accessed November 11, 2014).

Kelling, G. L. and M. H. Moore. 1988. *The evolving strategy of policing,* vol. 4. US Department of Justice, Office of Justice Programs, National Institute of Justice. Washington, D.C.

Khashu, A., R. Busch, Z. Latif and F. Levy. 2005. *Building strong police–immigrant community relations: Lessons from a New York City project*. New York: Vera Institute of Justice.

Lum, C., M. Haberfeld, G. Fachner and C. Lieberman. 2009. Police activities to counter terrorism: What we know and what we need to know. In *To protect and to serve: Policing in an age of terrorism*, eds. D. Weisburd, T. E. Feucht, I. Hakimi, L. F. Mock and S. Perry, 101–143. New York: Springer.

Mastrofski, S. D. 2006. Community policing: A skeptical view. In *Police innovation: Contrasting perspectives*, eds. D. Weisburd and A. Braga, 44–77. Cambridge, UK: Cambridge University Press.

Mueller, J. E. 1973. *War, presidents, and public opinion*. New York: Wiley.

National Research Council. 2004. *Fairness and effectiveness in policing: The evidence*. Committee to review research on police policy and practices, eds. W. Skogan and K. Frydl, Committee on Law and Justice, Division of Behavioral and Social Sciences and Education. Washington, DC: The National Academies Press.

Ofek, A. 2004. *Community policing centers in the Israel police: An evaluation of research*. Ramat Hasharon: The Ofek Institute of Management and Research. [In Hebrew].

Perry, S. 2004. *The heroin market in Israel—The "economical behavior" of the "rational criminal" and enforcement policy*. Unpublished PhD dissertation, Hebrew University, Jerusalem. (In Hebrew).

Pines, A. M. and G. Keinan. 2003a. *Stress and burnout in the "border police" work*. Jerusalem: The Chief Scientist, Ministry of Public Security. [In Hebrew].

Pines, A. M. and G. Keinan. 2003b. *Stress and burnout in the Israeli policeman's work*. Jerusalem: The Chief Scientist, Ministry of Public Security. [In Hebrew].

Rattner, A. 2009. *Legal culture: The reflection of the law and justice system in the Israeli society mirror, longitudinal study from 2000 to 2009*. Sasa Center for Strategic Studies, Hebrew University of Jerusalem. [In Hebrew].

Regev, B. 2008. *Economic and quantitative aspects of white collar crime law enforcement policy*. Unpublished PhD dissertation, Hebrew University, Jerusalem. [In Hebrew].

Rix, A., F. Joshua, M. Maguire and S. Morton. 2009. *Improving public confidence in the police: A review of the evidence—Research report 28*. London: Great Britain Home Office Research Development and Statistics Directorate.

Samkin, G., C. Allen and K. Wallace. 2010. Repairing organisational legitimacy: The case of the New Zealand police. *Australasian Accounting Business and Finance Journal* 4:23–45.

Santo, Y. and N. Ali. 2008. *Israeli Arab society policing—Attitudes and expectations among the public Arab citizens of Israel*. Jerusalem: Chief Scientist, Ministry of Public Security. [In Hebrew].

Schulhofer, S. J., T. R. Tyler and A. Z. Huq. 2011. American policing at a crossroads: Unsustainable policies and the procedural justice alternative. *The Journal of Criminal Law & Criminology* 101: 335–374.

Shadmi, A. 2001. Urban policing in Israel: A historical necessity in a new policing. *Police and Society* 5:49–70. [In Hebrew].

Shadmi, A. and E. Hod. 1996. *The history of the Israel National Police, vol. A: 1948–1958 (the establishment phase)*. Jerusalem, Israel: The Israel National Police. [In Hebrew].

Shalev, O. 2003. *Organizational change in Israel national police toward community policing: New era in control of police?* PhD dissertation, Hebrew University, Jerusalem. [In Hebrew].

Sherman, L. W. 1998. *Evidence-based policing*. Washington, DC: Police Foundation.

Sherman, L. W. 2002. Trust and confidence in criminal justice. *National Institute of Justice Journal* 248:23–31.

Shoham, E. 2000. The battered wife's perception of the characteristics of her encounter with the police. *International Journal of Offender Therapy and Comparative Criminology* 44:242–257.

Shoham, E. and Y. Regev. 2000. Police attitudes regarding wives' complaints of husbands' violence against them. *Police and Society* 4:135–153. [In Hebrew].

Skogan, W. G. 2006. The promise of community policing. In *Police innovation: Contrasting perspectives*, eds. D. Weisburd and A. A. Braga, 27–43. Cambridge, UK: Cambridge University Press.

Smith, R. and R. Arian. 2007. *Public attitudes towards the Israeli police 2006*. Ramat Gan, Israel: Smith Consulting and Research Inc.

Smith, R. and H. Yehezkel. 2008. *Public attitudes towards the Israeli police 2007*. Ramat Gan, Israel: Smith Consulting and Research Inc.

Sunshine, J. and T. R. Tyler. 2003. The role of procedural justice and legitimacy in shaping public support for policing. *Law and Society Review* 37:513–48.

Thacher, D. 2005. The local role in homeland security. *Law and Society Review* 39:635–676.

Tyler, T. and J. Jackson. 2012. Future challenges in the study of legitimacy and criminal justice. *Yale Law School, Public Law Working*. http://dx.doi.org/10.2139/ssrn.2141322 (accessed November 11, 2014).

Tyler, T. R. 2004. Enhancing police legitimacy. *The Annals of the American Academy of Political and Social Science* 593:84–99.

Tyler, T. R. 2009. Legitimacy and criminal justice: The benefits of self-regulation. *Ohio State Journal of Criminal Law* 7:307–359.

Tyler, T. R. 2011. Trust and legitimacy: Policing in the USA and Europe. *European Journal of Criminology* 8:254–266.

Weisburd, D. and S. Amram. In this book. The law of concentrations of crime at place: The case of Tel Aviv-Jaffa. *Police Practice and Research: An International Journal*.

Weisburd, D. and A. Braga. 2006. Introduction: Understanding police innovations. In *Police innovation: Contrasting perspectives*, eds. D. Weisburd and A. Braga, 1–23. Cambridge, UK: Cambridge University Press.

Weisburd, D. and T. Jonathan-Zamir. 2011. *The effects of policing terrorism on police effectiveness in crime fighting and public expectations of and attitudes toward the police: A multi-method study of the Israeli experience*. Final technical report submitted to the US National Institute of Justice (grant no. Z909601) and to the US Department of Homeland Security, the National Consortium for the Study of Terrorism and Responses to Terrorism (START) (grants no. N00140510629 and 2008-ST-061-ST0004).

Weisburd, D. and P. Neyroud. 2011. *Police science: Toward a new paradigm*. Washington, DC: National Institute of Justice.

Weisburd, D., T. Feucht, I. Hakimi, L. Mock and S. Perry. 2009. *To Protect and to serve: Policing in the years of terrorism, and beyond*, 1–9. New York: Springer.

Weisburd, D., B. Hasisi, T. Jonathan and G. Aviv. 2010. Terrorism threats and police performance: A study of Israeli communities. *The British Journal of Criminology* 50:725–747.

Weisburd, D., T. Jonathan and S. Perry. 2009. The Israeli model for policing terrorism: Goals, strategies, and open questions. *Criminal Justice and Behavior* 36:1259–1278.

Weisburd, D., O. Shalev and M. Amir. 2002. Community policing in Israel: Resistance and change. *Policing: An International Journal of Police Strategies & Management* 25:80–109.

Weitzer, R. and B. Hasisi. 2008. Does ethnic composition make a difference? Citizens' assessments of Arab police officers in Israel. *Policing and Society: An International Journal of Research and Policy* 18:362–376.

Welsh, B. C. 2006. Evidence-based policing for crime prevention. In *Police innovation: Contrasting perspectives*, eds. D. Weisburd and A. Braga, 305–321. Cambridge, UK: Cambridge University Press.

Yogev, D. 2010. Public attitudes towards the Israel police. *Mahshov*. Jerusalem: The Chief Scientist, Ministry of Public Security. [In Hebrew].

Yonay, S., A. Zamir and S. Levin. 2009. Deterring criminals through DNA sample. *The Essence of the Research: Studies and surveys of literature in the work of the Israel Police*. Jerusalem: Israel Police Strategic Research Department and Statistics. [In Hebrew].

Index

A Call for Authors
Advances in Police Theory and Practice

AIMS AND SCOPE:

This cutting-edge series is designed to promote publication of books on contemporary advances in police theory and practice. We are especially interested in volumes that focus on the nexus between research and practice, with the end goal of disseminating innovations in policing. We will consider collections of expert contributions as well as individually authored works. Books in this series will be marketed internationally to both academic and professional audiences. This series also seeks to —

Police Reform in China

The CRIME NUMBERS GAME
Management by Manipulation

Mission-Based Policing

The International Trafficking of Human Organs
A Multidisciplinary Perspective

- Bridge the gap in knowledge about advances in theory and practice regarding who the police are, what they do, and how they maintain order, administer laws, and serve their communities
- Improve cooperation between those who are active in the field and those who are involved in academic research so as to facilitate the application of innovative advances in theory and practice

The series especially encourages the contribution of works coauthored by police practitioners and researchers. We are also interested in works comparing policing approaches and methods globally, examining such areas as the policing of transitional states, democratic policing, policing and minorities, preventive policing, investigation, patrolling and response, terrorism, organized crime and drug enforcement. In fact, every aspect of policing, public safety, and security, as well as public order is relevant for the series. Manuscripts should be between 300 and 600 printed pages. If you have a proposal for an original work or for a contributed volume, please be in touch.

Series Editor
Dilip Das, Ph.D., Ph: 802-598-3680
E-mail: dilipkd@aol.com

Dr. Das is a professor of criminal justice and Human Rights Consultant to the United Nations. He is a former chief of police, and founding president of the International Police Executive Symposium, IPES, www.ipes.info. He is also founding editor-in-chief of *Police Practice and Research: An International Journal* (PPR), (Routledge/Taylor & Francis), www.tandf.co.uk/journals. In addition to editing the *World Police Encyclopedia* (Taylor & Francis, 2006), Dr. Das has published numerous books and articles during his many years of involvement in police practice, research, writing, and education.

Proposals for the series may be submitted to the series editor or directly to –
Carolyn Spence
Senior Editor • CRC Press / Taylor & Francis Group
561-317-9574 • 561-997-7249 (fax)
carolyn.spence@taylorandfrancis.com • www.crcpress.com
6000 Broken Sound Parkway NW, Suite 300, Boca Raton, FL 33487